The Sexually Abused Male

The Sexually Abused Male

Application of Treatment Strategies
Volume 2

Edited by

Mic Hunter

Lexington Books
An Imprint of Macmillan, Inc.
New York

Maxwell Macmillan Canada
Toronto

Maxwell Macmillan International
New York   Oxford   Singapore   Sydney

Lexington Books
An Imprint of Macmillan, Inc.
866 Third Avenue, New York, N.Y. 10022

Maxwell Macmillan Canada, Inc.
1200 Eglinton Avenue East
Suite 200
Don Mills, Ontario M3C 3N1

Macmillan, Inc. is part of the Maxwell Communication Group of
Companies.

Printed in the United States of America

printing number

2 3 4 5 6 7 8 9 10

Library of Congress Cataloging-in-Publication Data

The Sexually abused male / edited by Mic Hunter.
    p.   cm.
    Includes indexes.
    Contents: v. 1. Prevalence, impact, and treatment — v.
2. Application of treatment strategies.
    ISBN 0–669–21518–X (v. 1 : alk. paper). — ISBN 0–669–25005–8
(v. 2 : alk. paper)
    1. Sexually abused children—Mental health. 2. Adult child sexual
abuse victims—Mental health. 3. Psychotherapy. 4. Child
molesting—Social aspects. 5. Boys—Mental health. 6. Men—Mental health.
    [DNLM: 1. Child Abuse, Sexual—psychology. 2. Child Abuse,
Sexual—rehabilitation. 3. Men—psychology. 4. Sex Offenses-
prevention & control. 5. Sex Offenses—psychology. WA 320 S5195]
RJ507.S49S49   1990
616.85'83—dc20
DNLM/DLC
for Library of Congress   90–6352
                                                CIP

To
Eli Coleman,
who has supported and encouraged me throughout my career;
to Peter Dimock,
for the First Annual Conference on Male Sexual Abuse Survivors,
which led to this book;
to my favorite men,
Glen Burchell,
Steven Martinetti, and
David Richfield;
and to
Ken Holappa,
who has been like a loving brother to me.

Contents

Preface   ix

1. Abreactive Work with Sexual Abuse Survivors:
   Concepts and Techniques   1
   Katherine Steele and *Joanna Colrain*

2. Brother to Brother: Integrating Concepts of Healing
   Regarding Male Sexual Assault Survivors and
   Vietnam Veterans   57
   Mark C. Evans

3. Use of the Terms *Victim* and *Survivor* in the Grief
   Stages Commonly Seen during Recovery from
   Sexual Abuse   79
   Mic Hunter and *Paul N. Gerber*

4. Creative Approaches to Healing Sexual
   Abuse Trauma   91
   Darryl Dahlheimer

5. Crossing Typological Boundaries in Treating the
   Shame Cycle   99
   Jack Rusinoff and *Paul N. Gerber*

6. Integrating Psychotherapy and Body Work for
   Abuse Survivors: A Psychological Model   117
   Robert Timms and *Patrick Connors*

7. The Treatment of Male Victims with Mixed-Gender,
   Short-Term Group Psychotherapy   137
   Jeff Brown

8. The Role of the Nonoffending Parent When the Incest Victim Is Male   171
Anne M. Gresham

9. Healing Abuse in Gay Men: The Group Component   177
Stephen Parker

10. Identification and Treatment of Child and Adolescent Male Victims of Sexual Abuse   199
Mary L. Froning and *Susan B. Mayman*

11. The Treatment of Sexually Abused Preschool Boys   225
Sandra Hewitt

12. The Victim/Perpetrator: Turning Points in Therapy   249
Shirley Carlson

Index   267

About the Contributors   273

About the Editor   277

Preface

As someone who makes a living sitting across from people who were sexually abused as children and attempting to help them reclaim their lives, I am very glad that this book exists. Prior to beginning this project, I had spent several years reading the professional literature on sexual abuse to write *Abused Boys: Neglected Victims of Sexual Abuse*. The majority of what was available focused on defining sexual abuse, estimating how frequently it takes place and describing commonly seen symptoms. I longed for practical treatment information.

Fortunately, it was about this time that Peter Dimock contacted me about a group he was forming for therapists who treated male victims of sexual abuse. This consultation/support group led to the organization of a conference on male victimization, which then led to the creation of this book. The original proposal called for only one volume. After I discussed the project with the authors and other practitioners, however, it became apparent that an understanding of the factors that affect victimized males are so important to the application of the treatment material that two volumes would be required. I encourage you to read the first volume, *The Sexually Abused Male: Prevalence, Impact, and Assessment,* particularly the first three chapters. I know that you will then find the information in volume 2 even more useful and powerful.

When looking for contributors for this project, I was determined to find people whose main professional responsibility was the day-to-day task of working with sexual abuse victims. These are the people who know what works and what does not. I am very impressed with the skills of the people who agreed to take part. I have learned a great deal from working with them. They have my respect, gratitude, and affection.

The first three chapters in this volume provide a framework for understanding the mind-set of the sexually abused client and the recovery process he faces. The first chapter, written by Katherine Steele and Joanna Colrain, provides not only a description of abreactive therapy techniques but also an excellent overview of dissociation. An understanding of dissociation is necessary in the treatment of sexual abuse victims and is critical in getting the most out of the remaining treatment chapters. Mark Evans uses the post-traumatic stress disorder diagnosis and the experience of combat veterans as a model for understanding men who have been sexually assaulted. Paul Gerber and I provide an overview of the recovery process from sexual abuse using a grief model.

These overview chapters are followed by five broader treatment chapters. Darryl Dahlheimer encourages creativity in treatment planning and delivery. Jack Rusinoff and Paul Gerber discuss the pairing of shame and sexuality that is frequently found in sexually abused clients. Robert Timms and Patrick Connors describe the use of body work in the recovery process. Jeff Brown outlines his use of short-term group therapy with both men and women. And Anne Gresham provides a reminder concerning the often overlooked issues related to the nonoffending parent.

The rest of the book focuses on treatment strategies with various populations. Steve Parker describes his use of group therapy with homosexual men. Mary Froning and Susan Mayman focus their efforts on young male victims, as does Sandra Hewitt. And Shirley Carlson concludes with a chapter on when to begin treating the victim within the offender.

None of this material has been available in print before now. I am grateful that Margaret Zusky and the staff at Lexington Books were able to see the importance of this project and worked to make sure it was released in a timely fashion.

1

Abreactive Work with Sexual Abuse Survivors: Concepts and Techniques

Katherine Steele
Joanna Colrain

A breaction is the revivification of past memory with the release of bound emotion and the recovery of repressed or dissociated aspects of a remembered event. While abreaction is an integral part of most psychotherapeutic work, it is essential with sexual abuse survivors. It provides a psychic reworking of the trauma that identifies, releases, and assimilates the unresolved aspects of the abuse, allowing resolution and integration on both [psychological] and [physiological] levels. This chapter focuses on the specific type of abreactive work involved in the recovery and healing of dissociated memories of childhood sexual abuse.

Unresolved, unassimilated trauma creates dysfunction in the client's life, causing flashbacks, overreaction to stimuli, distortions of perceptions, and high levels of internal stress. Change and mastery evolve through the remembering, releasing, and relearning that occur during abreaction, so the trauma no longer has an unconscious effect on the client's behaviors and belief systems in the present. Planned abreaction can provide a step-by-step framework in which memory work can be done safely, giving the client mastery over what he or she could not control as a child.

Abreaction was originally described by Breuer and Freud (1957) as a cathartic technique for hysteria. Its use as an effective process with victims of trauma was proposed by Lindemann (1944). However, abreaction with combat veterans during World War I and World War II met with mixed results and fell into disuse for a variety of reasons. During the Vietnam War, abreaction again became an important part of the treatment for posttraumatic stress disorder (PTSD). During the 1980s, there was a renewed interest in the works of Pierre Janet (a contemporary of Freud), Charcot, Binet, Prince, and others (Ellenberger 1970; van der Hart and Friedman 1989). These men used abreactive work in the treatment of hysteria, which is the historical antecedent of what are now termed traumatic stress and dissociative disorders. In addition, the increasing knowledge about the relationships among trauma, PTSD, dissociation, and hypnosis—including their physiological components—has led therapists to reconceptualize the process of abreactive work, making it more effective with traumatized individuals (Kingsbury 1988; Nichols and Efran 1985; Ochberg 1988; Spiegel 1986a, 1986b, 1988).

Over the past decade, as additional victim populations have been identified and treated, abreaction has gained in popularity as an important component of the overall treatment. Currently, many clinicians agree that abreactive work is a necessary part of the assimilation process with most survivors of childhood abuse (Bass and Davis 1988; Braun 1986; Courtois 1988; Figley 1985; Gil 1988; Kluft 1984; Putnam 1989; Ross 1989; Spiegel and Spiegel 1978; van der Kolk 1987; van der Kolk and Kadish 1987). However, most of the literature on treatment of adult survivors of childhood abuse does not address the context and process of abreaction in detail.

The concept of abreactive memory work and the related concept of dissociation are often misunderstood and not used adequately by therapists who work with adult survivors of childhood abuse. Some therapists use abreactive work instinctively with abuse survivors without having a conceptual basis for their work; some understand the need for abreactive work but are intimidated by its intensity; some see it as a separate process to be done by a specialist, such as a hypnotherapist. Others are not aware of the need for abreactive work and focus on alleviating the secondary symptoms of the trauma without dealing directly with the past. While we believe that abreactive work is an integral part of the process of working with most survivors, it must be adequately timed, managed, and processed, or it may retraumatize the client, promote further repression and dissociation, produce negative transference reactions, trigger nontherapeutic regression, and even precipitate psychotic decompensation, self-mutilation, or suicide attempts. Thus, the appropriate use of abreactions is paramount for a safe and effective therapy.

This chapter delineates the context and process of abreactive work. Much of the conceptual basis and many of the techniques presented here have been derived from recent work done with multiple personality disorder (MPD). It is the authors' contention that survivors of childhood sexual abuse (and other types of abuse and trauma) may be placed on a dissociative continuum. MPD is the most extreme and pervasive form of dissociation, and during the 1980s, by far the most research and clinical work in the area of dissociation and abreaction was done with MPD. Thus, there is a wealth of information in the MPD literature that may be used with other survivors of childhood abuse. In no way is this meant to imply that all survivors of childhood abuse should be treated as multiples. Multiplicity is a specific diagnostic entity with its own indigenous phenomenology. Although a substantial minority of childhood abuse victims are multiple, the majority are not. Many concepts and techniques that have been developed for the treatment of MPD can, however, be modified for effective use with other dissociative clients.

Some abreactive techniques, such as those for facilitation and containment, are emphasized here, together with some of the more common and generally useful ones. What is most important is that the therapist understand the process and goals of abreactive work and the concept of dissociation. Then, both therapist and client together can use their creativity to develop techniques tailored to the needs of the individual client.

A number of the techniques presented in this chapter are hypnotic in nature. Hypnotic techniques are particularly useful in the management of abreactions because of the similarity between the dissociative state of consciousness present during abreactive work and the state of consciousness produced by hypnosis (Kingsbury 1988; Spiegel 1986a). There is evidence that childhood abuse victims are highly hypnotizable (and, thus, easy hypnotic subjects), although the reasons for this are not entirely clear. Calof (1987) has referred to the use of hypnosis with survivors of sexual abuse as an approach of "fighting fire with fire," meaning that hypnosis is the intervention matched most closely with the dissociative defenses of the client (Kingsbury 1988).

A note of caution: Hypnosis is a specialized therapeutic technique that should be used in a circumspect and carefully planned manner. Therapists should *never* attempt to use hypnosis without adequate training and supervision and should be well versed in indications, contraindications, proper induction procedures, and ethical considerations. Information and training may be obtained from the American Society of Clinical Hypnosis, 2250 East Devon Avenue, Suite 336, Des Plaines, IL 60018. A number of basic texts on clinical hypnosis also are available (Hammond 1988a, 1988b; Wright 1987).

Other important areas discussed in this chapter include the therapeutic use of the client's dissociative skills in the abreactive process, a conceptual framework for abreaction, and a review of countertransference issues that arise in doing abreactive work with survivors. Particular emphasis is placed on setting a safe context for abreactive work.

The concept of dissociation is vitally important in abreactive work and will provide a foundation for the understanding and management of abreactions. Activation of traumatic memories without adequate defenses will overwhelm and retraumatize the client. Dissociation is the defense the client used at the time of the trauma, and by accessing the trauma within this defensive structure, the client will retain the capacity to work through the abuse at his or her own pace.

What Is Dissociation?

Dissociation is a psychophysiological process in which there is a separation or nonintegration of emotions, thoughts, sensations, or behaviors from the current stream of consciousness. *DSM III-R* defines dissociation as "a disturbance or alteration in the normally integrative functions of identity, memory, or consciousness" (American Psychiatric Association 1987, 269). Ross (1989) defines it simply as a lack of association in which aspects of consciousness that are normally associated within one's awareness are compartmentalized into separate areas of consciousness so that there is no longer an association between one aspect and another. One is usually aware of one's thoughts, feelings, and sensations at a given moment. In a dissociative process, one or a combination of those aspects may be separated from the current field of consciousness.

For example, many individuals appear calm following a traumatic event such as a car accident in spite of the fact that they have just had a very frightening and even life-threatening experience. Such individuals have dissociated their intense affect from their current awareness. And, as those who have had such an experience know, intense affect is likely to find its way into conscious awareness sometime (hours, days, or weeks) after the original experience.

Dissociation occurs on a continuum of awareness that begins with full awareness and progresses through suppression to repression and then dissociation (Braun 1984a, 1988a; Hilgard 1977; Ross 1989). Repression, for the purposes of abreactive work, is considered to be a special case of dissociation with three basic differences:

1. Dissociation creates an amnestic barrier that prevents the interchange of memories and experience, whereas repression creates amnesia only for unacceptable impulses and affects.

2. Repression is a purely psychological phenomenon, whereas dissociation has both psychological and neurophysiological components.

3. Repressed material is pushed from the conscious arena into the unconscious at some time after a traumatic event, whereas dissociation occurs at the moment of trauma so that the conscious material becomes encoded into a separate consciousness rather than becoming unconscious.

Dissociation is a universal survival response. When an experience is more than a child's mind can tolerate, he or she must escape. The human instinct to survive is paramount. When a being is small in size; dependent on others for nurturance, protection, and connection to the world; and unequipped to integrate abusive traumatic experiences (because of a lack of experience and inadequate cognitive schema), he or she is left with no alternative except to dissociate, or to decompensate psychologically. In dissociating, the child disengages his or her feelings, sensations, behaviors, or cognitive knowledge during abusive events and deflects those into a separate consciousness in which the events are recorded and encoded.

Dissociation helps to preserve the basic ontological security needed to maintain a cohesive sense of self and experience. It is the mechanism that allows one to say, "It didn't happen to me." Yet dissociated aspects of the trauma leak back into consciousness in alternating cycles of numbing/denial and intrusion so that, ultimately, dissociation is not sufficient to protect the survivor from the impact of trauma (Horowitz 1973, 1976).

Dissociation is an interesting and challenging clinical phenomenon, but it is crucial for the therapist never to lose sight of the human being who has come for treatment. For survivors, dissociation is the way in which they have survived the intolerable. The very personal meaning and value of the dissociative process is best conveyed by the words of one of our former clients:

> I knew my ugly, bruised body couldn't go anywhere, so I just left it there, where it had been deposited by (the abuser). But I could and did leave. I simply let the soft purple fog engulf me, and I sunk deep into the darkness until the pain and fear and the taste of salty tears belonged to someone else, and I was free.

Types of Dissociative Experiences

Dissociation occurs on a continuum ranging from normal experiences to the extreme of MPD. Normal dissociation is an integrative function of the ego that filters extraneous stimulation from the field of consciousness to prevent sensory overload. Highway hypnosis, engrossment in a television program, and daydreaming are examples of normal dissociative experiences. The content of normal dissociation is very narrow and specific, its duration is brief, and the individual realizes that dissociation has occurred and quickly reestablishes control (Sachs and Frischholz 1989). Dissociation may be used as a defense during trauma or during an experience that is not in the normal range for a given developmental stage of life. It is considered to be dysfunctional when it becomes a primary defense rather than an emergency measure, when the individual cannot reestablish control, when there is no awareness of dissociation, when it is used in inappropriate contexts, and when its intensity and duration are disruptive to the individual's life.

Braun (1988a, 1988b) has described the BASK model of dissociation, which is conceptualized along four dimensions of experience: behavior, affect, sensation, and knowledge. During trauma, any one or any combination of these four dimensions may be dissociated from consciousness.

By using these four dimensions in abreactive work, the therapist can determine which are missing from the client's experience and, thus, which need to be accessed and integrated. For example, if a client reports a brutal rape very calmly, the therapist will recognize the missing dimension of affect. Sometimes a client will report with intense affect an episode of abuse that must have been physically painful, but the client will say his or her body felt "numb," hence missing sensation. Amnesia is the indicator for dissociated knowledge components.

Behavioral components often intrude into the present and can be puzzling and frightening to the client. For example, a client began a session by reporting an overwhelming urge to curl up on his side with his knees to his chest (behavioral clue). This was accompanied by a sensation of pressure and burning in his rectum (sensory clue). Following these clues, he was able to access the dissociated knowledge component, which was an episode of being sodomized by an uncle. Such combinations of sensory and/or behavioral clues that occur without a cognitive component are known as somatic or body memories and are extremely common in survivors of childhood physical and sexual abuse.

The degree and manifestation of the dissociation depends on a number of factors, such as the age of the victim, severity and length of abuse, number of abusers, family modeling of dissociation, genetic predisposition, presence of restorative factors in the environment, and presence of normal psychological building blocks. These include cognitive lines of separateness, imaginary playmates, state-dependent phenomena related to trauma, ego states, degree of separation-individuation, and maturity of self and object representations (Kluft 1984).

Dissociation may be temporal, as in amnestic episodes related to traumatic events, or spatial, as in out-of-body experiences and fugue states (Spiegel 1984). The continuum of dissociative experiences includes normal experiences such as hypnosis and automatism, out-of-body experiences, localized and generalized psychogenic amnesia, fugue states, object fixation, profound detachment or depersonalization, derealization, somnambulism, possession states, mystical experiences, ego states (Watkins 1979–80), and MPD. PTSD, a diagnosis often used for adult survivors of childhood abuse, also is considered to be dissociative by many leading experts in the fields of abuse and traumatic stress (Courtois 1988; Donaldson and Gardner 1985; Figley 1985, 1986; Gil 1988; Mutter 1986; Ochberg 1988; Price 1987; Putnam 1985, 1989; Ross 1989; Spiegel 1984, 1988, van der Kolk 1987).

Dissociation is present as a physiological process in a number of organic conditions. These include post–head injury amnesia, electrical injury, toxic conditions, petit mal seizures, infections, metabolic disorders, drug and alcohol use, medication reactions, and temporal lobe epilepsy. Such organic problems must be ruled out if a client is currently dissociative. There is some indication that the type of dissociation present in organic disorders is qualitatively different from trauma-induced dissociation (Loewenstein and Putnam 1988). Furthermore, those who use dissociation as a psychological defense have a history of dissociative episodes prior to physical injury or illness.

Assessment of Dissociative Phenomena

Since the recognition of dissociative phenomena is crucial for the effective treatment of abuse survivors, assessment strategies for the identification of a client's dissociative capacities are important. There is much information to be gained regarding the client's ability to dissociate if the therapist is alert to clues in the client's presentation, beginning in the first session. The survivor usually will understand questions about dissociative phenomena immediately if they are asked in nonclinical terms—for instance, "Do you have times that you feel lightheaded or spacy?" "Do you sometimes feel as though you're not quite real?" "Do you know how to 'check out' when you're nervous or afraid?" "Are there times that you can remember the beginning and the end of an event but not the middle?"

Table 1–1 lists some self-reported indicators of possible current dissociation. Table 1–2 lists some indicators of possible dissociation observed in session. These indicators will be useful in assisting the therapist in determining the nature of the client's dissociative experiences. These are not exhaustive lists but do include some of the more commonly found indicators. And, of course, the presence of some of these signs and symptoms may not necessarily mean that a dissociative process is occurring. Any one sign (with the exception of current loss of time and amnesia) may not be significant in terms of a dissociative process, but the therapist should be alert to clusters of these indicators. It is always important to rule out an organic process and Axis I diagnoses other than dissociative disorders. Yet dissociative symptoms very commonly have disguised presentations that mimic physical illness and/or other Axis I diagnoses. The presence of several of these indicators raises an index of suspicion about a dissociative process, and further inquiry should be made of the client.

One can expect more severe forms of dissociation and more frequent dissociation if one or more of the following apply:

1. There were multiple abusers.
2. The abuse was violent or sadistic.
3. The onset of abuse was at an early age.
4. The abuse extended over a period of time.
5. Family members modeled dissociation in their interactions with the client and with each other.
6. There was further trauma upon disclosure, or there was no disclosure.
7. There is a genetic predisposition to dissociate.
8. The client has no memory prior to the abuse, poor memory of the abuse, and/or poor memory of childhood in general.
9. The client reports current dissociative experiences, especially loss of time.

Table 1–1
Self-Reported Indicators of Possible Current Dissociation *

Impulsive behaviors/self-abusive behaviors
  Impulsive spending
  Sudden gambling, shoplifting, or promiscuity
  Substance abuse
  Overeating, binging, or purging
  Self-mutilation
  Compulsive exercising
  Accident-proneness
  Sexual acting out
Inability to remember recent events or parts of events
  Vague, fuzzy, or unclear memories of recent events
  Loss of time or inability to account for time
Depersonalization
  Feeling parts of one's body change
  Feeling outside of one's body
  Anesthesia and paresthesia
  Feeling of unreality
Unexplained or unusual phobias
  Panic attacks
Impaired concentration ability
  Limited coping abilities
Unexplained behaviors
  Finding oneself in an unfamiliar place
  Finding evidence of having done things that one does not remember doing
  Finding various articles in one's possession that one does not remember buying
History of disorganized behavior
  Inability to complete projects
  Needing lists and notes to organize
  Forgetfulness

---

* Many of these experiences occur in drug-induced altered states; therefore, it is necessary to inquire as to whether these experiences occur at times other than with the use of drugs or alcohol.

Upon receiving reports of any current dissociative behavior, further screening for MPD or another severe dissociative disorder is always indicated. The therapist should explore the extent to which the client is dissociating, how much awareness the client has that he or she is dissociating, and how much control the client has over whether or when he or she dissociates. This information can be gathered while asking about general coping styles and the presenting complaints. For instance, a client may report that he feels nervous around older men because his abuser was his grandfather. When the therapist asks him to give an example, the client replies that he went to a dinner party and was seated next to a man who was about seventy years old and kept nudging him with his elbow as he talked.

"And did you get nervous?" the therapist asks.

"Yes, I didn't want to sit near him," the client replies.

Table 1–2
Indicators of Possible Dissociation Observed in Session

Behavioral clues
  Staring
  Repetitive movements (such as rocking)
  Rigidity of the body
  Unresponsiveness
  Disorientation to time, place, or person
  Responses to visual, auditory, or tactile hallucinations
  Seizurelike behavior
  Signs of regression (childlike voice, posture, or habits)
  A subtle but definite change in face and/or posture that can be recognized in a client that you
    know well.
Affective clues
  Reports of feeling paralyzed, numb, terrified, spacy, floating, feverish, dizzy, cold, far away,
    icy, lightheaded, lost, confused, distant, disconnected, weird, or not feeling anything
  Affect that is incongruent in type or intensity with the current situation
  Labile (unstable) affect
  Rapid shutting down of affect
  Lack of affect
Sensory clues
  Limb paralysis
  Numbness, partial or complete
  Anesthesia
  Paresthesia
  Tingling or buzzing
  Trouble hearing
  Choking or sensation of suffocating
  Tightness in chest
  Tunnel vision or psychogenic blindness
  Pain in parts of the body, most notably pelvis, rectum, vagina, throat, jaw, wrists, ankles,
    neck, or abdomen
  Headaches
  Nausea
  Sensation of falling
  Coldness
  Stigmata, such as bruising, bleeding, or blistering
  Palpitations
Cognitive clues
  Verbal clues to past dissociation
    "I left my body and went to the ceiling."
    "I don't know if that happened to me or to my brother."
    "I saw it happen to this other little boy."
    "I knew it was happening, but I thought about something else."
    "I remember him walking in the door, and the next thing I remember, he was walking out."
    "He came over to the bed and turned out the light . . . and I went out to play."
    "It must have been scary because my sister started to cry."
  Intrainterview amnesia—evidence that the client does not remember portions of the session
  Microamnesia—extremely brief episodes of amnesia during which the client does not hear all
    or part of what was just said
    "Sorry, I missed what you said."
    "I didn't hear you."
    "I was thinking about something else."
  Tangential or circumstantial thought patterns
  Confabulation (building a story on minimal facts)

"And what happened? Do you remember anything else about that dinner?"

"No, I just had to sit there, and I really don't remember much, except how glad I was to leave."

As this is pursued, it becomes clear to the therapist that the young man had dissociated and the entire night was fuzzy except for being nudged by this man's elbow and feeling fearful, after which he blocked out all sensory and affective content.

Two reliable instruments are used to measure dissociative experiences. The Dissociative Experiences Scale (DES) is a short, self-administered screening questionnaire that gives a wealth of information on the types and frequency of dissociative experiences in a given individual (Bernstein and Putnam 1986; Ross, Norton, and Anderson 1988). The Dissociative Disorders Interview Scale (DDIS) is a structured interview that distinguishes among various *DSM III-R* diagnostic categories related to dissociation (Ross et al. 1989; Ross 1989, 314–334). Other instruments have been developed but have not been widely tested on clinical groups, and validity and reliability have yet to be established.

Theoretical Framework

There is now a wide acceptance that childhood sexual abuse is traumatic and harmful and that it often produces long-term sequelae in the adult survivor. The extent of negative effects depends to some degree on a number of external factors, such as age of onset of abuse, length and severity of abuse, and number of perpetrators. In addition, an individual's responses to trauma depend not only on the objective severity of the trauma but also on the subjective experience of what happened. Thus, different individuals may have different responses to the same traumatic event. In no way does this suggest that sexual abuse is not traumatic to some individuals, but it is important to be aware of the various possible responses. It is crucial for therapists to understand the individual's worldview and the personal meaning that individual attaches to the trauma.

How does sexual abuse traumatize the child? Childhood sexual abuse produces psychophysiological stress primarily related to activation of the autonomic nervous system (ANS). Psychologically, when an individual is unable to tolerate the trauma and a "fight or flight" response is not possible, he or she attempts to escape through dissociation. The individual either will have amnesia for the event ("It never happened"), will have an out-of-body experience, or will create an alternate personality ("It happened to someone else, not me"). There is a concurrent physiological process in response to the stress of the trauma. This process creates an altered state of consciousness in the victim that is a hypnoidal dissociative state (Rossi 1986; Rossi and Cheek 1988; Spiegel 1986b). In other words, a stress reaction creates chemical changes in the brain and body, which in turn produce dissociation. Dissociation is similar in nature to the altered state of consciousness produced by hypnosis. Thus, during trauma an individual is in a hypnotic state.

Traumatic experiences are encoded as state-bound information that is accessible only in the psychophysiological state of the individual at the time of the trauma (Braun 1984a, Eich 1980; Mutter 1986; Putnam 1985; Rossi 1986; Rossi and Cheek 1988; van der Kolk and Greenberg 1987). These states contain the dissociated aspects of the trauma. Since they must be accessed for the trauma to be resolved, the therapist who is skilled in recognizing dissociative states and phenomena will have myriad therapeutic options for abreactive work.

Childhood sexual abuse implies the loss of an internal locus of control, with resultant helplessness and the presence of disintegrative anxiety in response to the threatened annihilation of self (Figley 1985; Krystal 1968; Spiegel 1988; van der Kolk 1987). The victim becomes an object rather than a person (depersonalization), losing the self-identity and meaning that normally provide a structure for ontological and psychological security. It is not uncommon for physical security also to be threatened, so the individual literally has no arena in which to maintain the sense of safety and stability that are the necessary underpinnings of living.

Several basic assumptions allow us to maintain our psychological and ontological security in the world. These assumptions include the belief in personal invulnerability, the belief that the world is meaningful and comprehensible, and the view of oneself in a positive light (Janoff-Bulman 1985). They also provide the foundation on which we build cognitive frames to make sense out of our experience. Sexual abuse, as well as other childhood abuses, shatters these assumptions. The abuse is so overwhelming that a child's cognitive structures may be inadequate to process it, much like the analogy of a child attempting to assimilate the concept of infinity (Fish-Murray, Koby, and van der Kolk 1987; Jehu, Klassen, and Gazan 1985; Orzek 1985). The unprocessed traumatic experiences force survivors to maintain an unconscious awareness of their extreme vulnerability, of the dangers of their world, and of their own sense of worthlessness. Because survivors are unable to make sense of, and thus to integrate, the trauma, they continue to remain stuck in the helplessness, anxiety, and meaninglessness of the experience. This is the base for secondary symptom formation.

The experience of trauma and the ensuing shattered assumptions lead survivors into existential crisis (Steele 1988, 1989a, 1989b). The existential crisis will be contained in the worst subjective moment of the trauma for a given individual. An existential crisis is a critical period in which one confronts several issues (Frankl 1963; Grove 1987, 1988; Silver, Boon, and Stones 1983; Spiegel 1988; Steele 1989a; Yalom 1980):

1. Death (or annihilation, the psychological corollary of threatened biological death)
2. Meaninglessness
3. Isolation
4. Issues of freedom and responsibility

Most individuals face these issues symbolically; survivors of childhood abuse often encounter them in the form of literal experiences. It is just such moments that the client must access within the abreaction to resolve the traumatic experience.

The crisis of death is a moment in which one believes that one will die or be annihilated and is helpless to prevent it. The crisis of meaninglessness is a moment in which one's experience is so overwhelming that it makes no sense and cannot be categorized. In addition, one may lose a clear sense of identity both as an individual and as a part of a social setting that provides a context for meaning. The crisis of isolation is a moment in which one is alone at a time when connection with another is most needed. This crisis is often heightened because parents who should be the significant others with whom the child can connect often are the perpetrators of the abuse. The crisis of freedom and responsibility is a moment in which one is utterly helpless, when there is absolutely no internal locus of control at a time when one's own or another's physical and/or psychological integrity is threatened. As a result, individuals may acquire either or both of two defensive postures: (1) They may respond with helplessness to any choice points (learned helplessness), or (2) they may assume an omnipotent responsibility for what has happened, blaming themselves for causing the abuse.

Attention becomes focused and fixed during trauma so that the field of consciousness (that which is held within conscious awareness at a given moment) narrows. This limits the amount of information that can be processed by the individual. Simultaneously, the usual defenses and screening functions of the ego are overwhelmed, and the individual cannot modulate the impact of the trauma. The individual essentially becomes a "blank slate" on which traumatic experiences, including the shattered assumptions and existential crises, are imprinted. Imprints have potent and lasting effects because they are paired with powerful affects and limited attention at a time when the individual has no ability to defend against them. These imprints are frozen as state-specific information within dissociated states. During abreaction, the dissolution of the imprint will occur as its emotional energy is decathected and as the resulting cognitive distortions are reframed. Imprinting is an important concept because it explains the powerful effect of dissociated material on the individual. Stressors (triggers) that are similar in structure to the trauma activate ANS activity, which partially releases the encoding of the imprint, resulting in the intrusion of flashbacks, nightmares, and other derepression phenomena.

By virtue of the dissociative process that is used to defend against these intolerable dilemmas, the survivor becomes fixated in particular moments of unresolved existential crises that have been imprinted. These moments become frozen in time as state-dependent phenomena and thus are refractory to change except within the state in which they occurred. The survivor experiences a bind: Dissociation defends against the disintegrative anxiety related to the existential crisis, but it also prevents resolution by keeping the crisis out of conscious awareness.

The therapeutic goal of abreaction is to unfreeze this moment of ontological insecurity and bring it into conscious awareness so that it can be reexperienced in a different way within the context of therapy. The existential crisis must be alleviated during abreaction by recreating the trauma as a contiguous experience on a continuum of space and time with the four dimensions of BASK reconnected in the client's experience. As the BASK components are linked, they will add clarity and new perspectives to the memories. The existential crisis will become manifest during this process. Cognitive frames that have been formed during preabreactive work can then be added to create new perspectives from which the client can discover the resolution of the crisis.

The experience of trauma, including the shattered assumptions and the existential crisis, results in a traumatic triad of helplessness, terror, and meaninglessness (Steele 1989b). This triad becomes imprinted, thus forming a wedge in the space-time continuum in which time is expanded because of the intensity of the experience, then frozen in a dissociated state (see figure 1–1). Because of the dissociation of at least some aspects of this experience from awareness, and because of the powerful and concentrated imprinting of this experience on the psyche, this experience will continue to have a powerful effect on the individual's life. This traumatic triad can be considered to be the abreactive target. If the client can be released from the "trap" of terror (disintegrative anxiety), meaninglessness, and helplessness, he or she can be empowered to resolve the trauma and to heal. The actual clinical process of accessing the abreactive target is discussed in the section "Alleviating the Existential Crisis."

Having provided a conceptual basis for abreactive work, the next logical step is to discuss the structure and planning of abreactions. For therapists who have witnessed spontaneous, unplanned, and distressing flashbacks by their clients, however, it is clear that abreactions are not always planned and that

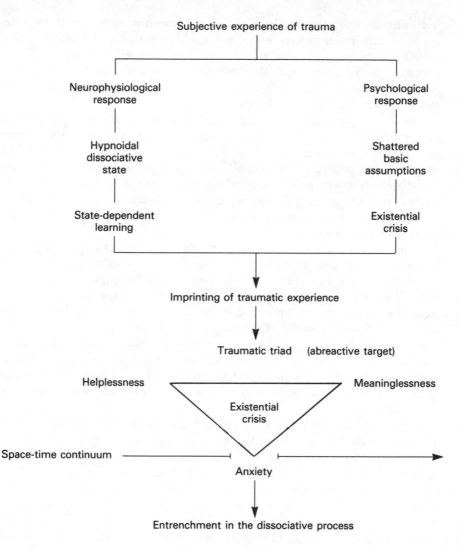

Figure 1–1. Dissociative Responses to Severe Abuse

flashbacks are usually an integral part of therapy with survivors of childhood abuse. Therefore, it is essential to provide some guidelines for understanding, framing, and containing flashbacks (spontaneous abreactions) before proceeding to planned abreactions.

Spontaneous Abreactions

What to Expect

The intense nature of many abreactions is often related to the fact that sensory-perceptual, affective, behavioral, or cognitive components present during the abuse (which have been dissociated and concentrated over a period of years) emerge with the full impact with which they were originally experienced. Abreaction is, in a sense, a time-distortion phenomenon in which the past is brought into the present, the present fades out, and the past becomes the experienced reality in the present. For the moment of the abreaction, reality becomes at least partially altered, and the client responds as though he or she were living in an experience from the past. In other words, during abreactions (spontaneous or planned), the client will be in an altered, dissociative state. Thus, it is crucial for the therapist to understand and be able to use dissociative phenomena therapeutically and to understand that abreactions are dissociative in nature.

Spontaneous abreactions are frequently experienced through conscious and unconscious flashbacks, which may occur during waking or sleep states (Blank 1985). Flashbacks are a reflexive, incomplete, uncontrolled, and fragmentary reexperiencing of trauma, with much of the content occurring unconsciously. Thus, despite the fact that catharsis and memory recovery may occur during flashbacks, these episodes are experienced as overwhelming and traumatic in themselves, and the original traumatic experience is not accessed in a linear fashion within a cognitive frame for understanding, which would promote resolution. Flashbacks can be very frightening, and without a cognitive understanding of the intense affects and sensory experiences that are part of spontaneous abreactions, clients often feel "crazy."

Conscious flashbacks include a cognitive component during which the client has at least partial conscious recall of the traumatic event. Additional dimensions of experience related to the trauma also are present, such as behaviors, affects, or sensations, including vivid multimodal hallucinations. There may be a disorientation to time, place, and person in which the client believes himself or herself to be living in the moment of the remembered trauma, without complete awareness of the present reality. Conscious flashbacks often are dramatic and easy to identify, although when they are misinterpreted by the therapist, they most often are labeled as psychotic episodes.

Unconscious flashbacks are more insidious and difficult to identify but are common occurrences in survivors of child sexual abuse, and their identification will greatly facilitate abreactive work. Unconscious flashbacks are the reexperiencing of some aspects of the traumatic event without conscious awareness. They are triggered by intrapsychic, interpersonal, or environmental cues of which the client is unaware. These cues are actually state-dependent stimuli that access the dissociated aspects of the original trauma (Eich 1980).

For example, a client experienced a panic attack as he walked down an enclosed concrete stairwell. He reported this in session and said he felt he was losing his mind, as he had never been afraid of stairs before. As the event was processed for clues that might have precipitated the panic, the client revealed that he had been eating a candy bar while walking down the stairs. It was discovered that as a child, he had been lured into a similar stairwell by a man offering him chocolate candy. He was subsequently brutally raped, and the complete cognitive memory of that trauma had been dissociated. It was the pairing of the two innocuous and specific environmental cues of chocolate and the stairwell that triggered an unconscious flashback. The panic attack was a reexperiencing of the affective response to the rape. Yet because the client had no conscious awareness of the triggering cues or of the trauma, he reexperienced the affect without the ability to process it. It was only when he was able to access the full cognitive memory along with the affect in an abreactive session that he was able to gain resolution. Following the abreactive session, he was no longer triggered by stairwells or candy bars.

Triggers also may be developmental or related to situational factors in the client's life that may symbolically or structurally recreate some aspect of the traumatic scenario (Gelinas 1983). These may include the onset of adult sexual behavior, marriage, death of a perpetrator or protector, divorce, child-bearing, one's child reaching the age of onset of the client's own abuse, weight loss, serious illness, or job changes.

The effects of triggers may intensify as clients become engaged in therapy and begin to focus on their history. They are more susceptible to triggers and resultant flashbacks when they are fatigued, stressed, or physically ill. Thus, the state of physical health, rest, nutrition, and stress reduction are all important issues to consider when the client is experiencing frequent, uncontrolled flashbacks.

Clients can be taught to recognize impending spontaneous abreactions in an effort to reduce their occurrence during the course of therapy. Signals often alert the client to an impending abreaction (table 1–3). He or she can learn to report early signs of impending abreactions to the therapist, and together they can plan a session to deal with the memory, or they can "contain" the memory by therapeutically using the dissociative skills the client already employs. It is useful to reframe cognitively the frightening signals of flash-backs as important messages that the client is giving himself or herself. The client can then acknowledge the signals as a sign of progress and can begin to have a sense of control as flashbacks become viewed more as a therapeutic instrument with which the client can cooperatively work rather than as an experience of total and meaningless dyscontrol.

Within a session, the therapist may recognize restlessness, hypervigilance, exaggerated startle responses, poor concentration, and evidence of increased

Table 1–3
Signs of Impending Abreactions

Dizziness or lightheadedness
Headaches
A subjective sense of "shifting" or "movement" inside the head
A sinking or drowning feeling
Telescoping or tunnel phenomena in which one feels physically distant from current reality
Confusion and/or disorientation
Hallucinations
   Auditory
   Visual
   Kinesthetic
   Rapid "snapshot" images of the abuse
Sudden and unexplained onset of dysphoria
   Free-floating anxiety and dread
   Panic attacks
   Irritability
   Depression with weakness and/or unusual fatigue
Secondary responses to dysphoria
   Self-mutilation or suicide gestures and attempts
   Missing or canceling therapy appointments
   Alcohol and drug use
   Binging and purging or anorexia
   Sexual acting out
Sleep disturbances
   Sleep avoidance
   Insomnia
   Hypersomnia (not common)
   Frequent sleep interruptions
Nightmares with specific themes related to abuse
   Night terrors
Phobic reactions to external stimuli
Physiological signs of automatic arousal, with or without associated feelings of panic
   Tachycardia (rapid heart rate)
   Palpitations
   Sweating
   Dry mouth
   Diarrhea, nausea, or vomiting
   Hyperventilation
   Hypervigilance and scanning
   Exaggerated startle responses
   Increased motoric tension and/or activity
      Agitation
      Pacing
      Restlessness
   Fight or flight responses
      Increased aggression
      Withdrawal

dissociation in a client just prior to spontaneous abreactions. Often the content of the session will trigger these, and the therapist will become astute in recognizing what material is most likely to produce spontaneous abreactions. He or she should approach these areas with caution in the beginning stages of therapy and at any other times that abreactions are not desirable (such as shortly before the therapist's vacation). Various types of acting out often precede abreaction, especially acts of self-mutilation, alcohol and/or drug use, binging or purging, and boundary testing with the therapist. Such acts temporarily relieve the internal pressure and dysphoria that are commonly experienced with the onset of abreactions.

When a client enters a spontaneous abreaction, the manner in which the therapist responds will affect the client's experience of the flashback. It is necessary for the therapist to remain calm and in charge. The therapist's own sense of helplessness, coupled with the contagious nature of the client's anxiety, will tend to increase the therapist's anxiety. The therapist should consciously relax his or her own body, breathe slowly and evenly, and help the client to pace his or her own breathing. The therapist should make eye contact if possible. This will provide a grounding in reality. It is helpful to speak slowly, clearly, and calmly. Suggestions given to the client should be simple, concrete, specific, and gently repetitious.

Containing Spontaneous Abreactions

The therapist faces a difficult and delicate choice point when confronted with a client who is in the midst of a spontaneous abreaction. Should the therapist help the client "get out" of it, or should the therapist facilitate movement into a therapeutic abreaction? The primary criteria for the successful management of flashbacks are as follows:

1. To prevent a retraumatization of the client
2. To ensure that the client has adequate ego strength and is oriented enough to the present to maintain his or her grounding in reality.
3. To modulate the intensity of the experience enough so that learning can occur
4. To provide a workable linear and cognitive frame within which to process the memory

If these criteria cannot be met within a given abreaction, then the therapist should make every effort to contain it until a later time.

In making the decision about whether to contain or facilitate a flashback, the therapist must consider a number of factors.

1. Is the timing right within the session? Abreactive work should not be started after the first third of a session. An ideal abreaction is begun with preparatory work in the first third, the actual abreaction in the second third, and closing and processing in the final third of a session. If an extended session

is needed, this should be planned ahead of time with the client's consent. Unplanned, prolonged abreactive sessions can give the client a sense of interminable pain.

2. Does the client have the ego strength to process disturbing memories and intense affects? If not, it is advisable to contain the abreaction until further ego strengthening is accomplished within the therapy. If the client is totally overwhelmed with intense affect and is not oriented to the present, it is advisable to distance him or her from such a malignant process.

3. Is the context for abreaction safely set? The internal and external context for abreactive work is critical, and no planned abreactive work should occur before this is well in place. Setting the appropriate context is discussed in detail later in the chapter.

4. Is the client asking to "get out," or is he or she willing to go deeper? It may be useful to say something like "When this happened back then, you had no choices. Now you have a choice about whether you would like to continue and find out what happens next." Lending some control to clients is critical in enlisting their cooperation in such a painful process and ultimately in empowering them.

5. Is the therapist grounded enough in his or her knowledge and skills to manage the process? Is he or she psychically and spiritually prepared for the intensity of the experience?

If flashbacks are interfering with both the client's everyday life and the therapy, the client can be taught to avoid for a time the environmental cues that are known to trigger abreactions. Bedrooms, basements, closets, beds, bathrooms, nighttime, and the many sensory cues related to sexual activity are common environmental cues for triggering abreactions for survivors. Obviously, one cannot avoid these entirely, but the anxiety and fear may be countered by providing rituals of safety for a period of time. For instance, nightlights, changing the color of sheets, an audiotape of a soothing voice giving orienting information, appropriate transitional objects, sleeping on the couch instead of the bed, and other temporary environmental changes may be used as stopgap measures. Cognitive framing and thought-blocking techniques may be somewhat useful at this point, but the underlying memories often must be addressed before this is entirely successful.

Temporary time-limited contracts may be made between the client and his or her sexual partner to facilitate the containment of flashbacks. These may include a period of celibacy, elimination of specific sexual activities, and other approaches that give the survivor more conscious control over the initiation, type, and frequency of sexual activity. Obviously, if the client is in an abusive relationship, sexual or otherwise, the current abuse must be addressed before any historical work is done.

Once clients have a moderate amount of ego strength, have been taught to recognize impending abreactions, and have experienced a number of planned abreactions, they can be taught to manage and process spontaneous abreactions outside of therapy. But this is usually a late development in therapy; in the beginning, flashbacks will simply retraumatize them. Most abreactions are frightening and painful experiences. Therapists must help clients to have control during abreactions in session for them to be willing to risk managing spontaneous abreactions on their own.

If the decision is made to help a client contain a memory, there are a number of ways to distance him or her from the flashback experience. If it is obvious that a client is experiencing flashbacks early in therapy, it is often useful to make a contract for him or her to attempt to separate cognition and affect and to hold the affect until it can be safely processed in the therapy session. This must be done prior to the moment when a client is actually in the midst of a flashback. To accomplish this, the therapist must enlist the client's dissociative skills. The effectiveness of such techniques depends to some degree on the dissociative ability of a given client. For example, one client who was having frequent flashbacks decided to (imaginatively) put all the accompanying feelings into a balloon and then send the balloon to her therapist's office, where she could access them during the following session.

If a client is at the point where he or she can begin to tolerate some of the effect, the following technique may be useful. The client is asked to imagine a container that can hold the feelings he or she is unable to tolerate. Then the therapist asks the client to gather all the feelings and put them into the container, except for a small amount (teaspoonful, cupful, handful, or the like) that the client actively chooses to feel.

As the client enters a spontaneous abreaction, the therapist may shift to the use of the third person, referring to the client as he or she. "And what does *she* experience now?" This creates an artificial dissociation between the adult client in the office and the inner child * who experienced the abuse years ago. This allows the client to observe and report the experience rather than being trapped in the affect of the past.

Further distancing can be accomplished by the use of past instead of present tense: "And so it *was* very scary for him *back then*." It is also important not to ask affectively directed questions, such as "What was he feeling?" but to focus more on cognitive themes such as "What was he thinking?" This will help begin to reduce intense affect by refocusing attention away from the affect and by adding a cognitive dimension to the experience.

---

* The term *inner child* is used here to denote the state of the individual during the remembered childhood trauma. The inner child is a common phenomenon in survivors of childhood abuse and represents a wide spectrum of dissociative responses that may range from metaphorical self-perceptions to ego-state phenomena to actual alternate personalities (Summit 1987).

Once this dissociation is accomplished, the therapist can suggest that the inner child ("the part of you that was there then") can go to a previously determined internal safe space. A safe space is an imaginative phenomenon created to assist the client in feeling safe, relaxed, and protected.

Safe spaces should be developed in the initial stage of therapy, prior to abreactive work. To create a safe space, the client is asked to imagine a place that is completely safe and comforting while in a state of relaxation. The client can be taught to relax and go to this space outside of therapy with practice. Once the client practices this on a regular basis, he or she may be able to use it when overcome by spontaneous memories or intense affects.

There are several keys to effective safe spaces:

1. The space must feel unequivocally safe to the client.
2. The space is more effective when it comes from the client's psyche rather than from a suggestion made by the therapist.
3. The type of safe space will change with the client's needs; thus, it must be updated and revised periodically.
4. Each aspect of the inner child (the part[s] of the client that hold the abuse memory) will need his or her own safe space.
5. The safe space must be elaborated through all five senses to enhance the effectiveness of the experience. For example, the therapist may ask about colors, descriptions of scenery, sounds, and smells.

Common safe spaces include hideaways in the woods or mountains, beaches, caves, rooms or a version of the therapy room, bubbles, or being with protector figures such as animals, people, or objects.

Other ways to create distance in a flashback include gradually moving the experience farther from the direct experience of clients by having them see it as a play they are watching from a front-row seat, then having them move to the back of the theater, then having it on a large movie screen, then moving it to a smaller television screen, and so on. Alternatively, clients may be able to imagine a book in a library that contains the abuse memories. Clients are instructed to close the book whenever they need or want to, and put it back on the shelf whenever they have read enough for one time (Braun 1984b). Or the memory may be put in a container with a lid that is under the client's control.

The therapist can reorient clients by reminding them to be both "here and there at the same time," while offering them a bridge to the present. Bridges may be auditory, kinesthetic, or visual. An auditory bridge can be created simply by talking to the client and saying, "As you hear the sound of my voice, let my words wrap around you and bring you back. Follow the sound of my voice back to now." Tactile bridges are useful but can be dangerous. If the therapist touches a client in the midst of an intense abreaction, the client may incorporate that touch into the abuse scenario and the therapist will become the perceived abuser. At first it may be more useful to ask clients to feel the couch, to feel that they have pants on, to feel something in the environment that was not likely to have been present during the abuse. After the client is oriented, the therapist may say, "And if you like, the adult part of you can hold my hand now as a reminder that part of you remains here in the present with me." This offers the client a choice about touch. Visual bridges may be used in a similar way: looking to see that he or she has pants on, looking around the room, looking at the therapist, and so on. It is useful to establish such bridges with the client before a planned abreaction begins.

It may be possible to suggest that the client change a small part of the image or experience as an entry into helping him or her get out of it. For instance, a client may be asked to change his or her position in the image so that he or she is watching the scene from above or from another angle. This is often quite difficult once the client is fully into an abreaction and is more useful in the early stages of a flashback.

Several other hypnotic techniques can be used to end a spontaneous abreaction. These are usually most successful when used within a planned, controlled abreaction but may be attempted to contain spontaneous ones. The therapist can attempt to limit the amount of time an intense affect is experienced by saying, "I am going to count from ten to one. You need only feel what you are feeling for ten seconds. As I count, you can feel less and less, until, at the count of one, you can move completely away from that feeling." Age progression can be used to move an individual through a traumatic event to its end. Sometimes an inner child state can be put to sleep for a brief period of time.

These are temporary, stopgap measures to be used when abreactive work is not desirable or useful. They should not be used to cut short abreactive work for the convenience or comfort of the therapist. Whenever possible, once an abreaction has started, it should be allowed to run its course.

Occasionally, once amnestic barriers begin to be breached in the course of therapy, a malignant derepression and flooding of memories may occur. If, in spite of competent containment measures, the client continues to have uncontrolled flashbacks or becomes overtly psychotic, a brief hospitalization and the adjunctive use of medication are indicated for the purpose of stabilization. Once the client is stabilized, additional containment and ego strengthening measures should be instituted before returning to abreactive work, and closer attention should be paid to pacing. Occasionally, a client will not be able to tolerate abreactive work. In this case, supportive rather than uncovering therapy is indicated, and the trauma should be sealed over as the therapy focuses on current issues that will maintain and improve the client's functioning capacities.

A Model for Planned Abreactions

Although abreactions may seem to be a confusing, frightening, and disconnected experience for the client (and sometimes for the therapist), abreactive
work should follow a logical process. If the therapist can guide the course of
each abreaction through this process, abreactive work should prove to be efficient and effective.

Of course, many abreactions do not contain an entire memory. The same
memory may need to be abreacted several times in order to access all the missing pieces (Putnam 1989). Not every memory will have to be abreacted; some
generalization begins to occur as various types of memories are processed
(Ross 1989). The therapist should understand that this process will take a
long time (months to years) and that it should not be hurried. Each client will
need and tolerate differing amounts of abreactive work, and even with good
work, this phase probably will seem to last longer than the client or the therapist wishes.

The logical question to ask is "When has enough abreactive work been
done?" The answer often comes in retrospect because new memories may
emerge over the course of therapy after the major portion of abreactive work
is thought to have been completed. Usually, however, some signals indicate
that abreactive work is finished. These include evidence of the following:

1. The client has a relatively continuous memory of the traumatic time
   period(s).
2. He or she is not currently dissociating in an uncontrolled or dysfunctional
   way.
3. He or she is not experiencing flashbacks or reliving the trauma in other
   ways.
4. He or she can remember and talk about the trauma without intolerable
   affect.
5. He or she has developed a subjective sense of the personal meaning of the
   trauma.
6. He or she expresses interest in and hope for the future rather than feeling
   overwhelmed by the past.

The conceptual model presented here can be followed both within a given
session during an abreactive event and through various segments of an
abreactive process that may occur over a longer period of time. The abreactive
process can be conceptualized as a model that has five basic components
forming the convenient mnemonic PEACE (Steele 1988, 1989a). This model
includes the following:

Preparing the context

Eliciting dissociated aspects

Alleviating the existential crisis

Creating a gestalt

Empowering the client

This conceptual model is based on a number of theoretical and clinical paradigms of trauma, including the following five components:

1. State-dependent learning (Braun 1984a, Eich 1980; Rossi 1986; Rossi and Cheek 1988)
2. Posttraumatic stress theory (Figley 1985, Horowitz 1976; Mutter 1986; Ochberg 1988; Spiegel 1984, 1988; van der Kolk 1987)
3. Cognitive distortion patterns in abuse victims (Fine 1988a, 1988b; Donaldson and Gardner 1985; Fish-Murray, Koby, and van der Kolk 1987; Jehu, Klassen, and Gazan 1985; Orzek 1985; Ross and Gahan 1988)
4. The BASK model of dissociation (Braun 1985, 1988a, 1988b)
5. Existential psychotherapy (Frankl 1963; Spiegel 1988; Yalom 1980)

The following sections address each of these five components in turn.

Preparing the Context (Preparation Phase)

Planned abreactions should not be undertaken in the early phase of treatment, although spontaneous abreactions may occur. The early phase of treatment includes the assessment period and the time in which a stable therapeutic alliance is being established, as well as a stabilization period for the client who enters therapy in crisis. A context of safety must first be established within the whole therapeutic process, as well as before, during, and after each abreactive event.

The therapist can do certain things to create a safe context for abreaction. Intrapsychic, interpersonal, and environmental issues are delineated below. This is not an exhaustive list but offers a basic framework for the creation of a safe and stable context for abreactive work. Such a context is crucial because of the rigorous and painful nature of abuse memory work.

Intrapsychic Safety

1. Simply talking about safety with a client introduces a concept and conveys a concern that the client has never, or rarely, experienced. From the very

beginning of the therapeutic relationship, the therapist must ask, "What would help you to feel safe now?" By doing so, the therapist is giving the client permission to begin to feel that he or she has a right to feel safe.

2. Helping the client to define and normalize dissociation and other survival mechanisms not only alleviates some of the client's fear that he or she is "crazy" but also lays the groundwork to enlist dissociative skills therapeutically to the advantage of the client.

3. Creating an internal safe space will allow the client to begin to learn to modulate intense experiences through imagery and relaxation and will provide a sense of internal safety.

4. Recognizing "triggers"—events, words, people, or objects that cause flashbacks—is an essential step in identifying feelings or thoughts that need to be "contained" or "saved" until later, thereby giving the client a sense of control.

5. The client must feel relatively secure that he or she will be believed. With each "telling," he or she will have fears about being punished, not being heard, or not being believed. The fact that the therapist will listen, believe, and not punish needs to be reinforced over and over again for the client.

6. The therapist needs an awareness of the individual's subjective meaning of "telling." There are many prohibitions against talking about the abuse (Lister 1982). These include issues of shame, guilt, and badness; injunctions against telling; split loyalties; religious taboos; and, in the case of cult abuse, internal cues for self-destructive behavior (Steele 1989a). These need to be cognitively and/or affectively addressed prior to abreactive work.

7. A working knowledge of the individual's defensive patterns will help in predicting stress reactions to an abreaction.

8. It is important to know the individual's general worldview and his or her awareness of family rules and messages (Harris and Colrain 1986). The context in which the abreaction is processed will depend in large part on the cognitive reframing that has already occurred (Courtois 1988; Donaldson and Gardner 1985).

9. The therapist must constantly modulate the intensity of the experience to what the individual can tolerate, always titrating the work against existing ego strength and building ego strength over the course of therapy.

10. General awareness of the cognitive content and identification of the missing pieces of abuse memories allow for more adequate planning and a structure within which to process abreactions (Courtois 1988; Putnam 1989; Ross 1989). Abreactive work that is not couched within an adequate cognitive schema can retraumatize the patient (Braun 1986; Comstock 1986; Kluft 1984, 1985).

11. The adjunctive use of medication may be useful to modulate secondary symptoms such as anxiety, depression, and insomnia. Chronic responses to trauma often are all or nothing. Indiscriminate and intense psychophysio-

logical responses (such as panic attacks) to all stimuli sometimes need to be decreased temporarily so that the individual may be amenable to therapy. Medication may be quite useful in reducing such intense responses. For example, clonazepam has recently been used successfully to mitigate the panic and nightmares related to PTSD (Loewenstein, Hornstein, and Farber 1988). It is important to note, however, that no medication ameliorates dissociative symptoms and none will substitute for appropriate containment interventions by the therapist.

12. To empower the client, the therapist must be willing to give him or her control whenever possible (without abdicating the therapy to the client) and to take the mystery out of the therapeutic process by educating the client about the purposes and functions of abreactive work. Empowering the client also means trusting the client's pacing.

Interpersonal Safety

1. The therapist must constantly give attention to issues of trust within the therapeutic relationship (Braun 1986; Kluft 1983, 1984, 1985). A solid therapeutic alliance is absolutely essential before abreactive work is undertaken. Traumatized clients cannot be expected to develop rapid, absolute trust in the therapist; this is an unrealistic goal and is often based on a counter-transferential need for the therapist to be liked and seen as good (Chu 1988b). In the beginning, however, the client must be able to give the therapist the benefit of the doubt.

2. The use of touch in psychotherapy is a controversial subject. Whether touch will be used in the therapy will be dictated by the beliefs and comfort level of the therapist. It is the authors' practice to use touch judiciously and with forethought. Survivors are often ambivalent about touch: They yearn for safe touch, and yet their experience has been that touch is frightening, painful, and/or intrusive. Therefore, the therapist should scrupulously examine his or her motivation to touch the client. Touch should never be given if it is for the benefit of the therapist, or if it obstructs therapeutic work by rescuing or prematurely comforting the client. It is essential that the client feel that he or she has control over not being touched. To maintain safe boundaries, there may be times that the therapist chooses not to touch the client in spite of a request to do so. For instance, it is common for survivors to have difficulty distinguishing between nurturing and sexual touch; it is important to make the distinction cognitively with the client before touch is initiated.

3. Maintenance of boundaries and the therapy frame will provide a sense of protection for the client and will relieve him or her of the responsibility of taking care of the therapist (Braun 1986; Chu 1988a; Kluft 1984, 1985). The therapist must be consistent and predictable and strictly adhere to clear boundaries, particularly in the area of sexuality. Breaking sexual boundaries with

any client is unethical and traumatizing to the client. Clients who have a history of sexual abuse are especially vulnerable to inappropriate sexual behavior from anyone in a position of power and trust (Pope and Bouhoutsos 1986).

4. Transference issues need to be worked through both prior to and after abreactive work (Braun 1986; Chu 1988a; Courtois 1988; Wilbur 1988). Survivors of childhood abuse will develop a traumatic transference during the course of therapy (Spiegel 1984, 1988). The traumatic transference is not only object relations based but also scenario based in that the client will unconsciously set up a double bind within the therapy session that reenacts episodes of abuse. The therapist will be seen as alternately withholding or punitive. This transference must be carefully monitored and interpreted, with "here and now" constantly distinguished from "there and then."

5. Resistance to abreactive work is almost universal because of the recall of deeply painful affects and sometimes horrendous memories. It is easy to imagine why clients would prefer not to remember much of what has happened to them. Resistance must be acknowledged and addressed rather than bypassed; vital information about the client and his or her response to the trauma is contained in such resistance. Chu (1988a) states:

> The resistance and the resulting crises of the patient in treatment are the substrate for the therapeutic process itself. . . . They [resistances] represent major opportunities for further understanding of the patient, as the patient and therapist together experience the vicissitudes of the patient's life. (p. 37)

At the same time, the therapist must gently and firmly guide (not shove) clients who are pain-phobic toward healing abreactive work. There is a complex, delicate, and ever-changing balance between respecting the client's resistance and guiding the client into abreactive work. The therapist must be exquisitely sensitive to this balance with each client.

6. Abreactive work requires that the therapist cultivate an acute awareness of countertransference issues related to the patient in general and to abreactive experiences specifically. Therapists ought to have a clear sense of their level of tolerance for such work. They need to develop ways of releasing and renewing to minimize the possibility of burnout and secondary PTSD (Braun et al. 1987; Courtois 1988, 229–243; Olson, Mayton, and Braun 1988; Putnam 1989; Ross 1989). Therapists who are working with survivors need resources for resolving countertransference issues, including personal therapy, group supervision, and/or individual consultation.

7. The therapist can use the concept of self as a grounding during and after abreaction and other methods of reality orientation to assist the client in distinguishing "here and now" from "there and then" (Comstock 1986; Putnam 1989).

8. The client ought to be encouraged to develop support networks within the family and within the community (Sachs 1986).

9. The client and/or the therapist can teach significant others about the purposes of abreaction and supportive measures they can provide the client.

Environmental Safety

1. The office of the therapist must be "abreaction-proof." This is merely a common-sense approach to basic safety issues. For example, sharp objects ought not to be openly available during a session in which the client may be very distraught or angry.

2. The therapist ought to be aware of the client's safety if he or she is driving to and from the office and should have the client arrange reliable transportation or provide time for the client to reorient before leaving the office.

3. It is important that a safe, structured environment outside the therapy hour be established and maintained. The client whose life is chaotic and unpredictable is a poor candidate for abreactive work.

4. A safe and trusting framework within the session needs to be created tailored to the individual's needs. For example, the client may wish to sit close to the door, have the blinds closed, or have the lights dimmed.

5. In planning abreactive work, the therapist must consider the age, life expectancy, quality of life, and physical condition of the client. Abreaction can be rigorous work, and sealing over, or modified abreactive work that includes techniques to minimize intensity, ought to be considered in some cases where the intense emotions generated by abreactive work would pose a threat to physical health (Kluft 1988, 1989). In the case of clients with imminent terminal illness, sealing over and focusing on improving the current quality of life is recommended, since abreactive work may take considerable time (months to years) and the client may find current concerns more salient and pressing.

6. When planning abreactive work, the therapist needs to be flexible concerning the length and spacing of sessions. Adequate follow-up sessions ought to be planned after intense abreactive work to help the client process what happened cognitively.

7. When the abuse has been exceptionally severe, sadistic, or ritualistic, such clients may require the protective environment of a hospital during abreactive work. Clients may become acutely suicidal or homicidal as they remember severe abuses. Contracts for no suicide or homicide are essential. Planned hospitalization to process such intense memories can be useful, but this option needs to be used sparingly and judiciously to avoid overwhelming the client. Clients who have experienced sadistic and systematic abuse are much more likely to be severely dissociated and fragmented; therefore, extra attention must be paid to ego strengthening, containment, and titration of affect. There are many specialized techniques for working with severe or ritualistic abuse victims, but these are beyond the scope of the chapter.

When working with clients with MPD, all of the above issues are applicable. There are also a number of concerns specific to MPD that are beyond the scope of this chapter. Several sources deal specifically with abreactive work in MPD (Braun 1986; Comstock 1986; Putnam 1989; Ross 1989; Steele 1989a).

Based on this context for abreaction, it is important to recognize a number of conditions that contraindicate abreactive work. These include the following:

1. The early stages of therapy
2. An unstable therapeutic alliance
3. Current and ongoing abuse
4. Current acute external life crises
5. Extreme age, severe physical infirmity, and/or terminal illness
6. Lack of ego strength, including severe borderline and psychotic states or pathological regression.

The provision of safety is an ongoing issue in treatment and ought to be continuously monitored. Once protection is ensured within the therapy, the actual abreactive work can begin.

Eliciting Dissociated Aspects (Identification Phase)

Dissociated aspects contain vital information that the client needs to assimilate the trauma. Successful abreactive work requires the reconstruction of the experience of trauma so that it may be reworked in therapy. Dissociated components of experience, including behaviors, affects, sensations, and knowledge, must be brought into the client's awareness in a timely manner. Thus, it is imperative for the therapist to elicit these aspects during the course of abreactive work. Any aspects that remain dissociated will continue to force the client to alternate between numbing and intrusive symptoms in order to ward off their impact. To elicit the dissociated components, the abreaction must first be initiated.

Five basic elements are involved in the initiation of an abreaction:

1. Contracting to work on a specific issue or memory
2. Developing a cognitive frame in which the memory can be processed
3. Using adjunctive modalities
4. Developing a safe context for a particular abreaction
5. Identifying missing BASK components

Some BASK components will be identified during the development of a cognitive frame, and others will be identified during the actual abreaction.

It is useful to contract with clients about doing abreactive work. This empowers them by giving them choices and a sense of control. Contracting may be as simple as asking whether the client would like to explore the memory. It may include considerations of timing (now or later) and the scope of the abreaction ("what happened with my brother but not what happened once my father came in with us").

When a client has blocked the memory of large portions of his or her childhood, a basic frame of reference, including time, place, and person, ought to be developed before any abreactive work begins. For instance, clients can be encouraged to explore what it was like at school; what the structure of a typical day might have been; what their favorite clothes were; what they liked to eat; what kinds of fun experiences they had; when they learned certain developmental tasks; who lived in their house; who slept in which room; when they might have moved from one place to another. Sometimes it is useful for them to collect stories about their childhood from friends and family (Herman and Schatzow 1987).

As clients become more familiar with the general historical context of their childhood, they can begin to explore more affectively loaded areas related to the abuse issues, such as what it was like to be with mother, father, or brother. Family photo albums can be brought to session, and as the client and therapist view the pictures and talk about the content and context of each picture, much information about the client's family life will be revealed. Gradually, as more information is gained in the early stages of therapy, the client will begin to develop more of an understanding of what it was like for him or her during childhood. This is the context in which the sexual abuse can be understood. For example, a client may remember that it was difficult to talk to his father, that in fact his father was quite stern and distant and they rarely talked at all. In the future, when he feels guilty that he did not tell his father about the sexual abuse by his mother, he will have a broader context in which to understand and process that experience.

For a planned abreaction it is useful to develop a cognitive frame around a specific memory or issue in the same manner in which a general frame for childhood was developed. As much knowledge as possible about the particular memory ought to be gathered prior to the abreaction (Sachs, Braun, and Shepp 1988). There are a number of ways to get such knowledge. Some of the most useful ones involve the use of adjunctive modalities.

Nonverbal modalities are especially helpful in working with abuse survivors. For many individuals, the task of "telling" horrendous memories is overwhelming and frightening, making verbalization difficult in the beginning. Injunctions against telling, including threats of death, are powerful imprints and inhibit survivors well into therapy (Lister 1982). Many trauma victims are alexithymic and do not have the vocabulary or cognitive structure to describe their internal affective experience (Krystal 1968).

Alexithymia is a syndrome commonly seen in severely traumatized individuals. Such individuals experience emotional states as undifferentiated, poorly verbalized, and primarily somatic, and there is a general inability to translate the somatic sensations into affective states. Thus alexithymic individuals are unable to utilize affects as signals about emotional states and therefore cannot describe how they feel (Krystal 1979).

Somatic and affective memories that are not coupled with cognitive content may be difficult to express verbally. And abuse memories that do not include eidetic images, such as preverbal memories or memories that are so dissociated as to be dreamlike, cannot be verbalized in the usual way.

Also, many abuse memories are quite fragmented and are thus difficult to communicate in a meaningful way. In such cases, a number of adjunctive, nonverbal modalities are useful in initiating abreactions. These include, but are not limited to, sandtray work (Sachs 1989); journaling (Courtois 1988; Sachs, Braun, and Shepp 1988); movement therapies (Chess 1989); music; the use of anatomically correct dolls and puppets; and artwork (Dyck 1988; Greenberg and van der Kolk 1987; Wohl and Kaufman 1985), including clay (Geeseman 1988), finger paints, drawing, and collages.

Journaling is one of the most useful ways to get cognitive material. A client may be asked to write about a specific time period or relationship or about a specific incident of abuse. To gain the cognitive information without the affective component, the client can be asked to write the memory as if it were a story that is about someone else.

Artwork is a powerfully effective way to gather cognitive material and to initiate abreactions. For instance, a client can be asked to draw a picture of himself or herself during the age(s) at which the abuse occurred. Critically important details which the client might otherwise have never thought to bring up with the therapist, may be revealed in such drawings. Clients also can "draw" feelings, giving them substance and form, thereby providing a concrete expression of, and sometimes containment for, the feelings. If the client is having flashbacks or dreams related to the abuse, he or she can draw the associated images.

Once cognitive framing and adjunctive modalities have been used to provide a structure for the abreaction, specific safety measures may be undertaken to ensure the abreaction. Guidelines for setting the general context for abreactive work are delineated in the section "Preparing the Context." Other interventions may be used to set the specific context for a particular abreaction. The therapist can arrange for preestablished cues, or "bridges" between the past and the present, that will orient the client. Clients can be given permission to stop the abreaction at any point. They also can be given permission to remember only what they are ready to remember.

Affect may be titrated by asking the client to imagine his or her feelings during the abreaction on a scale of 1 to 10, with 1 indicating minimal intensity of feeling and 10 indicating intolerable intensity. Prior to the abreactive work, the client can choose a point on this scale that will indicate the intensity of feeling that is subjectively intolerable. A client who has little tolerance for feeling may choose 3 as the point at which he or she needs to stop, but another client may be able to tolerate 9. Then, during the abreaction, when the client indicates (by raising a finger or by saying the number) that the feeling level has reached the predetermined point, the therapist can assist the client in moving away from the feeling and memory while inducing a deep relaxation. Once the client is relaxed, he or she can move back into the memory. This is basically a desensitization process and will allow the client to gain mastery in a stepwise fashion.

Clues to the dissociated aspects of traumatic experiences will be contained in the client's verbalized memories, affects, and somatic manifestations; in phobias, compulsions, and hallucinations; in dreams and nightmares; in nonverbal modalities; and even in the client's metaphors (Braun 1988a, 1988b; Comstock 1986; Grove 1987, 1988; van der Kolk 1987; van der Kolk and Kadish 1987).

BASK indicators of dissociation are listed in table 1–2. These clues will assist the therapist in determining the missing dimensions of experience within a given abreaction and will give the therapist an entry point into an abreaction. For example, in the process of talking about her adolescence, a client reported to her therapist that she used to push the bureau in front of her bedroom door each night. She also reported that she did not know why she had done that. In addition, until telling her therapist about it, it had never occurred to her that it was an unusual behavior. In this instance, the client had knowledge of a behavior that was disconnected from any cognitive understanding of the origin of the behavior.

To initiate an abreaction, the therapist asked the client whether she wanted to pursue the memory at that time. Once a contract was made with the client, she was asked to draw her bedroom, showing the bureau in front of the door. This elicited some anxiety. She was then asked to find a way to act out the behavior by pushing the bureau. The client chose to push a chair across the room to the door. As soon as she began pushing the chair, she began to reexperience the full affective dimension (terror) of the past experience. Once she had accessed the affect, she immediately gained the cognitive component and said. "Oh, I pushed the dresser against the door to keep my father out!"

Affective and sensory clues present in the client during the session may be used to initiate an abreaction. One of the most common ways to do this is to ask, "When have you felt that before?" or "Do you remember the first time you felt that feeling?" An affect or sensory bridge also can be hypnotically created (Watkins 1971). Once the client has entered the abreaction, the next phase may begin.

Alleviating the Existential Crisis (Resolution Phase)

During an abreaction, the client is in an altered state of consciousness, and contact with the present reality fades. The client loses a sense of chronological time as he or she moves into a state-bound experience. Prior to abreactive work, the client has been unexpectedly and chaotically thrown back in history during flashbacks and other intrusion phenomena. A planned abreaction must add a sense of continuity and finiteness that flashbacks have not provided. A time line of the trauma must be provided for the client so that he or she experiences the beginning and the end of the trauma (Putnam 1989). The client with dissociated traumatic memories does not have a sense of past and present relative to the trauma, so the abuse has a sense of timelessness. Flashbacks typically take a client back into the middle of an experience or provide only a fragmentary piece that is reexperienced over and over, thus making it seem interminable.

A time line can be provided by asking the client to go back in time to just before the trauma happened. This direction need not be specific (for example, telling a client to go back to 9:50 P.M. if the trauma happened at 10:00 P.M.). It is rare for the client to have a literal sense of the exact time of abuse, especially when it occurred over a period of years. Yet the unconscious of the client will consistently be able to provide a point in time from which to begin the abreaction. Once the abreaction has begun, the therapist can continue to provide a linear frame by asking, "And after that, what happened next?" (Grove 1987).

Abreactions typically follow a curve of intensity (Ross 1989). The peak of the curve will correlate with the most intense moments of the episode for the client. The traumatic triad of anxiety, helplessness, and meaninglessness will be found at the apex of the curve, and the existential crisis will manifest itself at this point.

The therapist can recognize the peak of the curve through verbal and non-verbal communications from the client. Existential crises often can be detected through themes the client will verbalize (Steele 1989a). Typical examples include the following:

- Death—"I am going to die"; "I wish to die"; "I can't stand the pain."

- Meaninglessness—"Why is this happening?"; "Why me?"; "No, it can't be my dad doing this to me!"

- Isolation—"I am alone; there is no one who can/will help"; "I am bad/dirty/guilty/different and can't be with others in a meaningful way"; Nobody could ever love me after this."

- Freedom and responsibility—"Could I have stopped it?"; "I *should* have stopped it!"; "It shouldn't have felt good; I must have wanted it"; "If I hadn't stayed home that day it wouldn't have happened"; "I should have fought harder."

Nonverbal clues to the peaking of the experience will be related primarily to the client's increasing affective response to the memory. Behavioral manifestations such as curling up, holding the crotch, sitting in the corner, and other behaviors generated by the client in a protective effort may be evident.

A wish on the part of the therapist to stop the abreaction and comfort the client often is a countertransferential clue that the abreaction is reaching its peak intensity. It is not easy to be with a human being who is suffering so intensely, and the therapist's wish to rescue may rise along with the intensity of the abreaction. Rescuing the client before he or she has achieved resolution, however, will result only in the abreaction having to be repeated again at another time. The fact remains that the client was not rescued from the abuse, and any attempt by the therapist to correct for that prior to resolution of the "stuck point" will be ineffective and obstructive to the client's progress.

It is, however, a positive and humane response to feel discomfort and empathy in the presence of such intense anguish. This response can be used in many constructive ways with the client and should not be suppressed. The client will not progress very far unless the therapist is caring and empathic. The empathic presence of the therapist creates a continuous experience during the abreaction, and his or her effective guidance of the abreaction is, in itself, a different and healing experience for the client. It is crucial that the therapist learn to distinguish between times when an abreaction ought to be titrated or stopped for the benefit of the client and times when there is a temptation to do so for the therapist's personal comfort.

As the abreaction reaches its peak, clients often stop the experience themselves. Or they may avoid the worst moment, focusing instead on an image or feeling that was experienced just prior to or after the worst moment. If the therapist feels that the client is missing a piece of the memory, it is sometimes helpful to ask the client whether there is anything else about the memory that he or she needs to have. The client then can review the entire memory as though it were a movie. Suggestions to view it from different angles may be helpful (Putnam 1989). This will continue to add small (and sometimes surprisingly large) pieces of experience to the abreaction in order to complete it.

The client must gain enough information from the memory, and be able to transfer enough knowledge from the present, to resolve the existential issues. For instance, the client must discover that he or she did not actually die. This will be, in the peak moment of an abreaction, quite a revelation. It is at such a moment of realization that a new imprint is formed. The knowledge and experience gained at this moment lay a foundation for further cognitive restructuring after the abreaction. For instance, clients must learn that the isolation imposed by the trauma does not last forever, that there is some subjective meaning to their experiences, that choices are now available to them, and that the responsibility for the abuse is placed with the perpetrators rather than with the victims.

As the intensity of the abreaction increases, the client should be able to release the accompanying affects in a cathartic experience. Often, the affect has been too intense to allow for adequate processing, and the client simply avoids anything that triggers it. Therefore, titrating it to a manageable level will enhance the client's ability to release it. Some techniques to modulate affect are discussed in the section on containment of spontaneous abreactions, and Kluft (1989) has described additional techniques.

Issues in the management of intense rage reactions often emerge during the course of abreactive work. Rage responses are common and can be frightening to both the client and the unprepared therapist. It is the therapist's responsibility to provide an environment conducive to the safe and appropriate expression of rage. The client cannot heal without processing such intense affect. If the client has difficulty with impulse controls, therapeutic work on building controls should precede intense abreactive work. Even in clients who generally have good impulse control, however, the memory of extreme injustices and pain can evoke powerful rage reactions.

It is useful to assess the ways in which the client generally manages anger within the context of his or her life and to build on appropriate management skills. If the client has a history of violence, the therapist should be aware that rage reactions may be especially intense, and issues that trigger anger should be approached slowly and with caution.

Clients often fear their own anger; it feels overwhelming and bad. These issues must be addressed cognitively as well as experientially in the context of the therapeutic relationship. The therapist must give permission for the client to be angry, while setting limits on destructive behavior toward self, others, or property. Appropriate limit-setting will be reassuring to clients who fear their own rage.

There are numerous techniques to manage such reactions without shutting them down. Young (1986) and Sachs, Braun, and Shepp (1988) have advocated the judicious inpatient use of voluntary physical restraints with the informed consent of the client during intense abreactions in which the client may be acutely suicidal or homicidal. This method is used primarily with severely dissociated clients who have experienced extreme abuse. Watkins (1980) has described a silent abreaction in which rage work is done internally in a hypnotic state. The advantage of this technique is that it can provide release in a client when movement or noise cannot be supported by the environment and in a client who is unable to express intense emotion outwardly. Sachs and Hammond (1988) use a hypnotic technique in which the client is encouraged to scream, with the suggestion that as he or she screams, the body will become heavier and heavier. The more the client screams the less the body will move.

A similar hypnotic technique involves having the client imaginatively go to a "control room" where there is a lever or switch that suppresses physical movement. The client is allowed to express intense feeling, but whenever he or she senses that the anger is getting out of control, the client can pull the lever to suppress physical expression. The client ought to be taught to recognize physical sensations that precede impulsive physical expressions of rage; such signals will alert him or her to the need to add controls within an abreaction (as well as in other situations). This, in itself, is an experience of mastery for the client.

Schrader (1989) has described an innovative outpatient technique for rage release that integrates concepts from bioenergetics and gestalt and psychomotor therapies. She used a network to gather a number of therapists together to contain a client physically during a carefully planned, extended abreactive session. The session began and ended with cognitive framing for both the therapists and the client. The therapists served not only as containment figures but also as positive support figures for the client. This allowed for maximum motoric discharge of energy along with affective catharsis, a combination that is very effective in creating new imprints for the client. This technique had the added advantage of providing a support system and network for the participating therapists.

Once the client has reached and at least partially processed the existential crisis within a particular abreaction and has discharged the affect, the intensity of the experience will begin to decline naturally. When is a particular abreaction complete? As the therapist begins to notice the descending curve of the abreaction, the client's affect also will decrease. The whole story will have been told, the dissociated aspects will have been released, and the client will not have a phobic avoidance of the memory. The client will often experience a visible physical relaxation and display evidence that he or she is oriented to the present. There may be a verbal expression of a new insight, with relieved affect, crying, or laughing: "Oh, I didn't die"; "Somebody did come"; "It wasn't my fault." Once the curve of the abreaction returns to the baseline, the next phase of abreactive work can begin.

Creating a Gestalt (Assimilation Phase)

To create a complete experience from an abreaction, the knowledge and experience gained from resolution of the existential crisis must be assimilated into the client's cognitive context in the present. In the preparation phase, the therapist and client build a knowledge of the client's worldview and his or her understanding of family rules and messages. This body of knowledge is based first on the subjective experience of the child who lived in the family and then is broadended through more objective, detached, adult observations made by the client. It is helpful, when broadening this context, to be able to recognize statements that come from the client's belief system and to clarify with the client the validity of such beliefs.

For instance, a client was talking about his relationship with his mother. He said that as a child, he never complained about anything to his mother because there were always others who were worse off in life than he. When questioned about that statement, he said that his mother spent most of her time doing volunteer work with the elderly and constantly told him how much they needed her. He had learned from experience that his problems could never match those of the people his mother tended and that he was selfish to feel any need. He generalized this belief to the point that any of his needs were unacceptable to him and he was unable to express needs within the context of a relationship.

Dysfunctional beliefs are formed not only by the client's perceptions of the sometimes confusing and chaotic world of his or her family but also by injunctions from the family or perpetrators. The assimilation phase focuses on cognitive restructuring of imprinted injunctions that are revealed in the abreactive work.

Injunctions are negative verbal and nonverbal commands or messages received during the trauma that are globally internalized and lived out. These injunctions are actually hypnotic in nature, since they are given in double-binding or abusive situations when the client is in a confused, suggestible, and dissociated state (Calof 1987) and thus are imprinted in the psyche. They are activated in the present by ANS activity in response to intrapsychic or environmental triggers. Since these imprints are usually encoded on an unconscious level, they are incorporated into the client's belief system without knowledge of their origin. To restructure the resulting cognitive distortions and behavioral concomitants, it is necessary to identify and bring to consciousness these injunctions (table 1–4).

Injunctions may be external or internal. *External injunctions* are those the victim receives from the abuser, such as "You're a bad boy; this is your fault." *Internal injunctions* are responses to abuse that occur as a result of the internal, subjective experience of the trauma. They are, in essence, messages reflecting the victim's understanding of the impact and meaning of the trauma. For instance, the victim may think to himself or herself during the abuse, "I am going to die. I will never get over this." Because these messages were received in a highly receptive hypnotic state, and because they were linked to powerful affects that were occurring simultaneously, they are deeply embedded. Injunctions are state-dependent phenomena and thus must be accessed in the state within which they were encoded. Once this state has been accessed within an abreaction and the associated affects released, the encoding is made available for restructuring. Old imprints can now be linked with new information gained from the abreaction and from imprints formed within therapy.

Table 1–4
Imprinted Injunctions and Resultant Cognitive Distortions

I: You want this to happen, you love it.
C: I wanted it, therefore I am bad.

I: If you tell, Mother will hate you; Mother will kill herself; I will kill you; I will kill myself.
C: I have the power to destroy my family; their survival depends on me. Telling the secret equals death.

I: If you don't do this, I will do it to your sister or brother.
C: I have the power to keep my family safe; it is my sole responsibility. I must sacrifice myself.

I: You're disgusting, you're dirty; you're shit.
C: I am bad to the core. This happened because I deserved it. I must never let anyone know me, or they will find out how bad I am. I don't deserve anything good in life. I deserve to be punished.

I: Don't make a sound; don't let Father hear us.
C: It's dangerous to speak, show feelings, or ask for help.

I: You're so pretty (handsome) I can't help myself.
C: I'm seductive and manipulative. I can't control myself. It's my fault that he lost control. I deserve to be punished. I must make myself unattractive.

I: Come here and let me love on you. You know I love you.
C: Love hurts. Sex and nurturance are the same.

I: I'm going to teach you to be a man (woman).
C: Being a man (woman) means being hurt or hurting someone else. Also, I'm not a man (woman).

I: Don't cry or I'll give you something to cry about.
C: What I experienced wasn't that bad. Showing my pain or fear is dangerous.

I: Shut up! You know I'm not hurting you.
C: I can't trust my own experience. Someone else must tell me what is real.

I: If you say no again, I'll ask your brother to come in and help me.
C: I have no power. I'm always outnumbered. I don't have the right to say no.

I: We don't talk about our family with anybody else. It's none of their business.
C: I have to look happy and be nice. I must never tell. This has never happened to anyone but me. It's so bad I can never tell.

I: We take care of each other because no one else will.
C: I cannot trust anyone outside the family.

I: Don't say those things about your uncle.
C: No one will ever believe me or help me. Maybe I just imagined it.

I: You only have three A's on your report card; wait for me in your room. You're going to pay for this.
C: If I'm good, maybe he won't hurt me. If I'm perfect, no one will see how bad I am inside.

Note: I = imprinted injunction (message from the abuser); C = resultant cognitive distortion.

For instance, many clients have the imprinted external injunction "If you tell, I'll hurt/kill you." The resultant cognitive distortion is "He will always know if I tell, and something bad will happen to me; therefore I must never tell" and "I am still vulnerable to being hurt by him." New information gained in an abreaction leads the client to the following constellation of restructured beliefs: "I was very little and helpless then, and now I am an adult and can protect myself"; "The past is not the present"; "It is safe and important to tell."

These beliefs are encoded verbally (symbolically) and experientially as the story is told within the abreaction without the client's getting hurt. This experience occurs in the specific state in which the original imprints were encoded. Thus, new imprints are formed and linked with the old imprints. These new imprints can be activated each time old injunctions are triggered, so old imprints lose their potency and are gradually extinguished. New imprints must be reinforced over and over in the course of therapy in order for them to replace old injunctions completely.

This process frees the client to change behaviors that were previously dictated by internal injunctions. The following example illustrates a behavioral change that results from restructured beliefs. A client, as an adult, was very paranoid, lifted weights, and carried a knife (although he had never used it). He believed that he could have and should have fought off his uncle, who anally raped him when he was ten. He said that he could have hit the uncle with something or he could have escaped.

In the abreaction of that particular memory, he gained the knowledge that his uncle had locked the door, hidden the key, and held a knife to his throat. He reexperienced the terror of a small boy who was brutalized by a two-hundred-pound adult. Only when he had these pieces and the associated imprinted injunction ("If you fight me, I'll kill you") could he understand that there were good reasons why he could not fight back and begin to let go of the shame of submitting. He could understand his excessive need to defend himself as an adult in the context of having been terrorized as a helpless child. As this new information was gradually assimilated, he began to feel safer in the world. As he began to experience himself as a full-sized and quite powerful adult rather than a small "weakling," his weight lifting became less obsessive, he stopped carrying a knife, and he became less paranoid.

The belief that the victim should have resisted the perpetrator is one of the most difficult ones to restructure for male clients. In this society, men and boys are not supposed to be victims. If they are victimized, they are taught that it is because of their own inadequacy (Lew 1988).

A difficult internal injunction to restructure, for both males and females, is some variation of "It felt good, so I must be bad/responsible." When pleasure is paired with pain, survivors feel an intense mixture of confusion, shame, guilt, and a sense of betrayal by their own bodies. Abreactive work will usually reveal that the child did not want the abuse and was coerced, sometimes by verbal persuasion or bribery and sometimes by sadistic brutality. It is useful to allow clients to acknowledge their pleasure rather than reassuring them that they probably did not feel much pleasure. In fact, the physical sensations may have been quite pleasureable.

In addition to accepting their experience in a nonjudgmental way, the therapist needs to understand and be able to explain the physiological sexual response cycle. The body has a standardized response to stimulation that is natural and normal, regardless of the source of stimulation, and perpetrators often use this knowledge to make the child less resistive ("See, you really do like it"). The distinction can be made with clients between their body's automatic reactions and their wishes and psychological reactions.

Sometimes clients will report that they initiated sexual activity in a desperate attempt to get nurturance and affection. It is helpful for the client to hear that nurturance is a basic human need rather than an indulgence. (This fact will often come as a surprise to many survivors.) Children will seek nurturance in whatever ways are available to them. The responsibility for the abuse, regardless of the initiator, still remains with the one who is endowed with power and trust in the relationship.

Ending an Abreaction

To end an abreaction, the therapist must reorient and ground the client, process or contain residual affect, provide a healing experience, and solidify the learning that has occurred during the abreaction.

The client should be reoriented to the present. It is sometimes helpful to ask the client, "Are you here?" A dissociated client will readily understand this question. If the client answers negatively, the therapist may ask, "Where are you?" The client may still feel pulled into the past or may be having a dissociative response to the intensity of the abreaction. Bridging techniques into the present, as previously discussed, can be useful at this point. It is important to give the client ample "reentry" time, allowing him or her to sit in another room after the abreaction if needed.

Grounding the client may be useful to reduce the "spaceiness" related to dissociative tendencies after an intense abreaction. Clients may be asked to feel their feet on the floor, press their tongue to the roof of their mouth, feel the couch supporting them, and so on. It is especially useful to ask clients to keep their eyes open, providing a visual and perceptual grounding in the present. Clients can be asked to describe the room or clothes that they or the therapist is wearing.

Residual affect may indicate that the abreaction was not fully completed or affectively processed. Obviously, all affect regarding an intense memory will not be released in one session. Extremely intense affect should, however, have been released during the abreaction, and the residual should be much more moderate and manageable to the client. In addition, feelings of terror, shame, and humiliation and issues of helplessness and responsibility should be thoroughly processed within the abreaction so that they are not the major affective issues to be processed afterward. The feelings most likely to remain following complete abreactions are grief and anger. Clients frequently need time after the abreaction to give expression to those feelings.

Positive healing experiences solidify learning and are an important part of the assimilation process. A healing experience also can help to reorient and ground the client. Asking the client to draw a picture of his or her inner child in a safe place can provide comfort and safety. Simply reading to a client a short children's story with a relevant therapeutic message can soothe and ground the client and add metaphoric cognitive content to the abreaction (Davis 1988; Ray and Lyn 1989). A guided visualization can be useful if the therapist has enough knowledge of the client's safe place or safe image (that is, an image that has been used successfully before or has been practiced by the client). The image also can originate with the client at the moment. The therapist may touch or hold the client to provide comfort and reassurance following intense abreactions.

The client remains in an altered state immediately after abreactive work, so when healing experiences are given at that time, they are especially powerful and can provide positive imprints in the present. Cognitive work often can continue during a healing experience. For instance, once a client is in a safe space and is feeling relaxed and comforted, the therapist may gently ask, "What have you learned, or what do you know that is different now?" Learning is a crucial part of abreactive work.

The new learning can be solidified by placing it on a time line that extends into the future (Comstock 1986). This encodes the possibility of choices and the ability to determine the direction of one's own life. The therapist can use age progression to reinforce the restructured imprints and beliefs by saying, "Now that you know (what was learned in the abreaction), go forward in time and see what your life will be like and how it can be different for you."

If an abreaction needs to be interrupted due to time constraints, give the client a fifteen- to twenty-minute warning, ask him or her to find a temporary stopping place, and use containment techniques, such as putting the memory in a box or time lock. The client needs to be given sufficient time in the session to reorient and, if necessary, should have a room in which to rest afterward. A follow-up session ought to be scheduled as soon as possible to complete the abreaction.

Once the abreactive event is completed, the client still has much work to do to assimilate the new learning and experiences gained in the abreaction into the context of his or her current life. This will occur gradually over the course of therapy.

Empowering the Client (Application Phase)

In the application phase, the client moves from the identity of victim to that of survivor and then gradually (for most individuals) to that of thriver. The mastery gained by the successful navigation of abreactions will provide a base for the development of empowerment. The client is empowered by integrating dissociated elements (the missing cognition, affect, sensation, or behavior) and new imprints into present-day life. Clients can begin to rebuild shattered assumptions, developing a sense that their lives can be safe, predictable, and meaningful.

As abreactive work helps survivors distinguish between past and present, and as dissociated elements are reintegrated, clients slowly begin to live more in the present and are less restricted by unresolved aspects of the past. In addition, clients gradually will come to appreciate and accept themselves—including the disowned parts that were trapped in the past—as old feelings of shame, guilt, responsibility, and badness are defused and restructured. The inner-child aspects of the adult can become an integral part of the individual's life, adding spontaneity, playfulness, creativity, and a wide range of affective responses.

Behavioral change follows the cognitive restructuring and affective catharsis of abreaction. As clients begin to experience the truth of what happened to them as children and realize that they had no choices and no escape, no power and no blame, they can begin to act as powerful and self-nurturing adults in the world rather than as helpless, victimized children who blame themselves.

Clients are empowered as they learn that feelings are neither lethal nor omnipotent. With the release of fear, shame, rage, humiliation, isolation, and hopelessness comes the release of joy and creativity, as well as the capacity to love and be loved. Newfound hope and joy can be enhanced through involvement in hobbies or other activities. And as clients reestablish their identities, they may discover new hopes and buried dreams that they can now pursue. Many clients will change careers or return to school as the past becomes resolved and more of their psychic energy is freed to be invested in the present.

The client must learn to experience and express positive as well as negative affects. Postabreactive work involves intense grieving and rage about the irreplaceable losses of childhood. Issues of abandonment and loss may surface on many different levels over the course of therapy and will appear in the transference relationship with the therapist. The consistent caring and predictable boundaries of the therapist will provide a safe structure in which the client can work on such terrifying and painful issues.

It is important for the client to become familiar and comfortable with his or her body. Sexually abused clients often have a split between mind and body that must be healed. Their bodies have often been painfully abused. This pain is dissociated, as the client simply separates an awareness of his or her body from consciousness. Clients often report that they do not feel their bodies; they may ignore signals from the body such as hunger and pain. Many sexually abused clients view the body as the enemy who has betrayed them and caused them great shame. As clients restructure beliefs about their current safety and about their physical responses during the abuse, they will gradually develop an awareness of their bodies and come to accept the responses of the body, sexual and otherwise, as an integral and important part of their lives.

As clients begin to acknowledge their physical selves, they become empowered to make healthy life choices. As they integrate the abreactive work and develop a respect for their bodies, they are able to make changes in eating and exercise habits, sleep patterns, and self-defeating work habits. Relaxation techniques and meditation can be used for ego strengthening and stress reduction (Flannery 1987).

Sexual issues must be resolved over the course of therapy (Maltz and Holman 1987). Phobic avoidance of sex or counterphobic promiscuity must be addressed. Clients may have disorders of desire, orgasmic difficulties, and other sexual disorders. Specific phobias that trigger memories should resolve as abreactive work resolves abuse issues. Clients must learn the difference between sexual and nurturing behaviors and how each can be asked for and given appropriately. Emphasis should be placed on sexual activity as pleasureable, respectful, and voluntary. Couples therapy can be a useful adjunct at this time, focusing on sexual and other relational issues.

Issues of spirituality often evolve during the course of treatment. For many clients, feelings of betrayal and abandonment by God may emerge. Clients may find spiritual awareness through nature, community, and other nontraditional avenues, as well as through more traditional means. The client may struggle with issues of sin, responsibility, forgiveness, good and evil, and the meaning of suffering, as well as others. It is important for the therapist to support clients in their search for healthy spirituality, regardless of the therapist's personal beliefs.

Clients will learn to cope with stress and fear in ways other than dissociating. As clients begin to believe they have needs and have a right to get their needs met, they can work on gaining assertiveness and limit-setting skills. Clients whose boundaries have been violated often do not have a sense of limits in relation to self or other. Abreactive work, and the therapeutic relationship, will help them learn to set appropriate limits and to be respectful of their own and others' boundaries. As they build a trusting relationship with the therapist and develop self-esteem, clients slowly learn to trust others, to build a support system of friends, and to develop a sense of community. As dissociative barriers erode, clients can more easily learn from experience and can develop good judgments about relationships. They can learn to discriminate between people who are safe and those who are not. Victim behaviors are reduced in intimate relationships as well as in the world.

It may be useful at this point to reiterate that the abreactive process is not linear. The application phase does not begin only when there is no more abreactive work to be done. Each abreaction must be carried through to empowerment in whatever small way possible. At some point in the therapy, the major portion of the work will shift to empowerment issues, though some memories may still need to be abreacted.

A Clinical Example of the Abreactive Process

To illustrate the phases of abreaction and how they might be integrated within one abreactive session, we will describe a complete abreaction. This example was chosen because of its brevity and simplicity. It occurred with a client who had been in therapy for eighteen months. The general context for abreactive work had been established previously. The client came into session visibly upset and crying. She said that the previous night she had heard someone say something about "putting something big into something small." She immediately felt "awful, bad, and ugly—like I had black slime inside me." The client was asked if she could draw the black slime. She drew an orange outline of a person with no hands or feet and with hollow circles for eyes and mouth. Every other part of the inside was colored black. A cognitive frame was set by the therapist by gathering information about the picture. The client was asked to tell the therapist about the picture: How old was the person in the drawing? What was she doing? What was happening around her?

The client replied that the figure in the drawing was four years old. "She's pinned against the wall, feeling helpless. She's floating over her body." (This was a clear indication that a dissociative episode had occurred.) The therapist then began to define the parameters of the dissociative episode (when it began and ended, how much cognitive information the client was able to access, and which BASK components were missing).

The therapist asked, "What do you think was happening when she couldn't stay in her body?" The client did not know, indicating that the cognitive dimension of the experience was not yet accessible to her. The therapist then asked her if she would like to find out what happened. A contract was established for the abreactive work, and the abreaction proceeded. The client wanted to explore her feelings but was unsure about how much of the memory she wanted to know. It was agreed that she could stop the abreaction at any time by simply saying stop or by raising her finger.

The therapist initiated the abreaction by saying, "So, as you would like to find out why she's floating over her body, you can let yourself go back to the time when you were four and you felt pinned against the wall and helpless and felt like black slime inside. You can let yourself remember only what you are ready to remember. And notice that you are also here with me now as you go back and remember. You can know that you may stop anytime you wish."

The client began to cry and said, "She's against the wall because something bad happened." The therapist said, "What might have happened that was bad?" The client was unable to answer. "Can you go back to the time just before she's against the wall and let yourself know what happened?" The client nodded affirmatively and, after a brief pause, said in a small voice, "I can't see anything." The therapist waited, and after another brief pause, the client exhibited overt signs of regression, which are common during abreactive work. She curled up on the sofa and began sobbing and mumbling like a young child. She then cried out in pain and put her hand to her crotch, having now gained a sensory component of the memory. The therapist reminded the client that she could be "here and there at the same time" and that the therapist was present with her.

At that point, the client sat up and said she wanted to stop. Her crying began to subside, and it was clear to the therapist that the client had accessed an experience that she was unable to process at that moment. The therapist respected the client's request to stop and gave her permission to distance herself from the memory by asking, "Can you tell me what's happening right now?" At the same time, the therapist was aware that the client had not yet completed the abreactive experience.

The client voluntarily returned to the memory and said, "I felt pressure on me. He was on top of me, and I couldn't breathe. And I was scared. He was smooshing me. And then it hurt, oh it hurt, like someone hit me with a hammer between my legs. And then I stopped because I felt like I was making it up." The therapist noted that the client had shifted from third person to first person. She was thus beginning to "own" the experience. The client also gave the therapist information about why she stopped the abreaction—because she feared she was making it up. A belief that the memory is "made up" is very common in survivors. Abuse memories often have a dreamlike or unreal quality due to the dissociative process. In addition, many clients defend against knowledge of the intolerable by not believing their memories. One of the hallmarks of dissociated clients is the remark "I think something awful happened to me, but maybe I'm making it up."

Responding to the client's first-person report of what happened to her, the therapist asked, "And who was it that was smooshing you?" The client began crying again. "My dad. It was my dad. I didn't want it to be true."

"What might happen if it were true."

"Then I'd be bad."

For this client, the existential crisis (the worst moment of the abuse) was contained in this statement. She had dissociated the memory in order not to believe she was bad, which involved the existential crises of isolation ("If I'm bad, no one will love me") and responsibility ("I'm bad because it's my fault").

"So what's it like when it's not true?"

"I feel crazy."

"So maybe feeling crazy, like you were making it up, is safer than feeling like you were bad?"

"Yeah, I don't want to be bad."

"And is there any part of you that doesn't want to be crazy?"

"Yes, right here." Without hesitation, she touched her heart.

With the client's "heart part," the therapist recognized the opportunity to offer the client a third option—something other than feeling bad or feeling crazy. "And what might the part that doesn't want to feel crazy do to comfort the four-year-old who does feel bad, like black slime inside?"

Again, without hesitation, she said, "It could be shiny and glow all through her body." The certainty in the voice of the client and her focus on what could be different were indications that the existential crisis was in the process of resolving and that a healing experience could thus be given without obstructing the process. The healing image came from the client, which made the experience more powerful and effective.

"It could be shiny and glow all through her body. Could you let that happen now? You can let that part be shiny and glow all through your body and comfort your four-year-old. And you can know that it was Dad and that you are neither bad nor crazy, but you shine and glow inside where black slime used to be."

The client was calm and relaxed. Her breathing slowed, and she began to smile a little, indicating that the abreaction was complete. The therapist said, "You can comfort that little four-year-old, and you can know that she isn't bad and she isn't crazy. She's just a little girl who got hurt very badly by her dad."

The client then drew a picture of the four-year-old with a yellow glow all though her body and took it home to hang in her room, reminding her that she no longer had black slime inside. After this particular abreaction, the client began to have other memories of more severe abuse. Her therapy at that point focused on containment outside of therapy and cognitive processing of the abuse memories. Although she had talked primarily about the abuse with metaphors in this abreaction, it was important later for her to verbalize what had actually happened in order to process fully her intense feelings of shame and badness.

Countertransference Issues

A final topic is the varied and intense feelings that arise in the therapist as a result of helping with abreactive work. Courtois (1988, 229–243) has offered a thorough discussion of typical countertransference responses to survivors. These include the following:

1. Dread and horror
2. Denial and avoidance
3. Shame, pity, or disgust

4. Guilt

5. Rage

6. Grief and mourning

7. Viewing the victim as exclusively needy or the survivor as exclusively self-sufficient

8. Believing that everyone is a victim

9. Language muting (that is, using euphemistic language to avoid the graphic details of the abuse ("the incident that happened" versus "the time your father raped you")

10. Contact victimization or secondary PTSD

11. Privileged voyeurism

12. Sexualization of the relationship

Unchecked countertransference issues may impede the progress of therapy in a number of ways. Some of these follow:

1. Stretching limits (taking too many midnight calls) and becoming resentful, withholding, or punitive

2. Ignoring interpersonal boundaries and thereby recreating boundary violation scenarios for the client

3. Expecting or needing the client to trust oneself and becoming resentful when he or she does not meet one's expectations

4. Ignoring gender issues that may have a powerful effect on the transference

5. Exhibiting caretaking behaviors that prevent empowerment of the client

6. Viewing the client as especially weak or strong, without consideration of the whole client, thus preventing the client from growing and developing

7. Viewing the client as especially strong and ennobled by the trauma, leading one to push the therapy too hard and fast

8. Colluding with the client's minimalization or denial, leading to a stalemate in therapy

9. Taking responsibility for the therapy and working harder than the client, engendering frustration and resentment in oneself and a more passive attitude by the client

10. Personalizing the client's projections rather than helping him or her sort out the confusion between the internal replay of abuse and the external trigger in the therapist-client relationship, thus resulting in one's resenting and dreading the therapy sessions

Progress in recovery for many survivors is made in small increments. Therapists who are new to this work often are impatient to "get to the memory work" and thus push the client into abreactive work, or they get frustrated because the client is "so resistant to therapy." When the therapist is not comfortable with the client's pacing, he or she may be ignoring some basic safety issues or a crucial transference or countertransference issue.

During many abreactions, the therapist must witness painful, wrenching affect and must hear intolerable, heinous abuses perpetrated upon children. The therapist is present in an intimate way with someone for whom he or she has a deep concern. This has to affect the psyche, if not the soul, of the therapist. The therapist's own existential crises will emerge, and he or she must deal with personal issues related to death/annihilation, meaninglessness, isolation, and freedom and responsibility. This personal struggle, which is universal, must be attended to outside the therapy hour. The therapist who is unable to deal with his or her own existential issues is not likely to be able to hear a client's deepest struggles. This may result in the therapist's avoiding abreactive work, consciously or unconsciously. Or the therapist may try to alleviate or fix the client's pain for his or her own comfort by prematurely bringing an abreaction to a close before the client has accessed the traumatic triad, thereby preventing any resolution for the client.

In addition to the emergence of the therapist's own existential crises, he or she also may have intrusive images or thoughts of a particular client's abuse outside the sessions (especially during sleep or sexual activity). And the therapist may be overwhelmed by the evil in the world, imagining an abuser behind every face at the supermarket. It is essential that the therapist hold on to his or her own ontological security—to be safely in a world that has meaning and hope. The hopelessness, cynical, or frightened therapist will be unable to hold any hope for the client's recovery—an essential, albeit intangible, part of the therapeutic process.

When working with survivors of childhood abuse, it is important for the therapist (regardless of theoretical orientation) to drop an analytic reserve and to be present for the client in a way that is genuinely responsive (as well as responsible) and empathic. At the same time, it is important that the therapist protect his or her own psyche by not overidentifying with, or absorbing all the pain of, the client. Some kind of protective visualization or ritual cleansing is often helpful. Some useful ways of releasing and renewing oneself after intense abreactive work with a client follow:

1. Listening to relaxing music
2. Using relaxation techniques, especially deep breathing, releasing affect and tension with each exhalation and breathing in comfort and relaxation
3. Exercising or taking a brief walk
4. Processing one's own feelings with an available colleague
5. Imagining a protective shield around oneself during abreactions so that

one does not "take in" the feelings of the client but is emotionally aware and available

6. Scheduling clients so that those who are doing abreactive work are spaced between "easier" clients

7. Scheduling breaks or time off immediately after abreactive sessions

8. Networking with other therapists who do similar work and are aware of the stresses

9. Carefully attending to one's own physical, emotional, and spiritual condition

Therapists must seek constantly to identify and separate their own issues from the client's issues through competent supervision or personal therapy. Therapists who are themselves survivors should be aware that new memories or feelings of their own may be unexpectedly triggered by the client's work. Such therapists should be adept at using for themselves some of the same containment measures that have been previously discussed, as well as receiving therapy to heal their own survivor issues.

Just as clients may have difficulty in distinguishing intimacy from sexual feelings, so can therapists. It can be especially difficult for some therapists to maintain clarity when the client (who may be covertly or overtly seductive) is having an erotic transference and when the therapy may, at times, focus on intense abusive experiences that were sexual in nature. It is crucial for the therapist to recognize and acknowledge to himself or herself (not to the client) the presence of any sexual feelings. Such feelings are to be processed in supervision or personal therapy.

As therapists, we cannot erase or compensate for the damages and losses of childhood our clients have incurred. Yet through the abreactive process, we can be present to validate their experiences, to alleviate their pain by helping them work through the trauma, and ultimately to empower them as healthy adults in the world. Perhaps the last word belongs to a former client:

> I never thought I'd make it through. I remembered stuff that was so awful and bad there were times I just didn't want to live. But during those times, my therapist hung in there with me. She kept telling me I'd make it, and she kept finding ways to help me get through the day. And I did, finally. Now I'm getting on with my life. Actually, for the first time, I have a life. What I've finally figured out is that it really is over, and I'm here now, and I'm very much alive.

References

American Psychiatric Association. 1987. *Diagnostic and Statistical Manual of Mental Disorders*. 3rd ed., rev. Washington, D.C.

Bass, E., and L. Davis. 1988. *The Courage to Heal: A Guide for Women Survivors of Child Sexual Abuse.* New York: Harper & Row.

Bernstein, E.M., and F.W. Putnam. 1986. "Development, Reliability, and Validity of A Dissociation Scale." *Journal of Nervous and Mental Disease* 174 (no. 12): 727–735.

Blank A.S. 1985. "The Unconscious Flashback to the War in Viet Nam Veterans: Clinical Mystery, Legal Defense, and Community Problem." In *The Trauma of War,* edited by S.M. Sonnenberg, A.S. Blank, and J.A. Talbot, 36–49. Washington, D.C.: American Psychiatric Press.

Braun, B.G. 1984a. "Towards a Theory of Multiple Personality and Other Dissociative Phenomena." *Psychiatric Clinics of North America* 7 (no. 1): 171–190.

———. 1984b. "Uses of Hypnosis with Multiple Personality." *Psychiatric Annals* 14 (no. 1): 34–40.

———. 1985. "Dissociation: Behavior, Affect, Sensation, Knowledge." In *Proceedings of the Second International Conference on Multiple Personality and Dissociative States,* edited by B.G. Braun, 63. Chicago: Rush University.

———. 1986. "Issues in the Psychotherapy of Multiple Personality Disorder." In *Treatment of Multiple Personality Disorder,* edited by B.G. Braun, 1–28. Washington, D.C.: American Psychiatric Press.

———. 1988a. "The BASK Model of Dissociation. Part 1." *Dissociation* 1 (no. 1): 4–23.

———. 1988b. "The BASK Model of Dissociation. Part 2: Clinical Applications." *Dissociation* 1 (no. 2): 16–23.

Braun, B.G., J. Olson, K. Mayten, G.T. Gray, and A. Pucci. 1987. "Post-traumatic Stress Disorder by Proxy." In *Proceedings of the Fourth International Conference on Multiple Personality and Dissociative States,* edited by B.G. Braun, 11. Chicago: Rush University.

Breuer, J., and S. Freud. 1957. *Studies on Hysteria.* New York: Basic Books. Originally published in 1895.

Calof, D. 1987. *Treating Adult Survivors of Incest and Child Abuse.* Workshop presented at the Eleventh Annual Family Network Symposium, Washington, D.C., May.

Chess, J. 1989. "Movement Therapy: An Integrative Approach to Remembering Preverbal Sexual Trauma." In *Proceedings of the Sixth International Conference on Multiple Personality and Dissociative States,* edited by B.G. Braun, 52. Chicago: Rush University.

Chu, J.A. 1988a. "Some Aspects of Resistance in the Treatment of Multiple Personality Disorder." *Dissociation* 1 (no. 2): 34–38.

———. 1988b. "Ten Traps for Therapists in the Treatment of Trauma Survivors." *Dissociation* 1 (no. 4): 24–32.

Comstock, C. 1986. "The Therapeutic Utilization of Abreactive Experiences in the Treatment of Multiple Personality Disorder." In *Proceedings of the Third International Conference on Multiple Personality and Dissociative States,* edited by B.G. Braun, 71. Chicago: Rush University.

Courtois, C. 1988. *Healing the Incest Wound: Adult Survivors in Therapy.* New York: W.W. Norton.

Davis, N. 1988. *Therapeutic Stories to Heal Abused Children.* Oxon Hill, Maryland: Nancy Davis.

Donaldson, M.A., and R. Gardner. 1985. "Diagnosis and Treatment of Traumatic Stress among Women after Childhood Incest." In *Trauma and Its Wake: The Study and Treatment of Post-traumatic Stress Disorder,* edited by C.R. Figley, 356–377. New York: Brunner/Mazel.

Dyck, P.B. 1988. "The Use of Art in the Treatment of Post-traumatic Stress and Dissociative Disorders." In *Proceedings of the Fifth International Conference on Multiple Personality and Dissociative States,* edited by B.G. Braun, 121. Chicago: Rush University.

Eich, J.E. 1980. "The Cue Dependent Nature of State Dependent Retrieval." *Memory and Cognition* 8: 157–168.

Ellenberger, H.F. 1970. *The Discovery of the Unconscious.* New York: Basic Books.

Figley, C.R., ed. 1985. *Trauma and Its Wake: The Study and Treatment of Post-traumatic Stress Disorder.* New York: Brunner/Mazel.

Fine, C.G. 1988a. "Cognitive Behavioral Interventions in the Treatment of Multiple Personality Disorder." In *Proceedings of the Fifth International Conference on Multiple Personality and Dissociative States,* edited by B.G. Braun, 167. Chicago: Rush University.

———. 1988b. "Thoughts on the Cognitive Perceptual Substrates of Multiple Personality Disorder." *Dissociation* 1 (no. 4): 5–10.

Fish-Murray, C.C., E.V. Koby, and B.A. van der Kolk. 1987. "Evolving Ideas: The Effect of Abuse on Children's Thought." In *Psychological Trauma,* edited by B.A. van der Kolk, 89–110. Washington, D.C.: American Psychiatric Press.

Flannery, R.B. 1987. "From Victim to Survivor: A Stress Management Approach in the Treatment of Learned Helplessness." In *Psychological Trauma,* edited by B.A. van der Kolk, 217–232. Washington, D.C.: American Psychiatric Press.

Frankl, V. 1963. *Man's Search for Meaning.* New York: Washington Square Press.

Geeseman, D.B. 1988. "Clay: An Adjunctive Tool in the Abreaction of Abuse." In *Proceedings of the Fifth International Conference on Multiple Personality and Dissociative States,* edited by B.G. Braun, 66. Chicago: Rush University.

Gelinas, D.J. 1983. "The Persisting Negative Effects of Incest." *Psychiatry* 46: 312–332.

Gil, E. 1988. *Treatment of the Adult Survivor of Childhood Abuse.* Walnut Grove, California: Launch Press.

Greenberg, M.S., and B. van der Kolk. 1987. "Retrieval and Integration of Traumatic Memories with the 'Painting Cure.'" In *Psychological Trauma,* edited by B.A. van der Kolk, 191–215. Washington, D.C.: American Psychiatric Press.

Grove, D. 1987. *Resolving Traumatic Memories.* Munster, Indiana: David Grove Seminars.

———. 1988. *Healing the Wounded Child Within.* Munster, Indiana: David Grove Seminars.

Hammond, D.C. 1988a. *Learning Clinical Hypnosis: An Educational Resources Compendium.* Des Plaines, Illinois: American Society of Clinical Hypnosis.

———. 1988b. *Hypnotic Induction and Suggestion: An Introductory Manual.* Des Plaines, Illinois: American Society of Clinical Hypnosis.

Harris, J., and J. Colrain. 1986. "A Model Training Seminar for Adult Incest Survivors." Paper presented at the Fourth National Conference on the Sexual Victimization of Children, Children's Hospital National Medical Center, New Orleans, May.

Herman, J., and E. Schatzow. 1987. "Recovery and Verification of Memories of Childhood Sexual Trauma." *Psychoanalytic Psychology* 4: 1–14.

Hilgard, E.R. 1977. *Divided Consciousness: Multiple Controls in Human Thought and Action.* New York: John Wiley & Sons.

Horowitz, M.J. 1973. "Phase Oriented Treatment of Stress Response Syndromes." *American Journal of Psychotherapy* 27: 506–515.

———. 1976. *Stress Response Syndromes.* New York: Jason Aronson.

Janoff-Bulman, R. 1985. "The Aftermath of Victimization: Rebuilding Shattered Assumptions." In *Trauma and Its Wake,* edited by C.R. Figley, 15–35. New York: Brunner/Mazel.

Jehu, D., C. Klassen, and M. Gazan. 1985. "Cognitive Restructuring of Distorted Beliefs Associated with Childhood Sexual Abuse." *Journal of Social Work and Human Sexuality* 4: 49–69.

Kingbury, S.J. 1988. "Hypnosis in the Treatment of Posttraumatic Stress Disorder: An Isomorphic Intervention." *American Journal of Clinical Hypnosis* 31 (no. 2): 81–90.

Kluft, R.P. 1983. "Hypnotherapeutic Crisis Intervention in Multiple Personality." *American Journal of Clinical Hypnosis* 26 (no. 2): 73–83.

———. 1984. "Varieties of Hypnotic Interventions in Treatment of Multiple Personality." *American Journal of Clinical Hypnosis* 24 (no. 4): 230–240.

———. 1985. "The Treatment of Multiple Personality Disorder: Current Concepts." In *Directions in Psychiatry,* edited by F.F. Flach, 11–25. New York: Hatherleigh.

———. 1988. "On Treating the Older Patient with Multiple Personality Disorder: 'Race against Time' or 'Make Haste Slowly?'" *American Journal of Clinical Hypnosis* 30 (no. 4): 257–266.

———. 1989. "Playing for Time: Temporizing Techniques in the Treatment of Multiple Personality Disorder." *American Journal of Clinical Hypnosis* 32 (no. 2): 90–98.

Krystal, H. 1968. *Massive Psychic Trauma.* New York: International Universities Press.

———. 1979. "Alexithymia and Psychotherapy." *American Journal of Psychotherapy* 33 (no. 1): 17–31.

Lew, M. 1988. *Victims No Longer: Men Recovering from Incest and Other Sexual Child Abuse.* New York: Nevraumont Publishing Co.

Lindemann, E. 1944. "Symptomatology and Management of Acute Grief." *American Journal of Psychiatry* 101: 141–148.

Lister, E.D. 1982. "Forced Silence: A Neglected Dimension of Trauma." *American Journal of Psychiatry* 139: 872–876.

Loewenstein, R.J., N. Hornstein, and B. Farber. 1988. "Open Trial of Clonazepam in the Treatment of Posttraumatic Stress Symptoms in MPD." *Dissociation* 1 (no. 3): 3–12.

Loewenstein, R.J., and F.W. Putnam. 1988. "A Comparison Study of Dissociative Symptoms in Patients with Complex Partial Seizures, Multiple Personality Disorder, and Posttraumatic Stress Disorder." *Dissociation* 1 (no. 4): 17–23.

Maltz, W., and B. Holman. 1987. *Incest and Sexuality.* Lexington, Massachusetts: Lexington Books.

Mutter, C.B. 1986. "Post-traumatic Stress Disorder." In *Case Studies in Hypnotherapy,* edited by T. Dowd and J. Healy, 34–45. New York: Guilford Press.

Nichols, M.P., and J.S. Efran. 1985. "Catharsis in Psychotherapy: A New Perspective." *Psychotherapy* 22: 46–58.

Ochberg, F.M. 1988. "Post-traumatic Therapy and Victims of Violence." In *Posttraumatic Therapy and Victims of Violence,* edited by F.M. Ochberg, 3–19. New York: Brunner/Mazel.

Olson, J., K. Mayton, and B. Braun. 1988. "Secondary Post-traumatic Stress and Countertransference: Responding to Victims of Severe Violence." In *Proceedings of the Fifth International Conference on Multiple Personality and Dissociative States,* edited by B.G. Braun, 120. Chicago: Rush University.

Orzek, A.M. 1985. "The Child's Cognitive Processing of Sexual Abuse." *Child and Adolescent Psychotherapy* 2: 110–114.

Pope, K.S., and J.C. Bouhoutsos. 1986. *Sexual Intimacy between Therapists and Patients.* New York: Praeger Press.

Price, R. 1987. "Dissociative Disorders of the Self: A Continuum Extending into Multiple Personality." *Psychotherapy* 24: 387–391.

Putnam, F.W. 1985. "Dissociation as a Response to Extreme Trauma." In *Childhood Antecedents of Multiple Personality Disorder,* edited by R.P. Kluft, 66–97. Washington, D.C.: American Psychiatric Press.

———. 1989. *Diagnosis and Treatment of Multiple Personality Disorder.* New York: Guilford Press.

Ray, S., and J. Lyn. 1989. "The Role of Children's Literature in the Treatment of Multiple Personality Disorder." In *Proceedings of the Sixth International Conference on Multiple Personality and Dissociative States,* edited by B.G. Braun, 121. Chicago: Rush University.

Ross, C.A. 1989. *Multiple Personality Disorder: Diagnosis, Clinical Features, and Treatment.* New York: John Wiley & Sons.

Ross, C.A., and P. Gahan. 1988. "Cognitive Analysis of Multiple Personality Disorder." *American Journal of Psychotherapy* 42: 229–239.

Ross, C.A., S. Heber, G.R. Norton, and G. Anderson. 1989. "Differences between Multiple Personality Disorder and Other Diagnostic Groups on Structured Interview." *Journal of Nervous and Mental Disease* 179: 487–491.

Ross, C.A., G.R. Norton, and G. Anderson. 1988. "The Dissociative Experiences Scale: A Replication Study." *Dissociation* 1 (no. 3): 21–32.

Rossi, E.L. 1986. *The Psychobiology of Mind-Body Healing.* New York: W.W. Norton.

Rossi, E.L., and D.W. Cheek. 1988. *Mind-Body Therapy: Ideodynamic Healing in Hypnosis.* New York: W.W. Norton.

Sachs, R.G. 1986. "The Adjunctive Role of Social Support Systems in the Treatment of Multiple Personality Disorder." In *Treatment of Multiple Personality Disorder,* edited by B.G. Braun, 157–174. Washington, D.C.: American Psychiatric Press.

———. 1989. "Utilizing the Sandtray Technique in the Diagnosis and Treatment of Dissociative Disorders: A Prescription for Its Use by Occupational Therapists." In *Proceedings of the Sixth International Conference on Multiple Personality and Dissociative States,* edited by B.G. Braun, 123. Chicago: Rush University.

Sachs, R.G., B.G. Braun, and E. Shepp. 1988. "Technique for Planned Abreactions with MPD Patients." In *Proceedings of the Fifth International Conference on Multiple Personality and Dissociative States,* edited by B.G. Braun, 85. Chicago: Rush University.

Sachs, R.G., and E. Frischholz. 1989. "Dissociation: Historical Issues and Their Impact on DSM-IV." In *Proceedings of the Sixth International Conference on Multiple Personality and Dissociative States,* edited by B.G. Braun, 199. Chicago: Rush University.

Sachs, R.G., and D.C. Hammond. 1988. *Hypnotic Techniques.* Workshop presented at the Fifth International Conference on Multiple Personality and Dissociative States, Chicago, October.

Schrader, S. 1989. "An Integrated Approach to Rage Release in the Outpatient Treatment of Multiple Personality." In *Proceedings of the Sixth International Conference on Multiple Personality and Dissociative States,* edited by B.G. Braun, 54. Chicago: Rush University.

Silver, R.L., C. Boon, and M.H. Stones. 1983. "Searching for Meaning in Misfortune: Making Sense of Incest." *Journal of Social Issues* 39 (no. 2): 81–102.

Spiegel, D. 1984. "Multiple Personality as a Posttraumatic Stress Disorder." *Psychiatric Clinics of North America* 7 (no. 1): 101–110.

———. 1986a. "Dissociation, Double Binds, and Posttraumatic Stress in Multiple Personality Disorder." In *Treatment of Multiple Personality Disorder,* edited by B.G. Braun, 61–78. Washington, D.C.: American Pschiatric Press.

———. 1986b. "Dissociating Damage." *American Journal of Clinical Hypnosis* 29 (no. 2): 123–131.

———. 1988. "Dissociation and Hypnosis in Post-traumatic Stress Disorders." *Journal of Traumatic Stress* 1 (no. 1): 17–33.

Spiegel, H., and D. Spiegel. 1978. *Trance and Treatment: Clinical Uses of Hypnosis.* Washington, D.C.: American Psychiatric Press.

Steele, K. 1988. "PEACE: A Model for Effective Abreaction with Dissociative Clients." In *Proceedings of the Fifth International Conference on Multiple Personality and Dissociative States,* edited by B.G. Braun, 134. Chicago: Rush University.

———. 1989a. "A Model for Abreaction with Multiple Personality and Other Dissociative Disorders." *Dissociation* 2 (no. 3): 151–159.

———. 1989b. "Unfreezing the Moment: Resolving the Existential Crisis of Trauma in the Dissociative Patient." In *Proceedings of the Sixth International Conference on Multiple Personality and Dissociative States,* edited by B.G. Braun, 125. Chicago: Rush University.

Summit, R.C. 1987. "The Hidden Child Phenomenon: An Atypical Dissociative Disorder." In *Proceedings of the Fourth International Conference on Multiple Personality and Dissociative States,* edited by B.G. Braun, 6. Chicago: Rush University.

van der Hart, O., and B. Friedman. 1989. "A Reader's Guide to Pierre Janet on Dissociation: A Neglected Intellectual Heritage." *Dissociation* 2 (no. 1): 3–16.

van der Kolk, B.A. 1987. "The Psychological Consequences of Overwhelming Life Experiences." In *Psychological Trauma,* edited by B.A. van der Kolk, 1–30. Washington, D.C.: American Psychiatric Press.

van der Kolk, B.A., and M.S. Greenberg. 1987. "The Psychobiology of the Trauma Response: Hyperarousal, Constriction, and Addiction to Traumatic Reexposure." In *Psychological Trauma,* edited by B.A. van der Kolk, 63–88. Washington, D.C.: American Psychiatric Press.

van der Kolk, B.A., and W. Kadish. 1987. "Amnesia, Dissociation, and the Return of the Repressed." In *Psychological Trauma,* edited by B.A. van der Kolk, 173–190. Washington, D.C.: American Psychiatric Press.

Watkins, J.G. 1971. "The Affect Bridge: A Hypnoanalytic Technique." *International Journal of Clinical and Experimental Hypnosis* 19: 21–27.

———. 1980. "The Silent Abreaction." *International Journal of Clinical and Experimental Hypnosis* 28: 103–113.

Watkins, J.G., and H.H. Watkins. 1979–80. "Ego States and Hidden Observers." *Journal of Altered States of Consciousness* 5: 3–18.

Wilbur, C.B. 1988. "Multiple Personality and Transference." *Dissociation* 1 (no. 1): 73–76.

Wohl, A., and B. Kaufman. 1985. *Silent Screams and Hidden Cries: An Interpretation of Artwork by Children from Violent Homes.* New York: Brunner/Mazel.

Wright, E.M. 1987. *Clinical Practice of Hypnotherapy.* New York: Guilford Press.

Yalom, I. 1980. *Existential Psychotherapy.* New York: Basic Books.

Young, W.C. 1986. "Restraints in the Treatment of a Patient with Multiple Personality." *American Journal of Psychotherapy* 50: 601–606.

2
Brother to Brother: Integrating Concepts of Healing Regarding Male Sexual Assault Survivors and Vietnam Veterans

Mark C. Evans

From a letter:

> You're not going to believe me. I didn't want to be there. I thought I was going to die. People didn't seem to care what I did or what happened to me when it was over. I shoulda let them kill me and be done with it.
>
> —*(Subject 6 to Subject 3*
> *March 4, 1989)*

From the reply:

> Your letter made me feel a lot better. It's weird that you understand how I felt even though everything was so different. You told me you were there before I was born. I don't want to hurt your feelings, but if you're still going through this much pain, what do I have to look forward to?
>
> —*(Subject 3 to Subject 6*
> *March 29, 1989)*

The complete text of the answer:

> Don't be so down! You have every one of us on your side every day. Don't quit and I won't.
>
> —*Subject 6 to Subject 3*
> *April 4, 1989)*

The first letter was written by a Vietnam combat veteran born in 1948, the second by a gang-rape survivor born in 1970. They took part in a 1989 experimental exchange of letters between male survivors of two different types of interpersonal violence and found that experiences were not so different after all.

The assessment and treatment models for returning Vietnam veterans have paralleled the experience of those treating the psychological wounds of sexual assault survivors. This chapter briefly reviews both treatment models and their separation in implementation. It also compares the symptomatologies and treatment protocols of rape trauma and delayed stress syndrome (DSS), both of which are considered posttraumatic stress disorders (PTSDs) (American Psychiatric Association 1980). Implications for treatment and suggested protocols also are included.

Why Study the Link?

The Vietnam War combat veteran represents a rare challenge and opportunity to those who study all types of posttraumatic stress, particularly that of male sexual assault survivors. Because most existing treatment procedures were developed for female rape survivors, models that fit more closely the gender identity of male clients are needed.

Prior to the Vietnam War, shared trauma of this scale had not been thoroughly documented. Veterans addressed their emotional needs openly enough for their experiences to be widely shared and for treatment schemas to be developed, used, and improved. Veterans represent a population of males who were victimized and have not hidden or denied it in the usual ways. Clinically, their experiences can be used to help make predictions concerning issues facing male sexual assault survivors, a group that has only recently begun to be studied. Although few longitudinal studies have been done among survivors who waited five or more years to disclose their victimization, numerous studies exist concerning Vietnam veterans.

Parallel Histories

Female and Male Assault Survivors

Assessment protocols for male sexual assault survivors evolved from efforts during the 1960s and early 1970s to identify and treat the psychological and physical effects of sexual assault on female survivors (Sutherland and Scherl 1970). The combined symptomatology was described as rape trauma syndrome (Burgess 1974). After this cohesive description was provided, refinements were made throughout the 1970s (Notman and Nadelson 1976; Burgess and Holmstrom 1974; Hilberman 1976; Groth, Burgess, and Holmstrom 1977; Feldman-Summers, Gordon, and Meagher 1979; Katz and Mazur 1979; Burgess and Holmstrom 1979a, 1979b). Features of this syndrome described in these works include its delayed impact on the survivor well after the traumatic incident (a sexual assault); the progression of identifiable stages; and strong emotional reactions, such as anger, fear, guilt, and feelings of vulnerability and helplessness.

Improved recognition of rape-related behavioral dysfunction, the growth of the feminist antirape movement, and the long-needed restructuring of women's history to break society's silence regarding sexual assault (Russell 1975; Brownmiller 1975) brought about a dramatic increase in reported rapes, from 37,000 in 1970 to more than 62,000 in 1980 (FBI *Uniform Crime Report* 1970, 1980). The integration of therapeutic treatment with confidential, peer-based programs to assist survivors through the rape trauma syndrome also was promoted (Bard and Sangrey 1979; Warner 1980).

A parallel movement was afoot to describe the long-term effects of combat trauma on returning Vietnam War veterans. As early as 1970, the efforts of veterans to deal with an unpredicted tide of emotion was documented (Bourne 1970). Early attempts to find help through peer-based programs also was described (Shatan 1973). Comparisons of veterans who served tours in the last years of the war with others who served earlier led researchers to predict that many soldiers would face a posttraumatic syndrome lasting years in duration and threatening the emotional stability of returning veterans with uncontrollable feelings of anger, fear of death, guilt, and alienation. The precipitating trauma for these emotions was described as an event, or set of events, that was outside of the normal human experience and threatened the physical and psychological well-being of the survivor (American Psychiatric Association 1980). The specific label delayed stress syndrome (DSS) was applied to this experience (Shatan 1975; Horowitz and Solomon 1975).

The veteran's self-help movement grew in strength during the 1970s, a number of books and movies made it possible to address the emotional wounds of the Vietnam War, and therapists improved their knowledge of DSS and its effects (Howard 1976; Nace, Meyers, and Rothberg 1977; Figley 1978; LaCounoiser, Godfrey, and Ruby 1980; Goodwin 1980).

In 1980, it appeared that the parallel tracks upon which so many worked in the healing process had come to a switching yard. The American Psychiatric Association, in its third update of its *Diagnostic and Statistical Manual of Mental Disorders (DSM III),* recognized Posttraumatic stress disorder (PTSD) as a valid psychiatric diagnosis.

Almost immediately, PTSD was used to describe survivors of both sexual assault and Vietnam combat. The diagnosis found acceptance among those treating Vietnam veterans (Langley 1982), with Brown (1984) noting that the veterans' "involvement in the guerilla warfare of Vietnam was outside the range of usual human experience." (p. 83–84).

Criticism was quickly registered, however, regarding the application of PTSD to the issues of sexual assault. Even before *DSM III* appeared, Katz and Mazur (1979) were questioning the methodology of studies that had been instrumental in bringing such recognition to rape trauma syndrome. Frank and associates (1981) found that the amount of force used in the assault and other factors significantly altered posttraumatic recovery. In a point/counter-point exchange with Ann Burgess in *Behavioral Sciences and the Law,* Raifman (1983) found no basis at all for a link between PTSD and rape trauma symptomatology, complaining that trauma other than that outside the normal human experience could cause the same symptoms as those described by the rape trauma syndrome. The following year, Lawrence (1984), in examining expert testimony concerning PTSD in criminal rape trials, found that the diagnosis was not a positive factor for the survivor, nor did it increase convic-tion rates for defendants.

Despite the Burgess (1983) rebuttal to Raifman and newer studies defend-ing the diagnosis of rape trauma survivors as suffering from PTSD, as well as its use in expert testimony (Burgess and Holmstrom 1985; Massaro 1985), the label was deemphasized. Subsequent literature, while focusing increas-ingly on the needs of male survivors, reversed the trend of the late 1970s to generalize the posttraumatic experience and sought no common ground between the men and women who experienced violence in Vietnam and those who found it in Chicago or Miami.

Male Assault Survivors and Vietnam Veterans

There appears to be a strong link between rape and warfare, as authors such as Susan Brownmiller (1975) have demonstrated. There is little question that the motivation to rape and to kill in battle come from the same root. The link between men as victims of sexual and military violence has only recently been discussed, although the view that the Vietnam veteran also should be recognized as a vicarious victim was expressed as early as 1972 in the veteran-organized Winter Soldier Investigation into the war (Vietnam Veterans against the War 1972).

During the years 1964 to 1975, some 8.5 million men and women played a role in the Vietnam conflict. Almost three million served a tour in the theater of operations, and 1.6 million endured direct combat and combat-related ex-periences. American forces suffered more than 56,000 dead and 300,000 wounded, more than 75,000 of whom were later classified as disabled. There were 2,493 declared missing in action (Veterans Administration 1981; Sheehan 1988).

War has always produced psychological injuries to its participants, in-cluding the fear of death or mutilation and witnessing the injury and death of comrades (Webb 1978), but the surreal conditions under which the conflict was fought have been cited as heightening the probability of posttraumatic stress. Vietnam marked the first war in which Americans fought against a guerrilla army without the support of the local populace and without popular support in the United States (Howard 1976).

Among specific factors in the psychological instability reported by participants are the following:

- Soldiers could not distinguish potential enemies from noncombatants (Keane and Kaloupek 1980)
- Most participants did not choose to be in combat (Lifton 1973)
- U.S. military personnel felt confusion and shame regarding U.S. involvement in Southeast Asia and their own role in the conflict (Caputo 1977)
- One-year individual tours often precluded emotional bonding and promoted the isolation of each service member (Bourne 1970)
- Traumatic situations in combat were entered directly from nonthreatening environments; the return to safety also was without acclimatization (Wilson 1978)

It is estimated that at least 500,000 (Goodwin 1980) and as many as 800,000 (Wilson 1978) returning Vietnam veterans suffered moderate to severe psychological adjustment problems as a result of these and other forces.

Meanwhile, in the United States, a different kind of war was under way. During the years 1964 to 1975, an average of 47,000 sexual assaults were reported to law enforcement agencies annually (FBI *Uniform Crime Report* 1964–1975). Although reporting of sexual assaults increased dramatically during these years, it is thought that, at best, only one in five actual rapes was reported to authorities (Burgess and Holmstrom 1974; Brownmiller 1975) and that more than 2.5 million American women, men, and children survived sexual assaults during the years of the Vietnam War. Among the recognized stressors reported by Burgess and Holmstrom (1974) by survivors are the following:

- Many entered the traumatic situation without sensing their departure from a safe environment.
- Survivors often faced threats of death and mutilation.
- Rape survivors were stigmatized by friends and family, losing access to emotional support.
- Many survivors felt confusion and shame due to the lack of support from law enforcement or medical authorities.
- Unable to distinguish potential attackers from those posing no threat, survivors suffered a generalized fear of others.

The separation in clinical treatment perceptions between these types of male-to-male violence has lessened as researchers have challenged the view that male rape, unlike the rape of women, is more sexual in manifestation (Warner 1980; Quinsey, Chaplin, and Upfold 1984). Recent longitudinal studies have found a shift in self-perception in men from masculine and dominant pattern to patterns that include weakness, fear, and ineffectualness (Cramer 1986). It is now recognized that male sexual assault, like military combat, is predominantly a projection of power and control (Groth, Burgess, and Holmstrom 1977). In both instances, survivors found themselves in a combat situation because they were specifically targeted by the perpetrator; in some cases, they simply fit the vulnerability profile and other needs of the attacker (Howard 1976; Groth and Burgess, 1980).

An intuitive grasp of the similarity of perpetrator intentions, basis in power issues, and traumatic environment has been shared by clinicians since that decade in which at least 250,000 men brought home the trauma of the war that Sheehan (19858) called "even more unexplainable than unwinnable" (p. 873) and in which at least 250,000 Americans passed through the United States' "combat zones" and survived sexual assault.

Comparing the Posttraumatic Stress Disorders of Two Syndromes

A basic assumption about PTSDs is that the individual possessed coping mechanisms before the traumatic event to meet the challenges of everyday life and its stresses. Crisis theory recognizes this dynamic homeostatis and posits that each person will use these skills to deal with emotionally hazardous situations. The individual cannot, however, anticipate or sufficiently prepare for either rape or wartime victimization, since these are outside the range of normal human experience. The survivor of the traumatic episode often feels as though he or she is unable to control his or her environment or actions. For both types of PTSD, reaction and recovery from the trauma have been documented to include three major stages—acute, reorganization, and integration—the symptomatology of which may be compared. Collective data suggest that these stages seem to occur on significantly different timetables (see table 2–1).

Survivors may move back and forth between these stages, and timetables for this movement are highly individual. The first stage of DDS among Vietnam veterans manifests itself an average of six months after the survivor departs the trauma-inducing environment, whereas the symptoms associated with the onset of rape trauma syndrome for male survivors often can be measured in minutes.

Other variables that strongly affect recovery are the following:

• *Pretrauma life style and life situation.* For example, a male rape survivor who was involved in a satisfactory and open relationship may be less

Table 2–1
Timetable for Recovery Progressions

Rape Trauma Syndrome		Combat Posttraumatic Stress Disorder
Acute stage	First 24 hours	—
Acute stage	2 months	—
Reorganization	4 months	—
Reorganization	6 months	Acute
Reorganization	1 year	Acute
Integration	18 months plus	Acute
Integration	2 years	Reorganization
Integration	6 years	Reorganization
Integration	10 years	Integration

vulnerable to a severe reaction to the assault that a recently separated or divorced survivor.

- *Stage of life.* Adolescence, adulthood, and parenthood all affect the way the survivor seeks to resolve issues surrounding the trauma. For example, PTSD symptomatology among Vietnam veterans appears to be most severe when it coincides with "Age Thirty Transition" (Levinson 1978), a time when males between ages twenty-eight and thirty-three may suffer life transitional crises.

- *Intervention.* The type and quality of crisis intervention given and, particularly, the amount of time between removal from the crisis situation and the intervention can affect PTSD symptomatology.

The Acute Stage

The acute stage is described as the set of reactions that immediately follows separation from the traumatic situation. While this is most often true for rape survivors and effects (including shock, fear, misdirected aggression, and denial) can be observed just after the assault, this stage often takes approximately six months to manifest itself in the affected veteran (making the term *delayed stress syndrome* very appropriate). This delayed response also has been observed in a significant number of male rape survivors. A sampling of effects on both types of survivor appear in table 2–2.

Shock, or battle fatigue, is a common reaction during the acute stage, although its manifestation varies widely with the individual. Hazelwood and Burgess (1987) point out that the survivor may be expressive (including those whose reaction is labeled "hysterical") or guarded or exhibit a mixture of social alienation and open expressionism. While Frye and Stockman (1982) document a similar range of responses among male combat veterans, a par-

Table 2–2
Acute Stage Symptomatology Compared

Rape Trauma	Combat Posttraumatic Stress Disorder
Shock	Shock
Fear of attacker	Fear of attack
Vulnerability	Little/no communication
Number to outside	Sleep disorders
Altered communication	Severe startle response
Physical pain	Fear of aggression
Misdirected anger	Misdirected anger
Guilt	
Flashbacks	
Humiliation	
Homophobia issues	Sexual dysfunction
Sexual dysfunction	Loss of support network
Disclosure issues	
Desire for retribution	
Disempowerment	
Denial	

ticularly common reaction is a "numbing to outside stimuli" and emotional disengagement (p. 113).

The Reorganization Stage

During the reorganization stage, long-term adjustment to the traumatic experience occurs. The survivor appreciates the full impact of the rape or combat experience physically, socially, and psychologically. The complete range of reported symptomatology/presenting complaints appears in table 2–3.

Among the issues arising during this stage are sleep disorders, serious social/behavioral problems, sexual dysfunction, and close support network alienation. Guilt and the role it plays in the survivors self-perception and the perception of the survivor by his support network also are important issues.

Sleep Disorders. Somatic complaints, while manifested in the acute stage of PTSD, particularly when the survivor is in denial, are often cited by both types of survivor during the reorganization stage. The most prevalent sleeping disorders include hypervigilance during sleep, dreamlessness, insomnia, altered sleep schedules, and nightmares. Survivors also report use of sleep to avoid facing emotional, relationship, and vocational challenges.

Social and Behavioral Issues. Social and behavioral problems are cited by many PTSD survivors seeking therapy. Often these behaviors are treated as primary concerns when they may be manifestations of PTSD instead. These include substance abuse, including alcohol, illegal drugs, and/or prescription

Table 2–3
Reorganization Stage Symptomatology Compared

Rape Trauma	*Combat Posttraumatic Stress Disorder*
High stress levels	Self-alienation
Sense of loss	Suppressed anger
Somatic symptoms	Somatic symptoms
Generalized fear of attack	Catastrophic nightmares
Self-blame	Fear of own aggression
Alteration of social life style	Substance abuse
Sleep disorders	Goals abandonment
Eating disorders	Chronic unemployment
Hypervigilance	Sleep disorders
Phobias	Eating disorders
Sexual dysfunction	Legal difficulties
Criminal justice concerns	Financial difficulties
Realignment of support network	Violence
Depression	Sexual dysfunction
	Physical pain
	Frustration with government
	Depression
	Cognitive deficiencies

medications; relationship or marital problems; legal difficulties, particularly for combat veterans, including convictions for offenses such as drug possession, assault, burglary, and public intoxication; and vocational problems, which may include diminished work performance and even chronic unemployment. One rape survivor summed up these issues in a letter to a veteran buddy:

> You can get wrapped up in things a lot worse than your attack. It took me a long time to get the picture. I wasn't doing drugs before. I worked and made good money. Then I started having trouble with my boss and I was wondering what the hell was wrong with me. I was doing more and more coke and my girlfriend dropped out of the deal. She said I was lazy and screwed up. I believed it until a lot later when I talked to (rape) crisis. Now I know I was just trying to prove what I thought just after the rape . . . that my life was pure shit from here on. (Subject 1 to Subject 4; April 17, 1989)

Sexual Dysfunction. Sexual dysfunction is another recurrent issue in PTSD recovery. Dysfunction as a consequence of rape trauma has been reported frequently among male and female sexual assault survivors (Groth, Burgess, and Holmstrom 1977; Sarrel and Masters 1982). Rape need not be directly linked with sexual dysfunction. A recent study confirms that not only are men more conscious of their sexual identity than women but also men may be more prone to sexual identity crises in response to nonsexual stressors (Darling and Davidson 1986). Sexual dysfunction as a psychological response to wartime trauma has been reported by the significant others of Vietnam veterans (Brown 1984), but it is not clear whether such dysfunction is a result of witnessing or participating in rape or other forms of sexual exploitation and terrorism (Lang 1969; Terry 1984). Whatever its specific origins, PTSD-related sexual dysfunction has been described by Nace, Meyers, and Rothberg (1977) and others who have worked with veterans since their return.

Survivor Support Networks. Rape and combat survivors also share challenges in maintaining their support networks. Brown (1984) describes the victim blaming of Vietnam veterans, as well as the self-blame of veterans' significant others, who feel responsible for family problems that more accurately could be linked to PTSD (C. Williams 1980). A majority of participants in a Des Moines, Iowa, support group for friends and family identified themselves as being in crisis (Brown 1984). While Frye and Stockman (1982) found that the perceived helpfulness of friends and family was considered crucial to returning GIs in their readjustment, they found instead insensitivity toward the emotional impacts of the war, some to the point of total denial that a son, husband, or friend really served in Vietnam (see also C. Williams 1980; T. Williams 1980).

Similarly, Hazelwood and Burgess (1987) identified victim blaming, denial, and insensitivity as major support network issues among sexual assault survivors. There is, however, a significant difference in the area of retribution and protectiveness. While retribution is commonly discussed among families touched by sexual assault and legitimate anger is often focused on the assailant, these issues are not addressed often among families of returning military veterans. Instead, a veteran's increased potential for violence promotes a fear of the veteran, both in himself and among his friends and family (Brown 1984), complicating the issue of legitimate anger. To whom and for whom should anger be addressed? Are there courts to which the war veteran may turn to face the agent of his anguish?

Guilt. Guilt has been strongly identified during the reorganization stage of PTSD. Guilt patterns for both types of survivor revolve around two central questions:

1.   If I had done everything differently, could I have avoided this?
2.   Did I really do everything I could once I was in the situation?

Guilt among rape survivors, particularly among male survivors, has been well documented (Burgess and Holmstrom 1974; Warner 1980; Hazelwood and Burgess 1987). Many men have been socialized to believe that they are responsible for protecting their own body spaces, as well as the body spaces of women (Groth and Burgess 1980). Failure to stop an assault constitutes failure as a man. The prevalence of this attitude among both women and men was confirmed by Smith, Pine, and Hawley (1988). Male ejaculation during the assault can add the survivor's own body to these voices (Sarrel and Masters 1982). Burgess, Groth, Holmstrom, and Sgroi (1978) describe the association of rape survivors with the power of the aggressor. A history of rape fantasy by the survivor prior to his sexual assault also can be a source of guilt feelings (Groth and Burgess 1980) and may be an issue that is increasingly identified as victimization fantasies for men shift from woman as victim to man as victim (Cramer 1986).

Guilt linked to powerlessness also has been expressed by veterans (Williams 1980). A common manifestation of guilt is the feeling of loss and failure linked with the death and injury of so many compatriots in combat (Williams, C. 1980; Brown 1984). Guilt patterns among Vietnam veterans are almost identical when the veterans see themselves as the survivors of victimization by others. This changes significantly when a veteran's guilt originates in the victimization of others.

Atrocities, including rape, were committed throughout the war by U.S. military personnel who were simultaneously victimized by shifting civilian loyalties, lack of support, and incompetent leadership (Brownmiller 1975; Caputo 1977; Webb 1978). Reporter Daniel Lang's *Casualties of War* (Lang 1969) illustrates the aggressor-victim dynamic in the story of Phan Thi Mao, who was kidnapped, raped, and murdered by a U.S. Army reconnaissance team. Other atrocities were committed by men who later said they acted more out of fear than out of anger or retribution (Hersh 1972; Terry 1984).

Nowhere was this duality more clearly expressed than in the account of Luther Benton III, a hospital corpsman who was wounded in a confused attack on a combat hospital at Hoi An (Terry 1984). He describes the end of the firefight, when another corpsman pointed in the direction of the moaning, wounded attackers and called upon Benton to do something for them. He did, opening fire until all were dead. His guilt was immediate, as was the awarding of a Bronze Star.

Such accounts and studies by Haley (1974) and others have given social scientists considerable insight into wartime trauma and may make the association between guilt and aggression clearer.

Implications for Assessment and Treatment

Comparisons of treatment protocols for both types of PTSD survivors may help us better understand men under traumatic stress. This may be of value in determining which client issues are unique to the client, the gender, and the issue.

A review of the literature in both PTSD areas indicates that treatments ranging from behavioral intervention to psychoanalysis and self-help groups currently are used for Vietnam veterans and sexual assault survivors. It may be useful to address key areas of concern for clinicians and crisis intervention specialists working with male rape survivors. These include client assessment, crisis intervention, gender and survivorship issues, individual versus group treatment, and a description of a program for survivors of both sexual violence and combat in a self-help project.

Assessment

Assessment of any client needs to be a thorough but compassionate undertaking. This is complicated for the male PTSD survivor for a number of reasons, but the process for male survivors includes some basic features:

1. The needs of the client need to be identified through questions or personal inventories.
2. The client's concept of self-worth and its sources should be investigated.
3. The strengths and vulnerabilities of the male client need to be identified.

In doing this, it is important to be alert to the values of the survivor and the care giver, watching for self-stereotyping as victim or aggressor. The client's gender identity and the relationship it has to views of aggression, spatial rights, and homophobia also should be questioned.

This type of client is likely to have difficulty being expressive in answering questions, asserting personal issues, and disclosing trauma. Many men respond to gender socialization, which tells them not to talk about emotional issues and, if they must, to keep the details to a minimum. Viney and associates (1985) tested this as a gender issue. They found that men expressed fewer feelings of helplessness and more feelings of competence during short-term crisis intervention than during follow-up one year later. Such socialization to silence is common among male rape survivors (Warner 1980) and veterans.

Langley (1982) notes, "During the assessment, it is not uncommon to hear the veteran state that he has been experiencing these symptoms for long periods of time, but was afraid to report it because he feared being labeled crazy or psychotic" (p. 95). He found that veteran PTSD survivors often exhibited the following symptoms:

1. A fearful or suspicious veneer
2. A defensive stance
3. Fear of his own mood swings
4. An impaired self-concept

Brown (1984) found that the inability and unwillingness to communicate emotional needs was at one time functional: "Survival depended largely on their ability to repress emotions, especially the emotions of grief and bereavement for the death and destruction around them" (p. 98). This protective barrier, quite different from survivor denial, has been maintained by some veterans for up to twenty years, and "once put on hold, these emotions have become difficult for many veterans to come to terms with. Their ability to grieve current losses is often impaired because of unresolved issues of grief from the past" (p. 102).

Such long-term suppression of emotions without denials has been documented. Thomas (1989) reports disclosure by female rape survivors as long as thirty years after the event. "Solo survival," as one veteran termed it, is a common coping strategy for adults who were molested as children (Bruckner and Johnson 1987), even if their treatment issues did not involve events commonly recognized as PTSD producing.

In assessing the need of the male rape survivor within this context, it is important to look for signs of long-term covert suffering. Such internalization of posttraumatic stress has been identified among combat veterans (Goodwin 1980), rape survivors (Burgess and Holmstrom 1979a), and gay survivors of violence (Miller and Humphrey 1980). Some signs of long-term internalization follow:

- PTSD-related symptoms such as substance abuse, social problems, and somatic complaints
- A history of effective coping strategies in the client's adult past
- An "event year" in which his coping strategies became ineffective due to some outside circumstance
- Significantly altered communication styles

Assessment for the PTSD survivor also should focus on his support system. A systems approach (Janchill 1969) can be used to determine pretrauma functioning patterns, how the survivor receives from his support network, and the ways in which friends and family have reorganized themselves since the trauma. The survivor's significant other, who is affected greatly by his feelings of anger, fear, guilt, and powerlessness, is in particular need of recognition and support. Brown (1984) warns, "It is not unusual for the friend and family of the (survivor) to manipulate their view of the veteran situationally to fit their needs at the present or to rationalize particular episodes from the past" (p. 174). The male rape survivor receives more situational blame for his assault than do female survivors (Howard 1984), making this a vital area for investigation.

Crisis Intervention

Rape survivors have been through an experience that challenges their normal perceptions and coping mechanisms. It is not unusual for the male survivor to present his issues as a result of a crisis or to have crises throughout the recovery process. It is worth stressing that physical and behavioral manifestations of the crisis may not be readily linked to PTSD.

When providing intervention during crisis, a fundamenteal hierarchy of response has been helpful to the author and other care givers in meeting the needs of male survivors of different types of interpersonal violence:

1. Assess the needs of the survivor, beginning with his most pressing needs (personal safety, suicide, injuries, and drug or alcohol abuse) and moving on to primary emotional, support system, or behavioral points of crisis.

2. Provide emotional support to the male survivor. It is likely that previous outcry has never or seldom occurred; therefore, the survivor has not been able to receive validation of his needs for love and support. The care giver may be the only person in whom the survivor confides his PTSD-related concerns.

3. Empower the survivor to take control of his life whenever possible and to take ownership of his feelings. A new framework for defining manhood that honors feelings and assistance seeking can be worked out with the survivor.

4. Provide information of all types to the survivor. Shapiro (1980) confirms how little information society gives to men on sex and sexual assault–related issues. Langley (1982) notes that survivors stabilize themselves much more quickly when shown the origins and symptomatology of PTSD. McCormack (1982) has found cognitive intervention to be extremely effective for Vietnam veterans. The information given survivors should include, but not be limited to, descriptions of PTSD, books, articles, movies, and a review of client self-inventories. Information also should include simple but powerful statements such as the following: "You are not alone"; "You are not to blame"; "You can regain control." It is important to men, and especially to PTSD survivors, to give themselves permission to feel.

5. Referrals are important. The survivor needs tools to finish the rebuilding job in progress: Whom can he call when he is in crisis? Where can he find others with the same experiences with PTSD? What are his options for treatment? Referrals, while often critical, are given less emphasis than other crisis intervention steps because they are next to useless unless the survivor understands what he is getting, why, and what he can expect from them. That the referrals need be solid means that they should be well researched. People providing services in a rape crisis program should be scrutinized for their skills and experience with male survivors and male internalization of PTSD issues.

Therapists should be examined for their backgrounds and perspectives on men in crisis.

Crisis intervention can be effective if the survivor had a moderately high level of dynamic homeostatis before the combat or rape trauma. Timely and empowering intervention can help the individual regain control of his emotional environment so that his normal coping skills will be effective. Because PTSD results from confronting events that are not part of the normal human experience, crisis intervention cannot replace therapy, but it can help the male survivor stay the course through recovery.

Gender and Survivorship Issues

Two major areas of concern in treatment are gender and survivorship issues. The divergent paths of combat and rape trauma treatment have resulted in combat survivors' being more likely to encounter same-gender intervention and abuse survivors' more often receiving intervention from female care givers. In addition, combat survivors often are supported by other veterans, whereas sexual assault survivors are not. Does this make a difference in the effectiveness of rape crisis and therapeutic care givers?

Differing gender socialization and its effects on communication, expressiveness, and feelings of competence have been researched from a number of perspectives. If the primary avenue of access to treatment for male survivors is the local feminist-based rape crisis program, it is likely that the male survivor will encounter cross-gender intervention (Evans 1989). What are the possible effects? Should only male counselors work with male survivors? Do those counselors need to be PTSD survivors themselves?

It has been found that the gender and trauma experience of the counselor do not in large measure affect the client's view of the helpfulness of the counseling option. Rather, a combination of factors—the client's self-concept, the perceived gender characteristics of the counselor, and the counselor's expertise—determine the client's level of comfort with the intervention (Angle and Goodyear 1984). Further, Blier, Atkinson, and Geer (1987) found that although male counselors are preferred for treatment in assertiveness concerns, female counselors are preferred in treatment that addresses personal vulnerability and helplessness. Since both sets of concerns are present in PTSD, it would appear that gender differences offers both help and hindrance. Brown (1984) has found that women were effective counselors with male Vietnam-related PTSD survivors, and Evans (1989) found equal cross-gender effectiveness among sexual assault survivors.

The key issue in gender identification with the client, therefore, is not the gender of the client and the survivor but the gender attitudes. Difficulties may arise as a result of gender stereotyping. Studies such as that by Scales, Etelis, and Levitz (1977) have indicated that counselors prefer to address personal issues with female clients. This may be related to societal tendencies to see the male as more competent and therefore less deserving of intervention (Raboteg-Saric and Saric 1984). Men also receive more societal blame than women for being violently assaulted (Howard 1984). Such stereotyping often includes the perception of a decreased capacity for expression by many male trauma survivors. Tryon (1986) found that, regardless of client gender, counselors are more likely to find that the client needs intervention and follow-up if he or she is "expressive" and "disturbed."

How can a counselor or therapist be effective with male survivors? It is clear that, against gender stereotypes, men who survive sexual assault need special protection after disclosure (Sarrel and Masters 1982), but the therapist need not overidentify with the survivor's gender. According to Fong, Borders, and Neimeyer (1986), a counselor can be effective by maintaining flexibility in regard to gender roles and maintaining a high level of comfort with self-disclosure. Sipps and Janeczek (1986) contradict earlier studies by noting that the femininity or masculinity of the counselor does not have a significant effect on the client's expectations for successful therapeutic intervention. Professional expectations present a different problem, however. A study by Brems and Schlottman (1988) indicates that therapists-in-training using the Minnesota Multiphasic Personality Inventory perceived a difference in what constitutes mental health for men and women.

Group Treatment for Male Survivors

The most appropriate treatment for individual male survivors varies, but the long-term effectiveness of client-centered peer groups bears discussion. These groups bring survivors together to explore grief and loss issues. A group often recreates the camaraderie of the combat units in which veterans served. This closeness is important because, unlike many groups that honor the needs of gays, men of color, and the poor by providing separate therapeutic platforms, veteran's self-help groups reflect conscripted male America, in which a disproportionate number of black and Hispanic men encountered combat trauma alongside white soldiers (T. Williams 1980). It is not surprising that such groups remain the treatment of choice for veterans suffering from PTSD (Brown 1984).

Survivor groups for female rape survivors are common but groups for male survivors are much rarer. Adolescent males turn to their male peers for their identity, roles, and value systems (Shapiro 1980), and the group format has been shown to reduce the rigidity of male attitudes and behaviors (Parker and Huff 1975). Peer groups have been used increasingly for male sexual assault survivors, and they have been found to be effective. For instance,

Bruckner and Johnson (1987) report peer group success in their work with adult male survivors of incest.

Linking Arms: Female and Male Survivors

At the Houston Area Women's Center Rape Crisis Program, the author found a widening gap between the feminist female-based intervention offered and the gender needs of male sexual assault survivors who turned to the center for support with PTSD symptomatology. During self-assessment interviews, a majority of my female clients identified themselves as victims even before their sexual assaults. A majority of males identified themselves as survivors or fighters before their assaults. This corresponds with Figley's (1979) findings.

This led me to question whether female-oriented sexual assault programs are addressing the large number of male rape survivors. Care givers and therapists know that many women have faced the threat, if not the experience, of rape throughout their lives. Men, however, rarely acknowledge their vulnerability to interpersonal violence until it happens to them. They have different responses to the invasion of their personal space (Skolnick, Frasier, and Hadar 1977) or their bodies through rape (Sarrel and Masters 1982). Male survivors often express their belief that rape is an emasculating experience and that, given the preponderance of women-oriented therapists and rape crisis centers, they feel isolated, cut off from their peers, and unable to find a positive self-image to carry them through recovery.

In searching for a better-fitting paradigm for treatment, I brought the issue to a group of men who found a link. "What do you think of a man who has been victimized, feels depressed, has nightmares and flashbacks, and battles drinking and work problems, while trying to take care of himself and his loved ones?"

"We think he is one of us," answered a Vietnam veteran of the Houston chapter of the Special Forces Association.

The chapter, convinced that there was common ground between male and female sexual assault survivors, agreed to participate in special projects on behalf of the Houston Area Women's Center. Three veterans consented to take part in a four-letter exchange with three male rape survivors. These letters were exchanged through me. Numbers were substituted for names, and permission was given for the letters to be copied and studied. All six participants reported an improved self-image as a result of the communications. One Green Beret wrote:

> I told a buddy of mine once that I felt like I had been raped by 'Nam. I was trying to be funny, but now I know that it wasn't so funny. Maybe I was raped, and if I was, I've got a lot (of) company back here in the States to share it with. (Subject 5 to Subject 2; April 29, 1989)

Such programs, still to be developed by therapists specializing in sexual assault and other victimization issues, may be able to link all male PTSD survivors in support networks that can be added to current treatment plans and peer groups. A participating rape survivor described the desired effect of such exchanges:

> I learned to see myself in a different way. The guy I was writing to said something that did it. He said that most of the medals in the war weren't given to soldiers for killing the enemy. They got the medals for being hurt and then doing what they could to help everyone else who was in the same shape. Fits me to a T, don't you think? (Subject 1 to Author; personal communication, May 2, 1989)

Implications for treatment abound in such a thought.

In summarizing the special treatment issues for male PTSD survivors, it is clear that the gender and shared life experience of the counselor is not crucial to successful intervention. However, male survivors do need the participation of other men in the healing process. And a more global approach to men's trauma, which brings together male survivors of differing experiences, may offer a more positive self-image to the man within his gender community.

Conclusion

More than 200,000 Vietnam veterans are coping with the challenges of PTSD. Their war is over, but their recovery continues. At least another 200,000 men had the same experience without ever stepping foot in Vietnam. They were given no weapon, no helmet, no flak jacket. They were not told they were approaching the forward edge of the battle area. Finding themselves in a battle for their lives, they survived sexual assault.

Thousands of others, survivors of other trauma experiences, share the same symptomatology but not the same treatment. Perhaps men can join together in new treatment paradigms that link them to each other and enhance their self-image as survivors.

References

American Psychiatric Association. 1980. *Diagnostic and Statistical Manual of Mental Disorders.* 3d ed. Washington, D.C.

Angle, S.S., and R.K. Goodyear. 1984. "Perceptions of Counselor Qualities: Impact of Subjects' Self-Concepts." *Journal of Counseling Psychology* 31 (no. 4): 577–580.

Bard, M., and D. Sangrey. 1979. *The Crime Victims' Book.* New York: Basic Books.
Blier, M.J., D.R. Atkinson, and C.A. Geer. 1987. "Effect of Client Gender and Counselor Gender and Sex Roles on Willingness to See the Client." *Journal of Counseling Psychology* 34 (no. 1): 27–30.
Boune, P.G. 1970. *Men, Stress, and Vietnam.* Boston: Little, Brown.
Brems, C., and R.S. Schlottman. 1988. "Gender-Bound Definitions of Mental Health." *Journal of Psychology* 122 (no. 1): 5–14.
Brown, P.C. 1984. "Legacies of a War: Treatment Considerations with Vietnam Veterans and Their Families." *Social Work* 37 (no. 3): 372–379.
Brownmiller, S. 1975. *Against Our Will: Men, Women, and Rape.* New York: Simon & Schuster.
Bruckner, D.F., and P.E. Johnson. 1987. "Treatment for Male Victims of Childhood Sexual Abuse." *Social Casework* 68 (no. 2): 81–87.
Burgess, A.W. 1974. "Persistent Systems in Rape Victims." *Medical Aspects of Human Sexuality* 4 (December): 31.
———. 1983. "Rape Trauma Syndrome." *Behavioral Sciences and the Law* 1 (no. 3): 97–113.
Burgess, A.W., A.N. Groth, L.L. Holmstrom, and S.M. Sgroi. 1978. *Sexual Assault of Children and Adolescents.* Lexington, Massachusetts: Lexington Books.
Burgess, A.W., and L.L. Holmstrom. 1974. "Rape Trauma Syndrome." *American Journal of Psychiatry* 131: 980–986.
———. 1979a. *Rape: Crisis and Recovery.* Bowie, Maryland: Brady.
———. 1979b. *The Victim of Rape: Institutional Reactions.* New York: John Wiley & Sons.
———. 1985. "Rape Trauma Syndrome and Post-Traumatic Stress Response." In *Rape and Sexual Assault: A Research Handbook,* edited by A.W. Burgess, 37–43. New York: Garland.
Caputo, P. 1977. *A Rumor of War.* New York: Ballantine Books.
Cramer, P. 1986. "Fantasies of College Men: Then and Now." *Psychoanalytic Review* 73 (no. 4): 567–578.
Darling, C.A., and J.K. Davidson, Sr. 1986. "Coitally Active University Students: Sexual Behaviors, Concerns, and Challenges." *Adolescence* 21 (Summer): 403–419.
Evans, M.C. 1989. "Men as Providers of Direct Service with Rape Crisis Centers." Paper presented to the Texas Association Against Sexual Assault, Houston, March.
FBI *Uniform Crime Report.* 1964–1975, 1970, 1980. Washington, D.C.: Federal Bureau of Investigation.
Feldman-Summers, S., P. Gordon, and J. Meagher. 1979. "The Impact of Factors within the Rape Situation." *Journal of Abnormal Psychology* 88 (no. 1): 101–105.
Figley, C.R. 1978. *Stress Disorders among Vietnam Veterans: Theory, Research and Treatment.* New York: Brunner-Mazel.
———. 1979. "Treating Combat Veterans as Survivors." Paper presented to the American Psychiatric Society, Chicago, May 14.
Fong, M.L., L.D. Borders, and G.L. Neimeyer. 1986. "Sex Role Orientation and Self-disclosure Flexibility in Counselor Training." *Counselor Education and Supervision* 25 (no. 3): 210–221.

Frank, E., S. Turner, B. Stewart, M. Jacob, and D. West. 1981. "Past Psychiatric Symptoms and Response to Sexual Assault." *Comprehensive Psychiatry* 22 (no. 3): 479–487.

Frye, J.S., and R.A. Stockman. 1982. "Discriminant Analysis of Post-traumatic Disorder among a Group of Vietnam Veterans." *American Journal of Psychiatry* 139 (January): 52–56.

Goodwin, J. 1980. "The Etiology of Combat-Related Post-traumatic Stress Disorder. In *Post-traumatic Stress Disorders of the Vietnam Veteran: Observations and Recommendations for the Psychological Treatment of the Veteran and His Family.* edited by T. Williams, 10–11. Cincinnati: Disabled American Veterans.

Groth, A.N., and A.W. Burgess. 1980. "Male Rape: Offenders and Victims." *American Journal of Psychiatry* 137 (no. 7): 806–810.

Groth, A.N., A.W. Burgess, and L.L. Holmstrom. 1977. "Rape, Power, Anger, Sexuality." *American Journal of Psychiatry* 134 (no. 11): 1239–1243.

Haley, S.A. 1974. "When the Patient Reports Atrocities: Specific Treatment Considerations of the Vietnam Veteran." *Archives of General Psychiatry* 30 (February): 191–196.

Hazelwood, R.R., and A.W. Burgess, eds. 1987. *Practical Aspects of Rape Investigation: A Multidisciplinary Approach.* New York: Elsevier.

Hersh, S.M. 1972. *My Lai 4: A Report on the Massacre and Its Aftermath.* New York: Random House.

Hilberman, E. 1976. *The Rape Victim.* Baltimore: Garamond/Pridemark Press.

Horowitz, M.J., And G.F. Solomon. 1975. "A Prediction of Delayed Stress Response Syndromes in Vietnam Veterans." *Journal of Social Issues* 31 (no. 4): 67–80.

Howard, J.A. 1984. "The 'Normal' Victim: The Effects of Gender Stereotypes on Reactions to Victims." *Social Psychology Quarterly* 47 (September): 270–281.

———. 1976. "The Vietnam Warrior: His Experience and Implications for Psychotherapy." *American Journal of Psychotherapy* 30 (January): 121–135.

Janchill, M.P. 1969. "Systems Concepts in Casework Theory and Practice." *Social Casework* 23 (February): 74–82.

Katz, S., and M. Mazur. 1979. *Understanding the Rape Victim.* New York: John Wiley & Sons.

Keane, T.K., and D.G. Kaloupek. 1980. "Behavioral Analysis and Treatment of the Vietnam Stress Syndrome." Paper presented to the American Psychological Association, Montreal, September.

LaCounoiser, R.B., K.E. Godfrey, and L.M. Ruby. 1980. "Traumatic Neurosis in the Etiology of Alcoholism: Vietnam Combat and Other Trauma." *American Journal of Psychiatry* 137 (August): 966–968.

Lang, D. 1969. *Casualties of War.* New York: McGraw-Hill.

Langley, M.K. 1982. "Post-traumatic Stress Disorders among Vietnam Combat Veterans. *Social Casework* 98 (no. 4): 593–598.

Lawrence, R. 1984. "Checking the Allure of Increased Conviction Rates: The Admissibility of Expert Testimony on Rape Trauma Syndrome in Criminal Proceedings." *University of Virginia Law Review* 70: 1657–1704.

Levinson, D.J. 1978. *The Seasons of a Man's Life.* New York: Alfred A. Knopf.

Lifton, R.J. 1973. *Home from the War: Transformations of Vietnam Veterans.* New York: Simon & Schuster.

Massaro, T.M. 1985. "Experts, Psychology, Credibility and Rape: The Rape Trauma Syndrome Issue and Its Implications for Expert Psychological Testimony." *Minnesota Law Review* (no. 3): 395–470.

McCormack, N.A. 1982. "Cognitive Therapy of Posttraumatic Stress Disorder: A Case Report." *American Mental Health Counselors Associations Journal* (no. 4): 151–155.

Miller, B., L. Humphrey. 1980. "Lifestyles and Violence: Homosexual Victims of Assault and Murder." *Qualitative Sociology* 3 (no. 3): 169–185.

Nace, E.P., A.L. Meyers, and J.M. Rothberg. 1977. "Depression in Veterans Two Years after Vietnam." *American Journal of Psychiatry* 134 (no. 2): 167–170.

Notman, M., and C. Nadelson. 1976. "The Rape Victim: Psychodynamic Considerations." *American Journal of Orthopsychiatry* 40 (no. 3): 503–511.

Parker, C.C., and V.E. Huff. 1975. "The Effects of Group Counseling on Rigidity." *Small Group Behavior* 6 (no. 4): 402–413.

Quinsey, V.L., T.C. Chaplin, and D. Upfold. 1984. "Sexual Arousal to Nonsexual Violence and Sadomasochistic Themes among Rapists and Non-Sex Offenders." *Journal of Consulting and Clinical Psychology* 52 (no. 4): 651–657.

Raboteg-Saric, Z., and J. Saric. 1984. "Neke karakteristike osobe u nevolji i pomaganje u stvarnoj zivotnoj situaciji." *Revija za Psihologiju* 14 (December): 33–39.

Raifman, L. 1983. "Problems of Diagnosis and Legal Causation in Courtroom Use of Post-traumatic Stress Disorder." *Behavioral Sciences and the Law* 1 (no. 3): 115–130.

Russell, D. 1975. *The Politics of Rape: The Victim's Perspective.* New York: Stein & Day.

Sarrel, P.M., and W.H. Masters. 1982. "Sexual Molestation of Men by Women." *Archives of Sexual Behavior* 11 (no. 2): 117–131.

Scales, P., R. Etelis, and N. Levitz. 1977. "Male Involvement in Contraceptive Decision Making: The Role of Birth Control Counselors." *Journal of Community Health* 3 (no. 1): 54–60.

Shapiro, C.H. 1980. "Sexual Learning: The Short-changed Adolescent Male." *Social Work* 37 (November): 489–493.

Shatan, C.F. 1973. "The Grief of Soldiers: Vietnam Combat Veterans' Self-Help Movement." *American Journal of Orthopsychiatry* 43 (July): 640–653.

Shatan, C.F. 1975. "Through the Membrane of Reality: 'Impacted Grief' and Perceptual Dissonance in Vietnam Combat Veterans." *Psychiatric Opinion* 11 (November): 6–15.

Sheehan, N. 1988. *A Bright Shining Lie: John Paul Vann and America in Vietnam.* New York: Random House.

Sipps, G.J., and R.G. Janeczek. 1986. "Expectancies for Counselors in Relation to Subject Gender Traits." *Journal of Counseling Psychology* 33 (no. 2): 214–216.

Skolnick, P., L. Frasier, and I. Hadar. 1977. "Do You Speak to Strangers? A Study of Invasion of Personal Space." *European Journal of Social Psychology* 7 (no. 3): 375–381.

Smith, R.E., C.J. Pine, and M.E. Hawley. 1988. "Social Cognitions about Adult Male Victims of Female Sexual Assault." *Journal of Sex Research* 24 (no. 2): 101–112.

Sutherland, S., and D. Scherl. 1970. "Patterns of Response among Victims of Rape." *American Journal of Orthopsychiatry* 40 (no. 3): 503–511.

Terry, L. ed. 1984. *Bloods: An Oral History of the Vietnam War by Black Veterans.* New York: Ballantine Books.

Thomas, C. 1989. "Crisis Intervention Techniques and Disclosure Issues." Presentation to the Rape Crisis Program, Houston Area Women's Center, February 22.

Tryon, G.S. 1986. "Client and Counselor Characteristics and Engagement in Counseling." *Journal of Counseling Psychology* 33 (no. 4): 471–474.

Veterans Administration. 1981. *Management Brief: Data on Vietnam Era Veterans.* Washington, D.C.

Vietnam Veterans Against the War. 1972. *The Winter Soldier Investigation: An Inquiry into American War Crimes.* Boston: Beacon Press.

Viney, L.L., Y.N. Benjamin, A.M. Clarke, and T.A. Bunn. 1985. "Sex Differences in the Psychological Reactions of Medical and Surgical Patients in Crisis Intervention Counseling: Sauce for the Goose May Not Be Sauce for the Gander." *Social Science and Medicine* 20 (no. 11): 1199–1205.

Warner, C.G., ed. 1980. *Rape and Sexual Assault: Management and Intervention.* Germantown, Maryland: Aspen.

Webb, J. 1978. *Fields of Fire.* Englewood Cliffs, New Jersey: Prentice-Hall.

Williams, C. 1980. "The 'Veteran System' with a Focus on Women Partners: Theoretical Considerations, Problems, and Treatment Strategies." In *Post-traumatic Stress Disorders of the Vietnam Veteran,* edited by T. Williams, 111–113. Cincinnati: Disabled American Veterans.

Williams, T. 1980. "A Preferred Model for Development of Interventions for Psychological Readjustment of Vietnam Veterans: Group Treatment." In *Post-traumatic Stress Disorders of the Vietnam Veteran,* edited by T. Williams, 37–47. Cincinnati: Disabled American Veterans.

Wilson, J., ed. 1978. *The Forgotten Warrior Project.* Cleveland: Cleveland State University.

3

Use of the Terms *Victim* and *Survivor* in the Grief Stages Commonly Seen During Recovery from Sexual Abuse

Mic Hunter
Paul N. Gerber

Much of the nomenclature inherited from the women's movement is not fully applicable to and respectful of the individuality of our male clients. There is a need to expand and revise this nomenclature so that it is more gender appropriate. It is important to acknowledge that a significant number of females and males in our society are socialized differently. While a gender-neutral (humanistic) approach to sexual abuse may seem ideal, as a practical matter, we cannot ignore the gender differences that result from the socialization process. This process affects early development stages and this is applicable to treating males of all ages. The focus of this chapter is on the highly developed, covert, presexual conditioning process that is the mark of most sexual abuse of males.

Historical Perspective

Today maltreatment of children is generally defined as neglect and sexual, physical, and emotional abuse. In the first half of the twentieth century, child maltreatment, in the form of physical abuse, was brought to the attention of the justice system by the Society for the Prevention of Cruelty to Animals (later the American Humane Society). This marked the embryonic stage of public awareness of the problem, which evolved slowly and in a segmented fashion until the women's movement of the 1970s.

The women's movement clearly escalated public awareness and facilitated rapid change in legislation and research. Logically, since the majority of the members of the early feminist movement were women, the issues of female maltreatment became apparent first. The original focus of the women's movement was the disparity in the treatment of women in the adult population. The emphasis later expanded to include the issues of the maltreatment of children of all ages and both genders. The contemporary emphasis of child maltreatment has become highly focused on sexual abuse, particularly the abuse of females.

Due to their origins in the women's movement, the nomenclature and practice within the field of sexual abuse prevention, intervention, and treatment have a strong female orientation. Furthermore, until recently, research on the victimization of female children provided skewed data on the frequency, type, and gender preference of offenders. Current research is causing treatment professionals to reexamine the entire issue of victimization.

Gender Differences

Many authors (Courtois 1988; Bear and Dimock 1988; Herman 1981; Hunter 1990; Kempe and Kempe 1984; Lew 1988; Meiselman 1979) have already described the syndrome that frequently results from sexual maltreatment. The sexual maltreatment of children is visible by the distortion of human personality that often lies in its wake. Common symptoms include denial, repression, minimization, and self-blame. Self-defeating behaviors, such as poor school performance, the inability to maintain healthy relationships, addictive disorders, and repetition of the abuse scenario, also are observed frequently. Without appropriate intervention, these behavior patterns can be perpetuated long after the actual abuse has ceased. For the sake of brevity, the symptomatology that we describe here is not all-encompassing. There are as many responses to sexual maltreatment as there are victims.

The symptoms and behaviors previously described are manifested in both genders, but the socialization process of the broader culture results in gender-specific presentation of these symptoms. Early in life, male children are taught to individuate and separate. In contrast, female children traditionally have been encouraged to focus on relationships. Constant messages such as "Big boys don't cry," "You take care of your mother and sister while I'm gone," and "My little man" begin to erect barriers to intimacy and interdependency. The patriarchal family structure commonly found in the United States is apparent early on to male children, creating a false sense of power vested in them by virtue of gender.

This false sense of power and authority discounts the vulnerability and powerlessness of childhood. It is reinforced throughout society in books, television, films, and even toys. The dolls that male children play with are adult soldiers (for example, G.I. Joe) rather than babies whereas dolls made for female children are designed to be nurtured and cared for, their male counterparts need no such care, as they are armed and self-sufficient.

Negative gender roles continue to be reinforced throughout the maturation process. Sexism permeates the culture, including the treatment community. For example, we discuss the *male* sexual abuse victim and the *female* sex offender as if they were enigmas, much like saying *male* nurse and *female* physician. Current empirical data show that significant numbers of males are sexual abuse victims (Finkelhor 1979, 1984). Until recently, they have been overlooked because of sexist attitudes and the manner in which they display their pain. This display is often described as a mask, since it fits the female victim response model.

Reasons Why Helping Professionals Overlook the Sexual Abuse of Males

As we have discussed, American culture is sexist. Helping professionals exist within this culture and are bombarded with this message. Further, we have begun to address the issue of the sexual maltreatment of children only within the past two decades, so relatively little is known and few professionals have specific or adequate training in the field. In addition, people attracted to helping professions often are in search of a resolution or validation for their personal issues. Finally, much of the abuse perpetrated against males, particularly by women, is of a more covert nature, making it even more difficult to recognize (for example, children being sexually fondled in the guise of bathing or toilet training or gay adolescents being "assisted" in "coming out" by significantly older men who are in reality using them).

The nomenclature widely used in the media, the court system, and some client service agencies continues to include phrases that create barriers to those whose sexual maltreatment came in the form of seduction rather than violence. The terms *sexual assault* and *rape,* which are defined as forms of violence (McKechnie 1979), do not take into account the seductive and manipulative nature of the predatory conduct that is so common in our society. Empirical data indicate that rape is one of the least frequent sexual offenses particularly when viewed in terms of the number of victims per offender (Abel et al 1987; Becker and Abel 1984). These data account for all types of aberrant sexual behaviors, including nontouch crimes as exhibitionism and voyeurism and touching crimes such as forteurism and child molestation.

The use of language that focuses primarily on assaultive, violent attacks creates seemingly insurmountable barriers to those persons who were victimized in a more seductive fashion. Whereas assault is an overt physical act, seduction is a more cognitive covert process. To seduce is "to persuade to do wrong, as by offering something, to tempt to evil or wrongdoing, to lead astray, to persuade to engage in unlawful sexual intercourse, especially for the first time; to induce to give up chastity. Syn. -lure, entice, mislead, corrupt, tempt" (McKechnie 1979, 1,096). Fortunately, in recent years, comprehensive legislation and service agencies have begun using terms such as *sexual misconduct* and *sexual offenses,* which more clearly account for the full spectrum of sexual maltreatment.

Victims versus Survivors

Use of the Term Victim

Classically, a dictionary definition of a victim is someone who is "killed, destroyed, injured or otherwise, harmed by, or suffering from, some act, condition, or circumstance" (McKechnie 1979)? Conventional victimology views the word *victim* as shaming and keeping the client helpless, passive, powerless, and trapped by the abuse experience. Many females react to the term as an extension or affirmation of their place in a male-dominated culture. Since the feminist movement sought to empower women, the term *survivor* became popular as a way to neutralize the power imbalance between the two genders. This term was used to reframe the aftermath of the abuse in a less debasing manner.

Rigidly subscribing to the view that the term *victim* is inherently demeaning can, however, result in gender-inappropriate clinical practices. Our position is that the term clearly describes the human condition as a result of the traumatic occurrence, places the responsibility on the appropriate person, and has a highly useful place in the evolution of the therapeutic process, particularly with males, since traditional males are conditioned to believe that by virtue of their maleness, they are impervious to victimization. In contrast, traditional females are less likely to see the term as a threat to their gender identity.

Just as women have traditionally been socialized to accept the role of passive dependence, men have been socialized to accept the role of aggressive independent. Although we acknowledge the reframing that takes place by using the term survivor for women recovering from the effects of sexual maltreatment, it is our clinical experience that it can be detrimental to males when applied too early in the treatment process.

Using the term *victim* at the onset of therapy frames the experience as "What was done *to* you was not okay, and it was not your fault." Since men traditionally have not thought of themselves as people who could be victimized, applying the word to themselves triggers profound emotional reactions. These include fear, anger, hurt, shame, and sadness. Access to these emotions is more easily attained when the term *victim* is used rather than the term *survivor*.

Use of the Term Survivor

The term *survivor* was coined in response to objections to the cultural implications of the word *victim*. It was designed to empower women and encourage them not to view themselves as passive, immature, dependent, damaged "goods," or susceptible to ongoing abuse. Survivorship speaks not only to enduring but also to overcoming demeaning or destructive conditions. In an attempt to place the responsibility for the abuse with the offender, where it rightfully belongs, the term may inadvertently imply that because the victimized person was not at fault, he or she is not affected by it. Avoiding the term *victim* immediately sets up the potential for double message: If no trauma took place or no damage was done, there is nothing to survive.

Part of the task of the clinician is to identify sex negativity in the culture, particularly as it relates to one's sense of "maleness" or "femaleness," the propensity to blame those victimized, and other factors that contribute to the cllient's distorted view of reality. While a clinician is clearly a guide, there is an obligation to have a gender-specific knowledge base that allows one to teach and empower the client by transforming cognitive distortions into a more life-enhancing view of self. Our assertion is that there are utilitarian applications of both terms in the natural progression of addressing sexual abuse for both genders. Each word is representative of a growth stage. The ultimate goal of therapy ought to be to transcend survivorship and remove the abuse experience as an issue of identity. The individuality of personhood must be paramount. Again, the key is not only being gender respectful but also not replicating the trap of more dogma.

Assessment

During the assessment period, it is vital that the therapist give the client permission to disclose his history from his own vantage point. The therapist ought not to apply any labels. The therapist's task at this point in the relationship is to learn how the client cognitively and emotionally views his experiences. Due to the social training most men receive discouraging them from noticing their emotions and the defense of emotional numbing that victimized people often use to deal with trauma, the client may not be able to describe what he felt or is feeling concerning a given experience.

Taking a sexual history is a difficult task for many clinicians. By its very nature, it demands specificity that will be dulled by the client's resistance and the practitioner's level of comfort with the client's sexuality. This is further exacerbated by a need for the chronology to include the nuances of the history or the seemingly less germane issues in the endless quest for the traumatic events. The sum total of the client's experiences are relative, and the tendency to focus on the dramatic paints a distorted picture of the person's sexuality. For example, it is imperative to look at very early childhood memories of naive sexual experimentation. Intellectually, we are aware that children have a natural curiosity and participate in age-appropriate sexual experimentation, but how this is connected to a sense of shame or guilt is paramount in the inquiry. Too often clinicians accept behavior at face value without detailed exploration of the client's reality in relation to issues of shame, guilt, arousal, and resolution.

Even if the client comes to the therapist with the presenting issue of having been sexually abused, other factors in the client's life need to be assessed before a treatment plan can be developed. The issues of chemical dependence, other compulsive/addictive disorders, acute anxiety, depression, personality disorders, physical handicaps, low intellectual functioning, and low ego strength need to be taken into account. Rarely is in-depth psychotherapy focusing on the effects of sexual abuse successful while the client is active in an addictive pattern, clinically depressed, highly anxious, or suicidal. These conditions usually need to be addressed prior to making sexual abuse the primary focus of the therapy.

An Overview of Therapy as a Grief Process

Denial

Once the client has been given the opportunity to describe his history without the therapist's interpreting its meaning and any issues that might prevent the client from being able to function adequately have been addressed, the therapist's task becomes helping the client to clarify details, reframe experiences, and pointing out cognitive distortions. If the therapist attempts these interventions too early in the therapeutic relationship, the client will likely view the therapist as not listening or not understanding. Much of what treatment professionals label as resistance in clients is the result of impatience and not taking the time to hear the client's view of his life.

The therapeutic process of healing from sexual maltreatment can be understood as a grief process similar to the five stages described by Kubler-Ross (1969). The first stage is denial. The client will make statements such as "Nothing happened," "I don't remember enough," or "I'm just making it up." At this point, it is the therapist's task to label the experience as abuse and to use the term *victim,* even if the client balks at it. This labeling must be reinforced by providing information to the client on the covert conditioning that frequently takes place prior to any sexual contact.

Bargaining

In response to the therapist's use of the terms *victim* and *abuse,* as well as the additional information concerning sexual maltreatment, the client will begin to move into the second stage of grief. In the bargaining stage, the client will acknowledge that sexual contact has taken place and may even say that it was sexual abuse but will want to deny or minimize any negative effect that it had on him. Commonly heard phrases at this stage are "It happened, but it didn't hurt me," "It happened, but I asked for it," "It happened, but I'm over it," and "We both wanted it."

As the client repeatedly describes the experiences, it is the therapist's task to help identify emotions and to point out examples of how the victim mentality is operating in the client's view of the abuse situation. Many victimized persons still have affection for the person who abused them. It is vital that the therapist not bind the client so that he believes that he must choose between his loyalty to the therapist and his loyalty to the person who abused him.

It is particularly difficult for a client who was abused by a loved one to move out of the bargaining stage. To facilitate this movement, the therapist must assure the client that even if he hates what was done to him, he need not hate the person who abused him. Therefore, the therapist ought to avoid labeling the person who abused the client as an offender or perpetrator. Rather than labeling the person, the therapist should label the behavior.

As the denial and bargaining defenses begin to lessen, the client often experiences fear or terror. Fear is an appropriate emotional response to being violated and the realization of one's venerability as a child and even as an adult. Since males are socialized not to acknowledge their fear, when they eventually pay attention to this emotion, it is unfamiliar and can seem overwhelming. Therefore, the therapist must respect the client's response to fear. This is a time in the therapy process when many clients resort to defense mechanisms such as self-mutation, alcohol and other drug use, compulsive sexual behavior, or compulsive eating. At this point, therapist must be careful not to focus exclusively on the acting-out behaviors but instead be sensitive to the client's fear. Inappropriate confrontation can be a replication of the abuse of power that the client experienced during the sexual abuse as a child.

Part of the covert presexual conditioning process involves the manipulation of the child's emotions by reframing his emotional response in a way that will enable the abuse to take place. Therefore, the therapist must avoid reframing the client's fear as another emotion. There seems to be a tendency among many therapists to encourage clients to express anger rather than to be aware of their fear and its significance. Fear is the emotion that informs us when we are in danger of being maltreated. The awareness of having felt fear prior to or during the sexual experience is a powerful validation that it was in fact abuse. Unfortunately, because of the carefully honed methods used by many perpetrators, the victim believes that he was a willing participant, so he discounts his fear.

It is during the bargaining stage that many clients are tempted to seek prematurely to forgive or reconcile with their offender(s). This response may be due to their desire to put an end to the discomfort they are experiencing, or it may be due to pressure from family members or others to put it all in the past or to forgive and forget. At this point, it is the therapist's responsibility to take protective steps, even if the client is an adult. The victim may be repressing or minimizing the number and type of offenses committed. He is probably underestimating the offender's psychopathy. Many clients assume that sex offenders grow out of it and therefore pose no danger in the present.

Anger

During the anger stage, the client may be heard saying, "It happened, and I really didn't want it," "She had no right to treat me that way," "It did seriously affect my life," "I was tricked and lied to," "I was treated like an object," or "I was used." This is the stage when the therapist can safely begin using the phrase *recovering victim*.

When some clients become aware of the level of their anger, it triggers fear and shame. Many victims respond to their anger by fantasizing violence or other forms of abuse directed toward the person(s) who abused them or others in their environment. These thoughts frighten the client, who is afraid that he may act on these fantasies or that he is just as bad as the person(s) who abused him, which then triggers shame and self-loathing. Some clients then self-medicate by resorting to numbing behaviors such as the overuse of drugs, food, work, religion, or sex.

As children, most victims were told, overtly or covertly, that they had no right to be angry about the abuse since it never really happened or, if it did happen, it was not abuse. Even if it was abuse, they were told, they had asked for it. In extreme patriarchal systems, the message is that children have no right to be. In other words, children ought to be grateful for existing, they are property, and they can be treated in any manner that suits the parents, particularly the father or other men in the system.

At some point during the anger stage, a client often feels great anger not only toward the person who sexually abused him but also toward the adults in his life who did not protect him from the abuser. Even in cases where the perpetrator came from outside the family system, there is usually an aspect of victimization within the family in the form of neglect. Unfortunately, many families are so dysfunctional because of chemical dependence or other addictive disorders that awareness are generally dulled. The adults are so preoccupied with other matters that they overlook a stranger who is being sexual with one of the children, and the child falls prey to the overall superficiality of the parenting. Being a member of a dysfunctional family makes a child more at risk for being sought out by sexually exploitive adults. Since the child is unable to get his needs met within the family, he is more likely to seek adult attention outside the family, regardless of the personal cost to him. Succinctly put, exploitive attention seems better than no attention at all.

When the abuse is discovered or disclosed, parents often are more concerned that it will affect their family's image in the community than they are about the child's well-being. For example, they may be afraid that their child is, or will be thought of as being, sexually abnormal. Inappropriate responses often are born out of ignorance rather than malice.

Sadness

During the sadness stage, the client is becoming aware of the losses he has suffered as a result of the abuse and is saying, "I'll never get my childhood back," or "I guess we didn't have the special relationship she said we did." Sadness is an emotion not encouraged in American males. At the risk of sounding trite, the old adage "Big boys don't cry" is still alive in homes and institutions throughout our country. Even if the statement is never spoken, it echoes in the minds of parents, teachers, and coaches and is implied through their behavioral responses to youths. In the clinical setting, some therapists see sadness in males as self-pity and are intolerant of it, preventing their clients from fully grieving their losses due to the childhood abuse.

During this stage, the therapist can begin to stop using the phrase *recovering victim* and begin using the term *survivor*.

Acceptance/Forgiveness

In the acceptance stage, the client begins to reorganize his life so that he shifts his attention from the consequences of the childhood abuse to leading an enjoyable life. Physical, cognitive, or emotional scares may remain, but they will have a minimal effect on his ability to accept himself and interact appropriately with others. He may express the view that "the abuse happened, it affected me, I am a survivor, and I am healing" or "the abuse happened, it affected me, I have healed, and I am a person like any other." The therapist's focus is on healthy behaviors rather than on any label.

At this point, both the therapist and the client are comfortable using the term *survivor*. Signs that a client has not reached the acceptance/forgiveness stage are depression, bitterness, resentfulness, hypersensitivity, or vigilance for clues of abuse; a view of oneself as powerless or childlike; and self-destructive or other abuse behaviors.

Therapeutic Style

Some traditionally trained therapists wait for the client to initiate discussion of sexual abuse and other issues. Any attempt to lead the client to describe sexual abuse is viewed as agenda setting and disrespectful. Further, use of labels such as *sexual abuse, victim,* and *survivor* also are viewed as disrespectful, limiting the client and even revictimizing him.

We have a different view of the situation and believe that the client can experience the therapist's lack of direction as disinterest. Issue avoidance can reinforce shame and give the message that the sexual abuse is not important enough to waste time talking about. We believe that the therapist has a responsibility to model willingness and comfort when talking about difficult issues and to provide information that the client lacks.

In light of this view, we propose a pace/lead model to use when working with people who have experienced sexual trauma. This model is taken from our hypnosis training and is very effective. According to this model, the therapist's mission is to encourage the client to focus on the painful experience of sexual abuse while still respecting the rate at which the client is able to tolerate his increasing awareness of memories and feelings. The client's defenses are not to be peeled away until such time as he has other effective coping techniques, so that he will not become overwhelmed.

In hypnosis, *pacing* is heightening the client's awareness of an event that has just taken place—for example, "You may have noticed that you just blinked." A *lead* is a comment that suggests that the client become aware of something new—for example, "You may find yourself becoming relaxed." The hypnotherapist uses a series of paces and leads to facilitate the client's obtaining a trance and then provides suggestions that are more likely to be entertained by the client due to his state of relaxation and focused attention. People who have been sexually abused are usually excellent hypnotic subjects, since they spontaneously dissociate and frequently are in trance states in session even when the therapist has not used formal hypnotic techniques.

When working with clients recovering from sexual abuse, the psychotherapist can use the pace/lead model by commenting on some aspect of the client's past experience that the client is likely to agree with ("So it was then that she began to fondle you") and then encouraging the client to reframe the experience by providing a lead ("And that is sexual abuse"). By shuttling between pacing and leading, the therapist is providing information to neutralize sex-negative cognitive distortions and shame-based self-talk, and he or she is helping the client to answer the universal question "Am I normal?" means "Am I acceptable as a person after what was done to me?" These techniques can be used to facilitate the client's moving from one grief stage to another: (pace) "So he denied that he had touched you"; (lead) "And you may now notice clues that you are angry." The pace/lead model also can be used to help the client change his self-image: (pace) "So you told him you wouldn't tolerate being treated disrespectfully"; (lead) "You are beginning to see yourself as a survivor."

The grief stages and pace/lead model are two ways of conceptualizing the very complex dynamics found in clients who have experienced sexual abuse. They are useful tools but are not a replacement for a relationship with a nonintrusive, respectful person who listens and believes in the client.

References

Abel, G., J.V. Becker, M. Mittleman, et al. 1987. "Self-Reported Crimes of Nonincarcerated Paraphiliacs." *Journal of Interpersonal Violence* 2 (no. 1): 3–23.

Bear, E., and P. Dimock. 1988. *Adults Molested as Children: A Survivor's Manual for Women and Men.* Orwell, Vermont: Safer Society Press.

Becker, J.V., and G. Abel. 1984. "Methodological and Ethical Issues in Evaluating and Treating Adolescent Sexual Offenders." National Institute of Mental Health monograph, *Treatment of Child Molesters.* Grant #MH 36347, June.

Courtois, C. 1988. *Healing the Incest Wound.* New York: W.W. Norton.

Finkelhor, D. 1979. *Sexually Victimized Children.* New York: Free Press.

———. 1984. *Child Sexual Abuse: New Theory and Research.* New York: Free Press.

Herman, J. 1981. *Father-Daughter Incest.* Cambridge, Massachusetts: Harvard University Press.

Hunter, M. 1990. *Abused Boys: The Neglected Victims of Sexual Abuse.* Lexington, Massachusetts: Lexington Books.

Kempe, R., and H. Kempe. 1984. *The Common Secret: Sexual Abuse of Children and Adolescents.* New York: W.H. Freeman and Co.

Kübler-Ross, E. 1969. *On Death and Dying.* New York: MacMillan.

Lew, M. 1988. *Victims No Longer.* New York: Nevramont.

McKechnie, J., ed. 1979. *Webster's New Universal Unabridged Dictionary.* 2d ed. Cleveland: Dorset & Baber.

Meiselman, 1979. *Incest: A Psychological Study of Causes and Effects with Treatment Recommendations.* San Francisco: Jossey-Bass.

4

Creative Approaches to Healing Sexual Abuse Trauma

Darryl Dahlheimer

Sexual abuse is a shattering, disintegrating experience for humans and leaves wounds on three levels—spiritual, physical, and emotional. Many therapy approaches to survivors deal primarily with only one level, and the process can be a long and incomplete one. Survivors commonly say to me, "I feel like my life is a movie I watch," "There's a hole inside that never seems to fill," or "I want to feel alive again." The experience they are describing is having a blunted or missing part of themselves. Nontraditional methods in therapy can help client and therapist reintegrate the numb or blunted areas into a sense of wholeness and aliveness. The purpose of this chapter is to describe five examples of effective approaches and to describe a process for cocreating additional approaches with clients.

Examples of Creative Approaches

Adequacy Journal

Low trust, shame, and fear are among the most common and stubborn wounds to heal in the aftermath of sexual abuse, particularly abuse that has been buried and unprocessed for years. Verbal processing plays an important role in promoting understanding and in normalizing abuse reactions, thereby reducing shame ("Oh, good, I'm not crazy"). But relief on the insight level often does not get inside to deeper levels. For example, the survivor may report, "I understand that this is a reaction to the abuse, *but . . .*" and then report that he still cannot trust himself, views himself as dirty, and is frightened that his emotions will overwhelm him. Since the abuse happened to a child, it is recorded and experienced through a child's perceptions, including magical thinking about adults being powerful, godly figures and children's own distorted judgments based on limited information or downright lies told by adults. Building a bridge back to that child requires the adult survivor to become a compassionate and friendly ally to the child within so that at the deeper (child) level, the trauma can be released and new information can become incorporated. Keeping an *adequacy journal* is one tool that works. Even if the client has kept journals in the past, this one is new in that it is targeted toward the core issues.

Specifically, the survivor is instructed to write down all emotional and behavioral breakthroughs in one section of the journal labeled "progress." These breakthroughs come as a natural part of the growth process, but collected on paper, they become a critical mass of progress and a concrete, self-comforting resource that the survivor can read and reread. This process helps him build trust in the healing process and self-evaluation ("Gee, I can see that I *am* growing").

The second part of an adequacy journal is the daily recording of five things the survivor did well. Initially, he may need therapist prompting, validation, and permission to start small (for example, "Well, you were honest about your fear in today's session" or "It sounds like you tried out a new way to talk to yourself on the bus"). Giving credit for the effort, not just the outcome, is a helpful attitude to teach. This part of the journal is cumulative (5 competent moments per day times 30 days equals 150 self-messages of "I am capable") and builds daily habits of looking for self-competency. In addition to adding self-worth, this process reinforces the concepts that small daily steps count and that the perceived overwhelming wall of shame can be dismantled brick by brick, moment by moment. This kind of hope building is very important in countering the experience of trust shattering or physical violation that sexual abuse constitutes.

Spoken Autobiography

This tool can help the survivor gently perforate his wall of denial and self-blame by telling the truth concerning the abuse and believing himself. Although denial and minimization of sexual abuse experiences are common coping strategies for most survivors, these are particularly common among male survivors because of the mistaken belief in our culture that adult/child sexual contact is not as traumatic for boys and adolescent males as it is for girls. A *spoken autobiography* helps a survivor lift the numbness and denial surrounding past abuse and validate that the experience was indeed abuse and that it had consequences for his later functioning in life. In addition, feelings that were previously split off from recall are reintegrated.

The survivor is asked to write a complete sexual history, including family sexuality messages, first awakenings of his own sexuality (desires generally precede behavior), major experiences with interpersonal sexuality, masturbation experiences, and, of course, extent, duration, and circumstances of all sexual abuse experiences. It is helpful to encourage writing even a paragraph about each memory and starting to write a little at a time, although some men will write the complete description in one sitting. It is important to stress that there are many different ways to write and that the client cannot fail at this task (except by never starting).

After the autobiography is complete on paper, the survivor reads aloud from it, in sections or in total (a longer session than normal will be required). The therapist's job is to listen for feelings and periodically stop the reading to focus on connecting the underlying effect with the events being described (for example, "That kid wasn't merely abused; that was more like torture. Can you feel how scared you must have been?").

One positive result is that the survivor experiences relief at being understood and not judged by another person who now knows his entire story. Another outcome is gaining increased knowledge of what happened to him (all the abuse, put in the context of his sexual development) and at the same time gaining detachment from his trauma-as-identity. Something in the process of writing his experiences down on paper and reading them aloud seems to shift the client's perceptions away from being defined by the abuse (identity as a victim) and toward a healthy detachment (identity as a person who was victimized). Perhaps it is as simple as the shift from "That's myself" to "That's my story."

Finally, the spoken autobiography is an important tool for discovery of further abuse experiences that have not been labeled as such. Males who were sexually abused as children frequently are involved in quasi-consensual relationships with adults during their teen years. The childhood abuse left them prematurely awakened and confused sexually, and they are very vulnerable to exploitation by adults who have more information and power to coerce. A complete autobiography lays all this information on the table so that the therapist can educate and validate while discussing the contents. Many survivors report "aha" experiences as they are writing or reading their stories aloud, and previously forgotten details of the abuse can be keys to deconstructing the trauma.

Photographs

Sexual abuse is disruptive of bonds—bonds with the perpetrator, bonds with family members to whom the child looked for protection, bonds with justice and security in a world that is predictable. Overwhelming feelings of confusion, shame, fear, anger, and hurt force many child survivors to cope by splitting off feelings and events from their lives, a strategy that creates shut-down or numb areas in the adult survivor's life. The splitting and numbing creates interpersonal problems of attachment and bonding with both the therapist and the child inside. Use of *photographs* can restore object constancy and connection, similar to children's use of stuffed animals as transitional objects.

Photos can work in both directions in therapy. One survivor who would feel flooded within a few hours after our session asked for a photograph of me to carry with him. When anxiety arose, he would look at the picture and calm himself by thinking of what I would have said to him in each situation. The visual cue allowed him to experience the security of the relationship. Another survivor asked me to carry his kindergarten picture in my wallet, as he was struggling to believe that I (or anyone) truly cared about him. He reported feeling "important to someone" for the first time in his life when I enthusiastically agreed to carry him with me.

In addition to promoting object constancy, photographs are a major source of reality testing. Survivors who are exaggeratedly concerned with aspects of body image, weight, or appearance often take in a therapist's normalizing statements better if photos serve as a common focal point. Without photos, the focus of the body image discussion is the person's body itself, a circumstance likely to heighten shame (shame amplified by feeling stared at or exposed). Finally, photographs of the survivor as a child at different ages can promote self-empathy. Survivors connect by carrying their own childhood photos in a shirt pocket (over their heart) and periodically looking at or talking to that child. Many men have told me that seeing the photo helped them realize that they were kids, little kids, when the abuse happened and that they could see (for the first time) that they were not to blame because they could not have stopped the adult abuser. Again, shifting self-perceptions away from self-blame and rejection and toward a compassionate connection with the inner child will aid healing. Pictures of themselves as children before the abuse occurred also can help establish the idea that there is a healthy core self that still lives.

Touch Exercises

The meaning of touch varies among cultures and families, but there is a normal human need for nurture and touch. One of the wounds of sexual abuse is that touch becomes associated with fear (danger), shame (due to the secrecy component), and confusion (self-blaming or mixed signals when touch is forced or corrupted in the context of a prior nonsexual relationship). As a result, a shame/need bind occurs, and many survivors split off this wound into extreme solutions:

1. Totally avoiding touch (starving)
2. Acting out the need for touch in self-abusive situations such as compulsive/addictive sexual behavior (binging)
3. Exhibiting a repressive-impulsive cycle that uses both extremes (similar to a binge/purge/diet cycle)

To regain power in the area of touch, survivors need to experience nurturing, nonsexualized touch that is paired with care, pleasure, and safety. The concept of trust building on a body level can be brought up early on as part of an effective treatment road map. Survivors frequently need to be coached about the process of touch so that they know they can still be in charge of if, when, and how they are touched. Demonstrating different holding positions makes the concept less abstract. I use a teddy bear to demonstrate how each person would be sitting in the various options. One good security-building position is for the therapist and survivor to sit side by side, with the therapist's arm around the survivor's shoulders. Another is for the therapist to sit with his or her back supported (for example, against a wall) and the survivor to sit in front of him or her, facing the same direction (outward) and leaning back onto the therapist. The second option allows the survivor not to have eye contact while being held and allows him the options of having the therapist's arms wrapped around him or placed on his shoulders or of not being held at all.

Many survivors say that this safe touch is a first (never previously experienced). Others note fear or sexual arousal and need to talk about these responses. The therapist's tasks are to affirm that many feelings can come up and to encourage the client to let those old pairings (touch/shame and touch/fear) go and concentrate on experiencing the safety/care aspects. If the client is unable to desexualize the touch, it is an indication that this is not the correct point in therapy to do the exercise. The potential benefits for the client are many:

1. He experiences his need for touch.
2. There is increased trust of and bonding with the therapist.
3. There is a detangling of nurture needs and sexualized touch.
4. He learns how to get safe holding from trusted others.

Broken Record

This tool helps survivors to manage shame and actively build hope and esteem. While the thesis of this chapter is that words alone are insufficient, using specific affirmations repeatedly gives words more power to be internalized. A parallel process occurs in which the therapist repeats certain messages aloud during each session (proactively looking for openings during sessions where the messages can be inserted in a way relevant to the content being discussed). In effect, the therapist functions like a *broken record* that skips and repeats a portion over and over; the survivor begins to record these messages in his head and then practices playing them in his daily life (that is, he starts to look for openings in which to insert these new, healthy ideas). In the same way that the chorus section of a song makes that song memorable and easier to learn, simple, concrete, repeated messages can be the easiest aspect of psychoeducation to absorb. Although individuals vary in the ways in which they weave shame into their lives, the following three messages are useful, if not essential, to most survivors.

The first message says, "You completely make sense." Often a survivor's greatest fear is that he is secretly crazy because of the confusing nature of his postabuse reactions and defenses. For example, a survivor may be baffled by having a nightmare only hours after a particularly productive session. When the concept of detoxifying is explained ("You loosened up some old poisons inside, and they produced symptoms on their way out of you"), the survivor can see that nightmare as a sign of progress rather than proof of decompensation, and the result is an increased trust in his own process. Even if the therapist does not have a clear explanation of what has happened in a given situation, it is very useful to take the stance "You completely make sense," as this empowers the survivor to join with you in tracking down the reasons something occurred. It shifts the focus from searching for confirming evidence of one's own insanity to searching for lessons and new self-understanding. Many survivors can then make intuitive guesses about cause, and this helps them regain confidence that their life will not be a series of random and mysterious setbacks.

A second useful message is to teach the distinction between real feelings and phony feelings. Real feelings are those messages that come from the core (inner child, spiritual self, wise person) and can be described as one of the four basic feelings—madness, sadness, gladness, and fear—or a combination of two or more. Phony feelings are those shame-based messages that come from many faces of shame—hopelessness, badness, worthlessness, despair, numbness, repulsion, uselessness, self-contempt—or a combination of two or more. Teaching survivors to distinguish real versus phony feelings is essential in sorting out truth, as both sets of feelings are experienced internally, but one set is an inner lie created by the abuse. The goal then becomes (1) believing and listening to one's inner feelings (the basic four) as guides for living, and (2) noticing and consciously rejecting shame-based feeling equivalents as phony and a lie about oneself. This distinction gives survivors the power to reject toxic internal messages without closing down the abundance of intuitive, emotional, and spiritual-level messages inside them.

The third useful message is "You can heal." Again, because the abuse was initially processed through a child's eyes, concreteness and absolutism can pervade a survivor's beliefs about the abuse. One common fear is that "there's no way back" and that a part of him is permanently damaged or unrecoverable. It is important to say that in your experience, you have found that human beings have amazing untapped healing powers and, while it may take years of effort, the client can have a complete and happy life. I used to concede that there was one possible piece of permanent damage, and that was loss of innocence, as so many survivors led frozen or disrupted childhoods after being prematurely sexually awakened and/or betrayed by the abuse. However, several of my clients have every appearance of having regained their sense of wonder, trust, and openness (albeit not a naive openness). As one person put it, "I'm *having* a very happy childhood." This message of "You can heal" replaces fear with hope and refocuses the grieving process from "the wreck that's left of me" to the more appropriate "areas I still need to reclaim." Survivors also spontaneously break through into new areas of self-love, freedom from self-blame, body-image acceptance, and so on, and these moments can be highlighted as proof of the truth that they have the inner power to heal their lives.

A final aspect of using the broken record technique is to encourage the client to *write the messages down,* carry them with him, and even post them around his world (on the refrigerator or closet door or on the rearview mirror in the car).

In summary, when inner shame dialogue start to play, the client can use a broken record approach of answering the shame with concrete messages of truth, hope, and esteem. The key is repetition and initial modeling by the therapist to confront the survivor's shame over and over as it appears in content.

Cocreating New Approaches

In addition to using the five nontraditional techniques described above, I encourage you to be creative and discover new approaches that have special salience for your clients. Here are som ideas to begin this journey.

Art

Creativity, spirituality, and art are closely linked in all cultures. Art has the advantage of being both an avenue of emotional expression and a link between concrete images and the healing process (that is, both mobilizing feelings and providing tangible containers for those feelings that can be hung on to). One survivor whose abusers repeatedly commented on his small features and boyish looks found himself deeply ashamed of his small hands and feet and scared that others would notice them. Words alone could not break the shame, but intuitively he sensed that finger paints could. He made a footprint and a handprint using finger paints, with the declaration "shame-proof" written over all, and presented it to me. That creation led to more resolution than all the other approaches we had tried, and it came from the client's intuition backed up by the therapist's encouragement.

Another example of useful art is poetry, where words join the realm of images. One survivor who regularly had terrifying nightmares about his family was encouraged to write down images right after awakening. In the process of writing one poem, he was able to recall a hidden memory that his mother for years slept with a huge butcher knife under the mattress "just in case" she needed to kill her violent husband. This was significant in that he could then make a link to his own cutting behavior on his arms as learned behavior (not a sign of his "craziness") to numb the pain and provide a sense of security.

Toys

Many children's toys are delightful because they allow the client a sense of mastery and control over something. Dolls are an obvious way to play out better resolutions to past events. Things that can be built up and then destroyed over and over (such as, blocks, or clay) are healthy channels for anger release. One survivor would make people from clay and then cut them up in little pieces with a plastic knife as a way of dealing with his primitive rage inside. Another survivor bought a child's slate-erase board where messages could be written through a clear film but would disappear when the clear sheet was lifted. He would write old toxic messages of verbal abuse and then say good-bye to them as he erased them.

Listen to clients, encourage them that they hold the keys to healing deep within their intuitions, and share stories about other seemingly crazy ideas that survivors have tried and used successfully.

Conclusion

Creative approaches to healing sexual abuse trauma in male survivors have many advantages over approaches dominated by talking therapy. These advantages include the following:

1. They provide concrete experiences of healing to match the concreteness of the abuse.
2. They provide access to the "wounded child" within who does not trust words.
3. They allow for the greater behavioral involvement of survivors in their own healing.
4. They keep therapists fresh and open to new ideas, which can aid personal creativity and healing.

5

Crossing Typological Boundaries in Treating the Shame Cycle

Jack Rusinoff
Paul N. Gerber

T his chapter focuses on treatment of clients in whom shame and sexual arousal or sexuality are associated. We agree with Fossum and Mason's (1986) definition of the term *shame:*

> Shame is an inner sense of being completely diminished or insufficient as a person. It is the self judging the self. A moment of shame may be humiliation so painful or an indignity so profound that one feels one has been robbed of her or his dignity or exposed as basically inadequate, bad, or worthy of rejection. A pervasive sense of shame is the ongoing premise that one is fundamentally bad, inadequate, defective, unworthy, or not fully valid as a human being." (p. 5)

Male sexual abuse victims and offenders experience a deep, shameful affect connected with their sexuality. The clients we work with react and respond to the bond between shame and sexuality in different ways. For some men, sexual arousal becomes tied to repetitive sexual behaviors and fantasies. Similar patterns can be seen in behaviors such as eating disorders or self-mutilation. Identifying sexually compulsive/addictive patterns can only follow comprehensive, sex-specific psychotherapeutic assessment. Assuming that a comprehensive assessment is in place, the primary goal of this chapter is to provide some cognitive, behavioral, and spiritual therapies for helping these people separate their sexuality from shame.

Treatment professionals recently uncovered the fact that many adult males are victims of childhood sexual abuse. Survey research is beginning to corroborate the clinical observation that a sizable population of men were sexually mistreated during childhood (see, for example, Risin and Koss 1987). More and more, counselors, therapists, and social workers are showing an interest in helping these victims. This is evidenced by a current upsurge in workshops and conferences addressing the male victim. As professionals learn about the issues and problems associated with male victims, they also discover that there is often a fine line separating these victims from offenders.

First, it is common for specialists to agree that many sex offenders were themselves victims of sexual (or other) mistreatment during their developmental years (Becker et al. 1986; Groth 1979; Knopp 1984; Mayer 1985). It is clear that most male victims of childhood sexual abuse never become full-fledged sex offenders (Gilgun 1988; Lew 1988; Hunter 1990). However, male victims of childhood sexual abuse often report, sometime during their treatment, that they sexually acted out against another during adolescence or early adulthood. Many victims experiment briefly with victimizing others, then abandon this form of symptomatology in favor of other methods of coping with their abuse. For reasons not completely discernible at this time, other male victims continue to victimize others sexually.

It also is well known that many sex offenders are paraphiliacs (Abel et al. 1987; Knopp 1984; Money 1989). By definition, sex offenders tend to act in sexually compulsive and addictive ways. For example, exhibitionists and voyeurs often repeat their offenses over and over, even after serious legal consequences. Similarly, many male victims behave in sexually compulsive (Carlson et al. 1987; Dimock 1988; Lew 1988; Hunter 1990) and addictive (Carnes 1983) ways. Dimock (1988) provides some examples: "preoccupation with sexual thoughts, compulsive masturbation as often as four or five times a day, sexual acts with other men at pornographic book stores and restrooms, and frequent and multiple sex partners" (p. 207).

Additionally, male sexual abuse victims and offenders share a plethora of other symptoms. Mayer (1985) lists several common problems experienced by male victims: suicide, self-mutilation, depression, drug and alcohol abuse, negative self-image, fear of homosexuality, and emotional fixation at the age of being abused. Dimock (1988) adds male role confusion and relationship (intimacy) dysfunction. Certainly, many sex offenders are self-destructive in terms of suicide (Lanning 1987), self-mutilation, and alcohol or drug abuse (Mayer 1985). Perpetrators share the experience of shame (Knopp 1984; Langfeldt 1989; Mayer 1983)—that is, they almost always have very poor self-images. Further, they tend to be extremely homophobic (Groth 1979) and experience sex-role problems (Seely 1989). Male pedophiles are often labeled as fixated at an earlier stage of development (Groth 1979). Because offenders typically exhibit poor impulse control, sexual and emotional immaturity, and dependence, it almost goes without saying that they have relationship and intimacy problems.

Finally, a large group of men falls somewhere in the middle of the continuum between victim and offender (Dimock et al. 1988). With this clientele, it is difficult to tell whether the victim or offender portion is bigger. These men were all clearly victimized in their past, and they may act out in sexually compulsive ways, which may or may not be hurting others. Working with this sort of person can pose a dilemma for the treatment professional.

As we have seen, male victims and offenders of sexual mistreatment frequently have similar problems and dysfunctions. Also, whether someone is better categorized as a victim or an offender is not always clear. Although victims and offenders can have very similar issues, there remains some hidden variable or set of factors involved in victims crossing over the line into offenderhood.

This chapter explores the treatment of a problem common to male victims and perpetrators of sexual abuse. Although the separation of sexual arousal from shame is not the only goal of treatment, it is a major part of healing for both perpetrators and victims. Therapeutic techniques for helping these clients experience a healthier sexuality, free of shameful affect, are presented here via case studies.

For the sake of clarity and brevity, some categories or diagnoses are acknowledged rather than defined. It is the authors' combined experience that clients fitting into each of these categories have a shared reality in that shame, arousal, and sexualized fantasy merge, ultimately resulting in self-defeating, self-debasing behaviors. The behaviors resulting from the pairing of shame and arousal fall into the broad, politically loaded categories of deviation, variation, or normalcy, but the issue of secrecy would appear to have greater relevance to the shame cycle than to these three categories.

The literature on sexual victimization and the actions of the criminal justice system place people into one of two dichotomous categories—(1) victims of sexual abuse or (2) perpetrators of the same. Treatment professionals working with victims or perpetrators further classify their clients into various descriptive typologies. These categories often share a common thread of repetitive sexualized fantasy or behavior resulting from the pairing of shame and arousal.

Most politically dangerous in treating male and female victims of sexual abuse is inferring that arousal often arises out of sexual victimization. This is most likely to occur when the sexual victimization is masked as loving and follows a covert, presexual conditioning process. Professionals rightfully view sexual victimization as something horrible that happens to people. Yet many professionals cannot or will not grasp the fact that bizarre fantasies, aberrant behaviors, and cognitive distortions often are a predictable outcome. When the behavioral sequela becomes deviated or aberrant, there is an immediate tendency to push the client into the offender domain. There seems to be a resistance to exploring and treating deviated fantasy among victims, particularly those who are not yet behaviorally symptomatic. Too often the client's identity as victim or offender, rather than the presenting problem, dictates the treatment or therapeutic approach.

Because some victims have learned to combine their arousal with deviant or exploitive sex, they experience shame and keep it a secret. Victims who have not associated sexual arousal with aberrant sexual behaviors also are often ashamed of their sexuality because of the shaming experience inherent in all forms of maltreatment, especially sexual abuse. Routinely, there is a tendency for clients to keep secrets from therapists. This is partly due to subtle prejudices growing out of the belief system that does not recognize the close relationship between offender and victim experiences, the power imbalance notwithstanding. It also is due to the client's fear of exposure; the client fears that his therapist will not accept him when the therapist finds out about his sexual variations and deviancy (real or imagined).

Most of the ambiguities shrouding the issue of appropriate treatment are illustrated by part of the extensive clinical assessment of a thirteen-year-old male whom we will call "Fredrick."

Case History. Fredrick was referred to the Program for Healthy Adolescent Sexual Expression. The government referring source identified Fredrick as a perpetrator of sexual abuse. Background data identified Fredrick and his younger male and female siblings as all having been long-term victims of sexual abuse at the hands of their biological father. While each child had separate, individualized abuse experiences with their father, a secondary activity was to have all three engage in sexual activity with each other during bathing. The father would instruct the three of them to be sexual with each other, with the father viewing the behaviors. At the time of detection by the criminal justice department, all three children were behaving as abuse-reactive children. In other words, these children were exhibiting the behavioral sequelae often found in the wake of gross, long-term sexual maltreatment. After the father was removed, Fredrick continued his sexual behavior with his siblings, as he had been conditioned to do for years. This behavior resulted in Fredrick's being labeled an offender by the criminal justice system.

A lengthy and comprehensive assessment using testing, hypnosis, and group, individual, and family therapy identified two poignant issues. The intensity, duration, and frequency of the sexual behaviors between Fredrick and his siblings, orchestrated by his biological father, had created cognitive distortions to the point that all the children had normalized the behavior. Furthermore, the behavior had become ritualized for Fredrick because he was repeatedly eroticized during his latency years and adolescence. His conditioned behaviors were ultimately paired with arousal, orgasm, and ejaculation. Secondarily, Fredrick's individual sexual contacts with his biological father represented a repertoire of sexual fantasy exclusively focused on mutual oral-genital contact between him and his father.

This exclusive sexual fantasy occurred daily, always produced arousal, and often escalated to masturbation. The fantasy was so powerful that Fredrick was reported on one occasion when he masturbated publicly. He reported that he had become so lost in his fantasy that he dissociated from his surroundings.

It became immediately clear, as a result of the psychosexual assessment, that Fredrick had normalized his behavior and that of his siblings. At the time of the initial intervention, he had immense shame surrounding the behavior with his father. Fredrick's continued, repetitive masturbation to that exclusive image exasperated him, with his anxieties about this behavior escalating and resulting in persistent suicidal ideation.

Conceivably (given the diversity of philosophies and treatment approaches), Fredrick could be labeled with any number of diagnoses or classifications from mental health, social service, and criminal justice professionals. For instance, child protection professionals might label him a victim of sexual abuse, while the juvenile court migh label him an offender. A psychologist could diagnose him as having a paraphilia or a personality disorder.

This brings us back to the core issue of treatment considerations when shame is paired with arousal, fantasy, and behavior. The question remains of what might be seen as effective cognitive, behavioral, and spiritual therapies that will be specifically focused on the dissipation of the ritual and the residual affect of the loss of that ritual.

Two schools of thought about dealing with deviant or aberrant fantasies seem to exist. At one of the spectrum is the theory that fantasy by its very nature does not represent reality and therefore need not be expanded, modified, or eliminated. The key issue is to implant cognitive social inhibitors in the client, creating a clear distinction between the acceptability of aberrant fantasies and the unacceptability of aberrant behaviors. Aiding the client in eliminating his shame about the existence of the aberrant fantasies would be part of the task. Another issue is to teach the client to be in control of his fantasies instead of perceiving himself to be the victim of them.

The opposing view holds fantasy to be a rehearsal for reality. Some clinicians use masturbatory reconditioning or satiation to diminish deviant arousal. Behavioral and cognitive therapy used together help bolster social inhibitors and challenge the minimization and rationalization often associated with sexually deviant clients. The behavior therapies have been applied in a variety of formats in the treatment of sexual offenders (Abel et al. 1984; Abel et al. 1987). Empirical research gives strong support to its application in eliminating deviant arousal patterns and behaviors.

Our position is that similar therapies are appropriate for both the male victim who was eroticized to the abuse (and ultimately became fixated on the abuse experience) and the noneroticized yet shameful male victim. It is essential that the use of cognitive and behavior therapies be blended, including a focus on the client's spirituality or lack thereof. Arousal, fantasy, shame, and self-defeating behaviors are so interactive in the totality of the compulsive/ addictive cycle (see table 5–1) that using less than holistic therapy fails to meet the needs of the client. A significant amount of empirical data suggests that repetitive, deviant arousal to fantasy will rarely be treated effectively by the exclusive application of talk (cognitive) approach.

We want to acknowledge that some of these curative approaches may seem extreme if a treatment provider comes out of a more traditional psychotherapeutic approach to the treatment of victims. The literature focusing on masturbatory reconditioning and satiation is, unfortunately, offender and male oriented. It is the same research that brought forth empirical data confirming that large numbers of sexual abuse victims are male. Some male victims of sexual abuse make a clear transition from victim to offender. Another segment of that same population can become entrenched in self-defeating, compulsive, or otherwise problematic sexual behaviors that are not illegal. Still others retreat from sexuality in shame and therefore experience intimacy problems. The very nature of these powerful patterns demands a multifaceted clinical approach that goes beyond the victim/offender dichotomy to recognize core issues that cross typological boundaries.

Table 5–1
Cycle of Shameful Sexuality

Stage 1: *Negative behavior*
   Perceived attack, threat, or criticism (real or imaginary)
   Abuse behavior toward self or others (acting out)

Stage 2: *Shameful feelings*
   Feeling exposed/discovered as defective
   Painful feelings about self as total failure
   Self-devaluing cognition

Stage 3: *Tension and fear*
   Fear of rejection/abandonment and hurt
   Fear of more attack, threats, and criticism (real or imaginary)
   Unresolved conflict and unmet needs and wants

Stage 4: *Rage and defense/coping behaviors*
   Avoidance of pain, shame, and fear
   Denial, blame, minimizing, rationalizing, or justifying

Stage 5: *Negative behavior*
   Repeat of negative behavior (acting out)
   Beginning of new cycle

The Shame-Sexuality Cycle

Sexuality and shame appear to cycle around for male victims of sexual assault. The trauma of the assault(s) causes the victim to feel ashamed of his sexuality. Consequently, sexuality becomes an unpleasant, shameful set of experiences even when it occurs during appropriate situations.

People are not born ashamed of their sexuality or sexual behavior. They become ashamed of sexuality through direct (overt) or indirect (covert) sexual maltreatment and abuse. After a person has been hurt sufficiently sexually, he learns to associate the pain and shame of his traumatic experience with his sexuality. Once this association is in place, which often occurs after only one episode of sexual victimization, the victim experiences painful and negative affect connected with almost everything sexual. The victim's sexuality and sexual activity become damaged and problematic. Every time the victim masturbates or engages in any sexual behavior, he feels bad about himself afterward. When the victim engages in sexual behavior (for example, masturbation) to relieve the tension and negative affect that come from a previous sexual experience or from some other source of stress, he begins to reinforce a vicious cycle of repetitive shame and sexual behavior. Table 5–1, which illustrates this cycle, can be used to help clients gain a cognitive understanding of their problematic experience of sexuality. Such cognitive understanding is only a small part of the healing process involved in helping clients separate their sexuality from shame.

During the first stage of the cycle, the person is abused by someone else or by himself. This cycle is started by victimization and the role-modeling processes that take place during the maltreatment. The victim does not necessarily have to abuse himself or another person as a result of being victimized. However, many sexually abused children (especially very young ones) do act out their abuse to show parents what happened. Often the parents do not understand the child's behavior and further shame him for behaving sexually. The case history at the end of this section illustrates this point.

The shameful feelings of stage 2 are a natural result of being abused. As part of this shame, the victim naturally blames himself and experiences other self-devaluing cognitions. Because he has learned not to like all or parts of himself, he moves on to stage 3.

During stage 3, a period of tension and fear, the victim believes that he is unlovable. He fears that more abuse may come soon, and indeed it may. He finds that he is unable to ask for what he needs and wants and that he has great difficulty resolving internal and interpersonal conflicts. The more these issues build up, the more he needs to move into the next stage as a means of trying to cope.

During the fourth stage of rage and defense/coping behaviors, the victim attempts to deal with the three preceding stages. The intensity of this stage is often too much for the victim to bear. Although the defense mechanisms used during this stage meet some functional need in helping him cope, he eventually fails and ends up back in stage 1.

At this point, he engages in his acting out. The acting-out behaviors alleviate the shame, pain, and fear. This is similar to the relief the alcoholic feels when drowning his or her sorrows. It is also similar in that the cycle then repeats itself. When a male sexual abuse victim engages in sexual activity to relieve the pain, he receives a temporary payoff. He then experiences the consequences of getting stuck in this cycle, and the bond between shame and sexuality becomes stronger and harder to break. As this cycle continues, the victim becomes hooked on his dysfunctional sexuality.

Case History. When, in his early thirties, "Scott" became aware of having been emotionally, psychologically, physically, and sexually abused during his childhood. He was in crisis, both emotionally and financially. When he came in for his intake interview, he said that he had recently remembered having been violently raped at a party when he was in his early twenties. He also knew that his parents had grossly mistreated him during his childhood.

Scott had a physical disability and could not hold a job or exercise because of extreme, chronic physical pain. He also was recently separated from his wife and starting to go through divorce proceedings. He had sought counseling elsewhere but thought that his counselor did not understand him or believe that he was a rape victim. Among his presenting problems were shame and rage, fear of intimacy and isolation, distrust, grief over his recent losses, an unhappy childhood, a sense of being ugly, many sexuality issues, and sexual dysfunction.

After the interview, it was clear that Scott was motivated to change his life, yet he viewed himself as helpless and hopeless. He agreed to come in for individual and group psychotherapy. He was slow to warm up to the group and fearful of the other participants, especially the gay men. He also expressed some ambivalence toward individual counseling by not showing up for his second appointment. Also, during his initial sessions, he discussed relatively safe issues (such as his current crisis). He also used several local help lines for support.

When Scott felt more comfortable, he began to tell more of the sad story of his childhood. His father had physically punished Scott with extreme harshness and brutality. His mother had called him a murderer and rapist while he was in grade school and older. Sometimes he came home from school to find his personal belongings thrown all over the lawn. When he received straight-A grades, his mother told him that she would straighten out his teachers because he did not deserve good grades. Scott desperately wanted to please his parents and win their acceptance. He could never do anything good enough for them. Up to this point in therapy, Scott had said little about his rape.

When Scott came in for his tenth individual session, he claimed that he was on the verge of a memory but was not sure that he wanted to retrieve it. After some discussion of the implications, Scott agreed to try hypnosis. During trance, the suggestion was given that Scott could "go back then and there, to any place or time" where he might want to do some therapeutic healing. When asked, he stated that he was three years old and at his grandparents' place. He looked visibly upset and remembered his grandparents fondling his penis, then laughing at him when he erected. During the trance, he was able to take control and make his grandparents stop. Toward the end of his trance, suggestions were given for Scott to continue his healing process and to remember anything else he might need to when he was ready. After waking up, he claimed no previous memory of this event. On his way home, Scott remembered more from later on that same day; his grandfather had stuck his penis into Scott's mouth.

At Scott's next session, he said that he felt strange and different in a positive way. He did not specify what he meant, and he still appeared to be in crisis. He was able to connect a blocked sensation in his throat with his grandfather's oral abuse. At this time, it also became clear that Scott was blamed for his sexual behaviors (acting out the abuse) by his parents. They misunderstood, and subsequently his mother called him a rapist as a young child.

Scott used his group and individual therapy sessions over the next four weeks to grieve for lost childhood and continue to debrief his abuse. As he continued his recovery, several more rape incidents from his young adult years surfaced into his memory. He seemed more able to face them and get his pain out. Scott still had sexual problems and sexual shame.

During his sixteenth individual session, the therapist suggested more hypnosis. Scott agreed to undergo trance again and wanted to work on feeling less ashamed sexually. This trance experience consisted of asking Scott to bring up his sexual shame in his imagination. His shame was conditioned to a touch on his right knee. Then he was asked to bring into his experience feelings of self-control, and peaceful strength. Those experiences were conditioned to touching his other knee. After both the positive and negative states where adequately associated with touching his knees, the therapist touched both knees at the same time. During this triggering of competing emotional states, Scott looked surprised and bewildered. At the same time, the suggestion was made that the good experiences could "short out" the bad experiences. Scott nodded his head in agreement. After several minutes, the therapist let go and tested the work. Touching the right knee no longer brought back the shame with any power, but touching the other knee still brought back empowerment. Then the therapist suggested, while touching the left knee, that those feelings of strength could come back during future sexual experiences. Scott again nodded his head in agreement. Before reorienting, Scott was given posthypnotic suggestions to continue his healing and recovery process.

Two weeks later, Scott took time in group to discuss his progress. He reported that he no longer felt shameful about his sexuality. He stopped masturbating in a compulsive, unpleasant way with rageful fantasies toward his parents. (He had not specified that his masturbation was compulsive or that he had pernicious fantasies before this point.) Scott asserted that masturbation had become pleasurable and that he was now able to decide when he wanted to do it rather than feeling as though he had no choice. At that time, it seemed that Scott was no longer in constant crisis. He was more able to deal with his interpersonal dysfunction related to rejection fears.

The pace of Scott's recovery was dramatic, given the extent and long history of his victimization. The "shorting-out" technique involves principles of classical conditioning. It is interesting, but difficult to explain, why the elicited positive mental imagery shorts out the negative imagery and not the other way around. Some clients speak about their shorting out almost as if it was a spiritual experience.

Treating Adolescent Males

In treating adolescent males who have been sexually mistreated and/or who are sexually abusive, one quickly realizes that their knowledge and attitudes about human sexuality are usually grossly limited. Many of these boys are both underinformed and misinformed, particularly in the areas of sexual physiology as it applies to orgasm and sex when it is paired with intimacy. Schools and parents often boast of being open and informative in sexual discussions with youths, but close scrutiny of the youths' knowledge and attitudes often shows that the information has been largely about "plumbing," with a specific emphasis on reproduction and disease. This new social posture has changed the preceding attitude of "Sex is dirty; save it for the one you love!" to "Sex is a bodily function; don't talk about arousal or intimacy!" Although these "plumbing" lessons are better than the previous void in rhetoric, they are sorely lacking in a culture rampant with sexual violence, teenage pregnancy, sexually transmitted diseases, and the sexual mistreatment of children.

Adolescent male victims often have a very strong genital orientation when it comes to self-pleasuring and are extremely secretive about masturbation. Masturbation continues to be shrouded in myth and misinformation. Certain belief systems, including some religious philosophies, still contain mythical sanctions against masturbation. When youthful male victims are asked to describe how they respond to touch, fantasy, visuals, or other commonly arousing stimuli, their responses intimate that the question is nearly nonconceptual. They describe their responses, in rather halting and simplistic terms, as anything from a mild experience to one of major significance. Their explanations make it evident that, at least momentarily, they seem to be lost in the experience. While the intensity and duration of the experience seem to be directly related to emergence into puberty, a significant number of clients have described orgasmic experiences that were not paired with ejaculation during latency years.

Irrespective of a growing social permission or approval for self-pleasuring, many youths remained steeped in secrecy and shame regarding this alleged socially acceptable form of sexual expression. General misinformation, combined with the chiding of peers, often creates a sense of shame or guilt so intense that it neutralizes the pleasure. Some boys report becoming avoidant or totally eliminate self-pleasure from their repertoire of sexual behaviors. When societal circumstances are further exacerbated by sexual abuse experiences, the enormity of the shame experience becomes overpowering, and the unhealed repetition of compulsive masturbation can result.

Considering this spectrum of behaviors and responses, a rather simplistic group psychoeducational approach in a therapeutic environment can be very effective. This approach is particularly effective with youths whose shame experiences are connected primarily to feigned peer intolerance and misinformation.

A wonderful format for the psychoeducational process has been set forth by Masters and Johnson (1982) in their book *Sex and Human Loving*. Information paired with specific personalized knowledge about guilt and shame is important in creating an effective presentation. Adolescent clients report that information salves their consciences and allows them to enjoy self-pleasure free from any pervasive sense of guilt or shame. This is obviously done with permission to have their sexual fantasies, which are as rich and varied as the clients are as individuals. If the fantasies are a direct replication of a victimizing experience or are related to some other behavior that the client no longer wants as part of his repertoire, more intensive cognitive and behavioral therapies often are in order. Those particular fantasies too often are a rehearsal for reality and are not addressed effectively by the psychoeducational approach described here.

While explanations about arousal and orgasm vary greatly, it is important for a youth to know that the male body responds to stimulation with relative consistency and similarity. The client also needs to understand the uniqueness of his emotional and intellectual response while in the process of eliminating guilt or shame.

At this point, it is paramount to teach boys the difference between guilt and shame. These two concepts are abstract enough that they often are used interchangeably by adolescents. A simplistic explanation of guilt is that it is an emotional reaction to a known violation of a law or rule. There is some acceptance of the concept of deserving a reasonable penalty or retribution for this violation. Also, that awareness and these emotions are followed by some clear form of remorse, with a willingness to apologize or make amends when practical. Kids soon identify guilt when it is defined this way: "I did it. It was bad behavior. I'm not a bad person. I'm truly sorry. Life goes on." Shame can be differentiated from guilt by the fact that it is often experienced when the behavior is not necessarily a clear violation of a law or rule. The acceptance of a penalty is replaced by feelings that the person is deserving of punishment or retribution, which are combined with self-loathing. Apology and closure are lost in the unhealed repetition of demeaning oneself. Because of its emotional dynamics, the physiological response to shame is more evident than that to guilt. Clients often describe shame as an internal physiological reaction as powerful as or similar to nausea. Since many dimensions of human sexual response meld the physiological, emotional, and intellectual, our position is that following those few moments during orgasm in which nothing invades the experience, the shame returns with greater impact and intensity. This shame response destroys the glow of resolution that should follow a sexual experience.

When talking to adolescent males about arousal, it is best to use their nomenclature. They usually describe arousal as being "horny" or "turned on." The actual physical response is often described as a "hard on" or as a "stiffy" or "boner." Since adolescent males are so focused on their genitals, they are mildly amazed that arousal and orgasm are primarily function of the brain, with fantasies, visuals, and epidermal stimulation acting as its secretary. Among adolescent males, one of the greatest sources of embarrassment and curiosity is their propensity for spontaneous erection. When the width and breadth of causation is explored, there is often some relief in knowing that simple, seemingly unrelated events can bring about sexual arousal. They are particularly interested in knowing that they probably experienced sexual arousal prior to birth and will continue to have the experience, in varying degrees, until death.

Once the boys have learned the difference between guilt and shame and the incredible intricacies of sexual arousal, they need permission to make a choice about responding to sexual arousal by way of self-pleasuring. Particular attention should be given to exploring the entire body so that they do not become so focused on the penis. As part of individual therapy or as a group exercise, drawing the sexual response cycle usually marks the culmination of their learning experience. For those boys in whom the destructive forces of shame are paired with orgasm, it may mark the midpoint of their therapy.

First, a graph similar to that in Masters and Johnson's (1982) *Sex and Human Loving* (figure 5–1) is drawn. Descriptions from a variety of clients will be combined for this example. A young man is sitting in his room doing homework, which is part of his daily routine. This particular young man then experiences some distraction and boredom, whereupon his mind wanders to a young person of his fancy. The thoughts become sexual, and he experiences psychological stimulation. At some point during the excitement, the young man makes a decision to masturbate and moves to a more comfortable, private place in his home, where he will access his penis and begin to masturbate. This will take him into the plateau where arousal is greatly increased,

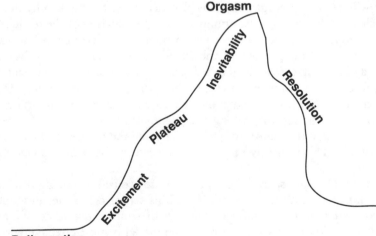

Figure 5–1. The Sexual Response Cycle

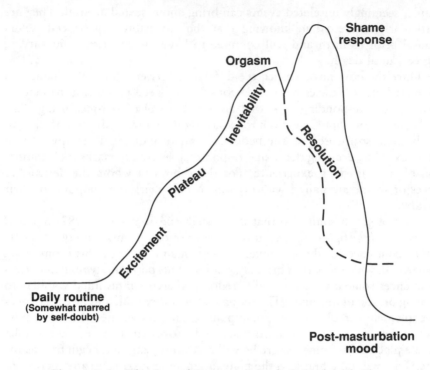

Figure 5–2. The Sexual Response Cycle Paired with Shame

and he will become preorgasmic. It is also beneficial for boys to learn about subtle changes that occur at this point, including elevation of the testicles and secretion from the cowper's gland, which many boys describe as "pre-cum." Some discussion about prolonging the self-pleasuring aspect during the excitement and plateau stages can lead to a discussion about premature ejaculation. Such a discussion always begs the question "Premature for whom?" During this discussion, some males may indicate that when they are close to orgasm, they stop masturbating to prolong the preorgasmic and ejaculatory period, only to realize that they have stopped too late and the orgasm and ejaculation are inevitable. This is clearly the point of no return. Orgasm and ejaculation will occur.

The sexual response cycle for those whose arousal is paired with shame looks significantly different (figure 5–2). This scenario includes descriptions from boys who have a significant amount of conflict regarding the act of masturbation. Since this psychoeducational model is most effective with less extreme cases, this scenario is appropriate, but the model should not be used in isolation of other therapies suggested for more disturbed clients. In this case, the young man can again be sitting in his bedroom when, as described earlier, his mind turns to sexual fantasies and he experiences arousal. Due to his conflict about masturbation, this potentially pleasant experience becomes sullied. During the excitement stage, he begins to masturbate, reaches the plateau, and, at the preorgasmic stage, decides he will deny himself orgasm and ejaculation in response to the ongoing conflict. He stops masturbating, only to realize he is at the point of inevitability; he attains orgasm and ejaculates. Immediately following orgasm and ejaculation, the boy experiences a rush of shame that, because of its powerful negative psychological reverberations, almost surpasses the intensity of orgasm and results in his plummeting into a mood that is lower than his premasturbatory mood.

At this point, masturbation can become compulsive. Since the act of masturbation can be intense enough to block the shame response and postmasturbatory mood temporarily, the youth may immediately distract himself with sexual fantasy or images and begin the sexual response cycle again. The goal with become the "fix" of the plateau and orgasm, which will obliterate the negative feelings. Unfortunately, the unhealed repetition of this pattern will be lack of resolution, with him again plummeting into the postmasturbatory mood as part of the shame response. This simplistically illustrates the beginning of a compulsive pattern.

Again, allowing for each person's individuality, it is inappropriate to label adolescent masturbatory behaviors as excessive or compulsive based only on frequency. Motive, mood, and the totality of the circumstances should be examined. Most often, an inquiry into a superficial skin irritation or more serious abrasive injuries to the penis may result in a client's disclosing that his masturbatory practices often cause these kinds of injuries. Humor may serve the therapist well in giving a brief lesson on friction, suggesting a moderate choice of lubrication somewhere between cooking oil and mother's expensive facial cream. Uninformed youths are easily led to the discovery of a common household commodity—hand lotion. This is also a particularly appropriate place to point out that males are not led by their penis but fully responsible for their sexual behaviors. Humor about the brain's seemingly being located in the penis rather than in the cranium usually drives the point home.

The explanations, permissions, and illustrations set forth here have been found to reduce the pairing of shame and arousal in adolescent male clients. While these are not empirical findings, they are shared clinical experiences that seem to be relatively consistent. Again, more intricate therapies, such as guided imagery, hypnosis, masturbatory reconditioning, aversive conditioning, or even chemotherapy, may be used at various junctures with more disturbed clients.

Conclusion

This chapter has focused on the treatment of the shame-sexuality bind that results from sexual maltreatment. We see the undoing of this bond as a central part of the recovery of male victims and recognize that there are many more facets to therapy. We hope this chapter generates ideas and questions for practitioners and researchers alike.

References

Abel, G.G., J.V. Becker, J. Cunningham-Rathner, and J.L. Rouleau. 1984. *The Treatment of Child Molesters.* NIMH Grant Publication, Emory University Behavioral Medicine Lab, Atlanta.

Abel, G.G., J.V. Becker, M. Mittelman, J. Cunningham-Rathner, J.L. Rouleau, and W.D. Murphy. 1987. "Self-reported Sex Crimes of Nonincarcerated Paraphiliacs." *Journal of Interpersonal Violence* 2 (no. 1): 3–25.

Becker, J.V., M.S. Kaplan, J. Cunningham-Rathner, and R. Kavoussi. 1986. Characteristics of Adolescent Incest Sexual Perpetrators: Preliminary Findings." *Journal of Family Violence* 1 (no. 1): 85–97.

Carlson, S., J. Dimock, J. Driggs, and T. Wesley. 1987. *Relationship of Childhood Sexual Abuse and Adult Sexual Compulsiveness in Males.* Workshop presented at the First National Conference on Sexual Compulsivity/Addiction: Controversies in Definition, Etiology and Treatment, Minneapolis, May.

Carnes, P. 1983. *The Sexual Addiction.* Minneapolis: CompCare.

Dimock, P. 1988. "Adult Males Sexually Abused as Children: Characteristics and Implications for Treatment." *Journal of Interpersonal Violence* 3 (no. 2): 203–221.

Dimock, P., J.S. Rusinoff, S. Carlson, and J. Michels. 1988. "Victim/Perpetrator— Perpetrator/Victim: Which One Do You Treat?" Paper presented at the Male Sexual Abuse Victims and Offenders: Controversy in Treatment conference, Minneapolis, October.

Fossum, M.A., and M.J. Mason. 1986. *Facing Shame: Families in Recovery.* New York: W.W. Norton.

Gilgun, J.F. 1988. "Factors Which Block the Development of Sexually Abusive Behaviors in Adults Sexually Abused as Children." Paper presented at the Male Sexual Abuse Victims and Offenders: Controversy in Treatment conference, Minneapolis, October.

Groth, A.N. 1979. *Men Who Rape: The Psychology of the Offender.* New York: Plenum Press.

Hunter, M. 1990. *Abused Boys: The Neglected Victims of Sexual Abuse.* Lexington, Massachusetts: Lexington Books.

Knopp, F.H. 1984. *Retraining Adult Sex Offenders: Methods and Models.* Syracuse, New York: Safer Society Press.

Langfeldt, T. 1989. "Developmental and Social Aspects of Sexual Violence in Boys and Men." Paper presented at the First International Conference on the Treatment of Sex Offenders, Minneapolis, May.

Lanning, K.V. 1987. *Child Molesters: A Behavioral Analysis for Law-Enforcement Officers Investigating Cases of Child Sexual Exploitation.* Quantico, Virginia: U.S. Department of Justice.

Lew, M. 1988. *Victims No Longer: Men Recovering from Incest and Other Sexual Child Abuse.* New York: Nevraumont Publishing.

Masters, V., and W. Johnson. 1982. *Sex and Human Loving.* Boston: Little, Brown.

Mayer, A. 1983. *Incest: A Treatment Manual for Therapy with Victims, Spouses and Offenders.* Holmes Beach, Florida: Learning Publications.

———. 1985. *Sexual Abuse: Causes, Consequences and Treatment of Incestuous and Pedophilic Acts.* Holmes Beach, Florida: Learning Publications.

Money, J. 1989. "Forensic Sexology: One Hundred Years and Six Principles of Causal Explanation." Paper presented at the First International Conference on the Treatment of Sex Offenders, Minneapolis, May.

Risin, L.I., and M.P. Koss. 1987. "The Sexual Abuse of Boys: Prevalence and Descriptive Characteristics of Childhood Victimizations." *Journal of Interpersonal Violence* 2 (no. 3): 309–323.

Seely, R.K. 1989. "Treatment of Offenders: Utilizing the Grieving Process." Paper presented at the First International Conference on the Treatment of Sex Offenders, Minneapolis, May.

6
Integrating Psychotherapy and Body Work for Abuse Survivors: A Psychological Model

Robert Timms
Patrick Connors

Increased public and professional awareness that sexual abuse occurs to males has led to a need for a therapeutic approach dealing directly with all the physical, emotional, and interpersonal consequences of childhood sexual abuse. We have developed a treatment approach using hands-on body work and intensive psychotherapy that we call the Psychophysical Model of therapy. Our model facilitates recovery of amnestic memories of abuse, safe expression of strong emotions, and awareness of body-image issues for abused men. This chapter describes the model, its development, and its applications for both individual and group therapy.

Special Needs of Male Survivors

Male survivors have specific therapeutic needs that historically have made it difficult for men to find help in dealing with this issue. For example, when psychologist Ed Tick (1984) became aware of his childhood sexual abuse and sought help for his emotional reactions, he had difficulty finding a therapist. The reactions were "I won't, don't, can't discuss or treat it. Some argued it was not a 'specialized topic'. Others steered its discussion into more generalized areas of emotional abuse" (p. 74). He finally found help at a rape crisis center for women. The senior author of this chapter also has described his personal search for therapy for his abuse (Timms 1989). Because of his frustration in finding a therapist willing and able to deal with his specific therapeutic needs, he eventually acted as his own psychologist in processing abuse issues. Until recently, the psychotherapeutic community has not been very responsive to the therapeutic needs of male survivors. This, according to repeated clinical reports, is even more characteristic of the many psychoanalysts who hold to the old theoretical belief that abuse memories are merely fantasies on the part of the client.

Professional literature on male abuse survivors has been sparse. Porter's brief book (1986) was the first specifically to address the issue of male abuse victims. Lew (1988) and Hunter (1990) have presented more comprehensive works. National conferences, such as the ones held in Minneapolis in 1988 and Atlanta in 1989, bring together experts in this area of study and treatment. Both male and female psychotherapists are starting to take adequate sexual histories and backgrounds of new male clients, sometimes using the guidelines developed by Dimock (1989) or Timms and Connors (1988), thus facilitating the identification of early sexual abuse for therapeutic attention.

Many men who are already in psychotherapy for a variety of health and personal problems are amnestic of abuse perpetrated against them (Timms and Connors 1989). Our clinical experience shows that many males who were abused in childhood suffer from depression, hypertension, cardiovascular disease, and/or sexual difficulties in adult life. These health issues indicate the profound impact abuse has on men's lives. As one survivor said in group therapy, "What happened to me changed *everything*. It affected every area of my life." We are convinced that complete therapy for abused males must be holistic, treating both the psychological and the physical consequences of abuse.

Therapists must learn to identify sexual abuse and help their clients reclaim the traumatic memory if it has been repressed. Clients can then work through painful, limiting emotions and behaviors and thus live more freely and fully. We have found it vital to combine psychotherapy with body work to facilitate amnestic recall and emotional expression in working with abuse survivors. Our Psychophysical Model of therapy, combining verbal psychotherapy with hands-on body work, is an approach that has had profound results with abuse survivors. Traditional psychotherapists have avoided work on bodily manifestations of emotional issues, but starting with Wilhelm Reich (1972), an increasing number of therapists are using body approaches in therapy.

In a related field, many massage therapists notice that emotions and memories sometimes emerge in their clients during body work. These emotions and memories may be related to earlier trauma, including sexual and/or physical abuse. Emotional release work, a specific use of massage to elicit blocked emotions and allow for safe release, has been a significant breakthrough in massage therapy and has potential value for psychotherapists.

Massage therapy, perhaps the original healing art form, gained in popularity and acceptance in the United States during the 1980s. For years, many women have sought massage for relaxation, health, and beauty reasons. They are now using it more and more for emotional release and support. For men, however, massage has served two limited functions: health club rubdowns and massage parlor prostitution. Thus, for many men, the healing benefits of therapeutic massage are essentially unknown.

Similarly, many women have been more open in seeking psychotherapy to deal directly with their memories, feelings, and experiences of abuse. Men in our culture generally are less expressive of their emotions and less willing to examine their behaviors. They also are considerably more likely to deny any problems resulting from early sexual abuse, even when they seek therapy for other issues. Denial in men is one of the major obstacles to therapeutic progress in working with abuse issues (Timms and Connors 1989).

Another difficulty in talking about sexual abuse with men in therapy comes from our clinical observation that at least 20 percent of abused men are partially or completely amnestic about their traumatic experience. Amnesia is an extreme form of denial. We find many clinical examples of men who have been through years of psychotherapy or analysis and have never recalled their sexual abuse. We think this is partially because the traditional approach of psychotherapy with men encourages them to talk about their feelings. Psychotherapy with men frequently flounders on the inability of the male to get past intellectualization and rationalization. As a group, men tend more toward "doing" than "feeling" and find it difficult to relate to talking about or feeling emotions. For abused men to get in touch with their memories and experiences of childhood sexual abuse, we believe a combination of body work and psychotherapy is required.

A major obstacle in using body work for psychotherapeutic purposes has been that most psychotherapists know very little about anatomy and thus either hold back in active physical intervention or run the risk of causing physical damage to the client. Massage therapists, though well versed in anatomy, have little training in handling emotional responses and no training in the process of "working through" the released emotional experiences. Finding one therapist with all this knowledge has been difficult, if not impossible. The model we propose uses two trained professionals—one skilled in psychotherapeutic work and emotional and intellectual integration and the other skilled in body work and emotional release.

The Psychophysical Model offers abused men help in eight areas:

1. The recalling of amnestic memories of abuse

2. The recovery of full awareness of the abusive experience(s)

3. Increased awareness of the long-term emotional, physical, and spiritual effects of abuse on adult behavior

4. Increased awareness and direct expression of emotions

5. A decreased feeling of shame and guilt in response to the abuse

6. The empowering experience of working through the terror and pain of the abuse in therapy and being able to live as a healthy, happy adult free of residual trauma

7. Improvement in body image and self-esteem, as shown by improved health, increased relaxation, and decreased stress

8. Diminishing of the protective armor, thus allowing the client greater flexibility in both giving and receiving emotional contact and support

We can best illustrate the clinical application of our model in detail by describing how we came to develop our integrated approach to therapy.

An Integrated Approach to Therapy

Case Report

Just as Freud developed some of his psychoanalytic concepts by self-analysis, our original concepts came from our own clinical work. Robert Timms was forty-six years old and suffered from uncontrolled hypertension (with no family history of blood pressure problems). He had periods of recurring depression, with no observable connection to external events. He had been in psychotherapy with several different therapists over a twenty-year period, with much improvement in many areas of his life but not in the areas of depression and health. About fifty pounds overweight, Robert was physically inactive. He was married and had two teenage sons. He traced the beginnings of his depression to the summer after his oldest son turned six years old. (This observation, made repeatedly in earlier therapy, had never been directly addressed.) Robert had no memory of any sexual abuse in childhood, but he was troubled by recurring violent dreams of physical attacks from behind by an unknown assailant, who either used a knife or attempted to strangle him with a cord or wire around the neck.

It became clear to Robert that verbal psychotherapy was failing, as he was gaining more weight, becoming more depressed, and continuing to have high blood pressure. Still not motivated to diet or exercise, he sought alternative approaches to help him relax and lower his blood pressure. When attempts at medication and biofeedback failed, he entered massage therapy. After the first session, his blood pressure reading was 120 over 75, about 20 points lower than usual for him. He elected to continue the body work with regular sessions twice a week.

After a few sessions focusing primarily on somatic sensations, deep emotions started to surface. With his extensive personal therapy background and his gestalt therapy training, Robert was able, with Patrick Connors's help, to switch between his "wounded child" ego state and his adult therapeutic self. The ability to dissociate from strong pain also helped in this process. Although we do not recommend this procedure as normal treatment, it worked for Robert and did allow us to develop our model. When the body therapist worked on the right side of the lower back, Robert began to experience agitation, anxiety, fear, and deep sadness. Initially this reaction was related to the memory of a traumatic surgery for a broken left arm at age twelve. All this was regularly processed verbally in the body-work sessions.

Emotions increased as the body work continued, and memories of being held down and hurt or being attacked surfaced. These memories were accompanied by intense crying, agitation, and fear. Finally, in a body-work session, Robert recalled a totally forgotten event: being brutally raped at the age of six by his favorite uncle. The uncle had then threatened to kill him if he ever told about the attack. Subsequent violent threats by the uncle had led to complete repression of the rape.

The results of uncovering the traumatic memory were tremendous. Robert sought out an individual psychotherapist during this time, but the therapist had no experience with adult males who had been sexually abused, and Robert remained essentially his own psychotherapist during this process. His feelings of being upset and depressed were offset by a strong sense of "finally understanding." A major understanding was of an earlier event in previous psychotherapy. Twenty years before, while in therapy, Robert had experienced himself as very regressed and small. Feeling terrified, he heard a voice say, "If you talk about this, you will die." He told this to his therapist, who only nodded and said, "Well, when you are ready to talk about it, you won't feel that way, so just forget it." He did—for another twenty years. There is no doubt in our minds that the repressed memory was trying to come out then and was actively discouraged by the therapist. This phenomenon has since been reported by many clients who wanted to tell a previous therapist about their abuse but found the therapist unwilling or unable to listen.

As the body work and therapy continued, the memory of the traumatic event became clearer. As is often the case in recovering memory of abuse, Robert at first tried to deny that it had happened, even when experiencing emotional pain and turmoil. Finally he realized he was not inventing the story but in fact needed to accept the reality of it and work on its impact on his life. The powerful doubting of the recovered memory is a common reaction for abused adults. This represents the last unconscious attempt at denial, as the protective part of the ego seeks to be certain that it is now safe for the survivor to express all the pent-up fear, terror, anger, and rage about the abuse. The cognitive period of uncertainty is usually simultaneous, with strong emotional expression of this pain, sadness, and anger. Even as the client is in the throes of powerful emotional pain that could not possibly be simulated, he may say, "But I don't think this really happened to me." What he means is, "I don't want to admit that this really happened to me. It hurt too much." The reality of the trauma must be fully acknowledged and accepted for healing to occur.

Robert's intensive body therapy continued for some months on a regular twice-a-week schedule. He continued to serve as his primary psychotherapist, while Patrick continued with the body work and assisted and supported him in the therapy. New insights continued to arise. One such awareness was the connection between the memory of the surgery for the broken arm and the sexual abuse. It became clear that the traumatic administration of the ether while being held down by orderlies revived the rape memory of being held down with his uncle's hand over his mouth. (This is a clear example of the role of muscle memory in our work.) The last memory Robert had as he became unconscious from the ether was recalling the rape and fearing he was being killed. He had worked on his disproportionate response to the trauma of the ether in psychotherapy before, but no one had ever noted that there seemed to be another issue under it.

Finally, Robert and Patrick felt the need to bring a female psychotherapist into the body-work session to help Robert express and work through feelings about his mother's and aunt's role in the rape. In this joint session, he used both therapists to help him express his anger and to release his pain and sadness. He finally was able to see his parents as people who would have helped protect him from the uncle if he had been able to tell what had happened. This joint session resulted in a lifting of the depression that had plagued him for years. He has not felt strongly depressed since that time. As a result of the expressive work, he was eventually able to forgive his uncle for the rape and feel free of the burden of victimization.

There also were significant physical changes as a result of the recall of the abuse and the subsequent emotional breakthrough. He started eating appropriately and lost fifty pounds over a nine-month period. He started a regular exercise program, which he has continued. He gave more attention to his appearance and dress, changing his wardrobe from somber, brown-tone clothing to brightly colored attire. The most important change was in his health. His blood pressure readings are now normal and have been stabilized for the first time in more than seventeen years, and his physician has taken him off blood pressure medication. He has maintained his new weight for more than two years.

The personal changes have been just as dramatic. Feelings of shame and guilt faded as self-esteem matured. A common pattern of dissociation, which had been noticed in the body work, disappeared with continued work. Feelings of numbness and blankness stopped. As a result, Robert's sexual life has become less inhibited and more satisfying. Lastly, he has become more socially and professionally active, productive, and happy. (We apologize for use of the pronoun "he" in much of the above report. It is very difficult to write clearly about a very personal experience in an objective way, particularly when there are two authors.)

Implications for the Psychophysical Model

With Robert being a practicing psychologist, the implications of his personal therapy for his professional work were clear from the start. Immediately, we started discussing how this type of work could be done with other clients who were known or suspected abuse survivors. This work led directly to the development of the Psychophysical Model. Several aspects of the model are demonstrated in Robert's case history.

First, the case illustrates that repressed or forgotten traumatic memories may be accessed through physical touch in a manner unavailable through verbal psychotherapy. We believe that strong emotional events leave lasting memory traces in the musculature and neural pathways between the musculature and the brain. Accessing the "muscle memory" kinesthetically and reactivating the full memory are major reasons for the use of touch in our model. Since about 20 percent of all abuse victims are totally amnestic of the traumatic event and many more are unclear about the full experience, the clinical need for drawing on this muscle memory is obvious.

Second, the case illustrates that working through abuse issues often requires physical expression of strong emotions (what some therapists call abreactive work—see Steele and Colrain in this volume) to allow the final release of the traumatic memories and feelings. While the more traditional verbal psychotherapies do not allow for this strong physical expression, the Psychophysical Model of therapy encourages it.

Finally, the case shows the deep connection between repressed emotional material and its impact on physical and emotional health. This is particularly true in cases of sexual abuse during childhood. We build on the psychoanalytic concept of repression in our emphasis on the muscle memory of the traumatic event as the key to recalling and working on the psychological memory. We also build on the work of early body therapists. Thus a short review of theories of repression and body therapy is needed, to place our work in historical perspective.

Historical Perspective

Freud wrote at some length about the purpose of repression in maintaining the ego. He maintained that repression cannot be used until there is a concept of conscious and unconscious, noting that "repression lies simply in the function of rejecting and keeping something out of consciousness" (Freud 1915, 89). Freud believed that pain alone was not a sufficient reason to repress events, though many repressed events are painful or traumatic. Masson (1984) has explored Freud's struggle with believing and reporting sexual abuse in his patients.

Freud's denial of the reality of incest set the stage for decades of denial of abuse and its consequences by mental health professionals. Nonetheless, Freud did make a major contribution by identifying a mechanism whereby certain traumatic events can be repressed into unconsciousness. He also described how the patient may turn the emotions inward if repression is not successful. Finally, Freud maintained that repressed material was always, at some level, seeking to become conscious again. Although Freud paid some attention to the body in relation to emotions, he did not focus on bodily reactions. But his contemporary Georg Groddeck did.

Groddeck (1923), in his major contribution to psychosomatic medicine, held that the unconscious expression of emotions is manifested through the body in every possible way. Though very controversial at the time, his work has long since formed the basis for the psychoanalytic approach to psychosomatic medicine. The psychosomatic approach holds that repressed emotions are directly related to conditions such as high blood pressure, sexual dysfunction, depression, low back pain, and headaches.

Following more directly from Freud, and aware of the work of Groddeck, was Wilhelm Reich. In his brilliant work *Character Analysis* (originally published in 1933), Reich (1972) developed his concept of character armoring and its relation to repression, personality structure, and the body. Starting from a basically psychoanalytic point of view, Reich gradually moved to a belief that the musculature of the body allows for emotional expression or withholding. Thus, chronic emotional withholding leads to chronic muscular tension. Eventually, direct manipulation of the muscles is necessary to facilitate expression of the withheld, or repressed, emotion. Character armor is the chronic muscular holding pattern based on an underlying inhibited emotion. Reich was a major influence on two schools of therapy—gestalt therapy, as formulated by Fritz Perls, and bioenergetic analysis, as originated by Alexander Lowen.

Lowen's work, now referred to simply as bioenergetics (Lowen 1975), has tried to recombine the mind and body in psychotherapy. Lowen writes about using body work to recall forgotten traumatic memories and gives vivid case examples, but he does not address working with sexual abuse survivors. Nonetheless, he has much to offer, particularly in his combination of deep body work with the principles of psychoanalysis. There are two reasons why his theories are not used more in work with abuse survivors. First, most therapists are not trained in psychoanalytic theory and technique. Second, the deep body work used in bioenergetics is experienced by many abuse survivors as intrusive and invasive, often leading to negative reactions rather than the desired healing.

A more helpful approach for working with abuse clients is Gestalt therapy, as expressed by Fritz Perls (Perls, Frederick, Hefferline, and Goodman 1951). It is a holistic, humanistic, existential approach to psychotherapy, with a strong focus on body awareness. This therapeutic approach, taught to young therapists more readily than Freudian psychoanalysis, has been a major influence on counselors in the past twenty years. It offers a particularly helpful concept for therapy with abuse survivors: unfinished business.

For Perls, any event in life not fully expressed emotionally and physically, and thus not integrated into the mainstream of life, remains unfinished. Unfinished business is manifest through blocking or denial of emotions. Finishing, similar to the analytic concept of working through, requires the client to relive the event with full emotionality and immediacy and find a satisfying outcome to the event, thus removing any need for repression or denial. The person is then free to feel his or her body and emotions fully, without painful inhibitions. This concept underlies much abreactive work in dealing with abuse survivors. Gestalt is a popular theoretical approach in groups for abused men and women.

Perls was a major influence on several body workers, most notably Ilana Rubenfeld and Eric Marcus. Rubenfeld (1990) combines Gestalt therapy and Feldenkreis-style body work (which she calls the Rubenfeld Synergy Method) and works with survivors of trauma, including Holocaust survivors. Marcus (1979) combines neo-Reichian body work with gestalt therapy and uses both in group therapy. The work of both these therapists has served as a background for our development of the Psychophysical Model using hands-on body work and psychotherapy with adult abuse survivors.

Finally, Reich's influence on three other body workers should be acknowledged. Kurtz and Prestera (1984) believe that past traumas are recorded in the body tissue, ready to be seen by therapists with trained eyes and hands and ready to be released by hands-on body work. Kelerman (1981) also advocates direct, hands-on body work for emotional release. His work is based more on a study of physical anatomy than on Freud. Our approach draws from the contributions of these three. Our concept of muscle memory of traumatic events is foreshadowed by Kurtz and Prestera, while our use of a body worker highly trained in anatomy is a recognition of Kelerman's approach.

Historically, here is where the road from traditional psychotherapy to body-oriented therapy combines with the road leading from massage therapy to emotional release work. *Emotional release* is a phrase used to describe a fairly common occurrence in massage therapy. As the massage therapist begins to work, the client will relax and let down some of his or her armor. Some observe that many clients spontaneously enter a light trancelike state. In such an open (even vulnerable) position, suppressed memories and accompanying emotions may surface for the client. We find that many massage therapists may be uncomfortable with emotions, leading them to change the topic or switch to another area of the body. For those who choose to learn how to work with these emotions, emotional release work becomes a form of massage with an intent to help the client become aware of and express emotional memories stored in the body.

Another form of massage therapy that can be useful in facilitating emotional expression is neuromuscular work. In this technique, patterns of trigger points (areas of high neurological activity in the muscle cells) are diminished, thus reducing the message relaying pain from the muscle to the brain. It works well with chronic or old pain and thus relates strongly to the stored emotional and physical pain of childhood sexual abuse.

This review of therapy and method explains two basic approaches: (1) psychotherapy with some awareness of the body and (2) body work with some awareness of emotional expression. Our Psychophysical Model proposes a combination of these approaches, using a trained body therapist as a coworker in the psychotherapeutic process. Of the available body workers, we believe that a massage therapist trained in emotional release work and in neuromuscular technique is the best choice.

Massage therapists, particularly neuromuscular therapists, are well trained in anatomy and know how to work in the deeper, structural layers of the body in such a manner as to promote release of stored traumatic memories without causing damage to the physical structure. This work can be done in such a way as to be both emotionally facilitative and noninvasive. Massage therapists, by definition, are comfortable with close human touch, something not always true of psychotherapists. In treating adults with a history of childhood sexual abuse, the selection of the appropriate massage therapist is paramount, since any touch must be nonthreatening and nurturing.

Selecting a Body Therapist

Clinical opinions about the appropriate gender of the body worker abound, but we know of no research investigating the assumptions generally held. The most commonly held assumption is that an abused woman should not work with a male body worker. Our clinical experiences negate this assumption. We believe that when the abuse was originally inflicted by a male, the healing process must include work with a male, to bring the experience full circle in a highly positive way. The presence of the male body worker provides a new opportunity for working through the original abuse issues and for viewing male contact in a positive way.

We think this is equally true in working with adult male survivors. Many abused men have residual issues or concerns about homosexuality. Some men are concerned that the body worker may be gay, and they may fear a repeat of their original abuse. In our model, we recommend the use of a heterosexual body worker. For most abused males, body work provokes enough anxiety in itself, without the added anxiety resulting from homophobia. For many abused males, any touch by another man is threatening and may elicit fear and old response patterns of shutting down emotionally and dissociating. These behaviors are most accurately seen and interpreted as responses to past abuse and not to current homosexuality.

It is a severe mistake to identify male abuse as a gay issue. It is important that therapy not add to the client's confusion or fears and that the therapist not add his or her own prejudices to the client's real issues. By having the body work performed by a male in a nurturing, supportive, and facilitative manner, the client can safely experience the memory of his trauma, along with the appropriate emotions, and can reframe the experience in a healing way.

Having male energy and attention as part of the healing process offers a model of adult helping and healing to the "damaged child" ego state. This helps the client reclaim his own adult sense of self, his masculinity, and his personal power. When the male body worker's touch is experienced as non-sexual, the client's general fear, homophobia, and heterosexism is decreased. In the body work, care is taken not to arouse the client sexually. No ethical body worker (or psychotherapist, for that matter) should have contact with the client's genitalia.

Determining the Client's Readiness for Body Work

According to our model for working with adult survivors of abuse, the psychotherapist has the responsibility for determining the client's readiness for body work. Some indications of readiness follow:

- A viable working therapeutic relationship between the client and the psychotherapist
- The client's willingness to be touched in a therapeutic manner (Some fear of touch may be present, but the client is still willing to try body work.)
- The client's clearly expressed commitment to working on his personal abuse issues
- A personal support system available to assist the client when strong emotions and memories surface
- Increased reporting of dreams with traumatic physical content, as well as dreams with a strong same-sex content in clients with a clear heterosexual orientation
- Increased experience of bodily discomfort without a known physiological cause

A clear cue for body work would be a client saying, "I feel that there is more here than I can remember." At that point, the therapist may want a nonverbal perspective for the therapy.

The Body Work

The initial presentation of body work to the client should be as clear and non-threatening as possible. We find it useful to say, "Many of our clients have found body work helpful in dealing with abuse issues for these reasons" (those listed in the section "Special Needs of Male Survivors"). Preparation should include reassurance that body work is a standard part of the treatment plan. Since many abused males have some difficulty understanding what is "normal" in life, it is important that the client not feel that he is being singled out for any special or unusual approach. When possible, an example or two of how other clients have benefited from body work will be helpful in preparing the client.

Regarding the client's first meeting with the body worker, it is best to introduce the worker to the client in a regular psychotherapy session, with no hands-on work occurring at that time. Within the safety of the session, the client can more readily open up to the body worker. The client reviews his history and therapy directly with the body worker. Procedures for the body work are then explained. When the client asks questions about body-work procedures, it is best for the body worker to assume his role in the joint work and respond.

A typical question is "Do I have to get undressed?" The fear behind the question should be addressed and reassuring information given. At no point in our body work is the client's full body exposed. In the massage sessions, most clients prefer to wear their underwear. A client is draped with a sheet, and a sense of privacy is maintained at all times. This is very important for people whose privacy was invaded during childhood. It is critical that the body work not add to the client's sense of being abused. In joint sessions when body work is performed in the presence of the psychotherapist, the client may remove only his shirt, or, if work on the legs is indicated, he may wear gym shorts. This gives the body worker complete access to the client and allows for the client's full movement and easy expression of emotion, while maintaining personal privacy.

Another frequent question concerns the body worker's sexual orientation. This should be answered directly and clearly. We encourage exploration of this question in therapy regarding its significance to the client. It often relates to a fear of sexual arousal when touched or a fear of emotional intimacy.

A Joint Effort

By having the body worker introduced within the context of the regular therapy session, the client's positive attitude (or transference) toward the therapist usually is extended to the body worker. This introduces a major component of our work—the model of two "good parents" to support, nurture, and help the client in his growth. The clear message is that the psychotherapist and body worker are a team, both committed to the client's growth and healing. This joint presentation reduces the potential for splitting the two therapists into the "good" and "bad" parent, a common therapeutic symptom in adult survivors of abuse.

We recommend that the client start with a series of four body-work sessions in the first month. Ideally, each should be scheduled as near to the regular psychotherapy sessions as possible. Feelings or responses arising in body work can be processed in psychotherapy while the emotions are clear for the client.

In the initial joint session, we explain to the client the need for close communication between the two therapists and obtain written permission for such sharing. We recommend that therapists and body workers using our model arrange weekly consultations. Often the body worker will be able to share useful emotional or behavioral reactions of the client. The psychotherapist also may want to suggest an area of the body on which the body worker should work, based on clinical material. For example, in one psychotherapy session, a client reported a dream in which his right foot was being attacked by several wild animals. When the body therapist worked with that area, memories relating to childhood sexual abuse by the father emerged with strong emotions.

Another important reason for regular communication is to evaluate early signs of transference. Body work can provoke a variety of emotions and memories, and some of these quickly become transferential in nature. The transference reaction of the client to the body worker may be positive or negative, may be idealized toward the therapist, or may even be sexualized. For example, one client had a negative reaction to the body worker in a joint session. The client, who had been physically abused by his father, felt a strong internal emotional reaction but did not communicate this in any way during the session. In his next individual psychotherapy session, he reported having felt as if he were a young child being hurt by his father while his mother watched. This was a reliving of what had happened in his family in real life and thus distorted his perception of what had happened in the joint therapy session. It would have been a useful experience in therapy if he had reported it when it happened. It became a problem when he kept it a secret, just as keeping abuse a secret creates problems. Instead of telling and working on his feelings, the client chose to see the body worker as a "mean parent." It took some time for the client to admit that the body worker bore a strong physical resemblance to the father. As this was processed in therapy, the negative transference toward the body worker began to resolve, and feelings of anger toward the father were expressed more directly. Thus, even a negative transferential reaction can be put to good therapeutic use. Clear, direct, and frequent communication between the two therapists will help both to stay open to the client's process.

Equally possible is a countertransference reaction on the part of either therapist. Every experienced clinician knows the personal risks involved in working with sexual abuse survivors. The client's experience has the potential of touching us in the deepest, most hidden parts of our being. Ganzarain and Buchele (1988) have reported some countertransference issues in group work with adult female survivors of abuse. They point out the anger that can arise toward the abuser or the victim. Frustration and sadness may be felt, and possibly even revulsion at some particularly cruel form of abuse. It is possible that either the body worker or the psychotherapist may start to feel sexual tension or attraction toward the client. This should be evaluated as a sign of countertransference. It is critical that every person working with abuse clients monitor his or her reactions and watch for any sign of countertransference. If this occurs for either the body worker or the psychotherapist, it should be discussed with the other colleague. If that is not sufficient to resolve the issue, the therapist needs supervision.

The therapists must be particularly vigilant about countertransference issues if one of them is a survivor of sexual abuse. It is critical that such a person have worked through his or her personal issues sufficiently so that he or she will not project them onto the client. It also is vital that the two therapists have a high level of trust in each other, both professionally and personally, which will allow them to help each other if countertransference issues arise.

Only the highest ethical standards are acceptable in doing psychotherapy and body work with survivors of childhood sexual abuse. We have worked with many men and women who have been reabused by other health and mental health professionals. Sexual abuse in psychotherapy is a common occurrence (Bates and Brodsky 1989). By its very nature, body work in psychotherapy offers temptations for abuse that some therapists have not been able to resist. Any sexual behavior in therapy with a client is abusive and must be prevented, even if the client invites it.

Clients in a dissociative state may behave in a seductive manner. This may represent an unconscious attempt on the part of the child ego state to replicate the abuse situation with a new outcome. When this behavior is unconscious, it is difficult for both client and therapist to address it. When the seductive behavior is conscious on the client's part, it often represents a desire for limit setting, which the client is unwilling or unable to accomplish. The therapist must set firm limits, with respect and regard for the client's emotions. Such limits, coupled with a gentle interpretation of the behavior, usually resolve the problem. More difficult cases call for active collaboration of the therapists; sometimes a consultant also may be needed.

Concerns about possible sexual implications of touch have caused many psychotherapists to avoid body work altogether. The solution is professional growth and education, not avoidance. Therapists should conduct themselves in a responsible, ethical, and appropriate manner with their clients. Integrity in the therapist will prevent exploitation of the client. Knowing that the therapist is clear on this issue will help reassure the client.

Group Therapy

Our Psychophysical Model also can be used in group therapy. We regularly work in groups of adult male survivors, using a psychotherapist and a body therapist as coleaders. We find group therapy to be powerful for abused men in many ways. In individual therapy, the client knows that his therapist will never reveal his secrets for legal and professional reasons. When an abused man enters a group, he is faced with revealing his secret to people he does not yet know and who are not required by law to keep his secret. In a very important way, this may be the first "telling" of the secret.

Joining a survivors' group is an open declaration that the client was sexually abused. Entering a group is a tangible sign that his denial of the abuse is ending and that he can work with his abuse issues more directly. This presents a major opportunity for the client to develop trust.

Trust is further developed in the group setting when the men share their personal experiences and discover many commonalities. The first commonly shared experience is simply being with other men who were abused. For the client, being in a room with seven other abused men is eye-opening. "I'm really not the only one!" is a common theme in the first session. As one of our clients said, "I'm sorry that each of you was hurt, but I'm glad to know I'm not the only man this ever happened to."

Men typically have difficulty expressing their feelings directly. In a new group, men often do not address their own feelings but hide behind a pseudo-anger that covers over their sense of shame and guilt. True anger arises as the trust level of the group increases. The first expression of anger is typically toward the abuser. Anger is then expressed at those family members who should have known what was going on and rescued him from the abuse. Anger toward the self is a constant during this part of the therapy. Eventually, feelings of sadness and loss emerge, with grief over the lost childhood and missed opportunities. Finally, as therapy continues, a deeper sense of caring, trust, and intimacy develops. The presence of the body worker allows for safe and controlled expression of strong emotions within the group setting.

Anger is usually difficult for men to experience directly in the group, since they fear loss of control. They often have a simplistic view of themselves as either very passive or out of control with rage. One of the therapists' roles in the group is to facilitate the safe, direct expression of anger in a way that will allow emotional expression and catharsis and lead to new personal and emotional awakenings. Commonly used methods for expressing anger safely include hitting pillows or a punching bag. Of course, no direct physical expression of anger toward other group members or the therapists is allowed.

Anger often is felt internally but not expressed externally. Part of the body worker's job is to assess where the client is blocking expression of emotions in his body and devise methods to help him express those emotions. Such assessment will be based on a variety of cues, including visual cues, Neural Linguistic Programming (NLP), intuition, past experience with similar clients, and awareness of empathic tensions in the therapist's own body. The body worker's awareness of his or her usual body state helps him or her recognize sensations that do not belong to him or her. In our experiences, the pscyho-therapist may be less aware of these proprioceptive cues.

In the case of anger, depending on where the blockage is, the body worker may provide resistance to the arms, hands, or legs. If the client reports feeling tension or anger in his arms or hands, the therapist may offer resistance by pushing against the client's hands or arms, or the therapist may hold the clien't arms while the client pushes out. Resistive contact also may include the body worker's containing the client while he kicks or pushes with his legs and feet. Part of the body worker's job is to oversee the client's safety during the expressive work. He must ensure that the client does not hit his arms, hands, or feet directly against the massage table or other furniture. By a careful and protective example, the clear message to the client is to learn safe expression of anger without harming himself or others.

One example of using body work to express anger and elicit a memory of abuse comes from our work with "Jack." This thirty-seven-year-old man had been in therapy for almost a year for depression and inhibited emotional affect. The following example occurred in a joint body work–therapy session.

As feelings of anger welled up in him, Jack started pounding on the massage table with his fist. When given a pillow to hit, Jack became more physically expressive and recalled a previously amnestic incident from about fifteen years before. At home, feeling angry, he had intended to scold his dog with a slight smack of his hand. Instead, he hit the dog so hard that he broke its back, and the dog soon died. Though deeply upset, Jack denied the consequences of his behavior to the point that, when a neighbor asked what had happened to the dog, Jack said it had been hit by a car. This response further anchored Jack's sense of guilt and shame, increasing his need to keep the secret.

Seeing that his behavior was so destructive, Jack felt that it was not safe to feel his anger at all, much less express it. Jack needed to give himself permission to feel anger and needed permission from us to express it. We provided a structure within which he could safely express his emotions. Following this expression, he could then mourn the loss of his pet, acknowledge his responsibility, and say good-bye to the dog. This, in turn, relieved some of his guilt and shame and led to an increased acceptance of self. This is an example of how body work and psychotherapy together can lead to a resolution of unfinished business.

Another example is the case of "Tom," a thirty-five-year-old man who often would smile or laugh inappropriately as a deflection of his true emotions. Further, he often felt inadequate, believing he could not do anything right. In a joint session, when the body worker started to press a point on Tom's left shoulder blade, Tom lurched upward and reacted with a nervous laugh. He caught himself, saying, "I'm not supposed to laugh, am I?" We went with his resistance and encouraged him to express himself the way he wanted to. His laughter immediately became wild and suddenly turned into a blood-curdling scream, with subsequent gagging. During the scream, he remembered having been severely beaten as a child by his father. As we processed more of his memory of the abuse, he remembered being told by his father that he could never do anything right. We helped him see that, by expressing himself the way *he* needed to, he "did it right." At the end of the session, he said that he felt like Superman.

Groups are the perfect setting in which to use a rage-reduction limit structure such as that developed by Pesso (1969) in his psychomotor therapy. In this approach, the client is given an absolutely safe manner in which to express as much anger as he feels, while the group members provide him with safe limits on his expression. This powerful technique is of great value in therapy with adult male survivors of abuse because it teaches them that their rageful feelings can be expressed safely. This technique is an example of the intense emotionally expressive work possible in groups using body work and psychotherapy.

Several issues arise early in group work with abused men. Most men report more compassion or anger toward other group members' situations than they feel toward their own. They also find commonality in feelings of low self-esteem and poor body image. Many men in group discuss early (or perhaps still current) embarrassment at undressing in front of others in gyms. This is related to feelings of shame about their bodies and the abusive episode(s). One man said, "It's as if someone who saw my body would know what happened to me." Some gentle, noninvasive body work early in the group experience helps ease such fears and moves the clients toward an increased acceptance of self.

The power of gentle body work and contact is best illustrated by an occurrence in one of our men's groups. In about the tenth session, "Sam," a rather withdrawn, passive, nonexpressive man, was unusually quiet in the session. Attempts to draw him out were not productive. As the group ended, Sam quietly started for the door. Patrick spontaneously went to him and asked if he wanted a hug. He accepted, with some emotion, and left. The next week Sam told the group that he had come in feeling suicidal the week before. He had intended to leave the group, feeling that no one liked or cared about him, get in his car, and drive away and commit suicide. The hug had changed all that, opening Sam up to contact and life.

It should be noted that a body worker typically has a different view about touch than does a psychotherapist. While many psychotherapists may be more conservative about initiating contact such as a hug, body workers typically see this as a natural, easy type of contact to make.

We find it easy to let the body work evolve spontaneously in the group. Since the group members know that one of the leaders is trained in body work, opportunities are soon forthcoming. Many men report chronic tightness in their neck, shoulders, back, and throat. This readily leads to a discussion of chronic holding patterns and an opportunity for some direct body work with group members. Many times body work is used in group in the form of a Gestalt experiment—that is, an opportunity for a client to explore his feelings in a way different from his usual style. This often leads to increased emotional awareness and expression, and thus to growth and positive change.

Stronger and more expressive body work emerges naturally as the group norm becomes supportive of deeper emotional expression. We find that our Psychophysical Model promotes greater personal sharing, more open expression of emotion, and more rapid growth in clients. We find, too, that as the group progresses, the men express more of a desire for the physical contact with each other, such as a hug after the expression of painful emotions.

Groups also help the men develop close emotional contact with other men and define the true experience of intimacy with another male. We see this intimacy as being a natural state of being alive and as being different from closeness. Intimacy means being truly yourself with another person and relating honestly with him or her in the context of a relationship. "Sharing out loud" the thoughts and feelings about abuse that the man has kept to himself helps bridge the gap between him and others and promote true intimacy. Such intimate sharing is what makes group therapy work so valuable and leads to deep growth for abuse survivors in recovery groups. Since the abuse was originally tolerated in silence, it broke off intimacy; reopening to being truly oneself with others brings profound healing. Most men have been accustomed to having this type of intimacy only with a woman, and thus they often confuse intimacy with sexuality. This confusion blocks true emotional intimacy with other males. In our groups, homophobic concerns fade away in the face of true caring and personal regard.

Who Can Benefit from the Psychophysical Model?

Regarding the types of clients who profit from our Psychophysical Model, we have worked with a variety of cases, ranging from limited impairment to severe dissociative conditions. Severity of psychological trauma is not a contraindication for body work; it is an indication to work more slowly, at the pace appropriate for the client. We realize that body work in dissociative disorders is controversial among some professionals, and we invite those persons to discuss our approach with us directly. We are always available for public discussion of our work and will discuss teaching cases in private consultations. To date, the only abuse survivors with whom we have not used our model are men who are offenders as well as survivors. At some point, this area also will need to be addressed.

Conclusion

We have been deeply moved at the rapid growth and progress made by our clients using both psychotherapy and body work. We believe that all work with abuse survivors should attend to the body as well as the mind and that the total person and his or her needs must be addressed. We invite all clinicians to explore this option for treatment. The many men and women who were sexually abused in childhood and who are ready for release from their lifelong anguish need the best treatment we can offer and deserve nothing less.

References

Bates, Carolyn M., and Annette M. Brodsky. 1989. *Sex in the Therapy Hour: A Case of Professional Incest*. New York: Guilford Press.

Dimock, Peter. 1989. *Treating the Adult Male Victim of Sexual Abuse*. Workshops presented at The Male Survivor conference, Atlanta, September 22.

Freud, Sigmund. 1977. *Introductory Lectures on Psychoanalysis*. New York: Liveright.

Ganzarain, Ramon, and Bonnie Buchele. 1988. *Fugitives of Incest: A Perspective from Psychoanalysis and Groups*. New York: International Universities Press.

Groddeck, Georg. 1923. *The Book of the It*. New York: Basic Books.

Hunter, Mic. 1990. *Abused Boys: The Neglected Victims of Sexual Abuse*. Lexington, Massachusetts: Lexington Books.

Kelerman, Stanley. 1981. *Your Body Speaks Its Mind*. Berkeley, California: Center Press.

Kurtz, Ron, and Hector Prestera. 1984. *The Body Reveals: An Illustrated Guide to the Psychology of the Body*. New York: Harper & Row.

Lew, Mike. 1988. *Victims No Longer: Men Recovering from Incest and Other Sexual Abuse*. New York: Nevraumont.

Lowen, Alexander. 1975. *Bioenergetics*. New York: Coward, McCann & Geoghegan.

Marcus, Eric. 1979. *Gestalt Therapy and Beyond: An Integrated Mind-Body Approach*. Cupertino, California: META.

Masson, Jeffrey. 1984. *The Assault on Truth: Freud's Suppression of the Seduction Theory*. New York: Farrar, Straus & Giroux.

Perls, Frederick, Ralph Hefferline, and Paul Goodman. 1951. *Gestalt Therapy*. New York: Julian Press.

Pesso, Al. 1969. *Movement in Psychotherapy: Psychomotor Techniques and Training*. New York: New York University Press.

Porter, Eugene. 1986. *Treating the Young Male Victim of Sexual Assault*. Orwell, Vermont: Safer Society Press.

Reich, Wilhelm. 1972. *Character Analysis*. 3d ed. New York: Farrar, Straus & Giroux.

Rubenfeld, Ilana. 1990. "Rubenfeld Synergy Method." In *Gestalt Psychology*, edited by Norman Shub, in press. Cleveland: Gestalt Institute of Cleveland Press.

Tick, Ed. 1984. "Male Child Sexual Abuse: The Best Kept Secret." *Voices: Journal of the American Academy of Psychotherapists* 20 (no. 3): 73–80.

Timms, Robert. 1989. "Courage to Continue: A Personal Statement about Sexual Abuse." *Pilgrimage: The Journal of Psychotherapy and Personal Exploration* 15 (no. 3): 2–6.

Timms, Robert, and Patrick Connors. 1988. *Integrating Bodywork and Psychotherapy for Adult Male Survivors of Abuse.* Workshop given at the National Conference on Male Abuse Survivors, Minneapolis, October 29. (Guidelines available from The Atlanta Center for Integrative Therapy, Inc., 20 Executive Park West, Suite 2025, Atlanta, GA 30329.)

———. 1989. "Sexual Abuse of Males: Ending the Best Kept Secret." *Voices: Journal of the American Academy of Psychotherapists* 24 (no. 4): 69–75.

7

The Treatment of Male Victims with Mixed-Gender, Short-Term Group Psychotherapy

Jeff Brown

"Edwin" was a thirty-four-year-old male who reluctantly presented himself to a therapist following threats from his partner that she could no longer stand the absence of intimacy in their life together. Edwin's primary motivation for seeking therapy seemed to be to appease his wife. He had grown tired of her constant complaints about his lack of emotionality other than infrequent angry outbursts, his periods of withdrawal, and his detachment and lack of interest in lovemaking or any other form of intimacy.

Indeed, when he observed other men with their partners, he had felt vaguely dissatisfied and self-deprecating. He loved his wife and wanted to make her happy, but he had long ago given up on the possibility that he could be like the other men he had observed or to whom his wife seemed to compare him. At his intake interview, Edwin revealed a history of sexual compulsivity during his college years, which included sexual interactions with males. Throughout his adult years, he had experienced frequent bouts of depression, withdrawal, and low self-esteem but assumed that "most everyone" had similar experiences. Upon further exploration, Edwin revealed that he had unsuccessfully attempted suicide during his college years. He also stated in an embarrassed voice that he often became frightened of small, dark rooms but that he had never told anyone because they would think he was not masculine. When the therapist questioned him about his abuse history, Edwin replied that he had no recollection of such experiences and that abuse did not happen to men anyway.

"Paul" was a twenty-nine-year-old chemically dependent gay male who had completed treatment approximately one year earlier. After detoxifying, Paul began experiencing flashbacks, nightmares, and unbidden emotional outbursts related to forgotten sexual abuse by his mother at age thirteen and subsequent sexual abuse by older men during most of his adolescence. Though less frequent, these flash-backs and nightmares continued following treatment. Initially, Paul had difficulty believing and acknowledging the abuse; he was particularly confused about his experiences with older males because he had felt sexual pleasure and had eventually initiated the sexual contacts. With time and discussion in treatment and with friends, he began to realize that he had been victimized.

After a year of sustained sobriety, Paul presented at intake concerns related to his discovery of sexual abuse. During the interview, it became clear that Paul had been affected by the abuse in a number of identifiable ways. Although it was probably not the cause of his chemical dependence, he had begun abusing chemicals shortly after the sexual abuse by his mother. At times he used these to deaden the pain or help him forget the abuse. Paul's sexual history was characterized by many casual, compulsive sexual acts with strangers, even though he was uncomfortable with this behavior and wished for longer-term intimate relationships. When he attempted these, they always failed. Some had involved forced sex by his partner.

Men like Edwin suffer in silence; men like Paul often feel alone, shameful, or unmasculine. Although it is changing, men as dissimilar as Edwin and Paul generally receive remarkably similar therapeutic interventions. For the most part, their hidden or spoken abuse histories are ignored or downplayed. Their symptoms are treated, but the possible meaning of the symptom patterns are overlooked. Perpetrator behavior is much more likely to be identified than victim issues.

Little has been written about the impact of abuse on males. Even less is available about effective treatment interventions with abused males. Many of the theories, goals, and models of trauma intervention were developed with female survivors in mind. In this chapter, I review the literature regarding the impact of abuse on male and female victims, current intervention theories, and guidelines and models of therapy with females and males. I then describe an abuse recovery group for males.

Problems Associated with Sexual Abuse Trauma

Research on the impact of abuse has centered on female victims of child abuse, most commonly incest. This research generally has been limited to a causal-correlational focus. Often it has been affected by a variety of research-related errors. Gold's (1986) review of research on abuse impact explains the problems and limitations of this research. He notes that the focus largely has been on selective subgroups such as college students, nonrandom volunteer samples, or women or men in therapy, which reduces the possibility of generalizing to other populations. Additionally, adequate control groups often are not used. Since no protocol or standardized measurement tools exist, the impact of abuse on survivors can be assessed only vaguely and without comparison to other groups.

Since so little is known about the impact of abuse on male victims, therapists and researchers must rely on clinical experience and information about female victims. Similarities and differences in the impact of abuse on males and females are not clear and have been established largely on a theoretical level. Researchers have identified the impact of abuse (primarily on females) in the areas of self-esteem, parenting skills, interpersonal relationship skills, psychosexual functioning, personality functioning, and dependence/compulsiveness. These effects are summarized below. Entries beginning with an asterisk refer to male or male and female victims; all others refer to females only.

Self Esteem

    Guilt, negative self-image, and associated depression (Tsai and Wagner 1978; Gelinas 1983; Kaufman, Peck, and Tagiuri 1984)

  * Lower self-esteem in both men and women independent of family income, emotional deprivation, and family practices (Finkelhor 1984)

    Loss of self-esteem, unresolved grief, and internalized anger (Benward and Densen-Gerber 1975).

  * Self-mutilation (Shapiro 1987; Olson 1990)

  * Low self-esteem (Gold 1986; Bruckner and Johnson 1987; Gil 1988)

Parenting Skills

    Difficulty providing structure and balance of affection and discipline (Gelinas 1983)

    Difficulty caring for children (Gil 1988)

Interpersonal Relationship Skills

    Unassertive behavior (Van Buskirk and Cole 1983)

    Marital discord (Rosenfeld 1979)

    Difficulty trusting men and women (Van Buskirk and Cole 1983; Tsai and Wagner 1978)

    Feelings of isolation (Tsai and Wagner 1979)

  * Difficulty maintaining healthy interpersonal relations (Benward and Densen-Gerber 1978; Lindberg and Distad 1985; Bruckner and Johnson 1987)

* Experienced violence of abusive partner in male victims (Olson 1990)

Difficulty developing trusting relationships (Gold 1986)

Fear of commitment, poor choice of partner, violent relationships (Gil 1988)

Psychosexual Functioning

More sexual symptoms, less responsive to sexual invitations, and less sexual satisfaction with current relationships (Gold 1986)

Significantly less responsiveness to partner (Tsai, Feldman-Summers, and Edgar 1979)

Less satisfaction with current sexual relationships (Rosenfeld 1979; Tsai, Feldman-Summers, and Edgar 1979; Van Buskirk and Cole 1983; Feldman-Summers, Gordon, and Meagher 1979)

Fear of sex, arousal dysfunction, and desire dysfunction in rape victims; secondary inorgasmia and primary inorgasmia in incest victims (Becker et al. 1982)

* Boys victimized by older men four times more likely to engage in current same-sex activity (Finkelhor 1984)

Frigidity (Lukianowicz 1972)

Precocious sexuality (Benward and Densen-Gerber 1975)

* Sexual dysfunction (unspecified) (Lindberg and Distad 1985; Bruckner and Johnson 1987)

* Prostitution and hustling in male victims (Olson 1990)

Dysfunction, sadomasochistic practices, desire disorders, and promiscuity (Gil 1988)

Personality Functioning

Characterological depression and impulsive/dissociative elements (Gelinas 1983)

Hospitalization for depression and suicide (Carmen, Rieker, and Mills 1984)

Depression (Bruckner and John 1987)

Elevations of Pd(4) and Sc(8) scales on Minnesota Multiphasic Personality Inventory (MMPI) (Tsai, Feldman-Summers, and Edgar 1979)

* In research of males, "Victim group differed significantly from the non-victim control group" on Pd, Mf, Pa, Pt, and Sc scales (Olson 1990) "even when controlling for the impact of treatment length." Author concludes that the "behavioral and maturity problems of the victimized study group, with thinking disorders likely in addition to the personality disorder, indicate a serious psychopathology (Olson 1990)

* Histories of suicidal/assaultive behaviors and criminal justice involvement (Carmen, Rieker, and Mills 1984)

* Involvement in criminal behavior and history of incarceration in males (Olson 1990)

   Hysterical characterological disturbances (Rosenfeld 1979)

   Anxiety disorders (Carmen, Rieker, and Mills 1984)

   Character disorders and psychiatric symptoms (Lukianowicz 1972)

   Antisocial behaviors (Benward and Densen-Gerber 1975)

   Impaired emotionality, including dissociative reactions, depression, and suicide attempts (Lindberg and Distad 1985)

   Dissociative reactions/multiple personality disorder (MPD) (Spiegel 1984)

* Bulimia or anorexia in males (Olson 1990)

Chemical Dependence or Other Compulsivity

* Significantly higher rates of illicit drug use among 145 male and female youths in a detention center who had histories of physical or sexual abuse (Dembo et al. 1985)

* Sixty-six percent of juvenile substance abusers had history of physical or sexual abuse (61 percent of boys and 75 percent of girls; more physical than sexual) (Sandberg 1986)

* Seventy-four percent of 35 recovering adult females had sexual abuse histories, 52 percent had experienced physical abuse, and 72 percent had experienced emotional abuse in comparison to a nonalcoholic control group in which 50 percent had experienced sexual abuse, 34 percent physical abuse, 44 percent emotional abuse (Covington and Kohen 1987)

   Forty-four percent of 118 chemically dependent females had histories of incest (Benward and Densen-Gerber 1975)

   Thirty-nine percent of 100 chemically dependent women had histories of incest versus 24 percent of a control group (Evans and Schaefer 1987)

* Male victims were much more likely to have struggled with compulsive behaviors, including chemical addiction and abuse, sexual acting out, compulsive spending, overworking, and eating disorders (Hunter 1989; Olson 1990)

* Problems with substance abuse in male victim clients (Bruckner and Johnson 1987)

In his summary of similar statistics, Coleman (1987) concluded that there is at least a 100 percent greater incidence of sexual abuse for chemically dependent women than for the general population.

Overview of Treatment Intervention Theory

Psychoanalytic Theory

Abuse trauma theory is a relatively new area of psychological study. Historically, trauma theory has been developed from research and clinical experience with Holocaust and disaster victims and individuals involved in military combat. Early formulations, on which much current theory is based, were developed by Freud (Horowitz 1986).

In his theoretical models, Freud conceptualized dual internal systems for managing trauma. Where external events were perceived as stressful or "signals of danger, fear, or anxiety" were present, internal structures functioned to regulate the amount of information available to the individual (Horowitz 1986, 86). Where traumatic memories were triggered, various forms of repressive defense mechanisms served to inhibit them. Intrusions of these memories and/or emotions occurred when the repressive mechanisms failed. Psychological intervention with traumatic memories focused on overcoming the repression sufficiently to reconnect with the material. Following this, the therapist would facilitate completing memories and assist the client in working through meanings and conflicts associated with the material.

Trauma Theory

For the most part, current psychotherapy with abuse survivors is based on the development and reformulation of Freud's work. Horowitz (1986) used these psychodynamic conceptualizations to develop one of the more comprehensive theories to date on impact, symptomatology, and intervention with trauma. Other theorists have focused on biological and behavioral elements in trauma formation. Burgess and Holmstrom (1974), Spiegel (1984), Gil (1988), Finkelhor (1981, 1984), and Finkelhor and Browne (1985) have studied the traumatic nature of abuse. A diagnostic category, posttraumatic stress disorder (PTSD) has been created to take into account these new areas of understanding (American Psychiatric Association 1987).

Horowitz's (1986) model integrates recent cognitive processing theory into psychodynamic trauma theory. A series of processes are expected to occur in the aftermath of a traumatic event so that individuals can find meaning and closure in the event. According to Horowitz, stressful events or trauma threaten individuals' "cognitive maps," which help them "organize their perceptions and plan their next moves" (p. 93). These cognitive maps include ways of conceptualizing themselves in the world, how others behave, types and meanings of relationships, and general beliefs about the way the world works. Following trauma, individuals continue to strive to make meaning of the event and find compatibility with their cognitive maps. At the same time, feelings such as fear and anxiety will be evoked as situations, people, places, and memories cue in the unresolved traumatic material. According to the model, these feelings may be sufficient to activate various internal mechanisms that reduce or eliminate the feelings or interrupt the memory. A repeating cycle of intrusion of the material and reduction/elimination/interruption following the intrusion occurs until the trauma is resolved.

Intervention based on this theory focuses on facilitating the client's natural tendency to find meaning and closure following a trauma. This primarily involves "completing integration of an event's meaning and developing adaptational responses" (p. 123). The therapist's role in facilitating integration includes intervening to reduce controls and the intrusion of the material or providing support, structure, and suppression of emotions, depending on the immediate status of the client.

Successful integration and adaptation are indicated by the client's ability to process the trauma in a realistic and accurate way with access to related emotions and without unrealistic acceptance of responsibility (Gil 1988). Furthermore, the client will be able to place the event in a past context and will not feel a need to repeat or create the same or a similar trauma.

In the previous example of Edwin, if there were enough corroborating data to indicate an abuse history, the clinician might assume that Edwin had sufficient defense systems of denial and repression to prevent any intrusion of the traumatic material. Preliminary intervention likely would focus on accessing the repressed memories via various abreactive therapies, such as hypnotherapy, and reducing the inappropriate use of denial and repression. Following intrusion of the material, the therapist would provide support, guidance, and appropriate structure so that Edwin would be able to work with the material without becoming overwhelmed or rigidly defensive.

In the example of Paul, preliminary intervention would involve assessing the nature and types of intrusions and the history of interruptions of the intrusions. Careful observation and determination of specific controls or defensive measures used would be essential for planning intervention. If dissociation was the primary control mechanism used, then the therapist might assist the client in developing more willful and adaptive use of dissociation. In exploring and working with the intrusions, the therapist would assist Paul in plotting a course while managing the material so that Paul would not be overwhelmed and consequently use his ability to dissociate.

Biological and behavioral models of conceptualizing PTSD treatment differ significantly from the psychodynamic models offered by Horowitz and others. Van der Kolk et al. (1986) hypothesize that traumatized individuals develop patterns of hyperarousal to stimuli perceived as traumatic. These patterns are similar in appearance and biological effects to learned helplessness in animals. These authors advocate treatment with a variety of medications to counteract the apparent effects of hyperarousal on the noradrenergic system, as well as training in relaxation and biofeedback and reeducation to decrease anxiety and overreaction to traumatic-appearing situations.

Those proposing a behavioral model suggest that individuals who are traumatized have learned whatever behavior is necessary to "avoid or escape exposure to conditioned and unconditioned aversive stimuli" (Fairbanks and Nicholson 1987, 46). Behavioral treatments include systematic desensitization, flooding, and stress management techniques to eliminate or reduce the conditioned avoidance and escape responses.

Trauma Theory Specific to Abuse Issues

A number of researchers in the field of abuse have reviewed the diagnostic indicators of PTSD and their applicability to survivors of abuse (Gelinas 1983; Tsai, Feldman-Summers, and Edgar 1979; Lindberg and Distad 1985; Donaldson 1983; Gil 1988). In a study of seventeen women who had experienced incest, Lindberg and Distad (1985) found that all of their subjects met the criteria for PTSD. Similarly, Donaldson (1983) found that 88 percent of her sample of forty women with incest histories met the criteria. Both researchers suggest that treatment be based on models similar to those proposed by Horowitz (1986).

Additionally, Spiegel (1984) argues that dissociative disorders most commonly associated with severe abuse trauma (including multiple personality disorder [MPD] are another form of PTSD. He notes, "The hypnotic dissociation becomes an attempt to anesthetize the pain by seeing it inflicted on a separate part of themselves" (p. 102). Steele and Colrain (1989) have placed trauma-related disorders on a continuum of dissociation, which includes PTSD, dissociative disorders, and MPD. According to Spiegel (1984), trauma resolution work with individuals with dissociative disorders parallels that with other trauma victims in its emphasis on integration and completion of disparate cognitive frameworks.

Lindberg and Distad (1985), Sutherland and Scherl (1970), and Burgess and Holmstrom (1974) observed phasic responses to abuse trauma in survivors. In female rape victims, Burgess and Holmstrom (1974) noted an acute phase, which began immediately following the rape and lasted two to three weeks, and a long-term phase, which followed. Sutherland and Scherl (1970) characterize the acute phase as punctuated with feelings of "shock, disbelief, and dismay" and periods of agitation, incoherence, and volatility (p. 504). The long-term phase appears to be similar to the "intrusion-repetitive" phase noted by Lindberg and Distad (1985, 332) and includes nightmares or dreams, guilt reactions, a variety of phobic responses, and sexual difficulties. Sutherland and Scherl (1970) hypothesize a middle phase characterized by "pseudoadjustment," in which denial and suppression assist to subdue the victim's feelings and interest in insight or further trauma resolution (p. 507).

Finkelhor and Browne (1985) propose a framework for understanding and working with childhood sexual abuse trauma that attempts to look more specifically at the implications for impact based on the dynamics present in the traumatic event. Impact is categorized according to the type of trauma that occurred: sexualization, betrayal, powerlessness, or stigmatization (p. 530). The authors recommend that intervention strategies be formulated to focus on the specific traumatic dynamics, as well as the family reaction to disclosure at the time and the "social and institutional response to the disclosure" (p. 538).

On the basis of the symptoms and abuse history he presented, Paul likely experienced sexualization and stigmatization as primary traumatic dynamics. Both his mother and the older men made efforts to elicit a sexual response in him, provided mistaken information about appropriate sexual behavior, and manipulated his developmental status in order to abuse him. The major taboos against sexual interaction with a child's mother as well as with men, the gender-related stereotypes about males and abuse, and the secretive quality of Paul's abuse contributed to a sense of stigmatization.

Developmental Theory

In her monograph on treating survivors of abuse, Hooker (1985, 1) proposes the "Victim Assessment Model, based on the developmental stage theory of Erik Erikson. Hooker's model describes specific behavioral patterns she believes to be associated with the lack of resolution of developmental crises in victims of abuse. Consistent with Erikson, she suggests that failure to resolve a particular developmental stage or crisis influences the capacity of the individual to resolve subsequent stages.

In Gelinas's (1983) review of the negative effects of incest, she proposes that many of the problems that follow sexual abuse trauma are symptomatic expressions of these developmental impasses, which are connected with the untreated trauma. She notes that these symptoms typically appear many years after the abuse trauma and often are precipitated by situations or events that demand functioning in areas (such as sexuality) that are disordered or impaired due to the developmental impasse.

Initial intervention using developmental models would focus on identification of the "problematic crisis or impasse" in the client. Following this, a clinician who utilized the model would theoretically be able to "discover the client's potential strengths or weaknesses, and anticipate possible resistance to certain therapeutic styles" (Hooker 1985, 4).

In the hypothetical model of Edwin, the unresolved developmental crisis would appear to be intimacy. Hooker notes "resistance to change during conventional therapy," primarily or totally repressed abuse memories, "denied feelings," "diffuse residual anger," and "lack of intimacy in the relationship" as behavioral patterns associated with this developmental crisis (p. 12). In this approach, Edwin would benefit from individual therapy that used psychodrama, was focused on the self, and was initially structured around surfacing the repressed memories. Following work on the repressed memories, intervention would emphasize expressing and validating anger and forgiveness of self and the victimizer.

Overview of Treatment Intervention Guidelines and Models

Despite the variety of theoretical positions taken in the treatment of abuse survivors, more similarities than differences are found with regard to the specifics of intervention. Similarities in descriptions of goals and rationale of treatment as well as the therapist's role are particularly apparent. More significant differences appear in conceptualizing group treatment and its structure and in determining the length of treatment.

Increased pressure for cost-effective intervention, as well as cumulative experience and knowledge in treating survivors, has led to a general movement toward more symptom-specific and goal-oriented intervention approaches. Various structured time-limited groups, phase-oriented treatments, and problem-based models have been proposed.

In her critique of the status of abuse recovery intervention, Altermatt (1985) is critical of this current direction of therapy, which involves "externally directed intervention" (p. 1). Altermatt believes that this type of intervention may recreate the imposition of power and control from outside forces. She suggests a return to an earlier emphasis on "giving control back to the victim" to facilitate the internal process of healing and a focus on his or her own process "without forcing resolution" (p. 1). Intervention from this perspective would apparently eliminate a focus on specific structures or timetables, deemphasize symptom frameworks, and emphasize support and empowerment of the client.

Goals and Treatment Themes

Whatever theoretical positions researchers take, a number of goals regularly appear in the literature. These are summarized here:

Disclosing the history of abuse (Ewalt and Crawford 1981; Tsai, Feldman-Summers, and Edgar 1979)

Learning to identify and express emotions connected with the trauma (abreaction) (Lindberg and Distad 1985; Ewalt and Crawford 1981; Courtois 1980; Tsai, Feldman-Summers, and Edgar 1979)

Eliminating irrational responsibility for the abuse (Lindberg and Distad 1985; Courtois 1980)

Acknowledging the abuse and grieving for the idealized childhood (Gil 1988; Tsai, Feldman-Summers, and Edgar 1979; Hooker 1985)

Reevaluating abuse experiences and meanings associated with them in a new context (Bruckner and Johnson 1987; Horowitz 1986)

Integrating dissociated parts (Spiegel 1984; Gil 1988)

Empowering the survivor (Gil 1988)

Increasing the survivor's sense of worth and competence (Horowitz and Kaltreider 1979; Lindberg and Distad 1985; Gil 1988; Bruckner and Johnson 1987)

Reducing self-destructive behavior patterns (Lindberg and Distad 1985)

Developing new adaptive behavior patterns (Horowitz and Kaltreider 1979; Horowitz 1986; Lindberg and Distad 1985)

Reducing isolation and increasing affiliation (Gil 1988)

Additionally, a number of clinicians and researchers have observed corresponding content themes and issues in individual and group psychotherapy. Although a number of these themes are noted by some observers and not others, those related to anger, relationship difficulties, sexuality, guilt and shame, low self-image, and self-disgust are repeated frequently in the literature. Recurrent themes specific to male survivors of abuse have been reported in the clinical and research literature as well.

Anger, rage, and resentment have been the most commonly noted responses in adult victims in therapy (Blake-White and Kline 1985; Donaldson 1983; Bruckner and Johnson 1987; Horowitz and Kaltreider 1979). In Donaldson's (1983) survey of women incest survivors, more than half of the respondents expressed anger that the abuse occurred, wanted to hurt the perpetrator, had generalized anger toward all men, and felt "explosive anger" (p. 17). Horowitz and Kaltreider (1979) note that anger in trauma survivors may take the form of "rage at those exempted," as well as "discomfort about" and "fear of loss of control of" aggressive impulses (p. 369). Males in Bruckner and Johnson's (1987) sample of male and female victims were particularly intense in their display of rage, which included fantasies as well as plans for and attempts at retribution. Interestingly, little has been written to make connections between this anger/rage and the underlying dynamics that these feelings serve (that is, the internalized victim-victimizer dynamic and shame-rage cycles).

As described earlier in this chapter, difficulties in relationships are well documented among sexual abuse survivors. Tsai and Wagner (1978) describe several factors that appear to contribute to relationship difficulties in female abuse survivors. These include mistrust of men, poor social skills, and patterns of reengaging in abusive relationships with men. Relationship problems also appeared to affect the development of trust and the disclosure of emotions in an all-male survivors' group (Bruckner and Johnson 1987).

When permission to discuss current sexual issues is provided in therapy, the variety of difficulties outlined previously often come to the forefront. Both Tsai and Wagner (1978) and Bruckner and Johnson (1987) emphasize the need for client information and education when working with sexuality issues. Exploration of perpetrator behaviors among male and female survivors is of particular importance and has until recently been largely ignored (Bruckner and Johnson 1987).

Themes of guilt and shame and consequent low self-image and self-disgust also are frequent among abuse survivors. Feelings of shame and guilt are generally the consequence of abuse experiences in which the victim was stigmatized, compromised, devalued, manipulated, disregarded, and humiliated. The victim is placed in a double bind: "In order to satisfy needs to belong, to feel whole, and to feel a part of something larger, [they] must substitute, throw away, and disengage aspects of self" (Brown 1987, 62–63). The victim develops an internalized belief that he or she is damaged or bad as a consequence of the abuse (Finkelhor and Browne 1985). Guilt and shame over surviving the trauma and feeling somehow responsible for it also are often present (Horowitz and Kaltreider 1979).

Although the literature regarding male abuse survivors is replete with inconsistent findings, certain recurrent themes that differentiate males from females have been reported. Most of these differentiating themes appear to be related to male socialization and its effect on perception of, impact of, and response to the abuse. Males are more likely to perceive the abuse as unique to themselves and to be isolated (Bruckner and Johnson 1987) partly because they equate abuse with an inability to protect themselves, a lack of masculinity, and homosexuality (Nasjleti, 1980; Bruckner and Johnson 1987). Consequently, they are much less likely to report the abuse (Finkelhor 1981; Fritz, Stoll, and Wagner 1981; Nasjleti 1980; Kaufman et al. 1980). Additionally, they are ambivalent about the abuse and its effects. Even though their perception is inaccurate, they often prefer to view the abuse as an initiation rather than a violation in order to maintain their self-perceptions of masculinity and power (Finkelhor 1981; Fritz, Stoll, and Wagner 1981).

These themes obviously affect the direction and focus of therapy and also may affect the specific intervention approach used. For example, when male survivors disclose their abuse histories as adults and are cognizant of the impact of the abuse, it appears that their action oriented role behavior and need to "assume control of their lives" result in a greater likelihood that they will publicly disclose their abuse and confront their perpetrators (Bruckner and Johnson 1987, 86). Their controlled emotional styles also may make it difficult to access affect in therapy (Kaufman et al. 1980; Nasjleti 1980; Bruckner and Johnson 1987).

Rationale and Models of Group Treatment

A number of theorists and practitioners have noted the value of group therapy for abuse survivors. In general, because of its use of the milieu, abuse-oriented group therapy challenges the isolation, shame, secretiveness, and lack of support/relationship skills that particularly characterize this population. Male survivors in particular view their abuse as unique and shameful and consequently lack the support of and identification with their own gender (Bruckner and Johnson 1987). Group therapy has been the modality of choice for developing an understanding of commonality of experience and thus reducing related shame and isolation, learning relationship skills and getting support, and experiencing feelings in a safe environment (Van Buskirk and Cole 1983; Courtois 1980; Blake-White and Kline 1985; Bruckner and Johnson 1987). In addition, group therapy can be particularly effective in avoiding the problematic transference and countertransference issues that often plague individual abuse-related therapy.

Various models of groups for abuse-related issues have been proposed. Length of the groups in the literature reviewed for this chapter ranged from four sessions in a closed model (Tsai and Wagner 1978) to more than fifty sessions (with an average of twenty sessions) in an open-ended ongoing model (Blake-White and Kline 1985). All-male, all-female, and male-female groups have been attempted, some with same-sex cotherapy teams and others with opposite-sex teams. The structure and focus of the groups has varied as well. Some models were structured around specific themes and topics decided by the group or the therapist(s) (Gil 1988; Bruckner and Johnson 1987; Tsai and Wagner 1978). Other models were structured around stages of individuals and/or the group (Blake-White and Kline 1985; Horowitz and Kaltreider 1979; Horowitz 1986). Pacing of individual work within the groups appears for the most part to have been imposed by the group leader; Gil's (1988) and Blake-White and Kline's (1985) groups apparently were paced according to the individual's self-identified need. Whatever the structure chosen, all the groups focused at various points on the abuse history and its impact on current functioning. Horowitz (1986), Horowitz and Kaltreider (1979), Tsai and Wagner (1978), and Bruckner and Johnson (1987) focused the initial session(s) on disclosure. Others proposed preliminary emphasis on related issues such as goals, self-image, intimacy, and/or group process (Gil 1988).

Abuse Recovery Model

As Altermatt (1985) has observed, early models of intervention with abuse survivors emphasized relative health and capacity to heal, responsibility to self, and lack of power/control in the position of victim. For many survivors, this facilitated a sense of empowerment, heightened self-esteem, and movement toward an internal locus of control. However, the overemphasis on empowerment through acknowledgment of and work with anger and rage at the perpetrator, as well as the focus on self-direction in the therapeutic process, at times led to overly generalized rage at all men or all women and a fixation and consequent incapacity to move past the angry feelings to the development of healthy relationships with both sexes. Secondary elaborations of the trauma, such as depression, sexual dysfunction, or more serious personality disorders, often were overlooked or misperceived due to this overemphasis. The overstating of victim-victimizer dichotomies missed important interactions and cycling between the two roles and ignored men who were victims, women who were victimizers, and many persons who were both (Evans 1987). Some individuals became overidentified with the victim role, while remaining unaware of their own victimizing behavior.

The growing body of knowledge regarding PTSD, dissociation, developmental theory, and work with victimizers has made symptom-specific and goal-oriented approaches, as well as more individualized interventions, possible. As Altermatt (1985) has noted, however, these approaches probably have contributed to a reinforcement of a victim stance in which the client feels helpless and increasingly dependent on the expert therapist rather than on himself or herself. The emphasis on symptoms, specificity, and therapist intervention may reinforce isolation, an external locus of control, and a withdrawal from community and personal resources.

The Abuse Recovery Model, originally conceived at the Program in Human Sexuality at the University of Minnesota's Medical School and Department of Family Practice and Community Health, was developed to take into account new areas of knowledge in the intervention process while at the same time emphasizing empowerment, active choice making, and use of personal resources. The treatment model uses the posttraumatic stress model as a theoretical basis for the development of structure and focus. The primary goal is integration of the traumatic experiences, mainly through assisting in identification and externalization, exploration of meanings, and reconnection of appropriate affect with these experiences. This reintegration of material will enable the client to reassess his or her life circumstance, make choices, and behave out of the present situation rather than out of the past.

Rationale and Goals

The posttraumatic stress model is viewed as an extension of our previous understanding of the natural and nonpathological process of healing trauma and is used to facilitate this process. The shifting of intrusion and denial during the initial phase in the abuse recovery group is reframed and worked with as part of the healing process. Through exposure to the feared traumatic memories during intrusion, the client is assisted in identifying and clarifying the traumatic material, developing boundaries helpful in managing the intrusion, reappraising the meaning of events, and developing adaptive responses (Fairbanks and Nicholson 1987; Spiegel 1984; Horowitz 1986). Further exploration of the abuse content is used to reduce shame, self-blame, and irrational responsibility for the abuse; encourage exploration of the contextual dynamics that reinforced the destructive qualities of the abuse; clarify the impact of the abuse; learn to identify and express emotions connected with the trauma; and grieve for losses. During denial, the client is encouraged to develop and practice ways to make himself or herself safe, use available supports (including group members), and recollect and reevaluate previous coping patterns.

A brief, structured, and individually focused context is used in the abuse recovery model to communicate expectations of the capacity to heal, accountability and responsibility to self for outcome, and use of community resources in the healing process. The short-term and time-limited aspects of the model were chosen to deemphasize pathology, reduce dependence on a group, and increase the likelihood that the client will maximize his or her ability to move forward in life. This communication of expectations and use of structure, as well as the emphasis on regularly determining and reevaluating goals, clarifying and practicing boundary setting, and self-definition of the therapy process and timetable, facilitate a sense of empowerment and competence. As stated previously, the client's active involvement in working with intrusion and denial also assist in empowering him or her.

Description

The original Abuse Recovery Model was based on an ongoing, time-limited (twelve-week) two-hour-session format with six to eight members who had been sexually abused as children. Membership in the group was coed, with a male-female therapist team cofacilitating. Since that time, the model has been adapted to a variety of circumstances and needs. A number of variations have been successful, including length of the group, closed structure, same-sex population, inclusion of victims of other types of abuse, and addition of an educational component. Other variations, most notably the inclusion of offender victims, have been less successful.

In all its variations, the group has focused on the past, present, and future as it relates to the abuse. In the past component, clients disclose and work through types of abuse, including covert, overt, and boundary violations, as well as sources of abuse. In the present component, clients identify victimlike patterns of behaviors, including caretaking, lack of assertiveness, setting oneself up, and problems with boundaries. In the future-oriented session(s), clients review the progress they have made, set new goals for themselves, clarify remaining issues that need to be addressed as part of their aftercare plan, and say good-bye to group members.

In addition to the limited content, a number of structural and procedural elements have been included so that the client can make as much progress as possible within the short time period. Before joining the group, new members are provided extensive information about rules and expectations to prepare them for the sessions, set a tone for the direction and type of work, and establish a context of explicitly stated boundaries, roles, and rules. Individual issues rather than group process is emphasized to encourage the client to get through the most of the personal material before graduating from the group.

Clearly stated, individually developed goals with specific client-determined time limitations are used and reviewed regularly to encourage this focus. As part of this process, clients are asked to determine the number of weeks they will work on the past, present, and future. In addition, time is divided evenly among the members, and all members are required to take time every week (each member determines how he or she will use that time). Most of the therapy work is expected to occur outside the group, given the limited time for each session and the short-term nature of the group. To facilitate work outside the group, packets of suggested homework are provided at various points during each client's progress.

Since the group is not primarily process oriented, the milieu of the group serves specific functions, which may differ somewhat from those of other groups. In particular, the use of group interactions to develop relationship skills and enhance intimacy is deemphasized though not excluded. Interactions and relationships in the group are used to facilitate practicing of assertiveness and boundary setting between members and with group leaders, to develop a sense of commonality of experiences, and to express feelings in a safe environment. Individuals are encouraged to use the group setting to check in on their progress, get support, discuss shame-laden material, work through impasses, and report progress on homework. Use of the group will vary greatly, since each individual determines what he or she will focus on and whether he or she will use the group primarily for reporting, receiving feedback, developing intimacy skills, or practicing assertiveness and boundary setting.

An educational component has been added in some groups lasting longer than twelve weeks (there is not enough time in groups that run twelve weeks or less). Information is presented to highlight material that might otherwise not get identified because of time restraints and to facilitate intellectual connections with personal issues. Typically, brief presentations and related homework materials are provided on a weekly basis on topics such as definitions of abuse, the abuse cycle, victim-victimizer connections, processes of healing abuse, anger and assertiveness, posttraumatic stress, dissociation, boundaries, codependence, the impact of abuse, and healing the inner child.

Same-sex and both-sex groups have been used with various goals in mind. Despite the deemphasis on group process in this model, same-sex groups can be powerful tools in creating a sense of identification, reducing isolation, and creating a safe place to discuss issues the members may not discuss in the presence of the opposite sex. All-male groups are more likely than both-sex groups to discuss issues of masculinity, fears of homosexuality, sexuality concerns in general, and perpetration issues. All-female groups appear beneficial for those who are extremely fearful of males or give up their power to males.

When the model is used with male-female survivor groups and other sex cotherapist teams, the goal is to reduce the overgeneralization of sex roles and victim/victimizer stereotypes. Participants in these groups are given opportunities to empathize with opposite-sex survivors, practice boundary setting, and challenge their own stereotypes. Opposite-sex therapists are used to model appropriate and compassionate male-female behavior, which hopefully will challenge the clients' views of both sexes and their capacity to relate to them.

Therapist Role

Given the deemphasis on group process and the short-term nature of the group, the therapist's role becomes more important. In most aspects, the therapist will be required to take a more active role in holding the client accountable for his or her goals and progress, modeling appropriate feedback and gender-role behavior, monitoring group process, and using the therapist's position to maintain a safe environment. The therapist also will be required to use the milieu of group members who are farther along in their recovery to draw parallels, provide direction, and model movement toward healing. However, because clients are encouraged and expected to make decisions about their process and direction, the therapist must be able to defer his or her power and knowledge in order to empower clients. At times this requires the therapist to withhold recommendations and advice and permit a client to make a poor decision. In this process, the therapist reframes all client decisions as choices, even if the client is choosing to let things happen. In the same way, the therapist must point out victimlike behavior in an objective, non-judgmental way.

Client Characteristics and Assessing for Placement

The specific structural and procedural qualities of the Abuse Recovery Model is of particular benefit to certain clients and is contraindicated for others. Consequently, a thorough assessment for placement is necessary to optimize the benefits of the model. Clients who are inappropriate for the group may find the process difficult and disturbing and may affect the quality, intensity, and focus of the group for other members.

The ideal client candidate will evidence a stable and relatively strong ego strength, with no evidence of personality disorder. Because of the intense short-term nature of the group, the client candidate will need to have active memory of at least some of the traumatic material, be functioning primarily in the intrusion phase, show by history a capacity to manage the material without severe decompensation, and not be involved in an active abuse situation or other crisis. Chemically dependent and compulsive individuals should have a history of stable sobriety and management of their behaviors, demonstrating a capacity to handle this painful material without relapse.

Since the group is structured primarily around individual work within a group, those clients who would benefit most from group process should be referred to other groups. In addition, the client must be motivated, capable of focusing on difficult material on his or her own or with the help of supportive others in the community, and able to manage several weeks of sustained painful and intensive focus, since so much of the work occurs outside the group itself.

Hypothetical client Edwin would likely be a poor candidate for the group, since presentation at intake showed no evidence of intrusion of abuse material, limited motivation to change, and a lack of clarity about his ego strength or the presence of compulsive/addictive behaviors. Hypothetical client Paul would be a good candidate for the group. Abuse material was readily available to him with ongoing intrusions, and he was highly motivated and stable, had numerous support systems, and showed a capacity for insight and work on his own.

Identifying the age of impact, numbers and types of trauma, secondary trauma in disclosure, patterns and levels of intrusion/denial, and types of defenses used with the traumatic material will provide a relatively complete picture of the abuse history so that determinations about severity, chronicity, and impact of the abuse can be made. In general, more severe and more chronic forms of abuse are associated with greater impact and secondary elaborations and with the likelihood that a personality disorder has developed. Consequently, these clients may require longer-term intervention (although they will benefit from placement in the group at an appropriate juncture). Group placement of the ego-weak client who shows evidence of MPD, severe dissociative difficulties, borderline or narcissistic personality disorders, or schizoid functioning will be problematic unless he or she is particularly responsive to the kind of structure and focus the model provides and the group is positioned to handle these differences.

Following assessment and determination of suitability for group placement, review of the client's current status and the group's condition will assist in making placement at the appropriate time. The client's presentation of contemporary symptoms, identified treatment needs, stage of healing, level of functioning, and type(s) of abuse experienced must be compatible with the current composition of the group and the capacity of the group to absorb new members. Wherever possible, placement of two members into a group at the same time should be considered so that they can establish some sense of safety, mutuality, and identification immediately.

Description of the Phases

Past Phase. As explained previously, the focus in the initial past phase of individual work in the group is on identifying and clarifying the traumatic material, elaborating the abuse content, learning to identify and express emotions connected with the abuse, and reappraising old coping mechanisms. Since prior assessment will exclude the denying client, a great amount of work is not needed to reduce primary defenses. The more subtle aspects of defenses, such as minimizing, intellectualizing, rationalizing, and dissociating, will likely be present and require the therapist's attention.

During the client's introduction into the first group, the client will be requested to disclose his or her goals and timetable, as well as some initial information about his or her abuse history. As always, decisions to disclose difficult material are framed as a choice that the client should explicitly make. Over the next several weeks and sessions, the client works with externalizing his or her history of abuse and the feelings he or she has or remembers having in the past. Homework is provided to assist in these efforts. Suggested homework includes journaling the client's history, collecting pictures from the period of the abuse and sharing them with the group, drawing pictures of the abuse, and writing unsent letters to people connected with the abuse. Clients also are encouraged to review lists of types of abuse (table 7–1), complete a brief abuse history (figure 7–1), and read a handout on the context of abuse (table 7–2).

Clients who have difficulty connecting with the emotional content may focus their efforts on writing letters to their small abused self, caring for a

Table 7–1
Continuum of Abuse

Sexual boundary violations
  Overquestioning child about sex
  Overconcern with child's changing body
  Sexual staring at someone's body
  Watching someone undress
  Sleeping with child
  Telling child inappropriate sexual secrets
  Sexual reading to child
  Use of inappropriate sexual language
  Parent showing his or her body parts to child
  Pornographic photography
  Jokes or comments about sexuality
  "Inadvertent" touch

Emotional boundary violations
  Unclear who is adult and who is child
  Parent's needs always come first
  Not helping child learn from mistakes
  Child as extension of parent
  Unconsenting sex with partner (date rape)
  Sexual "games" or "torture"
  Penetration with objects
  Disrespectful or power-based sadomasochism

Emotional abuse
  Blaming child for parent's problems
  Denying reality as child sees it
  Overprotecting or smothering
  Excusing child or blaming others for child's problems
  Love dependent on child's behavior
  Not talking about abuse
  Child has to watch others being physically, emotionally, or sexually abused

Physical abuse
  Slapping, spanking, scratching, or squeezing
  Beating with objects, cords, sticks, boards, or other objects
  Throwing, pushing, or shoving
  Burning, scalding, or freezing
  Forcing food, water, or excrement; starving
  Overworking

representative doll or stuffed animal, or visiting and observing children of an age similar to their abused age. Clients who are shameful about their disclosures and the abuse are encouraged to verbalize their shame and its meanings in the group, ask for corrective feedback, and monitor themselves for further feelings of shame (Brown 1987). In cases in which the shame is based on client self-blame, additional work on reframing previous accommodation

Age	Name of Abuser	Relationship	Type(s) of Abuse	How Ended
___	_____	_____	_____	_____
___	_____	_____	_____	_____
___	_____	_____	_____	_____
___	_____	_____	_____	_____
___	_____	_____	_____	_____
___	_____	_____	_____	_____
___	_____	_____	_____	_____
___	_____	_____	_____	_____
___	_____	_____	_____	_____
___	_____	_____	_____	_____
___	_____	_____	_____	_____
___	_____	_____	_____	_____

Directions: Use the letter abbreviations in the key below to tell what kind(s) of abuse you experienced.
Key: S = sexual abuse; P = physical abuse; E = emotional abuse; SP = sexual preference abuse; N = neglect; B = boundary violations.

Figure 7–1. Brief Abuse History

behaviors (such as hiding or initiating the abuse) as necessary for coping and survival and exploring the dynamics that produced the behaviors will be helpful in shifting the client's cognitive set and increasing compassion for self.

Later work in this phase usually focuses on further exploration of the material, the context in which it occurred, meanings associated with it, and issues of disclosure and confrontation. At times, a client may need assistance from group members or the therapists in broadening his or her awareness of the types of abuse he or she has experienced, particularly where subtle or unknown forms of abuse, such as emotional neglect, date rape, boundary violations, or covert abuse, have occurred.

As clients develop greater clarity, insight, connection with affect, and reduction of shame and self-blame, they may benefit from disclosure to supportive others in the community and confrontation of their perpetrator(s). Intervention with this issue generally includes assisting the client in assessing risks/benefits, developing boundaries about his or her disclosure, clarifying needs or wants related to the person to whom the client will disclose, and providing means to rehearse the disclosure through role play, letters, image work, and so on. Before considering confronting his or her perpetrator(s), the client must be assisted in exploring his or her anger, loss, betrayal, and pain.

Table 7–2
Context of Abuse

A history of abuse over several generations; dysfunctional family dynamics
  Some or all feelings not allowed or shamed
  Shame about sexuality, sexuality as dirty or bad, or lack of information about sexuality
  Appearance more important than people
  Children given adult role
  Emotional needs of child ignored or interfered with
  Child taught to ignore own needs and attend to others
  Lack of physical touch or nurturing
  Secret keeping
  Child not protected or made to feel safe
  Individuals scapegoated instead of looking at family problems
  Abuse treated as normal

Child's reactions
  Doesn't know what abuse is
  Learns to keep pain inside or keep it away
  Doesn't know what healthy sex is
  Learns to distrust his or her feelings, thoughts, and beliefs
  Feels alone, unprotected, and unsafe
  Expects to be blamed or blames self even if it is not his or her fault
  Learns to keep things to herself or himself

Hidden abuse/boundary problems
  Sexual boundary violations
  Emotional boundary violations
  Physical boundary violations

Overt abuse
  Sexual abuse
  Emotional abuse
  Physical abuse
  Verbal abuse
  Sexual orientation abuse

Includes material from Sterne, Schaefer, and Evans (1984) on the continuum of abuse.

As Bruckner and Johnson (1987) have noted, male survivors in groups will generally approach their past focus work differently than female survivors. In general, their disclosures initially will appear removed and dispassionate and will move toward an identification of anger and a desire for action that includes public disclosure and confrontation of the perpetrator(s). In my experience, feelings of pain, sadness, shame, and compassion for self will be much more difficult to access and will occur in the latter portions of the past phase.

Additionally, males appear to have a greater difficulty identifying with other survivors and viewing themselves as sharing commonalities of experience with them (Bruckner and Johnson 1987). These generalizations about males appear to be mitigated somewhat in male-female groups, since male members are able to observe and imitate female members' emotional disclosures and commonality-seeking behaviors. Therapist decisions about intervention and pacing will need to take into account these apparent differences.

Present Phase. The middle stage of individual work in the Abuse Recovery Group addresses the impact of the abuse on current functioning and behavior. In this context, current victimlike behaviors, belief systems, and self-talk, along with coinciding behaviors, are examined. Clients are provided a handout on the long-term effects of abuse (table 7–3) and an inventory of victim behavior (figure 7–2) to help them begin to identify and connect some of their current difficulties in living with the previous abuse. Intervention in the group milieu highlights ongoing victimlike behavior as it is presented to focus on setting boundaries, expressing anger and stating needs directly, and using assertive behavior. Homework assignments are given to develop skills in self-care, assertiveness, and direct expression of boundaries, needs, and feelings.

Since the short-term structure of the group makes it impossible for the client to implement behavior changes fully, the major focus of the client's work is on developing insight and clarity into his or her general victim stance. In particular, clients are encouraged to reassess their belief systems and corresponding self-talk that may support this stance. The clinician should draw on locus of control and learned helplessness theory (Seligman 1975) to assist the client in developing greater understanding of his or her personal meaning of the trauma(s) and the conclusions and beliefs that he or she has developed about the world and themselves. These often include themes of powerlessness and lack of choices in the world, inability to protect oneself and create safety, discounting of needs and feelings, and feelings of worthlessness. Sexuality-related themes include views of sex as power and control, equating sex and intimacy, poor body image and sexual self-esteem, and incapacity to set sexual boundaries. Constructs related to gender often are stereotypic and self-limiting and confound views of the abuse and the victim's responsibility for it.

With the assistance and support of the group, individual members who are in the present phase are encouraged to review and evaluate patterns of victimlike behaviors. Depending on individual circumstances, clients are asked to write sexual or relationship histories, assess elements of compulsive behavior or dependence in relationships, examine self-destructive patterns, review boundaries with regard to sexuality or other areas, or clarify current sexual functioning. Following this period of self-assessment, clients are supported to make small success-based behavioral changes. Individual assignments to say no, practice assertive behavior, draw new boundaries, state needs or feelings, or renegotiate sexual contracts are common in this phase.

As has been previously mentioned, interventions with victims often overlook elements of abusive or offending behaviors. While the majority of clients

Table 7–3
The Long-Term Effects of Abuse

Dynamics	Possible Effects	Behavioral Clues
I can't trust my experience of the abuse: "It only happened once"; "It was discipline"; "I didn't stop it"		
Secrecy	Minimization	Disconnected
Stigmatization/blaming the victim:	Making excuses	Unable to remember
Ignored	Dissociation/trance	Shutdown of feelings
Told to forget it	Rationalizing	Phobias
Told it was made up	Denial/forgetting	Fear of dark
Child's reality twisted	Becoming controlling	Rigid control of thoughts
Feelings expressed were disregarded or made fun of	Developing individual reaction to pain	Depression
Afraid of abuser/child threatened	Aggression/acting out	High pain tolerance
	Using chemicals	Anxiety response to any pain
Whoever I am, it will never be enough: "I hate myself"; "I don't deserve it"		
Abuse humiliating	Have low self-esteem	Self-blaming
Taught not to value self	Feel shameful	Self-destructive
Told you'll never succeed, called stupid, or told you're only good for sex	Lack sense of importance, personal worth, or competence	Cutting
Body objectified	Feel worthless	Suicidal
	Come to believe you don't deserve to be taken care of, deserve abuse	Depressed
	Blame self for abuse	Shameful
	Have self-doubt	
	See self as different and not as good	
People who love you hurt you; all relationships are abusive: "What I want in a relationship doesn't count"		
Betrayal	Relationship problems	Lack of trust
Unmet needs as child		Isolation
Trust manipulated		Codependence
Lack of support/protection		Confusion of sex and intimacy
Give up self to be loved		Repeatedly picking abusive partners
Intimacy sexualized		Overtolerant of abuse
		Passive/dependent
		Responsive to needs of others
The world is a dangerous place: "It's not worth trying"		
Powerless in abuse; no choices	Define self externally	Passive/controlling
Dependent on others' goodwill	See self as victim	No active choice making
Victimizer's needs and feelings imposed on victim	Distrust own feelings	Helpless
Attempts to protect self fail		Addicted/compulsive/codependent
		Cannot identify own needs, wants, or feelings

Table 7–3 (Continued)

Dynamics	Possible Effects	Behavioral Clues
Sex is a means of control, power, or hurt: "My sexual needs/feelings don't matter"		
Pairing of force, shame, and hurt with sexual development	Confuse love, intimacy, and sex	Block sexual needs/feelings
		Sexual aversion/dysfunction
	See desire as dangerous	Sexual compulsion
No sexual boundaries	Sexualize relationships	Promiscuity
Rewarded for sexual behavior inappropriate to age	Learn to disconnect from sexual feelings	Use sex to control
		Perpetrator
Intimacy sexualized	See sex as giving in/being forced	Poor body image
		Sadomasochistic
Introduced to sex on adult's timetable; no chance to explore sex naturally		Unable to set sex limits
		Problems pacing/initiating
		Sex only when using chemicals
Who I am in the world doesn't matter: "I don't know where I stop and the other person begins"		
Double bind: give up self to be loved	Boundary problems	Lack of sense of self as separate
Role reversal: who is the adult?		Boundary confusion
Repeated invasion of privacy, physical space, emotions, and sexual autonomy		

may not have histories of overt abuse, many will exhibit hurtful or passive-aggressive patterns of behavior (Evans 1987). These include attacking others when they feel shameful or blamed, inappropriate expressions of anger, attempts to hurt others or get even, acting like a bully, disregarding others' boundaries, setting others up to be hurt, using sex manipulatively or to get control, or purposely interfering with others' needs (figure 7–3). In the present phase in the abuse recovery group, therapists routinely point out abuselike behaviors and encourage members to evaluate patterns of these behaviors.

In the later stages of this phase, clients are asked to determine which behavioral difficulties will require further intervention and treatment. At this point, specific observations and direct advice from group members and the therapists are appropriate. Sex therapy, codependence treatment, eating disorders intervention, assertiveness training, and self-defense classes are the most common referral recommendations made. As always, the client may choose to bypass this advice or make other decisions.

At this same point, the respective group member is encouraged to evaluate his or her support system and ongoing needs for support following completion of the group. Where appropriate, members may join incest support or recovery groups or initiate new or more intimate connections with other abuse recovery members or friends in the community. This concluding element usually marks the transition to the future phase.

Figure 7–2. An Inventory of Victim Behavior: Self-Assessment in Preparation for Making Changes in Your Life

To help you in your personal inventory process, we provide the following list of victim behaviors and attitudes. Check those that are familiar to you and add any others of which you may be aware. No one is completely free of all of these behaviors; there is no need to shame yourself for having some of them.

Self-esteem

_____ Feeling as though you're bad, good for nothing, or defective

_____ Almost always not believing good things others tell you

_____ Needing to try harder or do better to make up for feeling bad or no good

_____ Regularly feeling down or depressed

_____ Self-cutting, self-abusive, or self-destructive

Sexual behaviors

_____ Afraid of or not interested in sex

_____ Problems responding to partner

_____ Difficulties getting/being turned on (aroused)

_____ Lack of sexual satisfaction with current/previous partner(s)

_____ Problems having orgasms (especially females)

_____ Not liking your body parts or sexual parts

_____ Confusing sex with love

_____ Having very strong reactions to certain sex acts

_____ Feeling like sex is dirty

_____ Sexualizing all relationships

_____ Mixing sex, affection, anger, power, and violence

_____ Feeling out of body during sex

General behavior

_____ Dreams or night terrors of being sexually abused

_____ Blocking out some time periods in early years

_____ Fear of being alone in the dark

_____ Sensitive to gagging or swallowing

_____ Unexplained anxiety attacks, bouts of crying, or fearfulness

Abusive/addictive behaviors

_____ Promiscuity

_____ Prostitution

_____ Drug/alcohol abuse or addiction

_____ Compulsive/addictive sexual behaviors

_____ Eating disorders

Boundary problems
_____ Fear of losing control
_____ Telling all
_____ Being sexually impulsive
_____ Having trouble stating needs, wants, and feelings
_____ Letting others walk all over you
_____ Talking on a close level on the first meeting
_____ Letting people go on too long doing or saying something that bothers you before stopping them
_____ Accepting food, gifts, touches, sex, and so on that you don't want
_____ Wearing too much or too little clothing for the time of the year

Assertiveness and self-care
_____ Giving in a lot; not standing up for yourself
_____ Aggressive behavior; bullying
_____ Becoming an abuser
_____ Feeling as though others dump on you or take advantage of you
_____ Giving too much without receiving from others

Relationships
_____ Choosing abusive partners over and over
_____ Becoming physically violent or verbally abusive when upset
_____ Putting trust in the wrong people
_____ Choosing partners who make you feel needed
_____ Becoming a martyr in the relationship
_____ Excusing the other person and blaming yourself for things that hurt you
_____ Always being understanding and forgiving
_____ Feeling isolated and lonely in the relationship
_____ Clinging
_____ Experiencing trouble trusting your own reactions, thoughts, and feelings
_____ Not expressing your needs and wants
_____ Rigid controlling of partner

Anger and rage
_____ Fear of becoming rageful
_____ Constant feelings of anger or rage that are overdone or inappropriate
_____ Ongoing abusiveness toward others
_____ Manipulative behavior instead of direct behavior toward others
_____ Cycles of anger and then helplessness/depression
_____ Anger toward all men or all women
_____ Sadomasochism that is based on feelings of anger, control, or power

Figure 7–3. Forms of Abusive Behavior

Self-abuse

_____ Cutting, burning, or mutilation

_____ Self-neglect, poor self-care, or withholding necessities from self

_____ Self-destructive acts

_____ Setting self up to be abused

_____ Sexual activities hurtful or demeaning to self

_____ _____

_____ _____

Abuse to others

_____ Ignoring/disrespecting others' boundaries

_____ Acting suggestively or using body position in inappropriate circumstances

_____ Setting people up to be hurt

_____ Withholding support, love, or affection out of anger, hurt, or power

_____ Manipulating others to get needs met

_____ Passive-aggressive or other indirect expressions of anger

_____ Making sexual jokes or using put-downs

_____ Treating others like objects

_____ Forcing or manipulating sex

_____ Using power to be sexual

_____ Engaging in sexual acts that involve control or rage

_____ Being a bully

_____ Not attending to needs of significant others

_____ Blaming or getting angry when shameful

_____ Getting needs met via indirect means

_____ Throwing things, making threats, or trapping another person

_____ Using physical abuse

_____ Using sexual abuse

_____ Using emotional abuse

_____ Attacking others to feel safe

_____ Getting even

_____ Interfering with other's needs

_____ _____

_____ _____

Table 7–4
Healing Abuse: Dynamics and Processes

Dynamic	Old Coping Response	Healing	Escalation Relapse
Pain internalized	Shut down	Reduce denial/ minimizing Share the pain	Use chemicals Exhibit compulsive behavior Offend Deny/hide pain Dissociate
Powerlessness/lack of choices	Controlling Passivity	Reclaim power Make choices Modify victim behaviors Evaluate and establish boundaries	Set self up to be abused Set loose/vague boundaries Tolerate abuse
Secrecy Shame, blaming, or scapegoating Fear abandonment or betrayal	Isolation Suspiciousness Lack of trust	Connect with others Share the secret	Have low self-esteem Be self-destructive Be depressed Be suicidal Withdraw
Intimacy sexualized Sexual boundaries invaded Sex paired with hurt, pain, or force	Block sexual feelings Dissociate	Set sexual boundaries Reclaim body/ sexuality Learn to connect love and sex Stop self-destructive/ compulsive sex	Return to compulsive sex Set loose sexual boundaries Offend Become asexual

Future Phase. For most individuals, the future phase is usually brief and very specific (average one to two sessions). Members are given handouts on healing abuse and relapse issues (table 7–4) and a summary of Gil's (1988) indicators of resolution of abuse issues (table 7–5) to enable them to review their goal status and progress, needs for further treatment and support, and relapse signals. Discussion and feedback from other members on these issues during group time is encouraged. In their final session, graduating members are asked to reflect on and celebrate changes made, receive encouragement from others, and say good-bye.

Conclusion

In the past several years, the Abuse Recovery Model has been used and adapted for use with a variety of individuals recovering from child sexual abuse and other forms of abuse. These groups have been found to be highly effective in helping individuals work through intrusive abuse material, connect with emotional content, clarify the impact of the abuse, and make

Table 7–5
Indicators of Resolution of Abuse Issues

Indicators that abuse is worked through and integrated
  Able to manage trauma in realistic way
    Experiences pain or loss that is raised
    Sees event accurately
    Does not feel unrealistically responsible
    Understands that trauma happened in the past
  No longer feels permanently immobilized by memory of the event
  Does not feel need to repeat the event (victim behavior, setting self up to be abused, choosing abusive partners)
  Feels in charge of life and able to make decisions
  Does not have regular intrusion of thoughts or nightmares related to the trauma
  Feels worthwhile, has something to offer, deserves good things
  Has grieved the loss of childhood and parents who were not ideal
  Has developed tools to manage depression
  Able to take care of self and yet depends on others when needs to
  Knows how to take care of own needs in a healthy way
  Able to express all feelings
  Has healthy support people

Indicators that trauma is not worked through and integrated
  Unable to process trauma in a healthy way
    Avoids thinking or talking about the trauma
    Cannot stand having feelings connected with the trauma
    Feels controlled, flooded, or trapped by abuse memories
    Feels rageful or victimized when remembering the past abuse
  Feels as though the past makes it impossible to live in the present
  Repeats patterns like the old abuse; tolerates abuse in present life
  Feels controlled, helpless, or victimized most of the time
  Sees no choices for self
  Abuse continues to affect current life (friendships, work, relationships, and so on)

Indicators of overly defensive managing of abuse trauma
  Avoids situations that seem like old abuse
    Controls exposure to similar feelings
    Avoids thinking about the abuse
  Pushes down or ignores feelings about the past abuse
  Uses defenses out of fear of becoming overwhelmed by feelings of abuse

From E. Gil, *Treatment of Adult Survivors of Childhood Abuse* (Walnut Creek, California: Launch Press, 1988), pp. 113–128.

behavioral changes. The short-term nature of the group encourages a hopeful yet realistic self-assessment of the abuse and its impact. A variety of structural elements are balanced with a distinct emphasis on empowerment and health so that members are able to move quickly beyond a victim stance in the world. Male members in these groups respond particularly well to this balanced emphasis and flexibility in approach, which allow them to capitalize on their need to take control and proceed in an action-oriented mode (Bruckner and Johnson 1987).

References

Altermatt, K. 1985. "Healing versus Treatment: Redefining Therapeutic Intervention with Adult Female Incest Survivors." *The MN Exchange* 8 (no. 1): 1–2.

American Psychiatric Association. 1987. *Quick Reference to the Diagnostic Criteria from DSM III R.* Washington, D.C.

Becker, J.V., L.J. Skinner, G.G. Abel, and E.C. Tracy. 1982. "Incidence and Types of Sexual Dysfunction in Rape and Incest Victims." *Journal of Sex and Marital Therapy* 8 (no. 1): 65–74.

Benward, J., and J. Densen-Gerber. 1975. "Incest as a Causative Factor in Antisocial Behavior: An Exploratory Study." *Contemporary Drug Problems* 4: 323–341.

Blake-White, J., and C. Kline. 1985. "Treating the Dissociative Process in Adult Victims of Childhood Incest." *Social Casework* (September): 394–402.

Brown, J. 1987. "Shame, Sexuality, and Intimacy." In *Chemical Dependency and Intimacy Dysfunction,* edited by Eli Coleman. New York: Haworth Press.

Bruckner, D., and P. Johnson. 1987. "Treatment for Adult Male Victims of Childhood Sexual Abuse." *Social Casework* (February): 81–87.

Burgess, A.W., and L.L. Holmstrom. 1974. "Rape Trauma Syndrome." *American Journal of Psychiatry* 131 (no. 9): 981–986.

Carmen, E., P. Rieker, and T. Mills. 1984. "Victim of Violence and Psychiatric Illness." *American Journal of Psychiatry* 141 (no. 3): 378–383.

Coleman, E. 1987. "Child Physical and Sexual Abuse among Chemically Dependent Individuals." *Journal of Chemical Dependency Treatment* 1 (no. 1): 27–38.

Courtois, C. 1980. "Studying and Counseling Women with Past Incest Experience." *Victimology: An International Journal* 5 (no. 2/4): 322–334.

Covington, S., and J. Kohen. 1987. "Women, Alcohol, and Sexuality." *Journal of Chemical Dependency Treatment* 1 (no. 1): 41–56.

Dembo, R., M. Dertke, S. Borders, M. Washburn, and J. Schmeidler. 1988. "The Relationship between Physical and Sexual Abuse and Tobacco, Alcohol, and Illicit Drug Use among Youths in a Juvenile Detention Center." *International Journal of the Addictions* 23 (no. 4): 351–378.

Donaldson, M. 1983. "Incest Victims Years After: Methods and Techniques for Treatment." Paper presented to the National Association of Social Workers, Washington, D.C., November.

Evans, S. 1987. "Making the Skeletons Dance." Paper presented at the Jamaica Conference on Victims and Victimizers, Runaway Bay, Jamaica, February 29.

Evans, S., and S. Schaefer. 1987. "Incest and Chemically Dependent Women: Treatment Implications." *Journal of Chemical Dependency Treatment* 1 (no. 1): 141–173.

Ewalt, J., and D. Crawford. 1981. "Posttraumatic Stress Syndrome." *Current Psychiatric Therapies* 20: 145–153.

Fairbanks, J., and R. Nicholson. 1987. "Theoretical and Empirical Issues in the Treatment of Post-traumatic Stress Disorder in Vietnam Veterans." *Journal of Clinical Psychology* 43 (no. 1): 44–55.

Feldman-Summers, S., P.E. Gordon, and J.R. Meagher. 1979. "The Impact of Rape on Sexual Satisfaction." *Journal of Abnormal Psychology* 88 (no. 1): 101–105.

Finkelhor, D. 1981. "The Sexual Abuse of Boys." *Victimology: An International Journal* 6 (no. 1/4): 76–84.

————. 1984. *Child Sexual Abuse.* New York: Macmillan.

Finkelhor, D., and A. Browne. 1985. "The Traumatic Impact of Child Sexual Abuse: A Conceptualization." *American Journal of Orthopsychiatry* 55 (no. 4): 530–541.

Fritz, G., K. Stoll, and N. Wagner. 1981. "A Comparison of Males and Females Who Were Sexually Molested as Children." *Journal of Sex and Marital Therapy* 7 (no. 1): 54–59.

Gelinas, D.J. 1983. "The Persisting, Negative Effects of Incest." *Psychiatry* 46 (November): 312–332.

Giarretto, H. 1978. "Humanistic Treatment of Father-Daughter Incest." *Journal of Humanistic Psychology* 18 (no. 4): 59–76.

Gil, E. 1988. *Treatment of Adult Survivors of Childhood Abuse.* Walnut Creek, California: Launch Press.

Gold, E. 1986. "Long-Term Effects of Sexual Victimization in Childhood: An Attributional Approach." *Journal of Consulting and Clinical Psychology* 54 (no. 4): 471–475.

Hooker, B. 1985. *Rx for Victims: A Clinician's Guide to Recognizing and Treating Victim Behavior.* Dallas: Thompson Publishing.

Horowitz, M.J. 1986. *Stress Response Syndromes.* Northvale, New Jersey: Jason Aronson.

Horowitz, M.J., and N.B. Kaltreider. 1979. "Brief Therapy of the Stress Response Syndrome." *Psychiatric Clinics of North America* 2 (no. 2): 365–377.

Hunter, M. 1989. "Use of the Terms "Victim" and "Survivor" in Stages of Grief Commonly Seen in Recovery from Sex Abuse." Paper presented at the Male Survivor: Assessment and Treatment of Male Sexual Abuse Victims conference, Atlanta, September 22–23.

Kaufman, A., P. Divasto, R. Jackson, D. Voorhees, and I. Christy. 1980. "Male Rape Victims: Noninstitutionalized Assault." *American Journal of Psychiatry* 137 (no. 2): 221–223.

Kaufman, I., A.L. Peck, and C.K. Tagiuri. 1984. "The Family Constellation and Overt Incestuous Relations between Father and Daughter." *American Journal of Orthopsychiatry* 24: 266–277.

Lindberg, F., and L. Distad. 1985. "Post-traumatic Stress Disorders in Women Who Experienced Childhood Incest." *Child Abuse and Neglect* 9: 329–334.

Listig, N., J. Dresser, S. Spellman, and T. Murray. 1966. "Incest: A Family Group Survival Pattern." *Archives of General Psychiatry* 14: 31–40.

Lukianowicz, N. 1972. "Incest. Part 1: Paternal Incest." *British Journal of Psychiatry* 120: 301–313.

Nasjleti, M. 1980. "Suffering in Silence: The Male Incest Victim." *Child Welfare* 59 (no. 5): 269–275.

Olson, P. 1990. "The Sexual Abuse of Boys: A Study of the Long-Term Psychological Impact." In *The Sexually Abused Male,* vol. 1, edited by Mic Hunter. Lexington, Massachusetts: Lexington Books.

Rosenfeld, A. 1979. "Incidence of a History of Incest among 18 Female Psychiatric Patients." *Journal of Psychiatry* 136 (no. 6): 791–795.

Sandberg, D. 1986. "The Child-Abuse-Delinquency Connection: Evolution of a Therapeutic Community." *Journal of Psychoactive Drugs* 18 (no. 3): 215–220.

Seligman, M.E.P. 1975. *Helplessness: On Depression, Development, and Death.* San Francisco: Freeman and Company.

Shapiro, S. 1987. "Self-Mutilation and Self-Blame in Incest Victims." *American Journal of Psychotherapy* 41 (no. 1): 46–54.

Spiegel, D. 1984. "Multiple Personality as a Post-traumatic Stress Disorder." *Psychiatric Clinics of North America* 7 (no. 1): 101–110.

Sterne, M., S. Schaefer, and S. Evans. 1984. "Women's Sexuality and Alcoholism." In *Alcoholism: Analysis of a World-Wide Problem,* edited by P. Golding, 421–425. Lancaster, England: MTP Press.

Sutherland, S., and D. Scherl. 1970. "Patterns of Response among Victims of Rape." *American Journal of Orthopsychiatry* 40 (no. 3): 503–511.

Symonds, M. 1976. "The Rape Victim: Psychological Patterns of Response." *American Journal of Psychoanalysis* 36: 27–34.

Tsai, M., S. Feldman-Summers, and M. Edgar. 1979. "Childhood Molestation: Variables Related to Differential Impacts on Psychosexual Functioning in Adult Women." *Journal of Abnormal Psychology* 88 (no. 4): 407–417.

Tsai, M., and N.N. Wagner. 1978. "Therapy Groups for Women Sexually Molested as Children." *Archives of Sexual Behavior* 7 (no. 5): 417–427.

Turner, S., and F. Colao. 1985. "Alcoholism and Sexual Assault: A Treatment Approach for Women Exploring Both Issues." *Alcoholism Treatment Quarterly* 2 (no. 1): 91–103.

Van Buskirk, S.S., and C.F. Cole. 1983. "Characteristics of Eight Women Seeking Therapy for the Effects of Incest." *Psychotherapy: Theory, Research and Practice* 20 (no. 4): 503–514.

Van der Kolk, B., M. Greenberg, H. Boyd, and J. Krystal. 1986. "Inescapable Shock, Neurotransmitters, and Addiction to Trauma: Toward a Psychology of Post-raumatic Stress." *Biological Psychiatry* 20: 314–325.

8

The Role of the Nonoffending Parent When the Incest Victim Is Male

Anne M. Gresham

In working with incest victims, both male and female, I have consistently been impressed with the importance of the nonoffending parent's role. Victims return for additional therapy years after completion of earlier therapy saying, "Something is still wrong?" When a full history of their lives and previous treatment is taken, the issue most taken often uncovered the impact of the nonoffending parent. My experience as a therapist has shown that when the incest victim is male, his issue often is totally overlooked by treatment professionals. In addition, it is common that the nonoffending parent of a male victim was more likely to have been abusive in other than sexual ways. This may be common for female incest victims as well, but I have noticed that it seems to occur more often among male victims.

In reviewing the literature, it is obvious that little emphasis has been placed on investigating and studying nonoffending parents, even in father-daughter incest situations. When this aspect of abuse has been studied, there has been much confusion and controversy. There is almost no discussion of the impact on male victims, nor is there any mention of differences between male and female victims. It is my hope that the therapeutic community will become more aware of these issues in the treatment of clients and that researchers will be challenged to investigate this further.

In this chapter, I refer to the nonoffending parent as female and to the offender as male. This is for convenience in writing and in no way limits the possibilities of males being nonoffending parents and females being offenders.

The Mother's Role

Numerous authors agree that the nonoffending parent plays a very important part in setting up the sexually abusive environment and in the recovery process for the victim (Justice and Justice 1979; Gelinas 1983; Spencer 1978; Meilselman 1978; Finkelhor 1979; Forward and Buck 1979; Maisch 1972; Weinberg 1955; Cormier, Kennedy, and Sancowicz 1973; Lukianowicz 1972; Kaufman, Peck, and Tagiuri 1954; Sholevar 1973; Garrett and Wright 1975; Summit and Kryso 1978; Walker 1984; Goodwin, McCarty, and DiVasto 1981; Goodwin, Cormier, and Owen 1983; and Vander Mey and Neff 1986). The mother in father-daughter or grandfather-granddaughter incest families is described as dependent, fearful, and viewing herself as inadequate to provide for her family or herself. Vander Mey and Neff (1986) state, "In fact, previous childhood experiences of mothers may be as important as the father's childhood milieu in predisposing a child to a high risk of incestuous victimization" (p. 61).

In most cases, the mother in this family was physically and/or sexually abused in her family of origin. This abuse has led the woman to see herself as helpless, worthless, inadequate, incapable, needy, and alone. Her needs have never been adequately met, and she believes that the only way they will ever be met is through another person—specifically, a man. She may remain passive throughout her life and submit to her husband's every need and desire to ensure that he will "keep her." She believes that she could not make it on her own, has no support system, and has no idea how to find support. Another scenario is the woman whose sense of inadequacy is met by marrying a very passive, immature man who needs her to take care of him. This gives her a sense of power and control over her life and others'.

In either case, the woman eventually may withdraw emotionally from her husband out of fear or anger, creating a situation in which she cannot meet his needs. He may then turn to their children. She cannot acknowledge his new dependence on their children because doing so will require her to confront her husband and take the risk of abuse, rejection, and further pressure. She already knows that she is inadequate to handle this, so she ignores, covers up, and represses her feelings and the facts. By the time the signs become blatant or the child reveals the incest, the mother has become emotionally unavailable to the family. She may deny the abuse, take the father's side, and reject the child. The mother in this case may contribute to the onset of the incest and its continuation, but she is not responsible for the abuse. It is the offender who touches the child.

Although this description presents a general idea of what is seen most often as the role of the mother in father-daughter incest situations, there are exceptions to the rule. Many mothers acknowledge the abuse immediately and handle it well. Others may be directly involved in the sexual abuse and are collaborative perpetrators. Little has been written about the family of the male sexual abuse victim. In what types of families are male children sexually abused, and what role does the nonoffending parent play? Looking at the types of offenders who are likely to abuse males may give some clues.

Types of Child Molesters and Rapists

Burgess et al. (1978) delineate two types of child molesters. The *fixated offender* is one whose primary sexual orientation is toward children. He identifies closely with the child victim and psychologically lowers his age to the child's, becoming a playmate of the child. He usually is not married, or if he is, he is married out of convenience or for protection. He is characterized by an arrested sociosexual maturity. He prefers male victims.

The *regressed offender* is one whose primary sexual orientation is toward age-mates, and sexual attraction to children is considered a temporary lapse of control due to external, situational influences. The regressed offender picks a victim, elevates her to adult status, and may even court her. This offender is usually married or has a long-term significant relationship. He prefers female victims.

Groth (1979) also delineates three types of rapists, which include child rapists. The difference between a molester and a rapist is aggression. The molester usually seduces or persuades his victims, whereas the rapist assaults them.

The first type of rapist is the *anger rapist*. He usually batters his victims in addition to abusing them sexually. His violence is retaliatory against some real or perceived wrong that he has suffered. A child victim is chosen to "get even" with an adult the child is related to or to "teach the child a lesson."

The second type of rapist is the *power rapist*. The offender uses whatever force or threat, including weapons, he can to gain the victim's cooperation. The victim may not be physically injured. This type of rapist chooses his victims based on vulnerability. He uses his power over his victims to cover up deep feelings of insecurity. He is in control.

The third type of rapist is the *sadistic rapist*. In this case, the physical force used to control victims is sexually arousing to the offender. The sexual act may be ritualized, and the victim could be tortured. He chooses his victims based on their symbolic nature—for example, a child who reminds the offender of himself as a child. In fact, child victims are usually the same sex as the offender.

According to Groth's typologies, the types of offenders who are most likely to choose male victims are: the fixated molester, the sadistic rapist, the anger rapist, and the power rapist. Groth states that of the five types of offenders, these four are the most dysfunctional and the least receptive to intervention.

The fixated molester is seldom married, but when he is, the marriage is for protection and/or convenience. The rapists may or may not be married. The obvious question is "What type of personal dynamics must a spouse have to maintain a relationship with an offender who may choose his son as a victim." In my clinical experience, I have found that the spouse must be equally dysfunctional and probably have been raised to accept violence and abuse as inevitable. She may be a person who also has the potential for acting out violence, who has less ability to be intimate in any relationship, and who may be even more withdrawn from their children. The nonoffending parent dynamics described above for father-daughter incest also seem to apply to father-son incest, but the dysfunction seems more severe.

Treatment

In the treatment setting, therapists need to ask questions about the behaviors of the nonoffending parent. Too often it seems that the therapy focuses on the referring offense, and other potentially damaging abuses may be over-looked. Even in father-daughter incest cases, the daughters often have more anger toward their mothers for issues of nonprotection than they do toward their fathers. This seems natural when considering how unpredictable, uncertain, and unsupportive their mother's behaviors have been. At least the victim knows what to expect from the offender. How much more devastating it is when the nonoffending parent also is abusing the victim.

The first step in treatment of the abuse victim is to believe him or her. One of the first and most devastating problems is that the nonoffending parent does not believe the victim. Even if the parent does believe, he or she may quickly side with the offender against the child. Some nonoffending parents do, of course, believe, and the therapist should not jump to conclusions too quickly. If the nonoffending parent also is abusing the child in some way, the likelihood of the parent's supporting the child is seriously diminished.

Another issue for therapists to address with victims is the guilt, shame, and responsibility the victim feels for causing the problem. Offenders often directly or indirectly blame the child for the abuse. In any case, depending on the age of the child, he will naturally take responsibility for the abuse due to normal developmental issues. The message the victim needs to hear is that he is not responsible for the abuse. That message is particularly effective when it comes from the nonoffending parent, but when that parent also is abusing the child, this message must come from the therapist.

The next issue victims need to address in their recovery is secrecy. Offenders encourage their victims to keep the secret, on pain of some undesirable consequence. Nonoffending parents often support the principle of secretiveness by promoting a "keep it in the family" rule and by modeling a "keep it to yourself" attitude. The victim's recovery process must include the discovery that in telling the secret and opening himself up to others, he can gain intimacy instead of abuse. In my experience, the turning point toward recovery often occurs when the victim's nonoffending parent truly hears the victim's story, feelings, and thoughts and when that parent acknowledges also having feelings that have been kept secret. If that parent also is abusing the victim, this alliance may not be possible.

One of the last issues to address in therapy is powerlessness. The victim needs to learn that he can have power over his life and that others do not control him. He must come to a point of understanding that not everyone will abuse him, and that if he says no, most people will respect his wishes. If a victim has at least one parent with whom he can ally himself, he can have a safe home base from which to venture out. When both parents are abusive, that safe base is particularly hard to find.

When the victim is a child undergoing family-based treatment, it is generally accepted that it takes approximately twice as long (two years) to treat the offender than it does to treat the classic nonoffending parent. This implies that offenders are more dysfunctional and/or more difficult to treat than nonoffending parents. Victims, depending on their age, generally spend less time in treatment than do nonoffending parents, implying that their issues are more easily dealt with.

There are several reasons why this occurs. One is that the victim may have one supportive parent. The victim needs to know that someone is behind him, and when he knows that person is his parent, his recovery can progress very quickly. If that other parent also is an offender, treatment for the parents may take a very long time, and the victim may have much more difficulty because of the wait. The recovery process also will be jeopardized by the fact that the victim has never had anyone close who was not abusive, and the safe home base may never be found.

Further Research

Further research on the role of the nonoffending parent is strongly suggested. This research will aid in treatment of all incestuous families. Research on any differences in the role of the nonoffending parent for male victims versus female victims also will be valuable. Are male victims of incest, as opposed to female victims, more likely to have two abusive parents? What effect does having two abusive parents have on victims? Are there differences in the treatment needs of the entire family when the victim is male? These and other questions must be answered. It is my hope that this chapter will lead to such research, answering as many questions as possible and making us aware of the questions we may not be asking our clients.

References

Cormier, Bruno N., Miriam Kennedy, and Jadwiga Sancowicz. 1973. "Psychodynamics of Father-Daughter Incest." In *Deviance and the Family,* edited by Clifton D. Bryant and J. Gipson Wells, 97–116. Philadelphia: F.A. Davis.

Finkelhor, David. 1979. *Sexually Victimized Children.* New York: Free Press.

Forward, Susan, and Craig Buck. 1978. *Betrayal of Innocence: Incest and Its Duration.* New York: Penguin.

Garrett, T.B., and Richard Wright. 1975. "Wives of Rapists and Incest Offenders." *Journal of Sex Research* 2 (May): 149–157.

Gelinas, Denise J. 1983. "The Persisting Negative Effects of Incest." *Psychiatry* 46 (November): 312–132.

Goodwin, Jean, Lawrence Cormier, and John Owen. 1983. "Grandfather-Granddaughter Incest: A Trigenerational View." *Child Abuse and Neglect* 7: 163–170.

Goodwin, Jean, Teresita McCarty, and Peter DiVasto. 1981. "Prior Incest in Mothers of Abused Children." *Child Abuse and Neglect* 5: 87–95.

Burgess, Ann Wolbert, A. Nicholas Groth, Lynda Lytle Holmstrom, and Suzanne M. Sgroi. 1978. *Sexual Assault of Children and Adolescents.* Lexington, Massachusetts: Lexington Books.

———. 1979. *Men Who Rape.* New York: Plenum Press.

Justice, Blair, and Rita Justice. 1979. *The Broken Taboo: Sex in the Family.* New York: Human Sciences Press.

Kaufman, Irving, Alice L. Peck, and Consuelo K. Tagiuri. 1954. "The Family Constellation and Overt Incestuous Relations between Fathers and Daughters." *American Journal of Orthopsychiatry* 24: 266–279.

Lukianowicz, N. 1972. "Incest Part I: Paternal Incest." *British Journal of Sociology* 120 (March): 301–313.

Maisch, Herbert. 1972. *Incest.* New York: Stein & Day.

Meiselman, Karen. 1978. *Incest: A Psychological Study of Causes and Effects with Treatment Recommendations.* San Francisco: Jossey-Bass.

Sholevar, G. Pirooz. 1973. "A Family Therapist Looks at the Problem of Incest." *Bulletin of the American Academy of Psychiatry and the Law* 3 (March): 25–31.

Spencer, Joyce. 1978. "Father-Daughter Incest: A Clinical View from the Corrections Field." *Child Welfare* 57 (November): 585–587.

Summit, Roland, and JoAnn Kryso. 1978. "Sexual Abuse of Children: A Clinical Spectrum." *American Journal of Orthopsychiatry* 48 (April): 237–251.

Vander Mey, Brenda J., and Ronald L. Neff. 1986. *Incest as Child Abuse: Research and Applications.* New York: Praeger Publishers.

Walker, Lenore E. 1984. *The Battered Woman Syndrome.* New York: Springer Publishing Company.

Weinberg, S. Kirson. 1955. *Incest Behavior.* New York: Citadel Press.

9
Healing Abuse in Gay Men: The Group Component

Stephen Parker

> There is more than sex to having a gay heart.
>
> —*Group Client*

T his chapter examines an approach to working with gay male survivors in outpatient group therapy as an important component of their total recovery program. It first focuses on how a minority sexual orientation affects the dynamics of abuse and the recovery from abuse. It then explores the effect of orientation on a model for group therapy. Finally, it discusses the experiences of a three-year-old ongoing therapy group for gay men with survivor issues.

The Limitations of Terminology

The term *victim* is not used in this chapter because of its limited utility as a concept in treatment. In my work, this term has proven to be disempowering as an identity label and invites dichotomizing of those traumatized by abuse into impossibly discrete victim and perpetrator categories. This begs the complexity of the question in ways discussed in chapter 5 of this book. The term *survivor* is used here for reasons explored in chapter 3.

Victimization is broadly defined in this chapter. Too often the impact of trauma is measured by the presumed objective severity of the event rather than its subjective impact. As Egendorf (1986) notes, "Events are not experiences unless a human being is present, not just as another factor in the equation but as the essential requisite" (p. 120). The sexual component is often not the most damaging component of a traumatic experience, although I have observed a predisposition among many to assume that sexual abuse is per se more serious than verbal or emotional abuse. This will vary greatly depending on the person experiencing the event. My compromise is to limit the literature review to sexual abuse and later in the chapter to make broader observations about victimization that apply to sexual as well as other forms of abuse.

Another terminological problem involves how the use of the identity label *gay* begs the fabulous complexity of the orientation question. The word is used here in the sense of a self-identification based on a man's lifelong subjective experience and not as an objective assessment of the type suggested by Klein (1978) or Coleman (1988). As a result, the terms *gay* and *bisexual* are conflated to some degree. This reflects the fact that making a distinction has not been an issue in the group's work rather than any argument that these terms are interchangeable. In a technical sense, they are not. To follow Kinsey's figures (Kinsey 1948), roughly half the general male population has a lifelong orientation that is entirely heterosexual, and 4 percent have an orientation that is totally homosexual. If approximately 10 percent of this population calls itself gay, then from a technical standpoint, many on both sides of this false dichotomy are fudging the evidence.

Finally, I welcome the demise of the term *homophobia* and use the clearer concept *heterosexism* in its place. The former does not work much like a phobia, and constructing the concept in this way ignores the vital dimension of the misuse of power informed by prejudice. Functionally, the phenomenon is much more akin to racism or sexism than to any *DSM III* (American Psychiatric Association 1980) disorder. The resultant transformation of "internalized homophobia" into "internalized shame due to heterosexism" makes the process clear and understandable. The reader is referred to Neisen (1990) for a detailed discussion.

Literature Review

The literature on gender differences among those traumatized by abuse is a recent phenomenon that grew out of a reassessment of psychological thinking and science spurred by the women's movement (Brown 1988). It became clear that some parts of psychological theory did not coincide with women's deeply subjective experience of their lives. Men's complementary awareness of the shortcomings of generic and gender-blind theories has been slower to develop. Browne and Finkelhor (1986) note the lack of empirical work on the incidence and emotional sequelae of sexual abuse in males. (This is updated by Urquiza and Keating in chapter 4 of volume 1 of this book.) If we add to this specialization of emphasis the consideration of sexual orientation, the literature practically disappears.

Briere et al. (1988) compared the symptomatology of forty males molested as children to that of forty females on standardized scales measuring dissociation, anxiety, depression, anger, and sleep disturbance. They also compared the men and women regarding suicidality and ratings of the extent of abuse. The results indicated no gender differences on ratings of suicidality or on the standardized scales, but the male clients obtained these scores based on less extensive abuse. One tentative inference made was that sexual abuse may be somewhat more traumatic for men than for women.

In his account of a group for thirteen male incest survivors, Singer (1989) describes low self-esteem, substance abuse, self-destructive behavior, intimacy dysfunction, and "sexually related issues" (p. 469). All the clients had histories of depression with suicidal ideation, and many recognized how their experiences had set up a pattern of subsequent revictimization. Lew (1988) also includes a long list of symptoms in his book (pp. 25–26), although the book's purpose as a guide for recovery precludes a quantitative focus on or differentiation among gay, straight, and bisexual clients (see also Hunter 1990).

Anderson (1982) discusses the impact of same-sex assault on gay male victims in terms of a redoubling of shame-bound isolation, denial, intensification of self-blame, and shame based on male-role expectations. He notes various anxiety reactions, including somatization, phobias, hypochondrial reactions, hypervigilance and scanning, chemical use and abuse, and retreat into asexuality. He also discusses depressive and self-destructive phenomena based on introverted rage. These seem to fit well with the profiles of both acute and delayed posttraumatic stress disorder (PTSD)

Gonsiorek (1989) observes the difficulties male survivors experience in understanding that they have been victimized. Many of these difficulties are based on male gender-role expectations. Because males are socialized to believe "that any power dynamic operates in their favor, they may have a high level of rationalization and denial that they are powerless and have been victimized" (p. 114). Furthermore, he observes that since men are likely to believe sex is a male prerogative, male survivors are likely to believe that any sexual activity was their choice, even when the activity happened in the context of therapy. The fact of victimization is ego-alien, as are the psychological effects, resulting in a double barrier of defense. Regarding the impact of orientation on these dynamics, Gonsiorek argues that heterosexual men may have greater difficulty recognizing sexual manipulation for the foregoing reasons. Gay men's responses, he hypothesizes, may be more like those of heterosexual women abused by male therapists, especially if they experienced manipulative sex during their coming out.

Myers (1989) describes a sample of male sexual assault victims, a majority of whom (8 of 14) identified themselves as homosexual (with one bisexual man). He notes the importance of repression, denial, and normalization as defenses. Four of the gay men blandly took the attitude "That's what you get for taking chances. . . . Life's an experience. All . . . sustained damage to their subjective sense of maleness," and nine were in some confusion about their orientation at intake. He attributes this confusion to "stereotypical mythology" about gay men (p. 205). All had problems with self-esteem; four of the gay men had distinctly distorted body images; and four men, three of whom were gay, had sexual dysfunctions diagnosed. Half (7 of 14) were markedly mistrustful of adult men generally. For most of these men, an assault was their first sexual experience and was perpetrated by someone they knew outside the family. Most were slow to realize their victimization. Myers does not compare the gay and bisexual men to his heterosexual clients along this dimension.

The Current Study

Quantitative Data

The present sample includes twenty-seven men, ages twenty-three to forty-six (mean age at entry was 31.9), who were included in a chart review of a therapy group for gay men with victim issues. Not included were two men who dropped out within two sessions. Twenty-three of our clients were white (85.2 percent), three were black (11.1 percent), and one was Oriental (3.7 percent). Most were from middle-class economic backgrounds; eight were from blue-collar or farm families. Table 9–1 lists the frequency of some of the men's symptoms. Table 9–2 describes the clients' histories of victimization.

The sample followed many of the symptom patterns described previously. Depression and anxiety in various forms were extremely common and often severe. Almost one-fifth of the sample had made multiple suicide attempts. The popularity and explanatory power of PTSD notwithstanding, only six

Table 9–1
Frequency of Current Historical Symptoms

Depression	20 (74.1%) (8 as major depression, 1 as bipolar disorder)
Anxiety	14 (51.9%) (5 as generalized anxiety disorder, 6 as posttraumatic stress disorder)
Dissociation	9 (33.3%)
Suicidal ideation	18 (66.7%) (at least one attempt: 7 [25.9%]; more than one attempt: 5 [18.6%])
Impatient psychiatric hospitalization (excluding chemical dependence treatment)	8 (29.6%)
Chemical dependence	14 (51.9%)
Chemical abuse and dependence	18 (66.7%)
Impulsive sexual acting out	9 (33.3%)
Eating disorders	3 (11.1%)
Violent behavior	3 (11.1%)
Sexual intrusion on others	5 (18.5%)
Impulsive or addictive behavior, all categories	22 (81.5%)

Table 9–2
Victimization History
(N = 27)

	Intrafamilial	Extrafamilial
Sexual	13 (48.17%)	5 (18.5%)
Physical	18 (66.7%)	5 (18.5%)
Verbal-emotional	25 (92.6%)	7 (31.8%)

of the group members carried this diagnosis. This is very similar to the percentage (3 of 14) in the sample described by Myers (1989, pp. 206–207). Impulsive and addictive behaviors were the largest complex of symptoms (81.5 percent), with over half of the group diagnosed as being chemically dependent (and recovering). Alcohol was the most frequent drug of choice, followed by Marijuana and cocaine. Interestingly, only a small number of this group had crossed the controversial line between victim and perpetrator. This undoubtedly reflects the self-selection implicit in a self-referred outpatient population. Those with greater histories of perpetration are more likely to be court-referred elsewhere. The men in this sample had experienced more self-victimization than victimization by others. Their histories revealed that their families were much more dangerous and damaging than the world outside their families.

Case History

The quantitative description of the sample can be augmented by the story of "Nick," a qualitative composite of the gay male survivors in our group. (All clinical vignettes in this chapter are composites representing no individual client but remaining true to general demographics, the level of traumatization, and the process of recovery.)

Nick was a thirty-seven-year-old divorced white man from a middle-class family who had surrendered custody of his children at the time of his divorce. He was a veteran of Vietnam and was referred by a veterans organization because of persistent relapses in his recoveries from chemical dependence and PTSD, which seemed clearly related to sexual issues. Nick was uncertain of his sexual orientation despite a long history of romantic and sexual involvements with men and relative boredom in his experiences with women. Recently, he had entered a pattern of intrusive cruising and anonymous sexual encounters at a college athletic facility and in sexually oriented bookstores. Simultaneously, he had experienced a surge of impulses to drink and admitted that not dealing with his sexuality seemed to be putting his sobriety at risk.

Nick entered the group admittedly terrified of being with gay men. His individual work with a gay male psychotherapist had convinced him that he needed this experiential data, though he feared seeing in others the stereotypes he always feared in himself. He often dissociated or suppressed his affective responses to the other men. Nick observed his own "poker face" as he talked, noting how much it belied his inner experience.

In the first few weeks, Nick began to tell the parts of his story that related to his struggles with staying sober and his sexual acting out. Since many others in the group shared these struggles, it provided Nick an opportunity to feel included and to begin processing his confusion about his orientation. Because of his internalized heterosexism, Nick did not believe intimate, loving sex between men was possible. Over time, this belief abated with surprising ease. It was then possible for Nick to admit that he had actually loved several of the men he had been involved with and that his avoidant or violent behavior with them served to put his affection for them at a distance. One night he noted with a grin that his confusion seemed silly to him now.

Nick risked disclosing his fear of striking his children in moments of intense frustration. He spoke about his mother's alcoholic rages and the beatings he took, sometimes with a two-by-four, to protect his siblings. He began to contract with members of our group and his Alcoholics Anonymous (AA) group to call them when his desperation approached unmanageability. Over several months, he developed a capacity to contain his rage and the impulsive or addictive behaviors that helped him medicate it away.

At this point, Nick began to identify strongly with other members' grief about the loss of their families and especially their fathers. By now, Nick was able to let his sadness and shame be seen and heard by others, and many grief issues began to surface. Some of these were familial, and some concerned his experiences in Vietnam.

More painful than the physical damage inflicted by his mother were his father's accusations that he deserved the beatings he received for being a "sissy." (Nick also had vague memories of sexual contact with his father, which he initially discounted.) This assault on his self-esteem prompted Nick to escape from his family at the first opportunity, at age fifteen. He lived on the streets for a time and finally decided that the military might make him the man he believed he could never make himself. This decision brought him to Vietnam, where he kept his homosexuality as secret as he, until now, had kept his veteran's status in the group. He told a story about a man with whom he had had a romantic and sexual relationship in his military unit. His partner was perceived as gay; Nick was not. He had always grieved his partner's death in combat. About a year earlier, he had overheard at a unit reunion that his partner had been killed by others in the unit because he was a "fag." By now, Nick was able to grieve with openness and intensity.

In the ensuing weeks, Nick began dating several people and experienced several disappointments. Each time, he experienced paroxysms of self-blame and self-criticism, with the inevitable impulses to act out sexually or use chemicals. The group kept him aware of what he had been doing differently and how they were seeing him change and give himself a better chance to get what he really wanted and needed. When he became angry in group, they gently challenged him to reach for the emotions behind the anger, and he was able to let them come. Twice he experienced from each side of a relationship his old pattern of preemptory rejection of his partner. This awareness allowed him to make amends to the other person and, more importantly, to himself.

He finally found himself in a relatively functional relationship. Whenever his trust in this new person proved well placed, his eyes would suddenly fill with tears of gratitude and an even clearer recognition of how much he had lost in his early years. He recognized how much he had internalized, especially his late father's contempt, and how he had kept it alive in his self-dialogue. Nick also began to let go of his rage at God for allowing such suffering to exist. He became better able to separate the spirituality that catalyzed his recovery from the institutionalized culture of heterosexism he had encountered in his religious training. This enabled Nick to feel a quiet, genuine pride in being male, gay, and a veteran.

The Dynamics of Abuse

The central proposition suggested by my clinical experience is that aspects of trauma that are inherently linked to a gay (or bisexual) male client's orientation cannot be healed unless and until that orientation has been adequately mirrored and affirmed in some primary empathic relationship. It is almost universally impossible for parents to provide that mirroring to a male child. When the mother is the primary caretaker, there may be mirroring of same-sex desires for a female child. Probably there is also greater shaping toward emotional merger. Male children are more likely to be shaped toward separation from a primary care giver, especially when the care giver is the father. Given this process and a father's likely internalized shame about any same-sex desires, appropriate mirroring is highly unlikely. The self-psychology of Heinz Kohut (1977), elaborated by Carmen De Monteflores (1986), provides some insight into how societal heterosexism becomes internalized in this way:

> Following the example of any minority child, what kind of empathy is possible from parents who perceive their own differences as deficiencies which are mirrored in their children? . . . These chronic narcissistic injuries may contribute to intrapsychic structural vulnerabilities in the emerging selves of children, so that a social problem [heterosexism] is perpetuated as a serious intrapsychic conflict. (De Monteflores 1986, 85)

Limit the essential component of a nuclear sense of self as gay—that is, that those inarticulate or unconscious desires constitute an acceptable or positively valued special difference—the person must repress, dissociate, split, or otherwise defend against powerful feelings of homoerotic desire and traumatization. That one can be symbolic of the other requires that both be fended off together. The result is a fragmented sense of self that occurs when the inner urge to competence, what Kohut (1977) labeled "creative-productive initiative" (p. 76), is met with abuse or abandonment. The natural affective results of this narcissistic injury are shame and rage. These affects occur as natural consequences of the disintegration of one's sense of self rather than as the results of aggressive or sexual drives. Miller (1981, 1983, 1984) eloquently illustrates how this very old misunderstanding of the inner forces the impel children's (and clients') growth and development has embodied a "poisonous pedagogy" that has resulted in "society's betrayal of the child" and the betrayal of the inner child by psychotherapy during its early decades (Miller 1983).

Nick had done much healing through the services of the referring organization. He even had the good fortune of working with a gay therapist individually. It became clear, however, that he needed the additional attention and affirmation of other gay men to come to terms with what emerged as a central theme in his early victimization—his homosexuality. The narcissistic injury in this early experience perpetuated a structural vulnerability in Nick's emerging self that intensified his traumatic experience of the Vietnam War. It may have created a template for his PTSD. The positive mirroring he received in his individual therapy allowed him to desire a test of his heterosexist stereotypes: Could he really become the kind of man he wanted to be and still be gay?

This leads to another important observation about the men in our group. The power of internalized negative stereotypes that participate in self-blame is very impressive. This is true enough for men who fear that they may be gay; for those who are certain, the effect is doubled. Their sexual acting out, which for many reasons became an approximation of intimacy with minimal emotional risk, is self-interpreted as a validation of the truth of those "dirty old man" or "sleazy young hustler" stereotypes and, consequently, as evidence of personal worthlessness. Implicit in these stereotypical self-accusations is a confusion between homosexuality and pedophilia that binds a gay survivor to believe, falsely, that abuse caused his orientation and that any efforts to explore his sexual orientation oblige him to perpetuate pedophilia. The larger culture's propensity to blame the victim becomes internalized and operates like a broken record. Nick's story is a clear illustration of how this works.

The prevalence of much chemical abuse and dependence among gay men has become almost a truism, and so it is not surprising that rates are high among the victimized subset of this population. The rule of thumb, based on a shaky assortment of small studies much troubled by sampling errors, has held that approximately one in three gay people are chemically dependent. A study in the Chicago area casts considerable doubt on this rule of thumb and appears to demonstrate that a carefully constructed sample reveals a rate of dependence no higher than that of the general population, with patterns of use and abuse well beyond the patterns of the general population (McKirnan and Peterson 1987). Neisen and Sandall (1990), in their study of the incidence of sexual abuse in an inpatient chemical dependence treatment center for gay and lesbian clients (n = 201), found that 42 percent of the male clients and 70 percent of the female clients had histories of sexual abuse. The percentage for the entire client group was 49 percent. Neisen and Sandall compared their study with a similar effort in a presumably heterosexual setting that found similar proportions of sexually abused clients. The evidence seems to suggest that higher rates of chemical abuse in gay and lesbian populations may have as much to do with sexual abuse as with sexual orientation.

In his excellent survivors' manual, Lew (1988) observes the tendency of gay survivors to wonder whether sexual abuse caused their orientation. Part of this worry is a result of the victim's self-blaming. Academically, the origins of sexual orientation are murky and mysterious, and they are likely to remain so, given the emerging probability of elaborate, multiple causation. Without joining this debate, it is enough to say that the results are inconclusive. Furthermore, this research effort has often been motivated by the heterosexist desire for a technology of orientation reassignment. Martin (1984) demonstrates how this technology has so far proven to be ineffective if not damaging. One could make the cynical observation that the inability of therapeutic abuse to reassign orientation may suggest the unlikelihood of sexual abuse as a cause. More to the point, I have observed in many clients an awareness of homosexual desires or gay identity that predates the onset of abuse. A careful sexual history can be a powerful tool for helping a man understand that his sexual abuse and the causation of his sexual orientation are probably separate issues.

These doubts are especially distressing when the sexuality of the abuse was, in part, enjoyable or was paired with otherwise rare emotional warmth. In the former case, enjoyment becomes a basis for the denial that what happened was abusive. In the latter situation, the client is set up to experience particularly intense sexualization of emotional intimacy later in life. One man the author interviewed suffered from both problems. He experienced intense sexualized attachment to a bitterly abusive relationship in the present. In his family of origin, the only time he was ever touched (he seldom ever saw his widely traveled parents) was when his grandfather cuddled him on his lap with his arms around the client and his hands cupped over and massaging the client's genitals. It felt so warm and so special that he could not afford to define what happened as abusive. This resulted in a belief that if he enjoyed it, it was not abusive and he was responsible. His situation illustrates the importance of careful language in assessment. It is often helpful to save the word *abuse* for later and ask instead whether anyone was ever sexual with a client when he did not want the person to be or in a way that felt "funny."

The most vital therapeutic strategy in addressing these concerns is the separation of issues of abuse from issues of orientation, leaving orientation concerns for later. Once the abuse has been sufficiently worked through, concerns about any causative relationship to orientation will usually have become insignificant, as they did for Nick.

Another important observation concerns the sexualization of intimacy in a particularly intense fashion in overattaching (dependent) or overseparating (avoidant or narcissistic) patterns (Colgan 1988). Sexualization of intimacy is certainly not unique to this population. It is an issue for heterosexually identified survivors and for nonabused gay and bisexual men, and it can probably be attributed in part to emotional neglect in all three groups. The difference is one of degree rather than kind. The pairing of intense sexual gratification with emotional warmth is a powerful learning experience. The effect is potentiated by the secrecy and shame a man may feel about his homosexual desires and emerging identity. The result is a behavioral exaggeration of the normal processes of merger and distance in the establishment of appropriate intimacy. It can become a relatively dependent pattern of overattachment that includes a swift progression to sexual expression of feelings and premature, incautious commitment that exceeds the limits of trust in a relationship. Under the influence of internalized shame due to heterosexism, it can become a powerful rationalization to deny or discount the validity of intimacy. This occurs introjectively in the case of asexual or avoidant styles or projectively in a more narcissistic or antisocial fashion (blaming and devaluing the partner, which might result in violence toward the partner). The borderline pattern encompasses both aspects in an extremely intense and rigid fashion.

The central feature in all these behavioral patterns is the way in which the failure of early mirroring of the elements of an eventual gay identity creates a structural vulnerability in a client's emerging sense of self, necessitating fragmentation of self whenever early abuse or abandonment is reexperienced symbolically. Nick experienced all these behavior patterns at various points in his adult life.

Finally, the role of grief and loss for gay and bisexual survivors must not be underestimated. This is again true for the larger population of survivors of abuse but is particularly intense and difficult when the nature of the abuse goes directly to core self-identification. Fortunato (1982) notes that his gay and lesbian therapy clients are immobilized in their adult development by grief and loss that they resist working through. In part, he argues, the resistance is an internalized version of the larger society's minimization of the extent to which gay men and lesbians are forced to give up most of the aspects of the American Dream that provide others with a sense of security, albeit false, against random trauma. Gay and bisexual men often become stuck in a bind of bargaining against the losses. They often end up living in "well-appointed closets" at the expense of a good deal of neurotic pathology (Fortunato 1982, 88).

Part of Nick's difficulty in establishing satisfying intimacy was due to his shame's prevented him from believing that his emotions were real and worthy of being validated. Until this validation was accomplished, he could not feel his own sadness and desperation at so many losses—family, comrades, career—and eventually move on to a different kind of self and object relationship. For some men in the group, the ongoing loss of their entire family of origin represents a major portion of their work.

The Role of Group Therapy

These observations of the dynamics of abuse in gay male survivors bring us to a consideration of the role of group therapy in recovery and to a consideration of how sexual orientation affects models of outpatient group psychotherapy with gay survivors. As a therapeutic modality for the treatment of abuse of any sort, group psychotherapy has several unique advantages. Its power to reduce isolation, enhance self-esteem, and provide a boundary laboratory where stereotypes and dysfunctional patterns of intimacy can be met with a more appropriate systemic response seems to operate at an order of magnitude above individual therapy alone. What individual work provides in depth and particulars, group work provides in breadth and enhanced power.

The intense insularity occasioned by internalized shame resulting from both abuse and heterosexism continually distorts a survivor's understanding of self and his interpretation of life events. The culture at large, due to its own heterosexism and its disinclination to validate a survivor's abuse, provides little opportunity for corrective experience. It is difficult for me to imagine a complete recovery without the sort of self-supportive resocialization a therapy group provides. Providing this resource in a gay-affirmative system is a critical feature of recovery for this population.

Nick had been involved in much group work organized around domestic abuse and chemical dependence issues and around recovery from PTSD associated with Vietnam. In most of these groups, Nick's shame-bound silence about his homosexuality was enabled by spoken or unspoken norms forbidding disclosure. The emerging affirmation of his orientation was assisted in individual therapy with a gay-identified social worker, but it became clear that when his recovery began to falter, his emerging self-identity required the systemic validation and resocialization a group could supply. The group became for him a nuclear family of choice.

Models of Group Therapy

Conlin and Smith (1982) and Schwartz and Hartstein (1986) both review the long history of efforts to co-opt group therapy in the service of orientation reassignment. With the declassification of homosexuality as a mental illness, the potential for gay-affirmative group therapy came to increasing recognition (Yalom 1975; Clark 1977).

The models discussed by Conlin and Smith (1982) and Schwartz and Hartstein (1986) differ in several respects, but they contribute a partial theoretical basis for the model chosen by the author.

Both previous models limited their populations to gay men. Conlin and Smith (1982) noted that generalized mixed therapy groups, in their experience, worked well for a gay man with high levels of "self-acceptance and adaptation . . . [who] presents with problems unrelated to sexual orientation" (p. 107). Where internalized shame due to heterosexism is a central concern, however, they recommend a homogeneous gay group. Lew (1988) notes that his groups of male survivors self-selected into gay and straight groups and that this division was, in retrospect, helpful. The longstanding efficacy of gay-identified groups in AA lends further support for a homogeneous population.

The groups conducted by Conlin and Smith (1982) were limited to twenty sessions and excluded clients with psychotic features, borderline personality organization, or high states of anxiety. The Schwartz and Hartstein (1986) groups were ongoing, with a minimum commitment of ten sessions and the expectation that clients would remain in the group for six months to two years. This allowed them to include people with more severe personality problems. The latter approach was more psychodynamic and the former more eclectic, with greater use of structured exercises.

Finally, the Conlin and Smith (1982) model occasionally included friends and family. They also conducted individual termination interviews. The Schwartz and Hartstein (1986) model discouraged contact outside the group and was based more on interpersonal dynamics than on exercises.

According to Schwartz and Hartstein (1986), the advantages of homogeneous gay male groups include visibility (gay members may hide in mixed groups); rapid group identification; relief from defending against overt heterosexist remarks and behavior from straight members; a supportive environment for surfacing internalized heterosexism, confrontation of stereotypes, and presentation of a range of life-style choices; and a particularly safe atmosphere to process sexual concerns in detail. To this list, I would add the provision of a gay affirmative family of choice. This is a specialized variant of Yalom's (1975) "family reenactment" factor among the curative features of groups (pp. 97–98). The group becomes a primary system that can mirror and affirm the client's sexual orientation in a way that most families of origin, and particularly most fathers, cannot. As the group facilitates identity formation and the integration of ego-syntonic sexuality, it becomes, in the best sense, a tribe of initiators into gay male adulthood.

The model used by the author is an ongoing group for six to eight gay men who commit to a minimum of twenty sessions. Commitments are reviewed in ten-session increments with the expectation that most members will stay for approximately six months to two years. Chemically dependent members are expected to have a stable and active recovery program, and members with histories of impulsive or addictive behaviors are expected to contract for abstinence or appropriate behavioral limits for their duration in the group.

The author has broken with Schwartz and Hartstein (1986) in encouraging members to socialize outside the group and to use each other for support between meetings. In my experience, the relief from isolation this provides and the added depathologizing normalization of an otherwise artificial social system far outweigh any problems encountered as a result of such contact.

Members contract not to be sexual with each other, to respect each other's privacy and confidentiality, and to come to sessions chemically free. To support group cohesion, members are asked to pay for sessions whether or not they are present.

The work in sessions can be in one of two modes. Members may bid for time to work individually on an issue with or without feedback, or they may designate individual time or an entire session to open processing. We have broken with Conlin and Smith (1982) in avoiding structured exercises. Members usually cohere in the group at quite different levels of commitment. They are coached never to pace their work faster than the boundaries of their own trust will permit. In my opinion, structured exercises push these limits too hard. Also, because of the obvious sensitivity and confusion about touch, any touching must be specifically requested and the experience processed. Every time I have been moved to offer physical comfort in group, my restraint has been rewarded by client feedback that he would not have been able to tolerate being touched at a moment of such vulnerability.

In the Northland group, the cofacilitators are gay-identified clinicians both within the group and in the larger treatment community. We share Schwartz and Hartstein's (1986) judgment that a person's "orientation *per se* neither qualifies nor disqualifies one to lead a gay therapy group" (p. 171). With this population, it does seem important that the facilitators are male. It is critical that leaders possess a personal and professional maturity that gives them a clearer awareness of how their own internalized heterosexism operates. They also should have a good working knowledge of the diversity of gay and bisexual male experience and of community resources. Most importantly, they should be well aware of the experiential sources of empathy in their own personal healing. These may be more immediately apparent for gay or bisexual therapists. For others, this awareness entails a capacity to bridge empathically from analogous experience (Parker and Thompson 1990). I suggest that if there are two facilitators, it is important to have at least one gay or bisexual therapist. This greately eases the cultivation of trust and cohesion in the group.

The majority of members over three years have been referred from the cofacilitators' individual caseloads, although outside referrals are increasing in number. When an outside therapist makes a referral, we establish reciprocal releases to coordinate treatment and minimize the intrusion of administrative problems (insurance concerns, legal issues, and the like). As we balance the population in the group, we do not make artificial distinctions between victims and perpetrators. The membership criteria are a recognizable pattern of victim behavior (broadly defined) or a history of victimization of any sort that is somehow active in the present. Considerations of personality problems or behavior are then assessed and discussed individually. Men with antisocial behaviors who have responded individually to treatment for their narcissism have been included in the group and have made excellent progress. The same can be said for men with borderline personality features.

Over our three years' experience with this model, it has become helpful to consider the development of work in the group from the perspective of an individual's moving through his work rather than from observation of the group system as a whole. There are two reasons for adopting this descriptive device.

The first reason concerns how critical issues (trust, conflict, cohesion, and so on) arise and are worked through in a cyclical fashion as the population changes over time. This approximates a kind of developmental steady-state equilibrium in which the group system regresses temporarily in its development roughly in proportion to the number of new members entering at the beginning of any given ten-week cycle. We have experienced major changes approximately every twelve to eighteen months. We also prefer to conceptualize trust, cohesion, and conflict as processes rather than systemic developmental attainments that function in different ways and for different purposes at different phases in the cycle.

The second reason for taking an individual perspective addresses the long-term nature of the group. Cycles of developmental working through notwithstanding, we are certain that larger and more subtle metasystemic changes occur over very long periods, but as yet we lack the longevity to observe such changes.

Initial Commitment and Trust

Members enter group therapy with their customary "dread" (Yalom 1975, 302) potentiated by the emotional effects of their internalized heterosexism. For many, the mere presence of other gay men in the first session entails contact with the limits of their vulnerability. This is especially true for men whose sexuality has distanced them emotionally from others (overseparators). Expectations of rejection or disgust at seeing their stereotypical images of themselves mirrored in others begin to dissipate rapidly in confrontation with reality. New members are coached to lead with their fear and their perceptions of difference. Older members begin to introduce themselves and their work and also begin to enculturate the newcomers, usually including stories of their own struggles with trust and inclusion. This exchange assists newcomers in relatively rapid and unexpected identification with others' concerns and helps them manage their anxiety level by providing an experiential map.

One new member in his early forties had lived most of his life anesthetized by alcohol and extremely avoidant of any intimacy, especially with other gay men. He spent his first group session silently. He check out of the second, saying, "Well, I can't say I really like any of you, and basically I think you're all full of shit." The older members, taking this in stride, heard the fear and shame in his voice, reflected them back to him, and helped him to contain his rage. Within six weeks, his attitude had changed, and he became an enthusiastic motivator for the group's work.

In his early phase of work, individual time tends to be taken in small increments, and feedback is often excluded or requested almost as an afterthought. Group processing is usually oriented toward refinement and clarification of norms and rules, and conflict is tentative and initially mediated through the therapists. For example, members might request that the therapists facilitate cohesion by enforcing attendance rather than by members' processing their concerns with the other members involved.

It also is important to attend to those who cannot cross the group's external boundary. Work in individual therapy with those who do not commit is a major by-product of the group's work on trust and usually addresses new issues in an efficient way. The following example illustrates this point.

"Michael," a black man in his late twenties, was an individual therapy client for eighteen months before considering entry into the group. He had been abused sexually by his mother and several teachers, physically by his father, and emotionally by both parents. The last represented a lifelong, unrelenting assault on Michael's sense of his gender and sexual orientation. Severe depression, serious suicide attempts, bulimia, and substance abuse all figured in his history. Through his formidable skills as a survivor, he found a partner with whom he had formed a relatively well functioning monogamous relationship for two and one-half years. In his therapy, he had stabilized his depression, had successfully contained his addictive behaviors (he had many years of success treating his bulimia as an addiction), and was working on his family of origin in a way that both the supportive and resocialization features of a group would have assisted.

We discussed the group for some weeks. As the first session approached, he dreamed one night that he was in the group and very scared but had a great time and knew it was the right thing to do. In the last individual session before the group, we discussed his career dissatisfaction. I expressed my puzzlement that he was so underemployed in a low-level academic advising job when he had both interest and demonstrated talent in several artistic media. He then explained that one of the teachers who had abused him was an art teacher who followed him from school to school as he transferred to escape. He finally abandoned this vital, self-nurturing pursuit, which had kept him alive through high-school graduation. For the first time, he experienced a full return of the repressed affect that had created a crisis that had made it unmanageable for him to participate in the group. It was clear to us in retrospect that without approaching entry into the group system, he might never have contacted the repressed affect.

A subsequent effort to join the group also "failed" because of his surfacing another set of major familial abandonment issues and his sudden decision to take lessons in an art medium different from the one in which the sexual abuse had taken place. He had once again found his own way. It became a subject of much humor between us that he gained so much from the group not by being in it but by bouncing off its external boundary.

Cohesion

Schwartz and Hartstein (1986) observed the fluctuation of trust and cohesion in their ongoing therapy groups. Our experience has been similar. Part of this fluctuation is due to changes in membership. The therapists support cohesive behavior in part through the contract with each member to pay for a complement of sessions whether or not he is present. New members need to test the existing group's cohesiveness as part of the establishment of trust. Likewise, existing members often test newcomers.

We have observed individual patterns of absence without notice or a distributed pattern in which different members miss sessions for a variety of unimpressive reasons. The crisis that is thus engendered invites the crystallization of a cohesive family of choice within the group. By this is meant a sense of safe systemic intimacy within which the need for mirroring and affirmation of members' orientation can be met. Thus, healing and development, arrested by neglect and shame due to internalized heterosexism, are revivified, and the sequestered trauma of abuse becomes accessible. The presence of this form of familiar relatedness not only allows members to reenact their original family roles in a corrective system (Yalom 1975) but also provides a sense of family for the part of them that never had one. The group members become, in effect, a collective gay father to each other. The therapists' role in this process is containment of maladaptive familial defenses.

As individual familial dynamics surface in group interaction, and as the possibility of appropriate affirmation becomes real, members often develop problems with impulsive or addictive behaviors. In our group, these have included substance abuse, sexual acting out, domestic abuse, overwork, overeating, and impulsive spending. These behaviors seem to represent both a desperate and an ineffective effort at what Johnson (1987) describes as a "self-soothing" prerequisite to change and a last resort to identification as a victim, with the attendant sense of powerlessness. One member described his frustration at observing himself resisting the current of sought-after change by clinging, white-knuckled, to his rock of identification as a victim.

The presence of others involved in twelve-step programs has provided an experiential perspective on what these behaviors meant for those who moved beyond them. Members who struggle with impulsive/addictive problems receive further support in the form of behavioral contracting, with subsequent exploration of slips and supportive contacts with other members outside group time. This usually facilitates successful limit setting over time. This mixture of twelve-step recovery tactics and more traditional group interventions enables a correction for the shortcomings of both systems. Twelve-step spirituality assists clients with letting go and moving on; the more traditional interventions tend toward rigid and controlling notions of sobriety. This is particularly important in areas such as spending, sex, and eating, where sobriety in the sense of abstinence usually can be only temporary.

Deeper Work

When the family of choice has demonstrated sufficient cohesiveness and reliability, and when maladaptive coping has been sufficiently contained to enhance trust in self, then the group has been prepared for the most vulnerable and creative work. This often entails formidable grieving. Many individuals spend a year or more in preparation for this very intense phase, which usually lasts ten to twenty sessions. By this point, the formal structure of the group's functions has been individualized so that members are more likely to welcome extensive feedback or to engage others spontaneously in group processing. Perceptions of difference or resistance are usually self-interpreted in terms of historical familial dysfunction.

Members begin to recognize substantial and genuine changes in their relationships both within and outside the group. As they begin to experience more satisfying intimacy, members often describe a kind of poignant joy in which the real extent of the losses they have experienced becomes clear. It is common for descriptions of large behavioral victories to be rendered in tearful respect for a clear sense of the costs. Fortunato (1982) notes:

> It is not enough, in therapy, to help gay people transform a negative self-image into a positive one because the world into which they emerge is, quite literally, "out to get them." It's no paranoid projection; it's for real. Not only must gay people give up attachment to what might have been but wasn't, they must also let go of what might be now and isn't and what the future might have held but won't. (p. 89)

The usual vehicle for this work is a written or oral rendition of a member's story. Some choose to write their story on paper and read it to the group. Others tell their story extemporaneously. Nick illustrated his story with the few photographs he had from his family and his military service. He also began to write poetry again after many years. Drawings, paintings, poetry, music, and textiles are evocative complements to the verbal process of therapy. Egendorf (1986) notes:

> Retelling one's story is an ancient cure. . . . In expressing how it was and is, we make ourselves the witness—one who sees rather than one who has merely been tossed about by passing events. . . . The more we reach to make ourselves a witness to the past, the less we are its victim. . . . As the teller, we create a more expansive present . . . transforming memory from an intrusion to a reminder that the present is elastic and can expand to hold the time of our [whole] . . . lives. The more amply we reach out to grasp our past, the more we can look on old pain gratefully, recognizing it as the instigator that provoked us into growing to encompass it. (pp. 69, 73–74)

As the story becomes clear and repressed parts of the story return in the facilitative milieu of affirmation for orientation, a member often considers whether to confront the perpetrator(s) of his abuse, and, if so, how to do so. At the very least, it is vital that any internalizations of perpetrators be vigorously confronted. Gestalt techniques such as an unsent letter or empty chair have worked well. In this ways, clients' contained rage becomes an appropriately channeled source of power. Its mirroring and affirmation in the group assist in healing the structural vulnerabilities in a client's nuclear self (De Monteflores 1986).

This healing accomplished, clients can more clearly see what outward confrontation they could make with reasonable expectations of enhanced self-esteem. Confrontations have ranged from graveside visits to six-figure lawsuits. The consequences must be weighed carefully, however. Considerations include how much energy is used to maintain secrets and dysfunctional systems, what reactions people will manifest out of their own internalized heterosexism, and how far and in what ways survivors choose to be "out" to those involved in their histories. In many ways, a confrontation recapitulates the task of coming out. In fact, the construction of a similar type of risk hierarchy of confrontation tasks may well enhance survivors' skill building and self-esteem as they work from the least to the most risky tasks in a paced way.

Just as repressed trauma returns to a survivor's recollection, so also do forgotten moments of genuine warmth and appropriate intimacy that have become lost in a fog of shame. For men who have been sexually abused, this may herald the resumption of sexual development postponed by the impact of abuse. One man recalled having had a relatively healthy, playful, exciting, and noncoercive sexual experience in his latency years with a neighborhood age-mate while he was being abused sexually at other times by adults. This served as a strong anchor for the changes he stove to make in his primary relationship. Paradoxically, sex itself has sometimes become an odd kind of secret in the group when members are experimenting with new ways to connect sex and intimacy. This secret usually emerges from a group process session where it suddenly becomes apparent how little we have talked about the playful, humorous, and spiritual dimensions of sex. The gradual success of these experiments and others often brings clients to the realization that they have nearly completed their work in the group and that termination is approaching.

Termination

The emergence of significant changes in an individual's pattern of attractions, the discovery of new connections between sex and intimacy, and the revivification of primary relationships all engender tremendous excitement but also mean that a member's work is nearing completion. The serious prospect of termination usually generates one more surge of grief and loss. For many men, this has been the first interpersonal system in which they felt trusted, respected, and appropriately responded to and found it safe to take large emotional risks. For some, it has meant making a decision about whether to stay alive. They now contemplate reentering a world that is likely, on the whole, to remain hostile to their homosexuality. This transition reenacts whatever remains unfinished in a member's emancipation from the family of origin; the parts of that process that were previously sequestered by the secrecy (from others or self) of their orientation or their abuse can now be worked through. The poignance of this task notwithstanding, members are often surprised by the clarity and ease with which they are able to move on. One member realized that it was easier for him to leave a well-functioning relationship than a relatively poor one.

Termination is managed as both a part of a member's ongoing work and a part of a structured decision process about recommitment to the next group cycle. At session 7 in each ten-week cycle, members give a preliminary indication of their intentions. At session 8, they receive feedback from the group. In the ninth session, a final decision is rendered, and in the tenth session, we process the end of the person's work in the group. Long-term members who have considerable difficulty with relational closure often devote an entire ten-session cycle to this process. Usually we have experienced this as a rich retrospective of how members experience their lives differently.

The indicators of completion include, but are not limited to, changes in patterns of attraction, an increased tolerance for appropriate vulnerability in relationships, an enhanced sense of flexibility, acceptance of a more playful and intimate role for sex, an enhanced capacity to use anger in appropriate self-assertion and limit setting, and a greater sense of competence and confidence at work. One man was surprised to realize the extent of his unemployment and observed that, as he progressed in therapy, his income improved significantly. Another member, previously disabled by his depression, was able to hold a job for the first time in many years and shortly after termination entered a primary relationship now nearly two years along. The most important indicator is a greater sense of comfort with one's orientation, in whatever way that manifests itself. Often this will enable some greater degree of "outness" somewhere in a man's life.

To facilitate moving on, we always leave the door open to graduating members to return if the need arises. This is appropriate in working through emancipation. It also allows members to take a respite from group work and to return later to complete whatever remains unfinished. This is particularly helpful when the other option is to leave the group altogether with a sense of failure. This can entail remaining involved with active members socially, though under the same contracts concerning sexual contact and confidentiality.

In our group, ten members who terminated their group therapy were assessed by the cofacilitators as having completed all the work they set out to do. Each manifested a number of the qualitative changes listed above. Four of these ten men established relatively functional primary relationships that were quite different from their historical relational patterns. Seven stabilized their lives sufficiently to improve their employment situations, either by reversing underemployment and making major positive career changes or by containing their habit of overwork as a defense against shame. They participated in an average of forty-four sessions, with a range of seventeen to seventy-two sessions. (At this writing, the current membership averages thirty-eight sessions.) Four members left in a respite from the group; two of these subsequently decided not to return. Six members left for reasons other than termination or to take a respite. Their reasons included job relocation (1), the onset of severe (nonpsychiatric) medical problems requiring lengthy hospitalization (1), the conclusion (despite feedback) that therapy was not helpful (2), and the perception that the group (despite its best efforts) was too much like the family of origin (1). One member, near successful completion, dropped out for an unknown reason, and we have been unable to follow up on him.

Conclusion

This chapter has explored the dynamics of the victimization of men with a substantially homosexual orientation and presented a model for outpatient group psychotherapy with this population. In many respects, the dynamics observed are shared by other groups of survivors. Often the differences are matters of degree rather than kind. One qualitative factor was identified as critical to these differences of degree and central to a gay survivor's ability to heal. The structural vulnerabilities in a survivor's self-structure, promulgated by shame-bound internalization of societal heterosexism, create a template for traumatic experience. The healing of these vulnerabilities is critical to a recovery that will resist relapse.

In closing, I would like to offer deep thanks to the men who have opened their lives in the course of therapy. I join with Arthur Egendorf (1986) in saying that "my cover is that I do this work for a living, when in fact it fulfills my lust and craving" (p. 218) for a capacity to self-witness, for the kind of healing where

> pain too can spring out as the bearer of some secret truth. Some long-lived cause for distress suddenly shifts and becomes a source of renewed confidence. In this way, weaknesses become our strengths, mistakes our greatest teachers, wounds the new and sturdy foundation for carrying on. These are enlightening turns, for the burden of living falls away and darkness cedes to light. (p. 202)

References

American Psychiatric Association. 1980. *Diagnostic and Statistical Manual of Mental Disorders,* 3d ed. Washington, D.C.

Anderson, C.L. 1982. "Males as Sexual Assault Victims: Multiple Levels of Trauma." In *Homosexuality and Psychotherapy: A Practitioner's Handbook of Affirmative Models,* edited by J.C. Gonsiorek, 145–162. New York: Haworth Press.

Briere, J., D. Evans, M. Runtz, and T. Wall. 1988. "Symptomatology in Men Molested as Children: A Comparison Study." *American Journal of Orthopsychiatry* 58 (no. 3): 457–461.

Brown, L. 1988. "New Voices and Visions: Towards a Lesbian and Gay Paradigm for Psychology." *A.P.A. Division 44 Newsletter* 4 (no. 3): 12–16.

Browne, A., and D. Finkelhor. 1986. "Impact of Child Sexual Abuse: A Review of the Research." *Psychological Bulletin* 99: 66–77.

Clark, D. 1977. *Loving Someone Gay.* New York: New American Library.

Coleman, E. 1988. "Assessment of Sexual Orientation." In *Integrated Identity for Gay Men and Lesbians: Psychotherapeutic Approaches for Emotional Well Being,* edited by J. DeCecco and E. Coleman, 9–24. New York: Harrington Park Press.

Colgan, P. 1988. "Treatment of Identity and Intimacy Issues in Gay Males." In *Integrated Identity for Gay Men and Lesbians: Psychotherapeutic Approaches for Emotional Well Being,* edited by J. DeCecco and E. Coleman, 101–123. New York: Harrington Park Press.

Conlin, D., and J. Smith. 1982. "Group Psychotherapy with Gay Men." In *Homosexuality and Psychotherapy: A Practitioner's Handbook of Affirmative Models,* edited by J.C. Gonsiorek, 105–112. New York: Haworth Press.

De Monteflores, C. 1986. "Notes on the Management of Difference." In *Contemporary Perspectives on Psychotherapy with Lesbians and Gay Men,* edited by T. Stein and C. Cohen, 73–101. New York: Plenum Press.

Egendorf, A. 1986. *Healing from the War: Trauma and Transformation after Vietnam.* Boston: Shambala.

Fortunato, J. 1982. *Embracing the Exile.* New York: Harper & Row.

Gonsiorek, J.C. 1989. "Sexual Exploitation by Psychotherapists: Some Observations on Male Victims and Sexual Orientation Issues." In *Psychotherapists' Sexual Involvement with Clients: Intervention and Prevention,* edited by G. Schoener, J. Milgrom, J. Gonsiorek, E. Luepker, and R. Conroe, 113–119. Minneapolis: Walk-In Counseling Center.

Hunter, M. 1990. *Abused Boys: The Neglected Victims of Sexual Abuse.* Lexington, Massachusetts: Lexington Books.

Johnson, S. 1987. *Humanizing the Narcissistic Style.* New York: W.W. Norton.

Kinsey, A. 1948. *Sexual Behavior in the Human Male.* Philadelphia: Sanders.

Klein, F. 1978. *The Bisexual Option.* New York: Arbor House.

Kohut, H. 1977. *The Restoration of Self.* New York: International University Press.

Lew, M. 1988. *Victims No Longer.* New York: Nevraumont Books.

Martin, A. 1984. "The Emperor's New Clothes: Modern Attempts to Change Sexual Orientation." In *Psychotherapy with Homosexuals,* edited by E. Hetrick and T. Stein, 24–57. Washington, D.C.: American Psychiatric Association.

McKirnan, D., and P. Peterson. 1987. "Alcohol and Drug Use among Homosexual Men and Women: Descriptive Data and Implications for AIDS Risk." Unpublished manuscript, Department of Psychology, University of Illinois, Chicago.

Miller, A. 1981. *The Drama of the Gifted Child.* New York: Basic Books.

———. 1983. *For Your Own Good: Hidden Cruelty in Child Rearing and the Roots of Violence.* New York: Farrar, Straus & Giroux.

———. 1984. *Thou Shall Be Aware: Society's Betrayal of the Child.* New York: Farrar, Straus & Giroux.

Myers, M. 1989. "Men Sexually Assaulted as Adults and Sexually Abused as Boys." *Archives of Sexual Behavior* 18: 203–215.

Neisen, J. 1990. "Heterosexism: Redefining Homophobia for the 1990s." *Journal of Gay and Lesbian Psychotherapy,* in press.

Neisen, J., and M. Sandall. 1990. "Alcohol and Other Drug Abuse in a Gay/Lesbian Population: Related to Victimization? *Journal of Psychology and Human Sexuality,* in press.

Parker, S., and T. Thompson. 1990. "Gay and Bisexual Men: Developing a Healthy Identity." In *Problems Solving Strategies and Intervention for Men in Conflict,* edited by F. Leafgren and D. Moore, 113–121. Washington, D.C.: American Association for Counseling and Development.

Schwartz, R., and N. Hartstein. 1986. "Group Psychotherapy with Gay Men." In *Contemporary Perspectives on Psychotherapy with Lesbians and Gay Men,* edited by T. Stein and C. Cohen, 157–177. New York: Plenum Press.

Singer, K. 1989. "Group Work with Men Who Experienced Incest in Childhood." *American Journal of Orthopsychiatry* 59 (no. 3): 468–472.

Yalom, I. 1975. *The Theory and Practice of Group Psychotherapy.* New York: Basic Books.

10
Identification and Treatment of Child and Adolescent Male Victims of Sexual Abuse

Mary L. Froning
Susan B. Mayman

T he identification and treatment of child and adolescent male victims of sexual abuse has only recently been acknowledged as a subspecialty within the fairly new field of sexual abuse in general. Within that context, this chapter presents current thinking about clinical practice in this subspecialty.

The attitude about male victimization in American society has resulted in a silence about the sexual abuse of males that creates a barrier against even the youngest boy disclosing and then discussing his abuse. Without the identification and treatment of this trauma in a boy's history, however, future problems for him and for society are likely.

Review of Literature on Assessment and Treatment

The only book currently available that focuses exclusively on young male victims of sexual abuse is Eugene Porter's (1986) *Treating the Young Male Victim of Sexual Assault: Issues and Intervention Strategies.* This book provides an overview of issues specific to boy and adolescent male victims and primary treatment approaches in working with this population. Porter advocates group therapy and family therapy as the two most important treatment modalities for young male victims. His book offers a model for group therapy and includes stages of this model and specific interventions used in each stage.

A book that contains some chapters on the assessment and treatment of male child victims is *Males at Risk: The Other Side of Child Sexual Abuse* by Bolton, Morris, and MacEachron (1989). The approach described is structured using behavioral/cognitive techniques. The authors describe a three-faceted approach to treatment, focusing on changing beliefs and attitudes related to responsibility for the abuse, trust, and self-image and competency; affective responses, including fear and anxiety, anger, and grief; and behavioral responses, including aggression and sexual acting out.

For those who do not have a background in general treatment issues and techniques for working with child and adolescent victims of sexual abuse and their families, two books are recommended. The first is the *Handbook of Clinical Intervention in Child Sexual Abuse* edited by Sgroi (1982). In the chapter on treatment of the sexually abused child, authors Porter, Blick, and Sgroi (1982) identify ten impact issues and discuss treatment implications for each of these issues. The ten issues are as follows:

1. The "damaged goods" syndrome
2. Guilt
3. Fear
4. Depression
5. Low self-esteem and poor social skills
6. Repressed anger and hostility
7. Impaired ability to trust
8. Blurred role boundaries and role confusion
9. Pseudomaturity coupled with failure to accomplish developmental tasks
10. Self-mastery and control

This book also contains invaluable information about family treatment, incest offenders, sibling incest, and treatment for mothers of incest victims.

The second book focuses on very young children. *Sexual Abuse of Young Children: Evaluation and Treatment* by MacFarlane and Waterman (1986) addresses the more general assessment and treatment issues for this population.

Finally, Roland Summit's (1983) seminal article "The Child Sexual Abuse Accommodation Syndrome" also is highly recommended. It explains the dynamics of both the child's reluctance to disclose and his struggle to make sense of his trauma.

Disclosure of Victimization

Many professionals believe that the incidence numbers for male victims of child sexual abuse are low and do not accurately represent the scope of male victimization. In a study by Risin and Koss (1987), 2,972 men in a representative national sample were asked about their childhood sexual experiences. Of this sample, 7.3 percent reported an abusive childhood experience before the age of fourteen. The vast majority of these men (81.2 percent) had told no one about their sexual abuse.

The research literature is clear that boys are less likely than girls to disclose abuse (Nielsen 1983; Finkelhor 1984). Another interesting finding is that boys were more likely to be identified as victims through indirect disclosure (Reinhart 1987). Reinhart found that in a population of medical center referrals, 20 percent of boys versus 11 percent of girls were identified by a third party, with later confirmation by the child. Johnson and Shrier (1985) routinely asked about child sexual abuse during intake at an adolescent medical clinic and found that there were no disclosures by adolescents under fifteen years of age and only six of forty disclosures by patients under seventeen years of age.

The earliest article that addresses the silence of young male victims is Maria Nasjleti's (1980) "Suffering in Silence: The Male Incest Victim." Nasjleti found in her group work with sexually abused boys that they were consistently resistant to discussing their victimization. Her article explores the psychological factors involved in the young male victim's difficulty in disclosing and discussing his victimization. Nasjleti concludes that our society's role expectations of male children "create a climate conducive to their victimization, and in turn their victimization of others" (p. 274).

One reason for underreporting is that boys grow up with the male ethic of self-reliance (Finkelhor 1984). Therefore, they acknowledge victimization with difficulty, have to grapple with the stigma of homosexuality surrounding abuse by a male, and may have more to lose by reporting because disclosure might lead to a curtailing of their freedom and independence.

Another explanation for boys being less likely to disclose than girls might be that violence and threats are more common for boys. Rogers and Terry (1984) report that boys were significantly more likely to be threatened with harm than were girls (51 percent for boys versus 31 percent for girls), as do Pierce and Pierce (1985).

Some studies report more violence surrounding the abuse for boy victims than for girl victims (DeJong, Emmett, and Hervada 1982; Pierce and Pierce 1985). Kercher and McShane (1984) found that the use of erotic materials were commonly used with boy victims, a shame-inducing aspect that may retard disclosure.

Among professionals in the field of child sexual abuse, there is much discussion and speculation as to why boys do not disclose their victimization. Much of the discussion focuses on the socialization process of the male child, which includes the following:

- Societal pressure for male children to be strong and protect themselves
- No permission in society for males to be identified as victims
- Fear of being labeled "homosexual" or "gay" if the perpetrator was male
- Fear of embarrassment if the perpetrator was female (As continually reinforced by literature and film, a young boy is considered "lucky" if he is "seduced" by an older woman.)

- Behavioral indicators of sexual abuse may be more externalized (These acting-out behaviors are often seen by society, parents, and professionals as "normal" male behavior.)

Following are some case examples of disclosures of young male victimization:

Case 1. George, age five, was referred to treatment for sexually acting out, which included playing a game called "kissing penises and bums." A year and a half later, in treatment, he finally disclosed his own abuse.

Case 2. The sexual abuse of Adam, age five, was discovered after a juvenile sex offender was caught and listed Adam as one of his victims. The abuse had occurred when Adam was three and a half years old.

Case 3. Kyle, age four, and his twin sister were sexually assaulted by a twelve-year-old neighborhood boy. Upon returning home after the assault, the little girl immediately told her mother what had happened.

Case 4: David, age thirteen, disclosed his sexual victimization to his mother after they watched a television movie about AIDS.

To facilitate disclosure of male sexual victimization, those professionals who work with children must be open to hearing about male sexual abuse. When therapists and child protective service workers are referred young boys or adolscents who present with problems such as acting-out behaviors, running away, declining school performance, anxiety, and physical symptomatology, a thorough evaluation or interview should include asking questions about the possibility of sexual abuse. Whenever one child in a family discloses sexual abuse, both female and male siblings need to be interviewed and protected by child protective services and the police.

A 1985 study by Pierce and Pierce illustrates one of the ways that boys and girls differ with respect to the reporting of abuse. The study analyzed 205 cases of sexual abuse reported to a child abuse hot line over a four-year period and also examined previous calls to the hot line from these same male and female victims. The study found that approximately the same numbers of boys and girls reporting victimization of sexual abuse had previously been reported and the report substantiated by a protective services worker. The data suggested, however, that while a majority of previous reports for female victims had been for sexual abuse, a majority of those for males were for "family stress."

Male victims present in a different way than female victims. Professionals need to recognize these differences. Once the abuse is disclosed, the initial responses by parents and professionals must be those of validation, support, and protection, for it is within the context of this initial response that the healing process begins.

Evaluation

Significant with regard to the creation of a safe environment for treatment is that in cases reported to child protective services (that is, family or caretaker abusers), boys were much less likely than girls to be protected (Pierce and Pierce 1985). The authors found that 4 percent of the boys versus 20 percent of the girls were removed from the home. They also reported that boys were both less likely than girls to be referred for treatment and less likely to stay longer than a few months. Thus, the initial task of evaluation is to ensure that the child is safe and that his environment supports treatment.

The next step is the development of an appropriate treatment plan. Bolton (1989) recommends a multiremedial evaluation of male children that includes several excellent suggestions for testing instruments and questionnaires that will help in this process.

In general, however, one needs to consider several items during the evaluation process. Initially, a developmental evaluation should be conducted that will compare the child's chronological age with his effective emotional age.

For example, "Kenny" was a fourteen-year-old boy who initially was referred because his stepfather had abused his sister. It was later discovered that he had been sexually abused by his uncle. His therapist reported going to the waiting room to meet her client for the first time and finding him on his mother's lap. Using techniques designed for younger children was deemed to be more appropriate for this child, who could not tolerate "talking therapy" alone.

The age at disclosure is an important factor. The more distant the disclosure is from the beginning of the abuse, the more entrenched the child's response to it will be. Also, there are ages at which it is more difficult for boys to talk about abuse, particularly ages twelve to seventeen. Greater tolerance and slower work may need to be done with boys in this age-group who are discovered to be victims.

There ought to be an evaluation of the child's behavioral response to the abuse. Friedrich's Child Behavior Checklist and Child Sexual Behavior Inventory are helpful (Friedrich, Urquiza, and Beilke 1986). In addition, a developmental history from parents and teachers needs to be gathered. This is important to help sort out, if possible, the effects of abuse from preexisting issues. For instance, difficulty concentrating in school could be attributed to the abuse but also to learning disabilities or an attention deficit disorder that existed prior to the abuse.

Similarly, a family history will be important for delineating the effects of the abuse. Victimization outside the home may be an indicator of current or past abuse in the home. Thus, the possibility of incest should be explored during the evaluation.

Determination of previous abuse, either within or outside the family, will be a factor in the treatment plan. The experience of abuse with each perpetrator will bring with it unique consequences and must be evaluated separately.

The age at which the abuse began is an important factor, especially when it started at a very young age. The seduction phase of the abuse initially may be out of the child's consciousness, which may lead him to a greater feeling of blame for the abuse.

Characteristics of the perpetrator and the relationship of the child to the perpetrator also are significant. For instance, the sex of the perpetrator may be meaningful. As we will discuss later, the effects of a male versus a female abuser may be quite different. For boys, extrafamilial abuse seems to be more likely. In Rogers and Terry (1984), 78 percent of the abuse of boys occurred outside the family. Finkelhor (1984) found that 83 percent of boys versus 56 percent of girls were abused outside the family. Kercher and McShane (1984) found that boys were three times more likely than girls to be abused outside the family. In younger populations, however, the differences between boys and girls were not significant (Mian et al. 1986; Reinhart 1987).

If the offender is a parent or other family member, separation of the abuser from the child is obviously the first order of business. Visitation plans may need to be developed early in the process, depending on court involvement. No child should be forced to be in contact with a perpetrator unless he is emotionally prepared for that. If contact is desired by the child, it should be properly supervised and the effects on him monitored closely.

The type and duration of the abuse are considerations in treatment. Issues such as violence, use of drugs or alcohol, degree of intrusiveness, whether the boy was required to be active or passive during the abuse, frequency, and length of the abuse affect the course of treatment.

Whether the abuse has influenced the child's ideas or image of his body or of his gender identity should be determined. Drawings of himself may provide clues about this issue.

Community and parental support systems should be evaluated. The course of treatment will go more quickly and successfully if the child has as many adults as possible to provide ongoing support. Educating these adults during the evaluation process about the possible issues that may arise for the boy during their care of him will help create an extension of the therapeutic environment outside the therapy room.

Cultural differences may affect a community's or family's ability to deal effectively with the sexual abuse of a young male. In some cultures, for instance, the concept of male is more rigid than in general American society. This might cause a lack of support for the child unless the issue is dealt with sensitively and carefully. In other cultures, there is no permission for young males to regress as a way to cope with trauma. Thus, an explanation of regression to the caretakers at the time of the evaluation could prevent misinterpretation and perhaps even punishment of regressive behaviors by the child.

Presenting Issues and Potential Consequences

Once sexual abuse has been established, a boy or adolescent victim often presents myriad issues. The first may be denial and minimization of the effects of the abuse. The tendency to avoid the stigmatization of victimization may mean that the word *abuse* does not fit with the child's interpretation of events. He may claim consensuality or even (especially in the case of a female perpetrator) suggest that it was beneficial. A careful exploration of his view is the initial step in the process.

In addition, he may claim that the event(s) was abusive but had no effect on him—another avoidance of the victim role. Firmness may be necessary with both child and parent to help them understand the need for treatment as a prophylaxis against effects that are not yet recognized or have not occurred. A slow and careful psychoeducational approach is useful here. It is effective to use examples of the effects on other boys, emphasizing that they also initially thought that there was no connection between certain feelings or thoughts and the sexually abusive event(s).

Specific symptoms associated with child sexual abuse are many and varied, often masking the deeper concerns. For instance, drug and alcohol abuse or other acting-out behaviors may be defenses against overwhelming sadness, loss, shame, anxiety, and fear.

Concerns about gender issues are usually present, even though denied at first. If the abuser was a male, homophobic concerns may be present. These may be reinforced by internal or external communication that the victim failed to do the masculine thing—resist. As a result, there may be premature labeling of the victim as a homosexual by either caretakers or himself in an effort to bind the anxiety about this possibility. These concerns may extend to a repulsion with masturbation, as the victim associates the abusive experience with sexual pleasure. If the abuser was a female, questions of adequacy as a male may be present as a reaction to his confusion and anxiety at the time of the abuse. These feelings may cause an overfocus on sexuality, leading to promiscuity or even forced sex on females to prove sexual adequacy.

Sexual acting out is another presenting issue, including excessive masturbation or the tendency to use sexual language. Masturbation (penile manipulation or inserting objects into the anus) to the point of bleeding or pain must be dealt with immediately.

One troubling response to abuse is identification with the abuser, creating a victim-abuser cycle. This recapitulation of the victimizing experience may be an attempt to master the experience, to regain masculinity by identifying with the abusive male, and/or to avoid (in his own mind) the label of victim. Without intervention, this sexual reactivity may lead to a lifetime of abusive behavior. Unfortunately, the cycle can be stopped only if the victim has the courage to disclose or if the perpetrator is caught in the act. It is otherwise unusual for young reactive abusers to acknowledge their behavior.

Low self-esteem is an almost inevitable consequence of sexual abuse. Boys, in particular, must deal with society's beliefs about the powerfulness and invincibility of males. A victimized young male, then, feels a lowering of self-worth simply because the event occurred. In addition, the abuse experience may have included being tricked or fooled, which leads the victim to believe he was inadequate in some way. Self-blaming statements such as "It was my fault" and "I was *so* stupid" are common. Immediate reassurance, as well as education about the techniques used by child sexual abusers, help allay these feelings.

Infantile behaviors may be present, with regressions in speech and play patterns and a tendency to pursue relationships with younger children. This latter tendency may be a way to regain mastery and should be watched particularly in older boys to avoid possible victimization of younger children.

Paranoid and phobic behaviors are common. Feelings of helplessness and powerlessness caused by the abuse may result in these symptoms, as well as panic attacks when a situation triggers feelings similar to those that the child had at the time of the abuse.

Nightmares and flashbacks are common, as the child's unconscious attempts to resolve the frightening events of the abuse. Nightmares often take the form of disguised presentations. For example, common themes include being chased, punished, and isolated, fear of being controlled by larger, faster, and more powerful beings, and (for younger children) snakes or bees going in and out of holes.

Suicidal and homicidal thoughts and feelings are common in this population. In fact, such feelings may coexist as the young male struggles with assignation of responsibility and shame to himself or his perpetrator. Periodic questioning about suicide risk is recommended, especially in the beginning of treatment.

Concern about the body is another presenting issue. Boys may present with great concerns about their body image, leading to compulsive neatness or its opposite and overconcern with bodily strength. There may be enuresis and encopresis (the latter particularly associated with anal intercourse). Eye infections may be present, associated with touching penises with fecal material on them and then rubbing the eyes. Other physical complaints may have to do with the limbs, chest, head, and abdomen. With the advent of AIDS, many disclosures have been prompted because the young males have feared that they may have contracted the disease from the abuse. Testing for AIDS, as well as a medical examination to detect sexually transmitted diseases, scarring, and other damage, should be done early in the process. A sensitive examination will detect medical problems that need treatment, will be reassuring to the child, and may lead to successful prosecution of the offender.

Trust

One of the most powerful and traumatic effects of sexual victimization is the tremendous feeling of betrayal. Contrary to the myth that boys are assaulted more often by strangers or unknown pedophiles, most boys who are sexually abused know their abusers (Finkelhor 1981; Ellerstein and Canavan 1980; Risin and Koss 1987; Spencer and Dunklee 1986). This feeling of betrayal may be manifested by isolation from family and peers, difficulty with closeness and intimacy, trouble with authority figures, and anxiety about decision making.

One example is "Michael," age fifteen, who had been sexually abused by an adult male neighbor who was a volunteer with his Boy Scout troop. His abuser was one of the first people Michael met when moving into his new neighborhood. Besides helping him in Boy Scouts, his abuser also helped Michael to get adjusted to his new school and taught him to play tennis. In treatment, Michael presented himself as having difficulty in school, particularly having conflicts with male teachers. He described himself as having few friends because he felt so much older than his peers. Michael had just moved to the area and was very wary of meeting people. "I didn't make such great choices the last time," Michael stated, referring to his prior experience and abuse.

The Therapeutic Relationship

The therapeutic relationship is the best place to begin to address the issue of trust. With both children and adolescents, the therapist always should be on time and be consistent. It is important for the therapist never to make promises that he or she will not be able to keep. Trust grows with time. For many victims, this therapeutic relationship will be the testing ground for building future peer and adult relationships.

Believing the young male victim about the sexual abuse and supporting him also are imperative. The therapist needs to acknowledge the belief that the abuse occurred, as well as validate the victim's feelings associated with the abuse and empathize with the effects the abuse and its disclosure have had on his life. Giving the male victim as much control as possible within the therapy sessions will assist him in regaining some of the control he lost and begin to build a base of trust in the therapeutic relationship.

Difficulty with Authority Figures

When the young male victim reports difficulty with authority figures, the therapist can assist him in looking at this problem. The therapist first ought to normalize this response. It is helpful for the victim to hear that other boys who have been sexually abused experience the same difficulties. Next, the therapist ought to explore abuse triggers with the client:

- What is it about this person that you are having trouble with?
- Can you describe this person?
- When did you start having difficulty with this person?

The therapist can then assist the young male victim in making connections between feelings associated with the abuse/abuser and the current situation/adult. Sometimes this can be as simple as the young teenager who described the teacher with whom he was having difficulty as having "white hair like my grandfather." Once the trigger has been identified, the therapist can move toward engaging the young client in resolving the conflict.

Judgment/Decision Making

Male children who are sexually abused by someone they know and trust often begin to question their own judgment about people and situations. Adolescents in particular may begin to look cognitively at the issue of trust. They may believe that they will never trust any adult (or anybody) again. The therapist can help the adolescent to look at whom they do trust and the reasons they trust that person. By looking at what went into the decision to trust someone (who has not betrayed that trust by abuse or misuse), the adolescent can begin to establish some guidelines or parameters. Writing down these guidelines can give the young male victim something concrete and measurable to examine.

Extrafamilial Abuse

When the young male victim is sexually assaulted by someone outside the family, the abuser usually is known not only to the victim but also to the family. Many times this person is an authority figure or a friend whom the victim and his family trusted.

For example, "Steve" was a family friend of the Smiths as well as a teacher's aide at their son's school. When Steve began to spend time at their home and individually with their twelve-year-old son, "Mark," Mrs. Smith welcomed his involvement, as she felt that her husband worked too hard and was unable to spend enough time with their son. Mr. Smith also liked Steve and felt he could help Mark with his academic difficulties. Mrs. Smith began confiding in Steve about her concerns for Mark and allowed Mark to spend more and more time with Steve. Mark disclosed his sexual abuse by Steve after becoming fearful of contracting AIDS.

When the perpetrator is someone known and trusted by both the victim and his parents, the entire family will feel betrayed. In the above case example, both Mr. and Mrs. Smith entered individual therapy to deal with their feelings of betrayal and anger. In individual therapy, and later couples therapy, they began to look at their parenting and decision-making processes. It was only through their work in individual and couples therapy that the Smiths were able to join their son in dyad and family therapy and respond to his feelings of anger and betrayal.

Young children who, because of their developmental age, believe that parents know everything may be confused and fearful. It is imperative that the parents of such children be integrally involved in their children's therapy. The parents need to reassure the child of their support and protection. If the parents are not working on their own feelings about the abuse, they will not be able to provide this assurance in a consistent and solid way for the child.

In cases of assault by a stranger, the circumstances of the assault, rather than the identity of the assailant, may bring up the issues of trust and judgment, which can be just as powerful as feelings about the abuse and need to be addressed in therapy.

Intrafamilial Abuse

When the perpetrator is a family member (father, mother, sibling, stepparent, or other), the resolution of betrayal and the rebuilding of trust is a long-term process. In these cases, it is ideal to have a therapeutic team working with the family, with each family member having his or her own individual therapist. In this way, boundaries that were blurred and violated in the family will be clear and consistent in the therapeutic process.

The offender should be removed from the home, ideally with the court's support by a restraining order or other court order. Even if the perpetrator is a sibling, a separation is necessary for the victim's immediate safety and stabilization. (For the young offender, this separation, though painful and difficult, is often beneficial because it provides him or her with safety and a structure in which to begin his or her work in therapy.)

In one example, "Jonathan," age seven, was sexually abused by his stepfather, Mr. Collins, who confessed the abuse to his minister. Mr. Collins was removed from the home and ordered to begin treatment and to stay away from the home. Jonathan and his mother also began individual treatment. Mrs. Collins continued to see her husband outside of the home. Six months into treatment, Jonathan began playing with some action toys, creating and recreating a scene in which the "big monkey hurt the little monkey." Jonathan was unexpectedly unable to rescue the little monkey (which in previous sessions he was able to do, using the mommy monkey or the police doll). After talking to Mrs. Collins, the therapist learned that she had allowed Mr. Collins in the house while Jonathan was in school and that Mr. Collins had left a note for Jonathan in his bedroom. Before this incident, Jonathan had begun to have some sense of safety and protection, but this safety was shaken when his stepfather violated established boundaries. For Jonathan, it also shook his trust that his mother would protect him.

The initial steps for the offender to take in rebuilding trust are as follows:

1. Follow through with the rules established by the court and the therapeutic team (regarding visitation, phone contact with other family members, contact outside the home, and so on.

2. Participate fully in a recommended treatment program (in many instances a combination of individual and group treatment).

The therapeutic treatment team will need to assess each family member's treatment process on an ongoing basis to make any further decisions about visitation and reunification.

The young male victim may have feelings of anger and mistrust regarding the nonoffending parent. For many victims, the immediate concern is "Will he or she protect me?" For young children, this sense of protection will be manifested in their play. Adolescents may need permission to be angry at the nonoffending parent for failure to protect, as well as at the offender (see chapter 8). Here again, a combination of individual and dyad work is appropriate. (See chapter 8 for more on this topic.)

Externalized Affective Responses

As is obvious in our society, externalized affective responses are more common in males than in females. Thus, it is not surprising that the literature in child sexual abuse (Rogers and Terry 1984; Friedrich, Urquiza, and Beilke 1986) demonstrates an increased likelihood of acting-out behaviors among boys who are victims of sexual abuse.

Specific indicators seen to be consequences of the sexual abuse of boys include homophobic concerns, sexual behaviors, aggressive and controlling behaviors, infantile behaviors, setting fires, running away, and prostitution (Sebold 1987). Friedrich, Urquiza, and Beilke (1986) note that sexually abused boys, compared to conduct-disordered boys, were more likely to be rated by their caretakers on the Child Behavior Checklist as behaving like the opposite sex, playing with their own sex parts in public, playing with their own sex parts too much, having sexual problems, thinking about sex too much, and wishing to be of the opposite sex.

Johnson and Shrier (1985) note that sexually abused adolescents identified themselves as nonheterosexual more often than a control group. They found that 58 percent of the sexually abused boys versus 10 percent of the control group identified themselves as homosexual or bisexual. In addition, they found that 25 percent of the sexual abuse population versus only 5 percent of the control population reported nonorganic sexual dysfunction.

In a later study, Johnson and Shrier (1987) found that the sex of the perpetrator affected the victim's perception of sexual preference and sexual functioning. Some 28 percent of the boy victims identified themselves as homosexual or bisexual when offended by a female, whereas 57 percent of those with male perpetrators and 8 percent of the control group identified themselves as nonheterosexual. With regard to sexual dysfunction, 21 percent of those with female perpetrators reported such dysfunction, compared with 28 percent of those abused by males and 4 percent of the control group. It should be noted that none of the sexually abused boys had received treatment for their abuse, which had occurred between ages five and seventeen, and very few of them had disclosed it previously.

Homophobic Concerns

A sensitive exploration of homophobic/heterosexist concerns is vital. This exploration should educate the child about the development of sexual preference and emphasize the therapist's acceptance of whatever sexual preference may eventuate in the child's life. This issue needs to be raised beginning with latency-age children. One approach might include a question such as "Do you wonder if because you were abused by a man, you'll grow up to be gay?" Group or dyad work is very helpful with this issue, as the child will find out that others have thought about this possibility. Absent access to direct contact with other victims, the therapist might relate experiences that other boys have shared to help normalize the boy's concerns.

Mild repulsion about masturbation may need an educational intervention, including disabusing the victim of the common myth that only homosexuals can enjoy sexual acts they associate with gay men. The therapist can help the boy by explaining the body's normal physiological response to sexual stimulation. In severe cases, this pleasure blocking may require a formal desensitization process to replace the child's repugnance for pleasureable sexuality. An exploration of family values and educational efforts with the parents are necessary before proceeding with this issue.

Sexual Behaviors

Sexual acting out can be a serious problem and must be dealt with as soon as identified. No therapy can be successful unless this behavior is uncovered and resolved. Compulsive masturbation or masturbation in public places can be treated with a combination of education and behavioral techniques. One approach is a gradual structuring so that certain places and/or times are set aside to be masturbation-free.

In more extreme cases of abuse, boys may have been lured into child pornography and prostitution (see Nielsen 1983; Burgess 1984; Burgess et al. 1984). Old patterns may be hard to break, especially if the child is accustomed to significant financial rewards. Boys deep into child pornography and prostitution have been taught an exploitive view of sexuality that may be hard to change. Acceptance of the child by the therapist and resolving of the underlying shame may help focus the young male on the need to move on. Once the child is motivated to change, behavioral techniques may be necessary to extricate him from the culture that has rewarded him in terms of both acceptance and money. It is only at this point that the young male may be willing to help with identification of other victims or prosecution of the adults involved.

When the young male's sexual acting out involves a child or adult victim, the task becomes more complex. Helping the child expand his worldview to include choices other than being either a victim or an abuser is the framework for the more specific tasks of therapy. Work with the victim/perpetrator should focus on acceptance of full responsibility for the abusive behavior and resolution of his own victimization. Both are important deterrents to future abuse. The first helps to emphasize the seriousness of the negative effects on his victim(s); the second allows him to develop empathy lost through his own victimization.

The ability to victimize depends on a lack of empathy with the victim stemming from a denial process that began at the time of his own abuse. Returning to that earlier time through talking, visualization, hypnosis, drawing, doll work, and other techniques is a necessary step to help the young man reconnect with his feelings concerning the victimization. The self-blaming of a victim also may need to be resolved in this regard, as the young male believes the abuse happened because he was no good and acts out his negative self-image by doing the worst thing he can imagine. Education about the dynamics of an adult child molester is vital to help convince the victim that he was not responsible for the abuse but that he is responsible for breaking the cycle of reacting to the abuse by becoming an abuser. Distinguishing him from his abuser by emphasizing that his abuser did not try to stop can help correct the young male's vision of himself as a bad person.

Other Acting-Out Behaviors

Rogers and Terry (1984) view nonsexual aggressive and controlling behaviors as inappropriate attempts by boys to reassert their masculinity. Thus, to protect himself from further victimization, the young male attempts to establish his invulnerability to attack by picking fights or attempting to bully other children; destroying property; being confrontive and obtrusive with parents, teachers, and other adults; being chronically disobedient; and appearing to be seeking punishment as a way to project a masculine image to others.

For example, "John" was fourteen years old when his own sexual abuse was disclosed because he was found to have sexually abused his younger brothers. He had been abused by his grandfather, whom he had admired and respected. He was able to begin to take responsibility for his sexual abuse and agreed to be placed out of the home for several months while his brothers began the task of healing. Once home, however, he continued a pattern of emotional and physical abuse toward his siblings. After almost two years of treatment concerning his own feelings of victimization, a confrontation session with his parents refocused work on his abuser side and resulted in a significant reduction of the troublesome behavior.

Besides work to curtail abusive behavior, the therapist and caretakers can help channel the boy's need to reassert masculinity into more socially acceptable activities, such as sports (especially contact sports) and self-defense training (such as boxing and the martial arts). Martial arts training that focuses on self-esteem and internal feelings of power (such as tae kwon do) can be especially helpful.

Infantile behavior and associations should diminish as the young male feels safer. Working with parents and other adults to provide age-appropriate nurturance and reassurance can help reduce attempts to elicit those needs with regressed behavior. With adolescents, it is especially helpful to work with the child within, who may be frozen in time at the age of the abuse (see chapter 1). Externalizing methods such as drawing and playing with dolls and puppets to recreate the abuse can emotionally distance the victim from the traumatic experience so that he can begin to resolve it.

Behaviors such as setting fires and running away are most likely to be calls for attention prior to disclosure. Here work with the caretakers is important, as they may be exasperated with the level of dysfunction the child has caused in the family with these behaviors. Helping them understand the child's disguised presentation and encouraging attention for positive behavior can break the cycle of negativity.

Anger

Dealing with the many and varied manifestations of anger and rage are paramount in the therapy of boy and adolescent victims of child sexual abuse. Activity seems to help calm boys in therapy. With older boys this might include giving them things to handle, taking walks, and letting them draw while talking about the presenting issues. With younger boys, physical activity is helpful, letting them use foam bats and other nondestructive ways to express hostile feelings. Puppets and dolls also are useful in helping contain the anger of young victims. It is important for the therapist not only to be accepting of and comfortable with anger but also to be able to work alongside the child to help him learn how to express rage in a focused way. By joining with the child, the therapist helps to ease the shame of expressing anger.

Ten-year-old "Aaron" was abused by his maternal grandfather. Aaron had many positive experiences with his grandfather and thus had difficulty expressing his anger toward him. However, he talked about being "wild in the head." Once the therapist made the connection between the child's experience and anger, he could be led to focus on the reasons why he was angry. The therapist then modeled directing the anger by guiding the child to follow her lead and take turns hitting a pillow with a foam bat, saying, "I'm angry at Grandpa because he . . ."

It is hard for many boys to identify anger. In such cases, the therapist's job is to observe nonverbal behavior and connect it with the feeling of anger. Also, the therapist can help the child label a description of feelings with a word for those feelings, such as Aaron's "wild in the head." Once the feeling is identified, the therapist can show the child how to express anger, including screaming, fantasizing consequences for the perpetrator, drawing feelings and experiences related to anger, and writing letters to persons (which may or may not be sent) with whom the child is angry. Educating parents about how to direct and help their child contain his anger at home also may be helpful.

Redirection of responsibility for the abuse may lead to rage at the offender and thoughts of revenge or even homicide. The child's acceptance of negative fantasies toward the perpetrator helps to contain his anger, lest it be directed at substitutes. Successful prosecution of the perpetrator also can be a major palliative in reducing anger. Even failed attempts at prosecution, if handled with realistic expectations from the start, can be helpful.

Work with supportive parents is vital in regard to angry feelings. This work may be fairly complex, as the therapist must deal with the parents' natural confusion of feelings toward their son and the perpetrator. When their son is both a victim and a perpetrator, this work is especially complex.

Suicide and Other Self-Destructive Behaviors

Obviously, suicidal ideation and/or attempts must be dealt with directly, including direct communication with the child's caretakers. Suicide watches or hospitalization may be necessary during the initial period of stabilization after disclosure. Initial therapy focused on reduction of blame and around shame issues should reduce suicide as a risk.

Other self-destructive acts short of suicide also are common and may include nail biting, cutting of arms with sharp objects, masturbation to the point of injury, and promiscuity without protection. Once these behaviors are labeled as self-destructive, work toward the resolution of a need to be punished can begin. Again, resolving feelings of blame and shame ought to reduce these behaviors.

Body Concerns

Education is important in dispelling myths that if the boy had been more physically powerful, he could have resisted the abuse. This must be exposed as unlikely given that the abuser probably used differences in physical size and authority, as well as manipulation and trickery, to perpetrate the abuse. Having the boy draw a picture of his body may help the therapist notice which areas are at issue. Body-image issues also may be addressed by encouraging the child's involvement in body building or material arts training as a way to feel safer from attack. Obviously, this does not preclude the possibility that the child will be revictimized and cannot be offered as a guarantee against such an occurrence, lest the child endanger himself with a violent abuser or feel guilty about not protecting himself if he is victimized again.

Internalized Affective Responses

Powerlessness

All victims of sexual assault experience a sense of powerlessness. Boys who have been sexually abused experience it in many ways. During the sexual assault, they were helpless to control what was happening to their bodies and how their bodies responded. Since the perpetrator probably was someone older and trusted, the victim was powerless to say no. Their need for control and choice will be manifested in the therapeutic process as well as in their daily interactions. For many boy victims of sexual abuse, anger may be the emotion through which powerlessness is expressed. However, for some boy victims, powerlessness is internalized and acted out in numerous ways.

With the young male, the sense of powerlessness will result in control issues in and out of therapy. In session, the therapist should give the child as much control and choice as possible. However, limits and rules regarding safety need to be clear and enforced, as the victim can begin to heal only within a safe environment. Young boys usually act out their sense of powerlessness through repetitive play, which help them begin to regain mastery of their experiences.

For example, "Christopher," age nine, was sexually abused by his grandfather for four years between the ages of four and seven. For the first six months in therapy, Christopher would spend half of each session building elaborate forts with the big pillows and cushions in the playroom. He would then place toy soldiers around the fort. After building the fort, Christopher would go inside. It was only after this weekly ritual that Christopher would talk to his therapist from inside his fort. With time and permission for this weekly ritual, Christopher eventually was able to talk about his abuse without his protective fort.

The therapist also needs to provide education and support for the parents, who may be confused about their child's behavior at home. Parents who were physically affectionate with their child may find him resistant or fearful. Parents may find the child victim's need for control disrupting the whole family. During the evaluation stage, the therapist ought to anticipate this behavior and then provide education and support to the parents.

Adolescent male victims may be able to articulate their state of powerlessness and helplessness. For adolescents who were not small children at the time of the sexual abuse, the therapist needs to provide education about the dynamics of victimization. Many adolescents struggle with acknowledging their victimization, but this is an important step in the therapeutic process. Young children and adolescents who are not able to acknowledge their victimization are at high risk to become victimizers. If the young male victim is unable or unwilling to do this important piece of work in therapy, the therapist ought to be concerned that he may be offending others.

The therapist can help the adolescent victim to look at things over which he does have control in his life. Sometimes it is helpful to make a list of these things. The therapist can discuss with the adolescent client appropriate ways to be assertive and aware of one's own power without needing to be powerful over others.

Some boy victims find that becoming involved in the criminal prosecution of their perpetrator is empowering. For some children and adolescents, this may mean testifying in court. For others, it may mean writing a letter to the judge or completing a victim impact statement. Some boys are able to become empowered when they disclose the details of the abuse and realize that by their disclosure, they may have protected other children as well as themselves.

Therapists should be creative in thinking of ways to help empower the young male victim. One therapist helped a child create a comic book hero character of himself telling about his abuse and helping other children. Two of the authors' adolescent clients made a videotape about their feelings of being sexually abused for a national conference on male survivors of child sexual abuse. The feedback from the participants was powerfully gratifying for the clients and their parents.

Shame

Shame is connected with several aspects of sexual victimization. For boys in our society, being labeled a victim is shameful. For many boys, this shame forces them to maintain their silence for so long. In whatever way the abuse was disclosed, the therapist needs to validate that it is good that the abuse is no longer a secret. Assisting young male victims in talking about their abuse and their feelings is the first step to lifting some of this shame. Again, the therapist can be creative and innovative, especially with the young child. Although adolescents may be able to articulate what happened, young children may find this more difficult. Using play as a medium, the therapist can help the child tell about the abuse using puppets, dolls, drawings, and toy telephones.

Young male victims may feel shameful about how their body responded to the abuse. Many boys experience erections and have other pleasurable sensations while being sexually abused. Educating both older and younger boys about physiology and normalization of the boy's response is important. One therapist explained it this way to a nine-year-old client: "If someone pokes you in the eye, it will probably tear up. If someone tickles you, you'll probably laugh. If someone touches your private parts, it will probably feel good."

Fear and Anxiety

Victimized children display fear and anxiety as a reaction to being abused. For some children, this will be manifested in regressive behaviors such as thumb-sucking and bed-wetting.

Intrusive thoughts, such as nightmares and flashbacks, can inhibit the young male from resolving issues of fear and power. Working with a nightmare, especially a recurring one, to help the child confront the powerful figure in the dream can reduce the anxiety in his waking life. Other ways of resolving nightmares include concretizing the dream by having the child draw pictures of it or creating a ritual around putting it away where it can no longer "escape." Education about flashbacks can help mitigate their effects. In addition, if flashbacks become disabling, medication might be an option (for example, clonazepam has been used in the treatment of adult posttraumatic stress symptoms, including flashbacks).

Male children particularly may react to fear and anxiety by acting tough and even engaging in risk taking or dangerous behavior. "Adam," age five, had been sexually abused by a juvenile sex offender when he was three-and-a-half years old. He came into therapy saying, "I'm tough," and would display his muscles. His play within the sessions was aggressive. When talking about being abused, however, Adam stated that after the abuse happened, he "ran all the way home." His therapist responded by connecting the action with a feeling: "You must have been afraid." The therapist also had Adam's father join his son for a session to talk about fear. Adam's father was able to say it was okay to be afraid even as an adult and give some examples of things that he was afraid of.

Parents also can be asked to institute safety rituals at home for the child.

Something as simple as saying the same reassuring sentence to the child every night can alleviate anxiety. Parents may need to step in and stop dangerous behaviors as well as consistently reassure the child of their protection.

Adolescents also experience fear and anxiety as a result of their sexual victimization. "Michael's" mother called his therapist after Michael, age fifteen, had become extremely upset and anxious. While working for a local pizzeria, Michael had been asked to deliver fliers to a strange neighborhood. His lack of trust in unknown adults triggered a panic attack. When Michael told his manager he did not think he could do this, she laughed at him and told him that fourteen-year-olds should be able to do this job. Michael was terrified of going into a strange neighborhood. He trusted his feeling of anxiety and said no. Yet his response was ridiculed by an adult, who did not know about Michael's victimization. Michael was reassured and felt protected when both his mother and his therapist validated his feelings and agreed with his decision.

Exploring with the adolescent which people or situations trigger his fear and/or anxiety is helpful. Adolescents can benefit from learning basic relaxation and breathing techniques. The therapist also can ask the adolescent to think of a place where he always feels safe or create such a place in his mind. The adolescent can visualize this safe place when he is feeling anxious or fearful. Again, as seen in the above case, parents are extremely important in helping the adolescent express his fears and feel protected.

Sadness and Loss

A victim of sexual abuse is also a victim of tremendous losses: loss of childhood, loss of innocence, loss of control and choice, sometimes loss of virginity, and often loss of an important person. Part of the healing process is acknowledging and grieving for these losses. For many boy victims, this will be an ongoing process. The very young victim may not be able to acknowledge these losses until he is older, but therapy should be a place where the boy begins to connect his experience with feelings.

The therapist needs to validate the feelings of young boy victims (for example, "It's okay to be sad"). Claudia Jewett's "Faces" (Jewett 1982) and Richard Gardner's "Bag of Words" (Gardner 1975) are two helpful techniques in assisting the child in identifying and expressing feelings.

The therapist can help the adolescent victim begin to label his losses and identify his feelings. The therapist also can be creative with adolescents by using artwork ("Can you draw a picture of what sadness looks like to you?"). Music is particularly helpful, as most adolescents are interested in it. The therapist can ask the adolescent to bring in a song that expresses his sadness, anger, or any other feeling. Even just listening with the adolescent to the kind of music he enjoys can be helpful in beginning to discuss feelings.

Loneliness and Isolation

Many victims and survivors of childhood sexual abuse feel lonely and isolated. In the past decade, support groups, conferences, newsletters, and books have emerged to break this isolation and loneliness for many adult victims and survivors. These resources, however, are more often targeted toward women than toward men. Resources for girl victims are still scarce, and those for boy victims are virtually nonexistent.

Obviously, the ideal resource for the young male victim who is feeling lonely and isolated is a therapy group for boys in the same age-group who have been sexually abused. Some therapists (Porter 1986) believe that group therapy is the best treatment modality for sexually abused boys.

If no such group is available, feelings of isolation and loneliness can be addressed in individual therapy. With adolescents, the therapist can provide education about the prevalence of the sexual abuse of boys. Adolescents also can benefit from reading the few books that are written specifically for or about boys who have been sexually abused (see the bibliography at the end of this chapter). If the therapist has other boy victims in the same age-group, some sessions with two (or more) victims can be extremely helpful in breaking down isolation. Networking with other local therapists may provide such an opportunity if the therapist's own caseload is more limited.

Younger boys may be more resistant than older boys to meeting others who have been abused. One therapist addressed the issue of isolation by asking her nine-year-old client how many children were in his class. When he said twenty, she placed twenty checkers on the table. She then pulled five checkers apart from the rest, saying, "Do you know that probably four other kids besides you have been sexually abused?" Thus, the therapist provided verbal and visual reassurance that he was not alone.

Family work is crucial, for as long as the sexual abuse is secret, the boy victim is alone. Individual work may be necessary for family members before family sessions can take place.

Countertransference

It is a challenge to work with boys who have been sexually abused, as only recently has this population begun to be identified and referred for treatment. Working with young male victims may elicit powerful emotions in the therapist that may be different from those elicited when working with female victims.

Some therapists may have difficulty hearing the details of same-sex abuse. Clinicians may be surprised at their sadness about a boy victim's trauma and loss. Perhaps this is because therapists are used to seeing girl victims and so, in some ways, have acknowledged and worked on those emotions. For example, some therapists find themselves unprepared for their own emotions when a boy cries in therapy.

For therapists who grew up in violent homes or for whom violence is a personal issue, witnessing the aggression and acting out of many boy victims may arouse deep feelings. Clinicians who find it easy to establish rapport and trust with girl victims may find themselves frustrated at the slow pace at which trust develops in boy victims, as well as the slow pace at which the abuse is disclosed and feelings are discussed.

Some therapists find themselves growing angry at a victim's parents for not providing their son with the same nurturance, protection, and supervision that they perceive the girls in the family receive. Other therapists find themselves feeling particularly angry in response to the fixated pedophile, who seeks out children to abuse sexually.

Many tactics can help the clinician to deal with the emotions that arise from working with young male victims. First, every therapist working in the field of child sexual abuse needs to explore his or her own feelings about any personal experience of abuse and his or her feelings about sexual abuse in general. Exploring one's own preconceptions about male victims and feelings about the male socialization process can help in identifying any misconceptions a therapist may have.

Second, getting supervision—individual or group—is invaluable in addressing and normalizing countertransference. Third, reading literature that particularly addresses the male victim also is helpful (see Hunter 1990). Finally, knowing and accepting one's own limits as a therapist and taking care of oneself are the main ingredients in being an effective and healthy therapist.

Transference

Young males who have been sexually abused can have several transference responses, some needing merely to be noted and others requiring therapeutic intervention. The primary transference can occur because of the gender match between the therapist and the abuser. Victims of male abusers may not feel safe being alone in an intimate situation with an adult male. Similarly, victims of female abusers may not feel safe with a female therapist. Since safety is the most important prerequisite for successful therapy with sexually abused children, this issue needs to be addressed at the time of the initial referral. If resolved successfully initially, it might need later discussion as issues of trust and safety arise. Anytime a child seems stuck in therapy, weakness in the therapeutic relationship ought to be explored as a possible contributor. For some young males who experience safety with an adult as a predominant issue, group therapy may be a viable alternative. For others, group therapy may actually be more threatening than individual therapy but may be added later as necessary.

Another transference issue may arise particularly in parent-child incest situations, where the child may have no parent who has been consistently nurturing and safe. Such a child may cling to the therapist as a parent substitute. With luck, there will be at least some caretaker with whom the therapist can work to provide the child with ongoing nurturance and protection. It is our experience that these situations occur more frequently with male than with female children because the environment is generally less protective and nurturing for male children, leaving a void that therapists are tempted to fill. It is, however, in the best interest of the child to find someone in his everyday environment to play this important role.

Countertransference issues are at work here as well. The therapist can be gratified that he or she is rescuing a child, but he or she also can be overly burdened by a child who seems to depend completely on him or her. Supervision and/or therapy is recommended to ensure that the therapist's issues do not interfere with treatment.

For example, "Tommy" was a five-year-old boy abused over a long period of time. The abuse was particularly violent and serious. At the first meeting, he grabbed his female therapist's breast in the waiting room, much as a toddler might. Age-appropriate limits had to be established and enforced to help this child mature. In this case, the therapist also had to resolve her countertransference issues toward the mother for failing to protect the child so that she could work productively with her to assume the maternal role for the child. Because of the neglect he had experienced, this boy also had developed an intense need to please as a way to elicit the attention of adults. The therapist had to help the child learn to express all of his emotions appropriately and to separate and individuate so that he could ask for and obtain the things he needed for emotional survival.

Conclusion

The identification and treatment of boy and adolescent victims of child sexual abuse is a complex and challenging task. It is, of course, in many ways similar to the treatment of girls. But there are some important differences.

Cultural taboos relating to males prevent young males (especially those between ages twelve and seventeen, who are just developing their identities as males) from either identifying themselves as abused or disclosing their abusive experiences. Even small boys are reluctant to admit that they were powerless to ward off the sexual advances of a perpetrator. Failing to acknowledge the reality of abuse situations and diverting psychic energy to keeping the abuse secret can have serious consequences for the emotional development of young males. Boys and adolescents tend to reassert the sense of masculinity lost during their victimization in inappropriate ways, often leading to the development of violent and delinquent behaviors. More than females, they tend to deny their victim status and identify with their abuser, which often leads to their perpetuating the cycle of abuse by acting out sexually or in other aggressive ways.

Disruptions in the development of sexual preference can occur for boys, especially those molested by males. Sexual dysfunctions have been noted in victims of both males and females. Whatever the sexual preference, a consequence of child sexual abuse for males seems to include the overprioritization of sexuality in relationships, which often disrupts the development of long-term intimacy.

Based on the literature review conducted for this chapter and the clinical experience of the authors, the following are recommended:

1. More public educational efforts about the effects of sexual abuse on young males to counter the current tendency of society to minimize these effects. This would include fighting the current stereotype that prepubescent or young adolescent males get "lucky" when they have a sexual experience with an adult female.

2. Community support for more protection of boys molested within their families and for more and longer treatment for all boys. This would include both individual and group treatment possibilities.

3. More professional literature written about boy and adolescent victims. In particular, there is a need for the dissemination of successful techniques for eliciting disclosures and for treating the effects of the abuse.

4. More research into the effects of sexual abuse on boys and adolescents.

5. As adult female survivors of child sexual abuse have come forward over the past several years, adult male survivors can help boys by acknowledging their abuse and its effects on their lives. Treatment professionals can help that process by telling the stories of the boys and men for them or by encouraging those victims who have the strength to speak out against the silence of male victimization.

We hope that this chapter will prompt thoughts and actions that will continue a dynamic process to provide evaluation and treatment of increasing quality for young male victims of child sexual abuse.

References

Bolton, F.G., L. Morris, and A.E. MacEachron. 1989. *Males at Risk: The Other Side of Child Sexual Abuse.* Newbury Park, California: Sage Publications.

Burgess, A. 1984. *Child Pornography and Sex Rings*. Lexington, Massachusetts: Lexington Books.

Burgess, A., C.R. Hartman, M.P. McCausland, and P. Powers. 1984. "Response Patterns in Children and Adolescents Exploited through Sex Rings and Pornography." *American Journal of Psychiatry* 141 (no. 5): 656–662.

DeJong, A.R., G.A. Emmett, and A.R. Hervada. 1982. "Sexual Abuse of Children." *American Journal of Diseases of Children* 136 (February): 129–134.

Ellerstein, N.W., and J.W. Canavan. 1980. "Sexual Abuse of Boys." *American Journal of Diseases of Children* 134 (March): 255–257.

Finkelhor, D. 1981. "The Sexual Abuse of Boys." *Victimology* 6 (no 1/4): 76–84.

———. 1984. "Boys as Victims: Review of the Evidence." In *Child Sexual Abuse: New Theory and Research*, edited by D. Finkelhor, 150–170. New York: Free Press.

Friedrich, W., A. Urquiza, and R. Beilke. 1986. "Behavior Problems in Sexually Abused Young Children." *Journal of Pediatric Psychology* 11 (no. 1): 47–57.

Gardner, R.A. 1975. *Psychotherapeutic Approaches to the Resistant Child*. New York: Jason Aronson.

Hunter, M. 1990. *Abused Boys: The Neglected Victims of Sexual Abuse*. Lexington, Massachusetts: Lexington Books.

Jewett, C. 1982. *Helping Children Cope with Separation and Loss*. Cambridge, Massachusetts: Harvard Common Press.

Johnson, R.L., and D. Shrier. 1985. "Sexual Victimization of Boys." *Journal of Adolescent Health Care* 6: (September): 372–376.

———. 1987. "Past Sexual Victimization by Females of Male Patients in an Adolescent Medicine Clinic Population." *American Journal of Psychiatry* 144 (no. 5): 650–652.

Kercher, G., and M. McShane. 1984. "Characterizing Child Sexual Abuse on the Basis of a Multi-Agency Sample." *Victimology* 9 (no. 3/4): 364–382.

MacFarlane, K., and J. Waterman. 1986. *Sexual Abuse of Young Children: Evaluation and Treatment*. New York: Guilford Press.

Mian, M., W. Wehrspann, H. Klajner-Diamond, D. LeBaron, and C. Winder. 1986. "Review of 125 Children 6 Years of Age and Under Who Were Sexually Abused." *Child Abuse and Neglect* 10 (no. 2): 223–229.

Nasjleti, M. 1980. "Suffering in Silence: The Male Incest Victim." *Child Welfare* 59 (no. 5): 269–275.

Nielsen, T. 1983. "Sexual Abuse of Boys: Current Perspectives." *Personnel and Guidance Journal* 62 (no. 3): 139–142.

Pierce, R., and L.H. Pierce. 1985. "The Sexually Abused Child: A Comparison of Male and Female Victims." *Child Abuse and Neglect* 9 (no. 2): 191–199.

Porter, E. 1986. *Treating the Young Male Victim of Sexual Assault: Issues and Intervention Strategies*. Syracuse, New York: Safer Society Press.

Porter, F.S., L. Canfield Blick, and S.M. Sgroi. 1982. "Treatment of the Sexually Abused Child." In *Handbook of Clinical Intervention in Child Sexual Abuse*, edited by S.M. Sgroi, 109–145. Lexington, Massachuetts: Lexington Books.

Reinhart, M.A. 1987. "Sexually Abused Boys." *Child Abuse and Neglect* 11 (no. 2): 229–235.

Risin, L.I., and M.P. Koss. 1987. "The Sexual Abuse of Boys." *Journal of Interpersonal Violence* 2 (no. 3): 309–323.

Rogers, C.M., and Y. Terry. 1984. "Clinical Intervention with Boy Victims of Sexual Abuse." In *Victims of Sexual Aggression,* edited by I.R. Stuart and J.G. Greer, 91–104. New York: Van Nostrand Reinhold.

Sebold, J. 1987. "Indicators of Child Sexual Abuse in Males." *Social Casework* 68 (no. 2): 75–80.

Sgroi, S.M., ed. 1982. *Handbook of Clinical Intervention in Child Sexual Abuse.* Lexington, Massachusetts: Lexington Books.

Spencer, M.J., and P. Dunklee. 1985. "Sexual Abuse of Boys." *Pediatrics* 78 (no. 1): July.

Summit, R.C. 1983. "The Child Sexual Abuse Accommodation Syndrome." *Child Abuse and Neglect* 7 (no. 2): 177–193.

Bibliography

Books for Young Male Victims of Sexual Abuse

Bell, R. *Changing Bodies, Changing Lives: A Book for Teens on Sex and Relationships.* New York: Random House, 1987.

Drake, E., A. Gilroy, and T. Roane. *Working Together: A Team Effort.* Gainesville, Florida: Child Care Publications, 1986.

Hall, L. *The Boy in the Off-White Hat.* New York: Charles Scribner's Sons, 1984.

Satullo, J., R. Russell, and P. Bradway. *It Happens to Boys, Too.* Pittsfield, Massachusetts: Rape Crisis Center of the Berkshires Press, 1987.

Talbert, M. *The Paper Knife.* New York: Dial Books for Young Readers, 1988.

Wachter, O. *No More Secrets for Me.* Boston: Little, Brown, 1983.

11
The Treatment of Sexually Abused Preschool Boys

Sandra Hewitt

T he treatment of child sexual abuse must be understood in a developmental context, whether the treatment is directed toward the child or toward the adult who was abused as a preschool child. Signs and symptoms of abuse, as well as understanding of the abuse, are shaped by the child's developmental stage at the time of the abuse. There is little difference between preschool boys and girls in the effects of developmental stages and the forms of therapeutic intervention used, but where there are differences, this chapter will highlight them. The first half of the chapter is devoted to a discussion of sexual abuse in a developmental context, and the second half deals with treatment strategies for the sexually abused boy.

Sexual Abuse in a Developmental Context

Birth to Eighteen Months

No one likes to imagine that sexual abuse occurs during infancy, but we know it does. In treatment, some offenders reveal that they began their abuse of a child during the child's infancy. Abuse may entail fondling a baby's genitals or sucking on an infant boy's penis. Sexual abuse of infants and toddlers up to eighteen months old is rarely if ever uncovered because the victim has no language. We substantiate children's cases based on their ability to verbalize; we cannot do so with infants. A case for intervention exists only if there is medical evidence (physical damage, presence of sexually transmitted disease, or discovery of sperm), if there is an eyewitness, or if there is a confession. All of these are rare. In fact even with medical findings, it is often difficult if not impossible to identify the perpetrators because the infant is unable to tell us who did it.

It is important to understand that the sexual abuse of infants may have several forms. A recent article by Haynes-Seman and Krugman (1989) details case histories of several parent-child interactions gleaned from a review of infants who were experiencing a failure to thrive. These case examples depict a very intrusive, sensual, sexualized involvement of a parent with a child. None of the examples would be considered sexual abuse as we legally define it, but the examples do show what could be thought of as the beginnings of such relationships. Sroufe and Ward's (1980) observations of mothers with their toddlers found that the mother's seductive behavior often did not respond to the needs of the child and was quite controlling and manipulative. Sroufe, Jacobvitz, Manglesdorf, DeAngelo, and Ward (1985) found early seductive behavior to be associated with attention deficit disorder and hyperactivity in kindergarten-age children. Thus, seductive behavior at these young ages can be associated with later behavioral adjustment difficulties. If the sexual abuse begins at these low levels, then our job in treatment is even more demanding, as we are attempting to change behavior whose roots may be deep in primitive infant-care giver behavior patterns.

Eighteen to Thirty-Six Months

It is very difficult to substantiate sexual abuse of toddlers. Much of the substantiation depends on the criteria noted above, but a child who is eighteen to thirty-six months old does have some form of language. Children of this age are just beginning to label things in their environment. They are building a vocabulary as they move from their sensorimotor world (Flavel 1963, 1968) into a world of verbal representation. The level of vocabulatory development is marked not by verbal expression but by a larger receptive, or understood, vocabulary. By the time a child is three years of age, he or she understands a great deal, and most children can express themselves very well. This verbal representation is one form of language. A second "language" encompasses the behavioral repertoire of young children. Any parent can tell you that toddlers are more effective at showing than at telling when they need to communicate things for which they have no words:

> "Nick" is eighteen months old and does not speak too clearly, but last night he had his first Popsicle, an experience he enjoyed very much. He watched his mother put the box with the rest of the Popsicles back in the refrigerator. The next morning Nick stood in front of the refrigerator, pointed, and said "More!"—one of his few words. Mom did not know exactly what he wanted, so she listened, held Nick, and opened the freezer. Nick peered inside. When he saw the box of Popsicles, he pointed and flashed Mom an eager smile. "More, more!" he said. Mom rewarded Nick with a Popsicle.

In like manner, children this age show good recall for objects in which they have been interested—for example, where Aunt Susan has the cookies or the pen in your purse. This capacity for recall and imitation can result in the spontaneous behavioral repetition of sexual interactions. It is very important when investigating sexual abuse at this age that this behavioral repertoire be acknowledged at least as strongly as the verbal statements the child makes. It is critical to document what the child says, in what context he or she says it, what the emotional or affect state was, and what the behavioral patterns have been.

Clinical experience with children eighteen to thirty-six months old at the Midwest Children's Resource Center (MCRC), a specialty child abuse service of Children's Hospital of St. Paul, Minnesota, has indicated a very wide range of verbal and nonverbal behaviors associated with abuse. Most of the abuse allegations evaluated in this age-group have involved females who often are bright and have good verbal skills. Young boys probably also are abused, but in this population, it seems that the greater language skills of females accounts for their more frequent referral for professional evaluation. The cases are difficult to substantiate, and the impact of the abuse varies. At MCRC, approximately six hundred children are seen each year for medical and/or psychological evaluation. Preschool children make up about 65 percent of those children. Two-year-olds have been seen in increasing numbers during the past few years because few child protection workers or police personnel feel comfortable assessing abuse at this age.

The importance of attending to nonverbal behavior in this population is well demonstrated in "Jamie's" case history:

Jamie's mother delivered him while she was incarcerated for the sexual abuse of an older daughter. Part of the plea bargain in her case was that she would terminate parental rights to her daughter if the charges of sexual abuse against her husband were dropped. After Jamie was born, he was placed in foster care but released to his father for weekend visits with his mother at the prison.

When Jamie was twenty-nine months old, his mother was released, having successfully participated in treatment, and Jamie was allowed weekend overnight visits with his parents. Jamie returned from the visits irritable, dirty, and sleepy. Development that had been proceeding well, except for some lag in speech and language skills, began to slow. Jamie also began to masturbate a lot, even to the extent that he would masturbate at the dinner table while food was present. (This is an unusual behavior; most children will not masturbate in the presence of interesting stimuli.) His masturbation often would leave him red and raw. (This is also unusual, as most children will not masturbate to the extent that they continue to hurt themselves.) Jamie's speech and language skills began to regress, and he added little expressive vocabulary. Besides being difficult to understand, Jamie would refuse to talk if he did not want to. Visits with his parents also initiated a time of skill regression in toileting, self-help, and interpersonal social skills, and his behavior problems escalated.

Because of these problems, Jamie was referred for evaluation of possible abuse. Despite being almost three years of age, he required evaluation skills geared more toward an eighteen- to twenty-four-month-old child. (Note that there is often a wide variation in developmental progress at these young ages; chronological age is not a guarantee of age-consistent functioning.) During the time of the evaluation, Jamie's foster mother recorded that he had gone into the bathroom, taken some of her hand lotion, applied it to his penis, and then masturbated. The foster mother reported that she had never applied lotion to Jamie's penis for medical or other purposes. A while later, he was observed holding the dog's head against his crotch so the dog would lick his exposed penis. This behavior was documented, and the level of concern (this is very unusual behavior) was communicated to the court. Unsupervised weekend visitation was then changed to supervised hourly visitation. The sexualized behaviors decreased markedly.

This example illustrates the form that behavioral enactment of sexual experience may take in very young boys. Even though this young boy could not talk, his behaviors were clearly indicative of aberrant experiences. Young boys of this age may display a marked interest in others' genitalia, have diapering problems, or act out aspects of an abusive situation (for example, trying to suck a woman's breasts when there is no history of breast feeding or trying to fondle a man's penis). All of these behaviors need careful evaluation in the context of the child's environment and developmental stage.

Children of this age do not give voice to their abusive experiences, so it is difficult to understand how they store their experiences and make sense of them. Because of their lack of verbal ability, many people believe that treatment for abuse experienced at these very young ages is not needed because the abuse memory will pass into the great void of inaccessible preverbal experiences, never to affect the child's life. Clinicians at MCRC, however, have encountered several children who were abused while very young (seven to fifteen months) act out or describe their early abuse at a later time. It seems very clear that some children store early abuse episodes with startling clarity.

The issue of very early abuse is problematic from a treatment standpoint. It does occur, it can be stored over the long term, and it can affect later behavior. Obviously, it is better if therapy can occur as close to the time of the abuse experience as possible because it is easier to correct the child's understanding of the abuse and to rectify misunderstandings and create appropriate boundaires at that time. Many children do not receive therapy, often because services for very young children are not available or because their caretakers do not see it as important. Also, the child may not be available verbally and conceptually for treatment. Treatment may need to be focused broadly on the child and his or her family. It may involve providing clear boundaries and a safe environment until the child is ready for additional forms of therapy.

Children at these young ages present with few words, a variety of behaviors, and a response frequency that does not fit well into the traditional investigative model. These children do not talk when the investigators come, they may talk about their experiences after the investigator leaves, and they may speak of these experiences to an unreliable reporter. Abuse is difficult to document, and it presents a challenge to treatment.

Three to Five Years

Preschool children understand their world in a way that is significantly different from the way adults understand their world. As with the ages above, a young child's world is very self-focused and based on concrete experience and perception. But as the child matures, a growing sense of the separation and differences between self and others emerges. As the child individuates, he or she gets better at describing other people and other events. Information is still stored very egocentrically; this creates the belief that "if I experience it, it's real, and the rest of the world understands things the same way I do."

Children of this age do not monitor other people's misperceptions, and an interviewer must take care to ensure that he or she is understanding information in the way the child means it. These children have not had a common socializing experience (such as school), and they reflect the wise diversity of their individual environments. They see the world revolving around them, and they expect that you see it the same way. For example, while walking in a grocery store, an overhead page announces, "Josh, please call number 64. Josh, please call 64." A preschooler whose name is Josh might turn to a parent and say, "Dad, they're calling me!" That is egocentrism.

A sexually abusive experience at this age often is understood as having been directed only toward the child, and thus the child must have caused it or been responsible for it. A nonviolent sexual experience may be understood as just one more life experience, with none of the values or sexual feelings adults ascribe to it. The experience may be openly replayed or demonstrated by the child devoid of a sense of shame or embarrassment. Often the child's sense of shame and wrongdoing comes from the reaction of the adults around him or her. When a parent learns of the sexual encounter, he or she may yell and scream, collapse, and cry, and the young child will form a sense of his level of wrongdoing based on the intensity of the parent's reaction. This sense of shame and guilt can affect the child's sense of self-worth over time.

Sexually abusive experiences at this age can shape the way a child interprets sexual information and expresses sexual behavior (for example, more genitally focused attention, more explicit sexual behaviors, or more interest in sexual material), and this in turn can affect other aspects of the emerging child. Child development expert Burton L. White (1975) argues that an individual's basic personality is shaped in the first three years of life. Early abuse can affect the emerging sense of self and world in a young child. Erik Erikson (1963) refers to the capacity to develop basic trust as the foundation of healthy psychosexual development. If a young child is abused by his or her primary caretaker, the child learns that those you trust may not be reliable in their interactions. Sometimes they may help, and sometimes they may hurt. Thus, as the older preschooler moves out to explore the world, he or she may be reluctant to trust others and thereby deprive himself or herself of important mentors in the learning experience. A child's capacity to explore and master his or her world may be seriously impaired if they cannot trust the adult "guides" in their world.

Socially, these young preschoolers are actively engaged in a search for peers to play with. On occasion, these peers may witness another child's abuse or they may also be part of it. It is important to check out the peer relationships in a young child's environment. Probably the most common form of peer involvement in child sexual abuse is that which occurs when one sexually abused child repeats the abusive behavior with a peer and an adult finds out. The newly abused child's parents are often very upset, seeing the other child as a perpetrator and unfit for any further contact with their child. It is rare for young children of this age to have a well developed capacity to "perpetrate"; most of these young children replay their experience of the world, and they do not have sufficient experience to make an active choice between one form of behavior or another. Their behavior is reflective of their experience. Although these children are not actively choosing a perpetrator style, there are some very young children who do act in powerful and abusive ways with other children, and they need specialized treatment. Work by Johnson and Berry (1989) outlines a treatment program for children who molest, encompassing children aged four to twelve. Troy and Sroufe (1987) have studied the play of preschoolers with abusive backgrounds. They paired these children with nonabused children as well as with other abused children. They found that although the abused children had experienced the victim role only in their abuse, they were clearly able to play out the victimizer role in certain play pairings. A child in an abusive experience learns two roles, even though he or she may have the opportunity to play out only one. In treating young children, care must be taken to understand that their aggressive, or acting-out, behaviors need to be processed against the background of their abuse experiences and not be treated only as behaviors that must be controlled or stopped.

Another significant aspect of emotional development at this stage is the ability of a child to take the role of another person (Flavel 1963), or to empathize. It is important to facilitate this development in the therapeutic interchange. One of the characteristics seen in many sexual abusers is the absence of empathy. Work at this beginning level could help to mediate against later acting out.

One other factor emerges for the three- to five-year-old. The child is now capable of discussing his or her multisensory store—that is, how the experience tasted, what it felt like, what it looked like, and how it smelled. Asking about these different senses may help the therapist to understand the full nature and extent of the abuse. Children at these ages do not tell their stories very well in the sense that they do not give the middle, end, beginning, and transitions or variations in logical order or sequence. Instead they relate it in bits and pieces. They also are incapable of clear enumeration (that is, one item goes to one number), and they have not developed a concept of time. It is common for a preschooler to ask, "It is tomorrow yet?"

All of these things make it difficult to assess some of the specific details of abuse. Understanding as much as possible about the nature and extent of the abuse and placing it in the child's current developmental context are critical to understanding the meaning of the abuse to the child. This lays the groundwork for effective treatment planning.

Earlier I noted that abuse experience may be stored at an early developmental stage and discussed at a later stage. At MCRC, it is common for children aged three or four to present with behaviors indicative of sexualized experience but with no current abuse history. The parent may recall, however, an earlier episode of abuse. In therapy, the child gives clear details of the abuse. The details may be fragmented, nonsequential, and short, or they may be longer strings of behavior. The child who enacts these scenarios is often very bright and has retained a clear memory of the event, even though he or she did not have the capacity to express it until now. Often the developmental issues of sexual interest, acting-out behaviors, and challenging authority will bring the issues of sex and behavior to the fore.

If the child recalls only fragments that are difficult to understand, sometimes adults who have knowledge of the child's history can provide explanations. This is "Mario's" story:

> For the third time, Mario's mother placed him in foster care because of her chronic drug problem. Mario was almost four, but he was delayed in many ways, such as speech and language skills, and there were concerns about retardation. Mom's use of cocaine or crack during her pregnancy also was considered. Mario displayed some unusual behavior with his foster mother. He would try to suck or touch her breasts, and he was very preoccupied with his genitals.

When observed with his mother during visits, he was noted to crawl all over her, to have few boundaries regarding touch, and to have little range of play behavior other than eating and snuggling.

Evaluation was geared toward an eighteen- to thirty-six-month age level because of Mario's delays. Besides documentation of a confusing blend of delays and strengths in Mario's development, the evaluation confirmed his unusual sexualized play behaviors. His limited statements and behavioral reenactments were seen as indicative of probable sexual abuse by his mother, but because of Mario's expressive problems and delays, this information went into the "suspected but unable to prove" category. It would have remained there had it not been for Mom's involvement in treatment.

Mom initially denied any sexual contact with Mario, but later, when she was being honest about her chemical use, her own background of abuse, and her feelings, she acknowledged sexual abuse of Mario beginning at age eighteen months, when she would fondle his penis in an attempt to arouse him. This behavior was fairly frequent during Mario's second year of life and episodic into his third year between foster care placements. Mother's own admissions, which were seen as valid disclosures, clearly depicted a sexually abusive relationship with her son starting at a very young age. Later matching of Mario's limited statements and behaviors with Mom's confession resulted in a startling similarity despite the young age at which some of the abuse had occurred.

It is important to note that adults in therapy who are struggling to recall what they think was past abuse may recall fragments of information but be unsure whether they were part of a dream or reality. It is quite possible that the recall comes from a very early memory store that was created during a developmental stage two levels below the current adult level. Looking back across the gap in the quality of perception and storage gives these fragments their dreamlike quality. Careful history taking about experiences at these young ages is important even in treating adult victims of abuse.

Treatment of the Preschool Male Victim

Four Type of Skills and Knowledge

Effective treatment of a preschool-age sexually abused child demands a complex blend of at least four types of skills and knowledge.

First, a detailed knowledge of child development is needed, for at no other time in the life span is there such rapid and wide-ranging growth as in the preschool years. It is essential that the therapist have a good understanding of the cognitive, social, emotional, and sexual development of children—not only what is expected as the norm but also where the child is headed in the next stage and what constitutes pathology in both developmental stages.

Second, the therapist must have skills in therapy with small children. Primary skills in play therapy are important, but observation, assessment, and parent consultation skills also are important. Because handicapped children often are at greater risk for abuse, some therapists need advanced knowledge of handicapping conditions and the ability to tailor their interventions to the strengths of the child's handicap.

Third, the therapist needs to have skills in working with a multidisciplinary team. Work frequently needs to be done not only in the context of this family but also with a day-care provider or teacher. Occasionally, consultation with extended-family members, friends, neighbors whose children are friends of the abused child, or other associates of the family is required.

Fourth, the therapist needs a good working knowledge of the various models that have been developed to describe the effects of sexual abuse and other types of trauma on children.

A discussion of all four of these areas is impossible here. Advanced training usually provides the therapist with the developmental background and some training in therapy, and experience helps hone networking skills. Academic settings have been slow to offer training in child abuse, so a brief overview of current models and processes for treating abuse follows.

Models for Treating Abuse

Many models address the effects of child sexual abuse and list key variables in the abuse that need therapeutic attention. Some of these models are presented chronologically here.

Porter, Blick, and Sgroi (1982) describe ten variables as important in the treatment of sexual abuse. These are the "damaged goods" issue, guilt, fear, depression, low self-esteem and poor personal skills, repressed anger and hostility, impaired ability to trust, blurred role boundaries and role confusion, pseudomaturity coupled with the failure to accomplish developmental tasks, and problems with self-mastery and self-control.

Finkelhor and Browne (1986) interviewed adult survivors of child sexual abuse and conceptualized four "traumagenic dynamics" of child sexual abuse: betrayal, powerlessness, traumatic sexualization, and stigmatization. Jones (1986) offers a five-part conceptualization of the traumatic experience of child sexual abuse: trauma, threat to ontogeny, neglect and emotional unavailability of the care giver, the child's feeling of exploitation, and the child's adaptation. Treatment is divided into three phases, with many of Porter et al's (1982) issues used as content focus.

MacFarlane and Waterman (1986) have written about the treatment of young victims. They integrate Porter, Blick, and Sgroi's (1982) issues into some general guidelines for treating young children. They also deal with issues such as assessment, the courts, and family involvement, all of which are important in treating young victims.

Burgess and Grant (1988) have developed a schema for thinking about the processing of trauma in children. This model can help clarify condition and treatment needs of the very traumatized child.

The MCRC Approach

Much of the theory concerning issues of sexual abuse was developed from information about adult survivors, and many of the therapy processes have focused on therapy with school-age children or adolescents. When designing a treatment program for a preschool child, the process should begin with an assessment of the child's status across several dimensions. At MCRC, a process of both objective and subjective assessment is used. If the therapist is not trained in assessment he or she ought to seek assistance on two levels:

1. Interpretation of parent report protocols obtained in the screening process
2. A full child assessment, as described below

The nature of the case and the availability of resources often determine the extent of the assessment support.

When a child is referred for therapy, the first step is a meeting with the primary caretaker to gather information about the child's developmental background and current status. Objective measures of development are obtained from the parent based on three tests; the Minnesota Child Development Inventory (MCDI) (Ireton and Thwing 1972), the Child Behavior Checklist (CBCL) (Achenbach and Edelbrock 1986), and the Child Sexual Behavior Inventory (CSBI) (Friedrich 1990). The first two measures are standardized tests. The third is an experimental scale that must be obtained from the author. Because these tests are completed by the parent, they suffer from the problem of parental bias. Results from these measures are matched with the clinician's own evaluation.

During the initial interview, it is important to gather a good developmental history on the child. Such a history should include information on prenatal, birth, and infancy events; significant medical problems; major separations from a primary caretaker; past levels of adjustment and growth, as well as regressions or problems in development; current status; and a clear account of what the parent saw that made him or her think that sexual abuse had occurred or was currently occurring. The last item should include documentation of the behaviors and statements of the child. The child's statements and behaviors should be interpreted in the context of the ongoing events in the child's life at that time.

Research on the memory of young children (Pearlmutter 1980) indicates that recall for very young children is related to a trigger event that calls forth aspects of a previous situation and brings that memory into focus. If the trigger event can be discerned, the clinician may be able to use that same cue to bring up information in the session.

After the intake interview, the therapist meets with the child. The foremost task of the first and possibly the second and third meetings is making friends with the child and establishing a comfortable and secure atmosphere. At MCRC, the early sessions also are used for evaluation of cognitive, behavioral, social, emotional, and sexual status. Some of this information is taken from the parent measures, but additional testing may be done. In addition, it is important to discern as clearly as possible the nature and extent of the abuse. Sometimes the child can do this himself or herself, and sometimes accounts need to be gathered from parents, police, or child protection reports. If the perpetrator is in treatment, clear and detailed accounts may be obtained from him or her. The perpetrator's report can be very helpful, not only because he or she was an eyewitness but also because the perpetrator is older and can give additional perspective on the child's reactions.

From these initial sessions, a fairly clear picture of the child's current status should emerge. Gaps or development lags are noted, and treatment goals are set to help restore the child to a more appropriate level of functioning. In treating the sexual abuse of young boys, the therapist must consider a treatment plan not only for the child but also for the family. For example, if the parents are very angry and/or depressed about the abuse, their reactions will affect the child and they need time and help to process these reactions. Preschool children are very alert observers of parent reactions, and often they will develop their own feelings of guilt, responsibility, or shame based on these reactions. When feeling such guilt and remorse about their child's abuse, parents may stop parenting for a period of time. For instance, they may suddenly stop enforcing common rules such as bedtime and excuse generally unexcusable misbehavior. From the child's point of view, this is yet another disruption in his or her life, as the child is suddenly unclear about limits and boundaries and may escalate his or her acting out to find new limits. Restoration of a routine and limits is very important in maintaining a sense of safety and security, following the abuse.

Setting treatment goals requires a complex synthesis of knowledge of child development, childhood psychopathology, the effects of child sexual abuse, common therapeutic techniques for treating young children, behavior management techniques, and family dynamics. Simply put, developing a treatment plan is a complex process. Little has been written about therapeutic interventions with toddlers or preschool-age children. The procedures and models outlined above provide the groundwork, but some adaptation needs to be made for very young children.

Intervention must be conducted within the context of the child's relationship with the primary caretaker(s) and the rest of the family. These children cannot exist outside of this relationship, and caretakers often are required to become cotherapists in the intervention process.

Parents vary widely in their ability to function in this role and in their own need for intervention. Some parents can function well with some crisis intervention and directed reading (for example, Hagans and Case 1988). Other parents require extensive therapy and remain emotionally unavailable to their children for a period of time while they are working through their own issues. Still other parents may not be able to participate at all in either the treatment process or the case plan. Many parents' reactions are similar to those described by Kubler-Ross (1969) in response to grief, and they may need time to work through them. Some couples may need marriage counseling, and sexual functioning often is suppressed as a reaction to the abuse. These aspects of parent functioning affect children of all ages, but the younger child, the more central the parents role, and thus the more clearly the therapist must define that role.

Therapeutic Interventions

Birth to Eighteen Months

Direct, cognitively based intervention is not possible at this age, so attention is directed toward the primary caretaker and toward restoring an environment that is safe, nurturing, protective, and able to provide clear boundaries. With the caretaker's assistance, the therapist carefully monitors the child's behavior. In many cases of child abuse, other areas of development are affected, and the child may experience developmental lags or difficulties as a result of the abuse. As the child becomes capable of exhibiting more behaviors, the quality of those behaviors must be monitored, with redirection and reeducation toward inappropriate behaviors.

Few children in this age-group are seen for therapy. Limited experience at MCRC and previous settings has suggested the following direct intervention. It is important to correct sexualized behavior toward adults, although children of this age are not capable of organized, directed, complicated sexualized behaviors. Tentative sexual behaviors should be gently redirected, as such behaviors can be disturbing to some caretakers and could interfere with the attachment process. In addition, some persons perceive such behaviors as indicative of an interest in sexual stimulation or games. This may predispose the child to abuse by other perpetrators who think the child is interested in sex and is sexually precocious.

Work with sexually abused infants and toddlers centers on the reestablishment of a safe, nonabusive environment; the facilitation of good primary caretaker attachment; and the redirecting and restructuring of overt sexualized behaviors. Remembering that early abuse may be stored and acted out or discussed at later ages is important, as the therapist and caretaker must remain open to providing individual therapy at a later date as the child might need it.

Eighteen to Thirty-Six Months

Again, intervention demands a close working relationship with the primary caretaker, which requires that the parent's capacity be carefully assessed. As with infants and toddlers, the child needs to be restored to a safe, nonabusive environment, and a healthy attachment relationship needs to be supported. Acting-out behaviors must be redirected and reframed. For example, in the story of Jamie earlier in this chapter, the foster parents directed Jamie to stop masturbating at the table and told him not to let the dog lick his penis. It is important that the child is not being abused when this restructuring and redirecting is done, or some important behaviors indicative of abuse can be suppressed. No shaming or judging should accompany this redirecting.

As these children grow older, some additional cognitive based intervention can be helpful. For example, as Jamie matures, his foster parents may tell him that such behavior is not acceptable and that someone tought him the wrong rules. Now that he knows the right rules, he is expected to follow them. This simple restructuring and reframing often helps control acting-out behaviors.

Older children in this age range may be in need of some of the affective discharge that is available in therapy. One twenty-four-month-old boy, after being physically mistreated by his day-care provider, could demonstrate his abuse only by having an adult doll hit a child doll. When he did this, he had a frown on his face and was concentrating intensely. A therapeutic intervention for him occurred when the therapist took the doll labeled as the sitter and told it in a stern voice that she could not hit Joey anymore. The child stopped, stared at the therapist, and smiled broadly. He picked up the sitter doll and held her up to the therapist so she could take her again. Joey clearly wanted the therapist to tell the sitter again not to hit Joey anymore.

Young children need to be supported in their sense of violation and their indignation that something wrong was done to them. Joey repeated his request for the therapist's admonition several times. Then his parents were invited into the therapy session and shown how to affirm their son's safety. The message was particularly powerful when Joey's father told the sitter doll that she could no longer hit Joey. The emerging sense of self among these young children needs to be recognized, supported, and affirmed.

Clear boundaries can be demonstrated for very young children by simple doll play. The therapist can say to a female baby-sitter doll, "Shari, you can't touch Travis's pee pee anymore. I won't let you do that, Travis won't let you do that, and his mom and dad won't let you do that. Travis says no, and you need to listen to him." After doing this with a young child in therapy, the child spontaneously added, "You go home. You can't play till you follow the rules!" This play helps to restore a damaged sense of self and offers the child a renewed sense of power.

Three to Five Years

MacFarlane and Waterman (1986) and Jones (1986) are especially useful resources for structuring therapy for children in this age-group. In addition to addressing the issues listed above (restoring a safe environment, encouraging good attachments, redirecting and reframing sexualized behaviors, and affirming the child's feelings and response), the therapist must remember that the three- to five-year-old is capable of more thinking and talking about the abuse. Although children may remain very egocentric, older children in this group may be aware of the perpetrator's feelings and motives on some level. They often need to play out the abuse as they perceived it, and they need assistance to make sense of the abuse and integrate it in healthier ways.

As stated above, therapy begins with the assessment of current status. Because sexual abuse carries the power of legal action, it often receives the most attention in this assessment. In addition, children who act out sexually or adults who have to deal with the idea of sexual abuse focus the assessment on the abuse rather than on other important factors in the child's life. In some cases, the sexual abuse may be of secondary or even tertiary concern. For example, a four-year-old child who has been living with an alcoholic mother who was involved in a violent relationship with her lover, may have more important issues concerning the loss of his primary parents, the behavioral sequela coming from a life of neglect, inadequate nutrition, lack of shelter, and the effects of witnessing the beating of his mother. It is important to place the sexual abuse in the context of the child's life experiences and look at it in relation to his or her other problems.

One way of considering how important the abuse might be in a boy's life is to consider the factors associated with trauma (Finkelhor 1986). Among these are the following:

- The relationship of the perpetrator to the child. Was he or she a primary caretaker, someone the child needed, loved, and trusted, or a more peripheral person such as an occasional baby-sitter?

- The degree of violence present. Was there a threat of violence against the child or his family, or was the abuse an encouragement of exploration with no threat?

- The level of support in the family. Do family members blame the child for the abuse and possible subsequent disruption of the family, or is the family protective and supportive of the child, with the parents venting their feelings when the child is not present?

- The length of the abuse or the degree of penetration. Was there intercourse or brief fondling?

Common Treatment Problems and Approaches

Not all abuse is the same, and not all children react to abuse in similar ways. The rest of this chapter deals with common treatment problems and strategies for dealing with those problems.

Sexual Acting Out

One of the most common treatment problems is sexually acting out with other children. Developmental stages can play a part in the timing of some acting out. Four-year-old children normally are involved in the exploration of boundaries and frequently focus on bodily functions and excretions. These children love to talk about "farting, pooping, and peeing"—discussions that are punctuated by raucous laughter. Four-year-olds also are exploring their parents' and others' limits and boundaries. Developmental factors help shape the form of intervention by recognizing the need for clear rules and structure for the expression of sexualized behaviors.

Sexual acting out is commonly seen around age four. Some of the normal sexual interest noted above is related to this timing. Experience with many preschoolers at MCRC has shown that abuse also may be acted out at age four, but as the child approaches age five and the different tasks required (starting school, separating from parents for greater amounts of time, increasing peer relations, and so on), the abuse becomes suppressed and acting out decreases.

It is common for preschool children to reproduce in their play with other children or adults things they have learned in other contexts. Again, developmental processes help shape the child's symptoms of abuse. Regardless of developmental stage or process, however, acting out of sexual abuse experiences with other children is not acceptable, and the child ought to be referred into therapy. The following questions can help the therapist learn about the basis for the acting out:

1. Is the child unclear about appropriate boundaries because of the abuse experience?
2. Is the child very eroticized and seeking sexual stimulation in the repetition?
3. Is the child repeating a situation that was difficult for him to master in order to regain a sense of personal power and control?
4. Is the child looking for affection through the contact the sexual behavior may bring?
5. Is the acting out a combination of one or more of the above factors?

A discussion of these factors and suggested forms of intervention follows.

Unclear Boundaries. The preschool child needs a clear sense of limits and rules. This intervention matches the preschooler's need for structure and limits. For some children, the process of establishing these limits and boundaries, plus reprocessing the abuse within a supportive family context, can contain the acting-out behaviors and help the child make new and more adaptive meaning of the abuse experience. Most often children who are responsive to this level of intervention are those who come from well-functioning families that are able to help process the child's abuse, which often is of a less traumatic nature.

Eroticized Play. Yates's (1982) work is helpful in understanding this process. The child needs to learn how to accept and manage his or her sexual feelings and behaviors in a nonexploitive relationship. Reaney (1987) discusses several goals for the eroticized child: parents' acceptance of sexual feelings through verbal expression, helping the child establish control over his or her own body, and rechanneling the child into developmentally appropriate activities. The parents may need additional work to help them understand their child's sexual behavior. Many families are very resistant to any form of sexualized behavior by their child. Giving a child permission to touch his or her own body in private may be more of an issue for the parents than for the child.

Repetition for Mastery. Repetitive play in therapy sessions may indicate the child's inability to achieve sufficient mastery over or comfort with the abuse to allow it to pass into long-term storage. Classical analytically based therapy holds that repetition compulsion is a sign of underlying conflict. In such cases, play therapy is needed to help the child play out and work through the abuse. Such play often is difficult for the therapist to watch, but careful observation of the child's depiction of his or her abuse can help the therapist identify where the child is stuck and where the therapist may offer interpretation that will help free him or her from the conflict. It is important to try to see the play issue from the child's point of view. A clear understanding of the child's perspective allows stronger intervention to grow.

If the play is violent or out of control, or if it leads to acting out outside the session, the therapist will have to set clearer limits to help the child remain within an effective "therapeutic window" (Cole and Barney 1987). This concept, taken from literature concerning adult survivors, refers to the range within which the patient can deal effectively with the abuse material. If the material is too strong, the therapist must help the child to maintain effective boundaries in dealing with it. On occasion, hypnotic techniques may be used if the material is extremely traumatic (Friedrich 1990).

Troy and Sroufe (1987) note that children reared with physical abuse are capable of taking the role of either victim or victimizer in their play with peers. Clearly, even though they had no chance to practice the victimizer role, they have internalized it and can reproduce it when needed. Boys often act out their abuse as part of a quest for the loss of power and control they have experienced. Macoby and Jacklin (1974) in an extensive survey of the research on sex differences, had basically one robust finding: boys were more aggressive than girls. Any parent who has attempted to provide his or her son with both "boys' " and "girls' " toys will tell you that the cars, guns, and swords are usually much more popular than the dolls and dishes. If part of the process of raising a male child is to help him learn how to handle his aggressive impulses appropriately, then the act of sexual abuse may have significant implications. During the abuse, the young boy loses his sense of power and mastery. He loses his strong self-concept, which embodies a sense of efficacy and control. Powerlessness then becomes one of the major therapeutic issues (W. Friedrich, personal communication, May 1987).

Therapy may revolve around restoring a sense of mastery and control and repairing the child's self-concept. Clinical experience at MCRC has showed this to be one of the most salient aspects of a young boy's treatment. One way to help the boy regain his sense of power is to discuss the abuser's use of tricks or misinformation to expose the boy to the wrong rules. The therapist must explain that the boy was too young to know the rules yet because he had not been taught all these things. The abuser did know the rules and violated them. The therapist can then reframe the boy as an expert on the rules and put him in charge of them. The child may have to role-play so that he can practice responding appropriately. The therapist also may have to teach some boys assertiveness. Helping the boy go from a victim of abuse to someone who is praised for his new knowledge of the rules and strength around them gives him a sense of having more power and control. This therapeutic strategy also is effective with boys whose boundaries concerning sexual touching have been disrupted by the abuse. This process of reframing and empowering reduces the child's need to replay the abuse as a way of regaining mastery and control. This represents a concrete application of therapy based on the traumagenic dynamic of powerlessness and stigmatization (Finkelhor and Browne 1986).

Another form of intervention for boys who continue to act out sexually is to put the boy in charge of his behaviors. The following case example demonstrates this intervention.

> One fall several years ago, I had about four boys, aged four to five, in individual therapy. All had been involved in sexual abuse by older adolescent boys. I helped the boys process the event. I worked with each family, and the boys' acting out of the abuse stopped. The abuse faded as a major topic in the therapy sessions, and the boys refocused on issues that were more developmentally appropriate.
>
> When the boys finished treatment, they were given standing permission to call me if they needed anything in the future. Several months passed, and in the spring, with the increased peer contact and mobility afforded by the warmer weather, I got calls from three of the boys' parents indicating that their sons were exposing their penises in inappropriate places, such as in the garage with a younger neighborhood boy. The boys came back in to see me, and we talked about the past abuse, the rules, and their feelings about their victimization, which we applied to their own victims. For two of the three boys, this did not make a great deal of difference.
>
> In one session with a boy who had been fairly active with his penis of late, I discussed the importance of his penis and the need to keep it safe: "Toby, you have only one penis, and it's the only one you'll get, and it's a very important thing to have. Why, without it you couldn't even pee. Although it's important now, it will be even more important to have when you grow up, and even more wonderful to have. You have an important job. You are in charge of keeping your penis out of danger. This means you have to be careful where it goes and that it is not in dangerous situations where you could get hurt, such as taking it out with younger and older boys. You are in charge of it. Do you think you can handle this?" I worked with the child to help him understand and master what he needed to accomplish this new task. Surprisingly, this worked well, so I repeated it with the other boy. It worked well with him, too. The penises stayed where they belonged.
>
> Later I discussed this seat-of-the-pants intervention with other therapists who treat male victims and offenders. They told me that it was not a bad intervention because it valued a special part of the boys' anatomy that had been devalued, and it also restored power

in an area that had been rendered powerless. Since that time, I have continued to use this intervention, and I have put several small boys back in charge of their penises with fairly good results.

I also have given boys permission to masturbate in appropriate places (after parental negotiation), using much the same language: "You are in charge of your penis, and it is yours to touch. But you must touch it only at the right times and in the right places. You can touch it when you're alone but not in school, because this is not the right place, and teachers won't like it. You may not touch it in public, because that's not the right place. You may touch it when you are alone, maybe in your room or in the bathtub. It's your body and that's fine."

Again, I must stress the need to help parents deal with their child's sexuality, as they seem to want to think of their preschoolers as asexual. One of the outcomes of sexual abuse is that it often awakens a premature sense of sexualization. I tell parents that they cannot take away that heightened sense of sexualization. They must help the child to manage it effectively. One way to do this is to allow the child the pleasure of touching his own body within an approved framework. For some very conservative parents, this is a very difficult adjustment to make.

Affection Seeking. For young children who do not have caretakers who can love them very well, sexual abuse may become associated with attention, personal contact, and a source of affection. The child must learn to separate erotic feelings from the need for affection (Kempe and Kempe 1984). Experience over thirteen years has shown such cases to be some of the most difficult to treat, and they have led to the most extensive history of future revictimization. The central therapeutic task here is work with an often damaged primary caretaker to help him or her develop some genuine affection. It also is important to help the child find out where in his environment his need for affection can be met.

Other Causes and Combinations. Some children may present with a combination of the above symptoms, and some children may have other reasons for acting out. Some children persist in acting out sexually inappropriate behaviors despite therapy to process their abuse and the use of various therapeutic interventions. These children may need interventions to suppress their sexual behaviors.

First, the therapist must be clear that the acting out is not coming from new abuse or from other old, unprocessed abuse. If it is, the therapist runs the risk of suppressing the expression of the abuse. When the therapist is sure that he or she has done as much as he or she can in therapy, the therapist may work with the parents to provide clear guidelines for appropriate sexual expression. With child and family, the therapist plans for appropriate consequences if this outline is not followed. The few cases in my experience in which this intervention has been initiated have involved families in which the child was never given much structure, and the few consequences for misbehavior were inconsistent or very ineffective. Often the family's response to the abuse was to stop disciplining altogether. Some of the therapy work involved helping the parents handle their guilt and to get back in charge. In these cases of repeated acting out, the therapy has focused on helping the parents monitor guidelines for behavior and enforcement of these guidelines. When this is done, the inappropriate sexual behavior usually stops; however, these boys and their families are monitored for a longer period of time than most children and families. Current long-term follow-up on a few of these cases has not uncovered any problems.

Aggressive Acting Out

A minority of young boys may act out aggressively, which may require a different treatment framework. The treatment framework developed by Johnson and Berry (1989) and the work by Gil (1989) may be useful. It is important to note the much of this work is directed toward school-age boys, and care must be taken to accommodate the cognitive and emotional structure and needs of this age group. Research by Friedrich and Luecke (1988) indicates that sexually aggressive boys often have histories that involve family violence and aggression. These factors are important to assess in the treatment of male victims and their potential to act out aggressively.

Group Therapy

I am not in favor of group treatment for most preschoolers as the initial form of intervention. I believe they demand a one-on-one relationship for effective intervention. I am aware that some systems are so overloaded that individual treatment for all sexually abused boys is not possible. In those cases, group treatment maybe the only form possible. I would caution that the best candidates for group treatment are older preschoolers and those with the fewest trauma indicators. If the family is functioning well and is able to support the child, then group treatment may have a place. A format for treatment groups has been published by Stewart and associates (1986).

Sex Education

Sex education often is required to correct the learning from the abuse experience. Teaching may be very broad or very specific. I make an effort to tailor the sex education to the form of the abuse and the parents' own values.

Calderone and Ramey (1982) indicate that by age five, most children should know the basic facts of life. Some families do not want me discussing this information with their four- or five-year-old. Sometimes I point out that their child has probably experienced a wider variety of foreplay than most couples will experience and that he or she has already been exposed to adult sexual practices. I say that I would rather teach them about sex rather than leave standing the education the child gathered from the abusive experience(s). Most parents finally agree. But what about the three-year-old child who was fondling his fourteen-year-old baby-sitter's breast? Does he need to know that penises go into vaginas? Again, Planned Parenthood (1986) indicates a preference for early education. But because the preschooler is so tied to his environment, these issues must be resolved with the parents.

Prevention Education

Prevention education is an important part of therapy, although there is controversy about the effectiveness of prevention education with preschoolers (Gilbert et al. 1989). The nature and extent of formal prevention-education efforts have yet to be refined successfully, but it is important to help victims of abuse understand the rules about touching and ways to help protect themselves if these rules are broken. This education must take place in a format that takes into account the child's intellectual and moral levels of development. In therapy, the therapist can tailor this education to each child and situation to ensure retention.

Dealing with the Child "Where He's At"

As a therapist, it is important to give yourself permission to treat what you can treat now and leave what you cannot treat for possible future therapy. Preschool boys are not mature, and the issues of sexuality that will come to the fore for integration during adolescence are dormant. My aim for therapy is to restore functioning to as close to "normal" for the child's age as is possible. I recognize that there may be issues that I cannot get to yet. One of these may be the issue of homosexuality. This question clearly has a male bias, and far more parents of preschool boys express concern about the effects of the abuse on their son's sexual orientation than do the parents of young girls. A preschooler does not understand the concept of homosexuality in the way that an adolescent or an adult does. As the boy grows older, the issue of homosexuality may become more salient for him.

Recently, I have tried to look ahead to the issue of homosexuality as a concern for a six-year-old boy who was abused repeatedly at ages three and four by a fourteen-year-old cousin. "Aaron" has already heard the words *faggot* and *gay* from his peers, in a derogatory manner, yet he does not know what it means to be gay. When he is able to understand the meaning more clearly, it is possible that he may put the understanding of male homosexual relations together with his experience and decide that he must be gay. Aaron's father and I have discussed telling Aaron about what the words gay and faggot mean, and we have decided the father will tell his son that some people choose this as a way to be but that it does not mean they are bad or weird. Just because someone tried these things with him does not mean he is gay. Gay is to choose a specific form of sexual expression, and Aaron will be able to choose his own way when he gets older. He is in charge, and if he wants any help in dealing with this, we are available.

I do not know the long-term effects this will have on Aaron, and I do not know the long-term effects of early same-sex experiences on sexuality. Some work indicates that 70 percent of male victims in treatment go on to have a homosexual or bisexual orientation (M. O'Brien, Program in Healthy Adolescent Sexuality, Maplewood, Minnesota. Personal communication, February 1989). Brody (1990) argues that early trauma can derail erotic interests by disturbing the links between sex and love. We know little about the effects of early sexual abuse on young boys.

It is important to tell the parents that their child may need therapy in the future and to let them see this as an appropriate and healthy thing. Young children operate at a very concrete level of thinking. When they shift cognitive developmental stages, as they will twice in the next ten years, they may need to reprocess the abuse within the level of understanding appropriate to the new stage, and in the context of the developmental issues that are attendant at that age. It is important that victims have permission to do this.

There are many questions crying for answers now in this field. Therapists working with young male victims also need to recognize that there is a dearth of answers regarding the long-term effects of such abuse, yet we continue to need to function in the present with incomplete knowledge.

Finally, it is important to know that the course of therapy with a young, sexually abused boy may not be smooth and linear (Friedrich and Reams 1987). There may be upsets and regressions. There is no clear and exact road map for work in this area. Over time, research can help delineate important issues and clarify the efficacy of certain interventions. Meanwhile, it is wise to keep abreast of the literature and to develop a circle of colleagues with whom one can share cases and gain support as well as input for work in this unmapped area.

References

Achenbach, T.M., and C. Edelbrock. 1986. "Child Behavior Checklist." Prepared for University Associates in Psychiatry, Burlington, Vermont.

Brody, J. 1990. "Scientists Trace Origins of Abberant Sexuality in Childhood." *The New York Times* (January 23d).

Burgess, A., and C. Grant. 1988. "Children Traumatized in Sex Rings." Monograph published by the National Center for Missing and Exploited Children.

Calderone, M., and M. Ramey.1982. *Talking with Your Child about Sex*. New York: Ballantine Books.

Cole, C., and E. Barney. 1987. "Safeguards and a Therapeutic Window: A Group Therapy Strategy for Adult Incest Survivors." *Journal of Orthopsychiatry* 157 (no. 4): 601–609.

Erikson, E.J. 1963. *Childhood and Society*. New York: W.W. Norton.

Finkelhor, D. 1986. *A Sourcebook on Child Sexual Abuse*. Beverly Hills, California: Sage Publications.

Finkelhor, D., and A. Browne. 1986. "Impact of Child Sexual Abuse." *Psychological Bulletin* 99: 66–77.

Flavel, J.H. 1963. *The Developmental Psychology of Jean Piaget*. New York: Van Nostrand Reinhold.

———. 1968. *The Development of Role-Taking and Communication Skills in Children*. New York: John Wiley & Sons.

Friedrich, W. 1989. "Child Sexual Behavior Survey." Prepared for the Department of Psychology, Mayo Clinic, Rochester, Minnesota.

———. 1990. *Psychotherapy Casebook with Sexually Abused Children*. New York: W.W. Norton.

Friedrich, W., and W.J. Luecke. 1988. "Young School-age Sexually Aggressive Children. Part I: Assessment and Comparison." *Professional Psychology* 19: 155–164.

Friedrich, W., and R.A. Reams. 1987. "The Course of Psychological Symptoms in Sexually Abused Young Children." *Psychotherapy: Theory, Research, and Practice* 24: 160–170.

Gil, E. 1989. *Child Abuse Treatment and Training Programs*. Gils and Associates, 2827 Concord Boulevard, Concord, California 94519.

Gildbert, N., J. Berrick, N. LeProhn, and N. Nyman. 1989. *Protecting Young Children from Sexual Abuse: Does Preschool Training Work?* Lexington, Massachusetts: Lexington Books.

Hagans, K., and J. Case. 1988. *When Your Child Has Been Molested: A Parent's Guide to Healing and Recovery*. Lexington, Massachusetts: Lexington Books.

Haynes-Seman, C., and R. Krugman. 1989. "Sexualized Attention: Normal Interaction or Precursor to Sexual Abuse?" *American Journal of Orthopsychiatry* 59 (no. 2).

Ireton, H.S., and E. Thwing. 1972. "Minnesota Child Development Inventory." Prepared for Behavior Science Systems, Minneapolis, Minnesota.

Johnson, T.C., and C. Berry. 1989. "Children Who Molest: A Treatment Program." *Journal of Interpersonal Violence* 4 (no. 2): 185–203.

Jones, D.P.H. 1986. "Individual Psychotherapy for the Sexually Abused Child." *Child Abuse and Neglect* 10: 377–385.

Kempe, R.S., and C.H. Kempe. 1984. *The Common Secret: Sexual Abuse of Children and Adolescents*. New York: Freeman.

Kubler-Ross, E. 1969. *On Death and Dying*. New York: MacMillan.

MacFarlane, K., and J. Waterman. 1986. *Sexual Abuse of Young Children*. New York: Guildford Press.

Macoby, E., and C. Jacklin. 1974. *The Psychology of Sex Differences*. Stanford, California: Stanford University Press.

Pearlmutter, M., ed. 1980. *New Directions for Child Development: Children's Memory*. San Francisco: Jossey-Bass.

Planned Parenthood. 1986. *How to Talk to Your Child about Sexuality*. Garden City, New York: Doubleday.

Porter, F.S., L.C. Blick, and S.M. Sgroi. 1982. "Treatment of the Sexually Abused Child." In *Clinical Intervention in Child Sexual Abuse*, edited by S.M. Sgroi, 109–145. Lexington, Massachusetts: Lexington Books.

Reaney, S. 1987. "Traumatic Sexualization of the School-age Child: Implications and Guidelines for Treatment." Unpublished manuscript, University of Minnesota.

Sroufe, L.A., D. Jacobvitz, S. Mangelsdorf, E. DeAngelo, and M.J. Ward. 1985. "Generational Boundary Dissolution Between Mothers and Their Preschool Children: A Relationship Systems Approach." *Child Development* 56: 317–325.

Sroufe, L.A., M.J. Ward. 1980. "Seductive Behavior of Mothers and Toddlers: Occurrence, Correlates, and Family of Origin." *Child Development* 51: 1222–1229.

Stewart, M., L. Farquher, D. Dichamy, D. Glick, and P. Martin. 1986. "Group Therapy: A Treatment of Choice for Young Victims of Child Abuse." *International Journal of Group Psychotherapy* 36 (no. 2): 261–277.

Troy, M., and L.A. Sroufe. 1987. "Victimization Among Preschoolers: Role of Attachment Relationship History." *Journal of the American Academy of Child and Adolescent Psychiatry* 26 (no. 2): 166–172.

White, B.L. 1975. *The First Three Years of Life*. Englewood Cliffs, New Jersey: Prentice-Hall.

Yates, A. 1982. "Children Eroticized by Incest." *American Journal of Psychiatry* 139 (no. 4): 482–485.

12
The Victim/Perpetrator: Turning Points in Therapy

Shirley Carlson

Therapists who work with victims and perpetrators frequently come to recognize that although not all victims become perpetrators, behind each perpetrator is some sort of victimization. Therapists, like social workers, judges, and probation officers, are justifyably wary of allowing this probable childhood trauma to serve as an excuse for the perpetrator's behavior. It is necessary to hold the perpetrator fully accountable and to protect society from his or her offenses.

The process of therapy continues beyond accountability and protection for society, however. Therapy seeks to set the perpetrator firmly on a road to recovery and in so doing to provide a better life for him or her and ongoing safety for the vulnerable. A significant portion of the recovery process consists of working through the underlying victimization, whatever its form may be.

In my experience in working with more than one hundred male sexual perpetrators (convicted of incest, child molesting, or rape), I have come to believe that it is essential to work on the perpetrator characteristics until the client arrives at a place where he is amenable to beginning treatment for his own childhood victimization. Certain signs, or turning points, indicate when the time has come to change course. To understand this process, we need to look at the perpetrator characteristics that will probably be present at the beginning of treatment. Although not all of these will be noted in each client, most will be observable to a greater or lesser degree.

Perpetrator Characteristics

1. *He is highly resistant to therapy.* He is probably court ordered and may have agreed to therapy as part of a plea bargain without really knowing what he was letting himself in for. Often he is outwardly compliant and may express an eagerness for help. But inside he is terrified—of change, of his emotions, and of the judgments of others.

2. *He is highly invested in controlling his situation, including his family, the group, the therapist, and the therapy.* The need for control may be related to the interior "terrors" mentioned above. It appears to be present in all perpetrators, although it may take many forms. His outward presentation may be sane and ratonal, pitiful, passive, or threatening. Most are inclined toward the passive/aggressive stance rather than the overtly aggressive. But the battle for control has started before he enters the room for the first time. He sets up power struggles, much as an adolescent does, and he seeks to win. He is accustomed to being in charge, whatever his style may be, and he does not want to give this up. He fights rules, limits, and boundaries, and his family colludes with him out of fear and familarity.

3. *He may deny his offense, minimize it, or admit to it without really taking responsibility for it.* There is almost always a significant difference between the perpetrator's description of his offenses and the victim's statement to the police. In my experiénce, reality turns out to be even more serious than the victim's statement. Victims appear to leave out material far more often than they invent it. When perpetrators become honest as treatment progresses, they often reveal that they had other victims as well. A perpetrator may even remember events that his victims have blocked from their memories. If he does admit to his offense, he probably will assign responsibility to others. The victim is a favorite target, along with the perpetrator's spouse. A common explanation by a perpetrator follows this script:

> My wife couldn't stay home—out every night to her clubs and classes. My daughter was in a real rebellious stage; she was defying all the rules. I thought she needed more attention, more affection. So I tried to give her that. God knows she wasn't getting much from her mother; none of us were. I don't really know. Maybe I went a little too far; maybe she misunderstood. I'll tell you one thing: My daughter is a real little flirt. You ought to see what she wears around the house. And her mother lets her get away with it.

Explanations such as this are used to justify offenses such as forcing oral, anal, or vaginal intercourse on the victim over a period of months or years.

4. *He presents himself as the victim (pseudovictim) and blames others for his problems; he feels sorry for himself.* Sometimes the litany seems endless: He had a "hanging judge," a chiseling lawyer, ungrateful children, an unappreciative spouse, a tough probation officer. All this has caused money problems, embarrassment, physical discomforts and loneliness. He feels abandoned, misunderstood, frustrated, and hurt. This is the fault of those who have failed him—his family, lawyer, and the courts. This stance is sometimes difficult for the therapist and group to handle without falling into the trap of

becoming sarcastic, abusive, or controlling and thereby adding to his "victimization."

5. *He has strong beliefs in the patriarchal system and a high need to be in an autocratic position.* Most perpetrators come from a family where Dad's word was law, and this law was not questioned by Mom or the children. Often a rite of passage for the older adolescent male was a violent confrontation in which he backed his father into a corner or shoved him against the wall, shouting, "I'm not taking any more from you!" At that moment, he became a dominant male in his own right.

Physical abuse and threats are common in sexually abusive families. Dad is seen as the most important person, whether or not he is successful in his career or is a competent provider. Boys may be either overvalued (in comparison with their sisters) or left alone to claw their way up to a position of authority. The act of sexual abuse of women and children puts an adult male in a position of ultimate power.

6. *He has a sense of entitlement and expects his needs to be put before the needs of others.* The perpetrator's sense of entitlement goes beyond the perks of the patriarchal system. He believes that he is entitled to feel good, or better, no matter what the costs may be to others. A slight discomfort for him is unacceptable, even if relief means a major discomfort for another. His dinner must not be late, no matter how ill his wife may be. The family tends to organize itself around the objective of anticipating and meeting his needs before he has a chance to feel them, thereby preventing abuse, rage, or temper tantrums.

7. *He has an external locus of control.* Others cause his feelings, should feel his needs, force him to act as he does, fail to deliver as expected, "ask for it," deserve whatever they get from him (abuse), mistreat him, keep him between a rock and a hard place, and so on. If only others would change, he would have no problems.

There is a villain present in his daily life, set up by him. In a short time, the group and the therapist become that villain. He is reactive rather than active; he acts from duress rather than from choice. His apparent inability to take responsibility for himself spreads beyond the abuse to all areas of his life.

8. *He may act remorseful, but he is actually feeling resentment and self-pity.* His affect may seem genuine: His voice quivers and tears fill his eyes. He probably does have some real concerns for the effect of this offense on the victim and on his family. But it is somehow difficult for the group to feel empathy or to reach out to him. There is a strange silence in the room. As he is encouraged to talk more, it becomes evident that the remorse is for himself—remorse that he has been caught, the consequences have taken place and continue to be forthcoming. The remorse now begins to seem manipulative and may, in fact, already have worked. Perhaps his sentence has been

reduced by the courts because he shows remorse. Often, at this point, he wishes to make a good apology to those whom he has hurt. It is best to be wary of encouraging this impulse, since it is often a way of coercing a token forgiveness from his victims, who feel abused yet again by this process.

9. *He is often "numbed out"—unaware of his emotions and needs.* This may be noticed as a lack of affect or as an inappropriate affect (for example, smiling when angry). Most perpetrators come from family systems in which emotions are not permitted or only one emotion is allowed (anger for men, hurt for women), and all other emotions must be channeled into the permitted emotion or suppressed. When asked how he feels, he does now know; he has never been taught to identify emotions. He has not been given appropriate ways to express his emotions. Often the only outlet for emotions is acting out or an explosion. For some, drinking provides an additional route.

10. *He is passive/aggressive in his anger expression and often denies his anger.* This is a family characteristic. Euphemisms such as "upset," "a little ticked," and "disappointed" are used frequently. Family communication is riddled with zingers, gotchas, zaps, and get-backs. Passive resistant forms such as lateness, procrastination, sexual coldness, silence, and ignoring are prevalent. All of these are practiced in group, often by all the members. A direct expression of anger as modeled by a therapist can be a revelation. In the clients' families, anger may have meant "kill" or permanent abandonment.

11. *He is very needy and is manipulative rather than direct in getting those needs met.* As has been stated, he may feel an aching emptiness inside, but he does now know his specific needs. So he manipulates to be taken care of, and he looks for fixes from others. Often his family rushes in to take care of him, but they miss the mark. He becomes more and more frustrated, and they feel more and more inadequate and guilty. Soon resentments escalate in all parties. He will continue this pattern in his relationship with the group and the therapist.

12. *He may have an idealized version of his childhood and family of origin.* Early autobiographical material may sound like a television show such as "Father Knows Best" or "Leave It to Beaver." This myth is supported by his parents, siblings, and other relatives. Anyone who deviates from the idyllic picture is extruded from the family. He may have a sibling who has been cast out, and he may fear that this will happen to him. The family's response to alterations of the myth exceeds punishment; it is abandonment and touches his deepest unmet needs for survival and security.

13. *He may be aware of dysfunction and abuse in his family of origin, and he may be presenting these (indirectly) as an excuse for his behavior.* There are many variations on this theme. He may live in the past to the point of obsession with past mistreatment. He may sincerely believe that he is not in any way as bad as his father. He may see abuse as a justifiable child-rearing practice: Spare the rod and spoil the child. He may be still caught between

an autocratic and abusive father and a weak, passive, and pitiful mother. He may have become an enthusiastic scapegoat, or black sheep. As I tell clients, "The family elects the scapegoat, and the scapegoat continues to run for office." He may be habituated to self-pity.

14. *He uses projection, denial, and repression as defenses.* He sees and condemns his negative qualities in others—sadly, often the victim. He may be very concerned that his teenage daughter is sexually active, which makes her a "slut." He perceives his passive wife as controlling. He ascribes qualities such as jealousy, lasciviousness, and stubbornness to others. Denial is ubiquitous—denial of emotions, culpability, responsibility, problems, and reality. He may repress significant data from his past, including long periods of time. For instance, he may not be able to remember his childhood at all, or he may not remember significant events such as the death of a twenty-one-year-old siblng when the client was ten years old.

15. *He has extremely low trust.* As a victim, he has had the experience of having those whom he trusted the most—his parents—turn against him with abuse and neglect. Imagine, then, how frightening the outside world must be. He avoids vulnerability, intimacy, and significant relationships. He may be superficially charming and even gregarious, but he keeps others at arm's length. He is committed, in spite of his loneliness, to going it alone. He trusts and depends on his children more than his wife. They are small and dependent and are less likely to hurt or reject him.

16. *He is isolated from himself and others.* Often he inhabits an imaginary world that is safer and more comfortable than the real world. He tends to be attached to certain fantasies of abuse and to be very reluctant to part with them. He sees these fantasies as "coming into his mind from the outside," and he does not take responsibility for them or believe that he has the power to stop them. When conflicts occur in his relationships with others, he retreats into himself as if into a moated castle with a drawbridge that can be pulled up. This process often takes place in group early in treatment. It is a safe haven.

17. *He is shame based, with low self-esteem.* His emotions, attitudes, and behaviors are guided by shame (a sense of himself as worthless, inadequate, hopeless, awful, perverted, or flawed) rather than by guilt (a sense of his behavior as being wrong or questionable). The deep sense of shame was originally put into him by his family, and he has fueled it over the years by negative self-statements and by self-condemnation because of his behaviors. It is impossible for him to admit to a mistake or to ordinary human failings. To him, to be human means to be bad. He works desperately to relieve his intense shame by striving for perfection, attempts to atone, attempts to exact forgiveness from others, blame and projection, denial, forgetting, and attempts to achieve.

18. *He prefers immediate gratification.* The interior world of a sexual

perpetrator is not a pleasant place, and he looks for relief through abuse, drugs and alcohol, eating, spending, exploding, or other forms of self-gratification. The future must be sacrificed to feed the demands of the present.

19. *He may seem to be eliciting abuse from others as a form of negative attention.* In some families, the only available attention is that received for negative behaviors. Forms of punishment or angry reactions are defined as love. Explanations of abuse may be given, such as "I'm doing this because I love you" or "This hurts me more than it does you." Sometimes parents feel remorse after abusing a child and seek to atone with apologies, promises, and gifts. Children who grow up with such a learning experience may continue to seek negative attention because it is better than nothing, all they know, all they believe is available, and all they think they deserve. Setting up the group and therapist to become angry and abusive is a common practice for such people and creates a struggle for group members who also come from abusive family systems and know the rules only too well.

20. *He has little sense of his boundaries or those of others.* The failure to develop a sense of boundaries represents a failure in his family system. From the beginning, his boundaries were not respected and were frequently crossed. The families of sexual perpetrators, past and present, may permit physical and sexual abuse, unwanted touching, intrusive comments and questions, merciless teasing, opening and reading of others' mail, walking unannounced into bedrooms and bathrooms, walking around partly clothed or naked, excessive control, verbal abuse, excessive caretaking, interference in others' affairs or relationships, speaking for others, defining others' reality, and negation of emotions. The sexual perpetrator is unable to say no and unable to hear or accept a no from others.

21. *Minnesota Multiphasic Personality Inventory.* The most common Minnesota Multiphasic Personality Inventory (MMPI) profile among the one-hundred sexual perpetrators I studied was the 4/8 (8/4), with the 4/3(3/4) the second most frequent. Subscale elevations often were noted in "need for affection," "overcontrolled hostility," "authority," and "narcissistic."

22. *Diagnosis.* Diagnoses most frequently come from the personality disorders section of the *DSM III* (American Psychiatric Association 1980) and *DSM III-R* (American Psychiatric Association 1987). Mixed features are common. Frequent diagnoses include the narcissistic, antisocial, passive-aggressive, borderline, obsessive-compulsive, avoidant, and schizotypal disorders.

Analyzing the Characteristics

As the preceding characteristics begin to emerge in the early days of treatment, it becomes apparent that the client's developmental process is incomplete. At times he may seem like a five-year-old, a seventh-grader, or someone of any age in between. The treatment plan must seek to supply an environment in which the victim/perpetrator can essentially grow up again, filling in the missing pieces of his experience. It is important to remember that he is irresponsible because he is still a child developmentally. Yet he has reached an age and position where society (rightly) holds him accountable. His development is incomplete due to the deficiencies in his family and environment. It is important to be aware of what he has missed:

1. He has not received adequate structure and limits.
2. He has been subjected to irrational punishments.
3. He has been protected from logical consequences.
4. He has been abused physically, sexually, verbally, and/or emotionally.
5. He has been shamed.
6. He has not internalized a value system (this is missing in his family).
7. He has, as a child, been placed in a parental or spousal role.
8. He has not received adequate nurturing.
9. He has not had an adequate male role model.
10. He has not been affirmed or encouraged.
11. He has not been listened to, believed, or validated.
12. He has not successfully bonded to a care giver.

Stages of Treatment

A workable treatment plan for the victim/perpetrator includes four stages, some of which will be concurrent.

Treating the Perpetrator Characteristics, Attitudes, and Self-Concept

Certain characteristics of the perpetrator must be addressed initially and focused on until their strength lessens.

Set Limits. The perpetrator needs a clear set of rules to guide his behavior. These provide a sense of security for someone who is out of control in many ways. These limits must cover areas such as contact with his victims, contact with family members, contact with children, chemical use, financial responsibility, and attendance at treatment. Consequences need to be clear. The client will respond best if he has a probation officer who can consult with the therapist and client to emphasize the importance of maintaining boundaries and limits. Attorneys, social workers, and employers also can serve in this capacity. Spouses cannot, as they tend to be caught up in the client's delusional system. The therapist needs to avoid power struggles and to avoid saving the perpetrator from consequences.

Provide structure. Goals, along with steps to achieve these goals, provide a needed guideline for moving from an immediate to a delayed gratification mode. Although the client may tend to produce shallow rather than thorough efforts, assignments are important. Assignments such as boundary setting, making lists of the consequences of the problem behavior, journaling, and writing an autobiography are helpful.

Limit involvement with the family. The perpetrator is overinvolved with his family. His energies are engaged in activities such as controlling and manipulating family members, seeking fixes, exerting pressure, shaming family members, and intruding on and interfering with others' lives. This dynamic obviously is not conducive to his recovery or to the recovery of family members.

Confront denial. This goal is best achieved in a group setting where both confrontation and encouragement come from peers. Confrontation from family members tends to be of limited value, since the perpetrator's power in his family is excessive and family members are often afraid to be honest.

Identity projection when it occurs. This chore tends to fall to the therapist, since projection is usually difficult for group members to understand. For example, the perpetrator may be comfortable in implying that his victim daughter is seductive, lascivious, bad, and a slut, and he may be very convincing in the portrait that he paints. Similarly, he may cast his wife as cold, uncaring, abandoning, and nonnurturing. Other children in the family may be presented as ruined by his wife's shortcomings. The perpetrator wears the white hat; he is the good guy. It is necessary that he bring these traits back to himself and own up to the fact that, deep down inside, he sees himself as lascivious, morally corrupt, cold, or cruel. Eventually this will be traced to his family of origin and to the messages he received from those who projected onto *him*. But that takes place in a later stage. In the early weeks, the issue of projection must be identified by all group members. As groups develop, members may be able to take over the job of confronting projection.

Confront the pseudovictim. The group can be very helpful in unmasking this sincere delusion. The perpetrator really believes that he has and is being victimized by his victim, his family, the courts, the group, the therapist, the treatment center, his lawyer, his boss, friends, parents, and siblings. Some are able to give up this stance more easily than others. Sometimes a steady but relatively gentle confrontation is enough. Others require more work. Pressure and time limits can be helpful. A client may need to hear that it is his obligation to make the group believe that he is, in fact, a sex offender and belongs in a sex offender group. And he may need to know that he has a time limit to accomplish this.

Reinforcing Positives and Building Strengths

The apparent ego strength of the perpetrator often is false. Inside he is lonely, isolated, alienated, and terrified of abandonment. He feels incompetent. The removal of his daily interactions with his family leaves a great gap. This area must be addressed before he can work on his own victimization.

Encourage him to build a new support system. Fellow group members are the obvious place to begin. A well-functioning group will take care of this with the exchange of phone numbers and invitations to social events. Twelve-step support groups such as Alcoholics Anonymous, Adult Children of Alcoholics, and Sex Addicts Anonymous provide another supportive environment. Many clients can be encouraged to fill some of their newly available time with bowling, softball, or church activities.

Encourage boundary setting. Most perpetrators have difficulty saying no to anyone in a position of authority. They tend to be exploited, feel resentful and self-pitying, and, in the past, probably have taken it out on others who are in a lower power position (wives, children, or other victims). Some group time may need to be spent in helping members to develop assertiveness skills. Respect for one's own boundaries appears to precede respect for the boundaries of others.

Encourage delay of gratification. Perpetrators lack alternatives to the fix. When a perpetrator finds himself struggling with unpleasant emotions, he is prone to break rules—perhaps to call one of his victim children and try to manipulate the child to take care of him or to contact a spouse and attempt to dump on her. Learning to call a group member instead leads to a better long-term solution. Group members can be very helpful to one another in suggesting alternatives.

Encourage giving and receiving feedback in group. Shame and low-esteem combine to prevent meaningful interactions among group members. Each group member needs to be assured that his comments are valuable to the group as long as they are not abusive or shaming. Interactions must be encouraged, as clients tend to be most comfortable in an approval-seeking dialogue with the therapist. Clients also need to learn to value the feedback of group members rather than relying on "pronouncements" from the therapist.

Reinforce all positive behaviors. It is important to reinforce all behaviors that may to lead recovery. Some of these may be admitting to problem behavior beyond what the client was arrested for, giving self-related feedback, completing assignments, owing up to responsibility (in any area of his life), expressing feelings appropriately, and asking directly for what is wanted.

Treating the Victim Within

The process of treating the victim within is similar to that of treating any victim of childhood trauma. The perpetrator behaviors have served to cover over the effects of his victimization, just as do other victim survival behaviors (such as chemical abuses, eating disorders, self-mutilation, or promiscuity). As these behaviors lessen, the underlying trauma begins to emerge. The victim within has a different set of needs than those of the client in the early perpetrator stage.

Provide ongoing support. Working through a childhood trauma is a frightening experience, and the client's needs may be more than the therapist can supply. This is where the value of the group, along with the value of outside support groups, becomes apparent.

Continue the educational process. The educational process starts at the beginning of treatment and continues throughout. Topics may include defining abuse; identifying emotions, symptoms of abuse, and characteristics of victims; and providing information on child development, alcoholism, forms of anger expression, family systems, and the recovery process.

Help client identify abuse and tell his secrets. Devices such as autobiographies or journals, art therapy, dream work, story telling, and guided imagery may help to bring out the secrets. Signs of repression often are present. These may include intense emotional content without data, lost time, flashbacks, incomplete memories, irrational aversions to a person or place, and body memories. The therapist or the group may notice that the story does not add up in some way, and this feedback can be helpful to the client. Others in the group may feel uncomfortable about an area to which the client has become inured and share this discomfort with him. Each individual process of telling the story is different, and each client struggles with the "don't talk" rules of his own family. Serious threats may have been made to ensure his silence, and opening up may take a long time.

Believe and validate the client. Being believed by the therapist and the group is a significant part of recovery. Victims struggle with doubts of their own reality, wonder if it is all a fantasy, and do not trust their own emotions. As they go through their process, being believed and validated by the group supports them until they can say with assurance, "This is what happened to me."

Recovery along these lines proceeds in the following areas:

Emotions. The client's emotions have been suppressed for years, and it may take several tellings of his story before he can show any affect. The client experiences his emotions as intense, explosive, and terrifying. He needs permission to feel and acceptance of these powerful emotions. He may need some help with pacing so that he does not become overwhelmed. Occasionally, a client may become severely depressed and need psychiatric consultation. If this happens, he needs to know that he is not crazy. Most clients can work through their emotions with support, at their own pace, and without medications.

Thoughts and Beliefs. Almost all victims seem to believe that the abuse that they suffered was their own fault. It is important to find out exactly how the client takes responsibility for the abuse that was perpetrated against him. Most victims need to be told over and over that the abuse was not their fault. This is crucial for the recovery of the victim/perpetrator because he often uses this faulty belief as permission to abuse his own victims. Many other faulty beliefs and much illogical reasoning are present in the victim/perpetrator, most of which came to him in his family of origin and were accepted by him as truths. Magical thinking, delusional thinking, and paranoid ideation all need to be identified and replaced.

Learned Behaviors and Coping Mechanisms. The victim/perpetrator needs to explore how he has carried out what he learned as a child. His victimization can be reframed as the source of his perpetrating behavior without making it an excuse or justification. An honest appraisal of his childhood role models (father and other male family members) often produces an awareness that he has done and is doing some of the same things they did. When he is in touch with his own feelings about being abused, he is in a better position to feel empathy toward his own victims or potential victims. The victim/perpetrator frequently has coping mechanisms that are common to many victims, and he may need help correcting patterns such as alcohol and other drug abuse, an eating disorder or compulsive spending. He may be troubled with other problem sexual behaviors such as exposing, voyeurism, or self-abusive masturbation. He may be in debt due to the purchase of pornography, or he may have health problems, such as sexually transmitted diseases.

Returning the Parental Role to the Client

Eventually the victim/perpetrator is ready to assume responsibility for himself. Oddly, in spite of the original resistance and the battle for control, when the time comes for him to begin the process of ending treatment, he may be frightened at the thought of independence from supervision. Probation often lasts beyond treatment but may end early after a successful completion. There are substages within this last phase.

Resumption of Family Life. This is best accomplished with small increments of contact, accompanied by family and couples counseling. The peer group is valuable for support, honest feedback, and confrontation.

A Client-Created System of Boundaries. The best boundaries are those created by the client. The more specific they are, the better. Clients need to consider areas such as appropriate dress, respect for others' privacy, and avoiding over-contact with potential victims (for example, coaching a children's softball team is not a good avocation for someone who has abused children). In parenting, the client must be clear about when it is his responsibility to provide guidance or limits for his children and when it is best to allow the children to learn from their own mistakes. He also needs to set limits with his family of origin.

A Client-Created Definition of Appropriate Sexual Behaviors. Again, each client needs to construct his own limits and controls. Each must decide what is best for him in areas such as masturbating, sexual fantasies, use of pornography, and choice of partners and practices. Group feedback is important in this area, as clients tends either to allow themselves too much leeway or to swing in the opposite direction and attempt to be nonsexual. The best criteria are pragmatic rather than moral: Does it work for me? How does this work for me? Does this lead me in a direction that will cause pain to myself or others?

A Client-Created Aftercare Plan. The client needs to identify how we will continue to get ongoing support and feedback after he leaves the treatment group. He needs to know what he will do if he begins to experience urges to act out illegally or if he has a relapse into problem behavior. He needs to identify how he will take care of himself in terms of his emotions, particularly anger, shame, and abandonment. He needs to know where he will get support in a crisis and where he will receive mentoring.

Closure. Graduation and good-byes are important. The client receives affirmation from the group and the therapist. The end of the therapy relationship is marked, along with the end of the special relationship present in the group. Although he may continue to see individuals from the group, the relationship is not the same, and this must be acknowledged.

Timing is important in working with the victim/perpetrator, and turning points can indicate the readiness of the client to proceed to a new stage. Clients frequently work in more than one stage at the same time. Clients also slip backward to an earlier stage of the treatment plan when the therapy becomes especially painful or when a crisis occurs in their daily lives. Sometimes it is difficult to believe that any progress is taking place, but most clients do move forward.

Moving from Perpetrator to Victim

Since the needs of the perpetrator stage (limits, structure, and enforced boundaries) are distinctly different from those of the victim stage (support, validation, and affirmation), it is important to know what developing characteristics may signal the readiness of a client to do productive victim work. Some indications of this readiness follow.

He begins to take responsibility (even minimally) for his abusiveness. Often this begins with a gradual cessation of behaviors such as blaming others, transferring responsibility, and stonewalling. This may be followed by a period of (apparently) honest confusion. He understands that he is responsible for what he did, but he does not have a handle on his process. It is important not to rescue him from this confusion; he is still hopeful of finding a solution that will save him from the intense shame and remorse that are in the wings.

He begins to develop support. Some signs are attending a support group that is or is not getting a sponsor, calling group members, spending social time with male friends or group members, giving feedback to others, and listening to feedback. Along with these activities, there will often be a decline in his involvement with his family, perhaps even some estrangement.

He expresses emotions that seem real rather than manipulative. This step is measured by therapist and group response. Empathy for him begins to replace wariness (the sense of being conned). Perhaps he can even express some honest anger without blaming, attacking, or being abusive. Or he may indicate only minimal affect, but it is experienced by the group as genuine.

He begins to question himself and to confront others in the areas of denial, repression, and projection. Again, he may appear to be in a state of honest confusion because he now doubts that which he had always accepted as reality. His rigid system of defenses is beginning to crumble, gradually, over time.

He begins to identify with others in the group and to apply their process to himself. It is at this point that admissions emerge, and they may be surprising to the therapist. These may be admissions of behaviors that were secret until now and that may include abuse for which he was not arrested. Additional rapes, perhaps, or child molestations, often at an early age, may come to light. He may be stirred by others' emotions. He may recognize a similarity between others' experiences and his own.

He begins to develop an inner locus of control. Often this appears as a statement that he understands he has a part in something or he knows he has or had choices. He may not know what his part is; he may not be able to list his choices. But something has definitely changed; his perception of reality has shifted. He still may ask what others think he should do, but he is beginning to understand that *he* is responsible for his actions.

These six characteristics emerge one at a time and imperfectly. He gradually seems to be more responsible, more adult. When all six are present, to one degree or another, he is ready to do true victim work. Without these characteristics, victim work is wasted and may serve only to reinforce his system of rationalization. These dynamics can be illustrated by a case history.

Case History

"Joe," a while male aged thirty-seven, was arrested for "French kissing" and fondling the breasts of a thirteen-year-old girl who was a friend of his twelve-year-old daughter. When the victim reported his behavior to her parents, they called the police. Subsequent investigation brought out the information that Joe also had abused his daughter for two years; the abuse included kissing, touching her breast and genital areas, and mutual masturbation. Joe was charged with several counts of criminal sexual conduct. He was allowed to plead guilty to a lesser charge (two counts) in return for a reduction of his sentence. He was sentenced to six months in the county workhouse, on work release, along with fifteen years of supervised probation. He also was required to attend a treatment program. Failure to complete the program satisfactorily would result in a sentence of twenty-two months in the state prison.

In his first session in the group, Joe stated that he did not believe that he had done anything out of the ordinary and that he thought that both of the girls had exaggerated to get attention. His anger was focused on his daughter's friend and her parents; he believed that they were retaliating against him because they were jealous of his business success. He believed that the thirteen-year-old friend had been a bad influence on his daughter and had led her astray. He speculated that the girls had been experimenting with drugs and thought that they were probably sexually active. He blamed his wife for not keeping a tighter rein on their daughter and implied that his wife was negligent in her duties. He said she was a bad housekeeper and spent money unwisely. When asked why he had pleaded guilty, he said that the system was against men and that his lawyer had not provided much in the way of legal counsel.

Joe talked rapidly in a high-pitched voice. Group members had to out-shout him to ask questions or give feedback. He frequently interrupted others and directed the group's attention toward his own issues. He allied himself with two other group members who saw themselves as victims of the system. This trio resisted feedback and supported each other's dysfunction.

Joe was court ordered not to have any contact with either of his victims. He was not allowed to call or visit his home without the written permission of the treatment center and his probation officer. After his arrest, he had moved in with his parents, who were solidly supportive of him and blamed his wife and daughter for his troubles. Within two weeks of his incarceration, he was able to obtain Saturday night overnight passes from the workhouse.

During his third week in treatment, a surprise visit from his daughter's social worker found him visiting in his family's home. He claimed that his wife had called him and pleaded with him to come over and repair the washing machine. She substantiated his claim, saying that she thought it would be all right since their daughter had agreed to stay in her room. The social worker reported him to his probation officer. His weekend passes were canceled, and he was warned that any further infractions would result in revocation of probation and commitment to prison.

Joe did not seem chastened by this consequence. He continued to define himself as the victim and now added his probation officer and the social worker to his list of victimizers. At this time, his alliance in the group broke up when one of his allies was sent to prison. The other ally became frightened and began to join with more functional group members. Joe continued as a lone wolf. He now began to set himself apart from other group members, some of whom were sharing their autobiographies. He claimed that his family had been kind and nurturing, unlike the abusive systems of the others. He continued to be intrusive in group. Since Joe did not seem to be progressing, it was decided to put him on probation. A session with his probation officer was held to clarify the consequences if he should be terminated. He was given three weeks to find a way to make the group believe that he was amenable to treatment. He was not permitted to have any time to talk about his complaints, and he was not allowed to interrupt others' time to switch the focus.

Joe appeared to be in a good deal of distress during the first week. Since his angry outbursts were no longer permitted, he sat in silence. He appeared depressed, but attempts by the group to draw him out were to no avail. Group members expressed their reluctance to spend any more time and energy on him.

Eventually he made a move. He called on of the more advanced group members at home on the weekend and asked to meet with him. He spent Sunday afternoon in a long discussion with two group members (this meeting was reported in group by the two members). Joe seemed less distraught and gave some brief but appropriate feedback in group, although he did not take any time to discuss himself. During the next session, Joe talked about his loneliness and confusion. Feedback from the group was positive, although members appeared wary. The next two sessions were similar, with Joe taking small amounts of time to ask for help in understanding himself. At the end of the three-week period, Joe's probationary period was extended for another month.

Joe's first break took place when he admitted that he had been beaten by his father on numerous occasions as a child. He attempted to defend his father by saying that he deserved the punishment, but the group would not agree that abuse is ever deserved. Questioning elicited that at times he was beaten to the point of having welts, bruises, and cuts. He then admitted that he had done this to his own son as well.

Subsequently, Joe admitted that both he and a younger brother had been sexually abused by a female baby-sitter. Until he received feedback from the group, he saw the baby-sitter's abuse as fun, a game that they had played. He then admitted that he had played these games with a younger sister and her friends and had been shamed by his mother and beaten by his father when one of the girls told her parents. During this time, he opened up and cried in the group. Group members were supportive of him.

By this time, Joe had completed his autobiography. He had maintained distance from his family and was attending an Adult Children of Abusers group. He was giving and receiving feedback in group and was no longer projecting onto his daughter and her friend. He was judged to be ready to proceed with victim work.

Most of Joe's victim work was accomplished using his autobiography as a framework. Joe was encouraged to write letters to his parents. He read these letters in group and experienced powerful feelings of shame, rage, and abandonment. He was surprised at the intensity of these emotions, since he had thought that he had a high regard for his parents. He resumed contact with his brother and sister, who gave him some validation by sharing their childhood memories.

Joe also wrote a letter to the baby-sitter who had played "games" with him. He no longer saw this abuse as fun, as he could now remember the shame, confusion, and powerlessness he had felt. He was able to see that much of his subsequent problematic sexual behavior might have stemmed from this experience.

Joe's belief system was based on the premise that abuse is the victim's fault. He had learned this from his father, who had verbally blamed his wife and children for the beatings he had given them. As this belief system shifted in Joe's mind, he began to feel intense remorse for his behavior toward his daughter, her friend, and his son. This was a very painful time for Joe. The group was supportive, although members did not attempt to take away his pain by rationalizing or minimizing his actions. Joe came to see that a number of his sexual behaviors were inappropriate or abusive. He was in the habit of harassing his secretary, and he frequently made suggestive comments to waitresses and female clerks. He was coercive with his wife when she did not want sex. Spending also was an area of concern for Joe. He ran up credit card debts and expected his wife to get the money to pay his bills by shorting herself and the children and working overtime at her job. He agreed to cut up his credit cards and take over payment of his bills himself.

Joe's reinvolvement with his family started with relationship work in a group of four couples who also had sexual abuse as an issue. The focus of the group was on honest communication, airing of secrets, and balancing of unequal relationships (where the male partner exercised excessive dominance). Family group followed, and Joe began spending time with his family, first in public places and then in short visits at home. In family group, the areas of focus were the same as in the couples group, with attention being paid to any verbal or emotional abuse from Joe to his children or wife. Joe continued in his men's group throughout this process, relying on it for support and feedback.

Before Joe's visits at home became more extended, he prepared a plan for appropriate behavior and boundaries in the house and presented it to his family. He also set up limits for his sexual behavior and shared this with his wife in the couples group. His final task was his aftercare plan, also shared with the family. These three plans were prepared with consultation and feedback from his men's group.

Joe moved home permanently. The family group continued meeting to process this change, and Joe remained in his men's group even longer. When he appeared to be able to handle living with his family again, he requested permission to graduate. He said his good-byes to the group and was discharged. He remained on probation for a period of time and continued to see his probation officer.

Joe's journey was not as smooth as the preceding description might indicate. He had periods of little progress and sometimes reverted to old behaviors for short periods. His treatment was lengthy, lasting more than two and a half years. He appeared to have made major changes in his attitudes and behaviors, and he has not come to the attention of the courts again. His experience in treatment followed a pattern that was similar to the patterns of many men in his group. His treatment plan was designed to address his perpetrator characteristics, his childhood victimization, his reunification with his family, and his ongoing growth.

References

American Psychiatric Association. 1980. *Diagnostic and Statistical Manual of Mental Disorders.* 3d ed., Washington D.C.

American Psychiatric Association. 1987. *Diagnostic and Statistical Manual of Mental Disorders.* 3d ed., rev. Washington D.C.

Index

Abel, G., 81, 100, 103
Abreaction(s): clinical example of, 44–46; conditions that contraindicate, 29; containing spontaneous, 18–22; countertransference issues, 46–49; definition of, 1; development of, 1–2; dissociation and, 3–10; environmental safety and, 28–29; hypnotic techniques and, 3, 35–36; interpersonal safety and, 26–28; intrapsychic safety and, 24–26; model for planned, 23–24; resistance to, 27; signs of spontaneous, 15–18; signs that abreactive work is finished, 23
Abreaction steps: alleviating the existential crisis (resolution phase), 33–36; creating a gestalt (assimilation phase), 36–40; eliciting dissociated aspects (identification phase), 29–32; empowering the client (application phase), 41–44; ending an abreaction, 40–41
Abuse Recovery Model: background of, 150–151; description of, 151–165; future phase of, 165; goals of, 151; past phase of, 155–159; placement of clients in, 154–155; present phase of, 159–163; role of therapist, 153–154
Acting-out behaviors: adolescents and, 210–211; preschool victims and, 239–244
Adequacy journal, keeping an, 91–92
Adolescent victims: acting-out behaviors and, 210–211; countertransference and, 219–220; disclosure of victimization, 200–203; evaluation of abuse, 203–205; fear and anxiety in, 217–218; feelings of betrayal, 207–210; feelings of powerlessness, 215–216; loneliness and isolation and, 219; masturbation and, 109, 113, 212; problems with treating, 108–113; rage/anger in, 213–214; responses to abuse, 205–207; review of literature on, 199–200; role of therapist with, 207–208; sadness and loss in, 218; shame and, 216–217; suicide and, 214–215; transference and, 220–221
AIDS, 206–207
Altermatt, K., 146, 150
American Humane Society, 79
American Psychiatric Association, 4, 58, 59, 142, 178, 254
American Society of Clinical Hypnosis, 3
Anger. See Rage/anger responses
Anger rapist, 173
Artwork, use of, 31, 97–98
Assessing a client, 83–84
Autobiography, keeping a spoken, 92–93

BASK model of dissociation, 5–6, 13, 32
Bates, Carolyn M., 130
Becker, J.V., 81, 100, 140
Beilke, R., 203, 210
Benward, J., 139, 140, 141
Berry, C., 230, 244
Bioenergetic analysis, 124
Blake-White, J., 147, 149
Blick, L.C., 200, 233, 234
Body work. See Psychophysical Model of therapy and body work
Bolton, F.G., 199, 203
Bourne, P.G., 59, 61
Braun, B.G., 2, 4, 5, 11, 21, 24, 25, 26, 27, 29, 30, 31, 32, 35
Bridges: auditory, 21; tactile, 21–22, 32; visual, 22
Broken record technique, 95–97
Brown, J., 148, 156
Brown, P.C., 59, 66, 67, 69, 71, 72
Browne, A., 142, 145, 148, 178, 233, 242
Brownmiller, S., 59, 60, 61, 67
Bruckner, D.F., 69, 73, 139, 140, 142, 147, 148, 149, 150, 158, 166

Burgess, A.W., 58, 60, 61, 62, 63, 65, 66, 67, 69, 142, 144, 212, 234

Calderone, M., 245
Calof, D., 3, 37
Caputo, P., 61, 67
Carmen, E., 140, 141
Cheek, D.W., 11, 24
Chemical dependence, abused persons and, 141–142
Child Behavior Checklist (CBCL), 234
Child maltreatment: definition of, 79; symptoms of, 80
Child molesters, types of, 172–173
Child Sexual Behavior Inventory (CSBI), 234
Children. *See* Preschool boys
Chu, J.A., 26, 27
Cole, C.F., 139, 140, 149, 241
Coleman, E., 142, 178
Colrain, J., 25, 144
Comstock, C., 25, 27, 29, 32, 41
Conlin, D., 187, 188, 189
Connors, Patrick, 118, 119, 120
Countertransference issues, 27, 46–49; in adolescent victims, 219–220; in body work, 129–130
Courtois, C., 2, 6, 25, 27, 31, 46, 80, 147, 149
Cramer, P., 62, 67

Davidson, J.K., Sr., 65
Davis, L., 2, 41
Delayed stress syndrome (DSS), 58; development of work on, 59
De Monteflores, Carmen, 183, 194
Densen-Gerber, J., 139, 140, 141
Development theory, 145–146
Diagnostic and Statistical Manual of Mental Disorders (DSM III), 3, 59, 254
Dimock, Peter, 80, 100, 118
Dissociation: assessment of, 7–8, 10; BASK model of, 5–6, 13, 32; definition of, 3–5; difference between repression and, 4; indicators of possible, 9; instruments for measuring, 10; normal, 5; organic conditions and, 6; self-reported indicators of, 8; temporal, 6; traumatic experiences and, 10–14
Dissociative Disorders Interview Scale (DDIS), 10
Dissociative experiences, types of, 5–6
Dissociative Experiences Scale (DES), 10
Distad, L., 139, 140, 141, 144, 145, 147
Donaldson, M.A., 6, 24, 25, 144, 147

Edgar, M., 140, 144, 147
Egendorf, A., 177, 194, 197

Eich, J.E., 11, 16, 24
Ellenberger, H.F., 1
Ellerstein, N.W., 207
Emotional release, 125
Environmental safety, abreaction and, 28–29
Erikson, Erik, 145, 230
Evans, S., 141, 150, 161
Existential crisis, 11–12, 13; alleviating the, 33–36
Extrafamilial abuse, handling, 208–209

Fairbanks, J., 144, 151
FBI, *Uniform Crime Report* of, 59, 61
Fear and anxiety, adolescents and, 217–218
Feelings in adolescents: of betrayal, 207–210; of fear and anxiety, 217–218; of loneliness and isolation, 219; of powerlessness, 215–216; of sadness and loss, 218; of shame, 216–217
Feldman-Summers, S., 58, 140, 144, 147
Figley, C.R., 2, 6, 11, 24, 59, 73
Finkelhor, D., 81, 139, 140, 142, 145, 148, 171, 178, 200, 201, 204, 207, 233, 238, 242
Fish-Murray, C.C., 11, 24
Fixated offender, 172–173
Flashbacks: conscious, 15; containing, 18–22; planning for, 13–14; signs of, 15–18; unconscious, 15–16
Flavel, J.H., 226, 231
Fortunato, J., 186, 193
Frankl, V., 12, 24
Freud, Sigmund, 1, 123–124, 142
Friedrich, W., 203, 210, 234, 241, 244, 246
Frye, J.S., 63, 66

Ganzarain, Ramon, 129
Gardner, R., 6, 24, 25, 218
Garrett, T.B., 171
Gay men, group therapy and: cohesion and, 192–193; effects of abuse on gay men, 183–187; example case history, 181–183; healing process, 193–195; information on current study, 180–181; initial commitment and trust needed in, 190–192; models of group therapy, 187–196; review of literature on, 178–180; role of group therapy, 187; termination from the group, 195–196; terminology used, 177–178
Gazan, M., 11, 24
Gelinas, D.J., 16, 139, 140, 144, 145, 171
Gender differences, sexual abuse and, 80–81

Gender of counselors and impact on recovery, 71–72, 126–127
Gestalt therapy, 124–125
Gil, E., 2, 6, 139, 140, 142, 143, 144, 147, 149, 150, 165, 244
Gilgun, J.F., 100
Godfrey, K.E., 59
Gold, E., 138, 139, 140
Gonsiorek, J.C., 179
Goodwin, J., 59, 61, 69, 171, 172
Gordon, P., 58, 140
Greenberg, M.S., 11, 31
Groddeck, George, 124
Groth, A.N., 58, 62, 65, 66, 67, 100, 172–173
Group therapy: preschool victims and, 244; Psychophysical Model and, 130–134; treatment intervention theory and, 149–150. *See also* Gay men, group therapy and
Grove, D., 12, 32, 33
Guilt: difference between shame and, 110; in rape survivors and veterans, 66–67, 148

Hammond, D.C., 3, 35
Hartstein, N., 187, 188, 189, 192
Haynes-Seman, C., 225
Hazelwood, R.R., 63, 66
Herman, J., 30, 80
Holmstrom, L.L., 58, 60, 61, 62, 65, 66, 67, 69, 142, 144
Homophobia: adolescent concerns, 211; use of the term, 178
Hooker, B., 145, 146, 147
Horowitz, M.J., 5, 24, 59, 142–143, 144, 147, 148, 149, 151
Houston Area Women's Center Rape Crisis Program, 73
Howard, J.A., 59, 60, 62, 69, 72
Hunter, Mic, 80, 100, 118, 141, 179
Hypnotic techniques, abreaction and, 3, 35–36
Hysteria, use of abreaction and, 1

Imprinted injuctions, 37, 38
Imprints, 12–13
Infants, abuse of, 225–226
Injunctions: external, 37, 38–39; imprinted, 37, 38; internal, 37, 39
Inner child, 20, 20n
Interpersonal relationship skills, abused persons and, 139–140
Interpersonal safety, abreaction and, 26–28
Intrafamilial abuse, handling, 209–210
Intrapsychic safety, abreaction and, 24–26

Jehu, D., 11, 24

Johnson, P.E., 69, 73, 139, 140, 142, 147, 148, 149, 150, 158, 166
Johnson, R.L., 201, 211
Johnson, T.C., 230, 244
Johnson, W., 109, 111
Jones, D.P.H., 233, 238

Kadish, W., 2, 32
Kaloupek, D.G., 61
Kaltreider, N.B., 147, 148, 149
Katz, S., 58, 59
Kaufman, A., 148, 149
Kaufman, Irving, 139, 171
Kempe, H., 80, 243
Kempe, R., 80, 243
Kercher, G., 201, 204
Kingsbury, S.J., 2, 3
Klassen, C., 11, 24
Kline, C., 147, 149
Kluft, R.P., 2, 6, 25, 26, 28, 35
Koby, E.V., 11, 24
Kohut, Heinz, 183, 184
Koss, M.P., 99, 200, 207
Krystal, H., 11, 30, 31
Kübler-Ross, E., 84, 236

Lang, D., 66, 67
Langley, M.K., 59, 68, 70
Lew, Mike, 39, 80, 100, 118, 179, 185, 188
Lindberg, F., 139, 140, 141, 144, 145, 147
Lister, E.D., 25, 30
Loewenstein, R.J., 6, 26
Loneliness and isolation in adolescents, 219
Lukianowicz, N., 140, 141, 171

MacFarlane, K., 200, 234, 238
McKechnie, J., 81, 82
McShane, M., 201, 204
Massage therapy, 118; emotional release and, 125; neuromuscular work, 125–126
Masters, V., 109, 111
Masters, W.H., 65, 67, 72, 73
Masturbation: adolescents and, 109, 113, 212; in preschool children, 227
Mazur, M., 58, 59
MCRC. *See* Midwest Children's Resource Center
Meagher, J., 58, 140
Medication, use of, 25–26
Meiselman, Karen, 80, 171
Messages in therapy, importance of repeating, 95–97
Meyers, A.L., 59, 66
Midwest Children's Resource Center

MCRC *(continued)*
(MCRC), 227, 228, 231; description of treatment by, 234–236
Mills, T., 140, 141
Minnesota Child Development Inventory (MCDI), 234
Minnesota Multiphasic Personality Inventory (MMPI), 254
Modalities, adjunctive and nonverbal, 30–31
Mothers, role of, 171–172
Multiple personality disorder (MPD), 2, 29
Mutter, C.B., 6, 11, 24
Myers, M., 179, 181

Nace, E.P., 59, 66
Nasjleti, M., 148, 149, 201
Neisen, J., 178, 185
Neuromuscular work, 125–126
Nicholson, R., 144, 151
Nielsen, T., 200, 212
Nonoffending parent: role of the mother, 171–172; treatment sessions and, 174–175
Norton, G.R., 10

Ochberg, F.M., 2, 6, 24
Olson, P., 139, 140, 141
Orzek, A.M., 11, 24

Pace/lead model of therapy, 88–89
Parenting skills, abused persons and, 139
Peck, A.L., 139, 171
Perls, Fritz, 124–125
Perpetrators. *See* Sex offenders
Personality functioning, abused persons and, 140–141
Photographs in therapy, use of, 93–94
Pierce, L.H., 201, 202, 203
Pierce, R., 201, 202, 203
Pine, C.J., 67
Planned Parenthood, 245
Porter, Eugene, 118, 199, 219
Porter, F.S., 200, 233, 234
Posttraumatic stress disorder (PTSD): abreaction and, 1; acute stage and, 63–64; compared with rape trauma syndrome and, 60, 62–74; crisis intervention and, 70–71; gender of counselors and impact on recovery, 71–72; medication and, 26; reactions and treatment for, 67–74; recognition of, 59; recovery progressions for, 62–63; reorganization stage and, 64–67; sexual assault and, 59–60; Vietnam veterans and, 59
Power rapist, 173
Powerlessness, feelings of, 215–216

Preschool boys, abuse of: acting-out behaviors and, 239–244; birth to eighteen months, 225–226, 236–237; eighteen to thirty-six months, 226–229, 237–238; group therapy for, 244; masturbation and, 227; prevention education and, 245; sex education and, 244–245; three to five years, 229–232, 238–239; treatment of, 232–234, 236–246; treatment of, by Midwest Children's Resource Center, 234–236
Prevention education, 245
Psychonanalytic approach to psychosomatic medicine, 124
Psychoeducational process, 109–110, 205
Psychophysical Model of therapy and body work: benefits of, 119–120; case example, 120–122; combining body worker and psychotherapist, 128–130; countertransference issues, 129–130; description of body work, 127–128; determining client's readiness for body work, 127; group therapy and, 130–134; historical perspective, 123–126; implications for, 122–123; selecting a body therapist, 126–127; special needs of male survivors, 117–120; who can benefit from, 134
Psychosexual functioning, abused persons and, 140
Psychotherapy, sexual abuse in, 130
Putnam, F.W., 2, 6, 10, 11, 23, 25, 27, 29, 33, 34

Rage/anger responses: in adolescents, 213–214; body work and, 131–133; common in survivors, 147–148; handling, 35–36; in veterans, 66
Rape, relationship between warfare and, 60–62
Rape trauma syndrome: acute stage and, 63–64; compared with posttraumatic stress disorder and, 60, 62–74; crisis intervention and, 70–71; gender of counselors and impact on recovery, 71–72; improvements in treating, 58–59; reactions and treatment for, 67–74; recovery progressions for, 62–63; reorganization stage and, 64–67
Rapists, types of, 173
Regressed offender, 173
Reich, Wilhelm, 118, 124
Reinhart, M.A., 201, 204
Repression: difference between dissociation and, 4; Freud on, 123–124
Resistance to abreactive work, 27, 84
Rieker, P., 140, 141
Risin, L.I., 99, 200, 207

Rogers, C.M., 201, 204, 210, 212
Rosenfeld, A., 139, 140, 141
Ross, C.A., 2, 4, 6, 10, 23, 24, 25, 27, 29, 33
Rossi, E.L., 11, 24
Rothberg, J.M., 59, 66

Sachs, R.G., 5, 27, 30, 31, 35
Sadistic rapist, 173
Sadness and loss in adolescents, 218
Safe spaces, creating, 21, 25
Sarrel, P.M., 65, 67, 72, 73
Scherl, D., 58, 144, 145
Schlottman, R.S., 72
Schwartz, R., 187, 188, 189, 192
Self-esteem, abused persons and, 139, 206
Sex, phobic avoidance of, 43
Sex education, preschool boys and, 244–245
Sex offenders: case history, 262–265; characteristics of, 249–254; common problems experienced by, 100; moving from offender to victim, 261–262; as paraphiliacs, 100; treatment for, 255–261; types of 172–173; as victims of sexual abuse, 100
Sexual abuse: gender differences, 80–81; history of, 79–80; indicators of resolution of, 166; long-term effects of, 160–161; in psychotherapy, 130
Sexual abuse trauma, problems associated with, 138–142
Sexual acting out: by adolescents, 211–212; by preschoolers, 239–244
Sexual boundaries, maintaining, 26–27
Sexual dysfunction, PTDS and, 65–66
Sexual response cycle, 111–113
Sexually abused males: common problems experienced by, 100; parallel histories between Vietnam War survivors and, 58–62; posttraumatic stress disorder and, 59–60; reasons why professionals overlook, 81
Sgroi, S.M., 67, 200, 233, 234
Shame: adolescents and, 216–217; definition of, 99; difference between guilt and, 110
Shame, separating sexuality from: behavioral and cognitive therapy for, 103–104; case examples of offender/ victim, 102–103, 106–108; cycle of shameful sexuality, 104–108; dealing with deviant or aberrant fantasies, 103; problems with treating adolescent males, 108–113
Shapiro, C.H., 70, 72
Sheehan, N., 60, 62
Shepp, E., 30, 31, 35

Shrier, D., 201, 211
Sleep disorders, 64
Smith, J., 187, 188, 189
Social and behavioral problems, PTDS and, 64–65
Society for the Prevention of Cruelty to Animals, 79
Somatic memories, 6
Spiegel, D., 2, 3, 6, 11, 12, 24, 27, 141, 144, 147, 151
Spirituality, issues of, 43
Spoken autobiography, keeping a, 92–93
Sroufe, L.A., 226, 230, 241
Steele, K., 11, 12, 13, 23, 25, 29, 33, 144
Stockman, R.A., 63, 66
Stressors/triggers, 13, 16, 25
Suicide, adolescents and, 214–215
Summit, R.C., 20n, 171, 200
Support networks, 66
Survivor(s): special needs of male, 117–120; use of the term, 82–83, 177
Sutherland, S., 58, 144, 145

Tagiuri, C.K., 139, 171
Terry, L., 66, 67
Terry, Y, 201, 204, 210, 212
Therapeutic process, steps in: acceptance/ forgiveness, 87; anger, 86–87; bargaining, 84–86; denial, 84; sadness, 87
Therapeutic styles, 87–88
Time lines, 33
Timms, Robert, 117, 118, 119, 120–123
Touching in therapy, use of, 26, 94–95
Toys, use of, 98
Transference issues, 27; in adolescents, 220–221. *See also* Countertransference issues
Trauma: sexual abuse and, 10–14; theory, 142–144; use of abreaction and, 1
Treatment: by Midwest Children's Resource Center, 234–236; for posttraumatic stress disorder, 67–74; for preschool boys, 232–246; for rape trauma syndrome, 67–74; sessions and nonoffending parent, 174–175; for sex offenders, 255–261
Treatment intervention theory: goals and treatment themes, 146–149; group treatment, 149–150; overview of, 142–146
Triggers, 13, 16, 25
Troy, M., 230, 241
Trust, developing, 26, 207–210
Tsai, M., 139, 140, 144, 147, 148, 149

University of Minnesota, 150
Urquiza, A., 203, 210

Van Buskirk, S.S., 139, 140, 149
van der Kolk, B.A., 2, 6, 11, 24, 31, 32, 144
Vander Mey, B.J., 172
Verbalizing memories, 30–31
Veterans Administration, 60
Victim, use of the term, 82, 177
Victimization: disclosure of, 200–203; use of the term, 177
Vietnam Veterans against the War, 60
Vietnam War survivors: parallel histories between sexually abused males and, 58–62; posttraumatic stress disorder and, 59–74

Wagner, N.N., 139, 148, 149, 150
Warfare, relationship between rape and, 60–62
Warner, C.G., 59, 61, 66, 68
Waterman, J., 200, 234, 238
Watkins, J.G., 6, 32, 35
Webb, J., 60, 67
Williams, C., 66, 67
Williams, T., 66, 72

Yalom, I., 12, 24, 188, 190, 192

About the Contributors

Jeff Brown, M.S., L.P., received his master of science in education–guidance and counseling from the University of Wisconsin–River Falls in 1981 and was licensed as a psychologist in the state of Minnesota in 1983. Since that time, he has specialized in therapy and training in the area of sexuality, including abuse-related issues. He is a member of the Scientific Society for the Study of Sexuality and the Association of Sex Offender Treatment Professionals. His work with sexual abuse began at the Family Renewal Program in Edina, Minnesota, one of the first programs for incest families in the country. He has supervised cases at Alpha House, a community-based inpatient program. While at the University of Minnesota Medical School's Program in Human Sexuality, he continued his work with sexual offenders, abuse survivors, individuals conflicted about their sexual orientation, and training in various areas of sexuality to the public and professional community. He is currently a consultant to the Pride Institute in Eden Prairie, Minnesota, an inpatient chemical dependence program.

Shirley Carlson, M.A., L.P., is a licensed psychologist in Minnesota. Her education includes an undergraduate degree in humanities from the University of Minnesota, a chemical dependency certificate from Metropolitan Community College, and a master's degree in human development from St. Mary's College in Winona. Her experience with abusive family systems includes facilitating an incest group in a program for runaway adolescents, advocating for battered women in a women's shelter, evaluating clients in a detox center, and working as a family therapist in a hospital-based family sexual abuse treatment program, where she worked with sex offenders. She is continuing her work with both victims and perpetrators in her private practice and as the director of Newstart Behavioral Counselors, which provides evaluation and education for adjudicated offenders.

Joanna Colrain, M.Ed., is in private practice in Atlanta, specializing in the treatment of child sexual abuse trauma and dissociative disorders. She provides supervision and consultation in these areas for hospitals and private clinicians. Together with Jim Struve, she has developed a hospital protocol for inpatient treatment of child sexual abuse survivors. For the past five years, she has been trainer and clinical supervisor for the Sexual Abuse Survivor Program of the Georgia Council on Child Abuse, Inc., where she has helped train more than six hundred clinicians and supervised more than eighty group facilitators.

Patrick Connors, L.M.T., is a licensed massage therapist. He began studying body work and yoga in 1975. Since 1987, he has been working in conjunction with psychologists in releasing repressed and amnestic memories from the body using movement, breath work, and therapeutic massage techniques. He is currently the director of admissions at the Atlanta School of Massage and is cofounder and director of body work of the Atlanta Center for Integrative Therapy. He also has a private practice in therapeutic massage. Along with Robert Timms, Connors leads workshops on the Psychophysical Model of working with adult survivors of physical and/or sexual abuse.

Darryl Dahlheimer, M.S.W., A.C.S.W., has learned methods of healing and preventing sexual abuse from direct work with children, adults, and families over the past nine years. He is currently employed at Family and Children's Service of Minneapolis. He works in the Gay/Lesbian Sexuality Program and the Family Counseling Program addressing physical and sexual victimization.

Mark C. Evans is a veteran of the U.S. Army's infantry, Ranger & Special Forces. He has been involved in rape crisis intervention since 1985. He is currently a rehabilitation counselor at New Medico Highwatch in Ossipee, New Hampshire, and is pursuing a doctorate in social psychology through Union Institute in Cincinatti, Ohio.

Mary L. Froning, Psy.D., is codirector of the White Oak Psychological Center in Silver Spring, Maryland, which is located in the Washington, D.C., metropolitan area. There she conducts a full-time private practice in general psychology. She received her doctorate from the Illinois School of Professional Psychology in Chicago. Her predoctoral internship was at the University of Maryland School of Medicine in Baltimore. In addition, she completed a two-year postgraduate externship in family therapy through the Family Therapy Practice Center in Washington, D.C., and has received the equivalent of two postdoctoral years of specialized training and supervised experience in child sexual abuse. She has specialized in the field of child sexual abuse for more than five year, during which she has evaluated and treated offenders, child and adult victims, and others affected by incest and other child sexual abuse. She has provided consultation and training for mental health organizations and has been involved in various theory-building and research endeavors and writing projects. She is cofounder of and professional consultant to the Coalition Against the Sexual Abuse of Young Children, a nonprofit educational group.

Paul N. Gerber, M.A., has two decades of criminal justice experience as a special agent for the Minnesota Crime Bureau and eight years of clinical practice, which combine to give him a unique perspective as an author, lecturer, and psychotherapist. Currently, he administrates an outpatient program for adolescent and latency-age male victims of sexual abuse. He also works with adolescent sex offenders at the Program for Healthy Adolescent Sexual Expression (PHASE).

Anne M. Gresham, R.N., M.S., is a psychiatric nurse specialist currently working as a psychotherapist at the Family Life Mental Health Center in Anoka, Minnesota. She graduated from Pacific Lutheran University in Tacoma, Washington, in 1974 with a bachelor of science in nursing and received her master of science degree from the University of Minnesota in 1983. Since that time, she has done outpatient mental health psychotherapy with individuals, couples, families, and groups. She also has extensive community education and professional training. Her specialty areas include hypnotherapy, compulsive disorders, sexual abuse, and premenstrual syndrome.

Sandra Hewitt, Ph.D., L.C.P., has worked with sexually abused children for the past thirteen years. She is the codirector of the Midwest Children's Resource Center, a specialty child abuse unit of Children's Hospital of St. Paul, Minnesota. Dr. Hewitt has a Ph.D. in educational psychology from the University of Minnesota. She has worked in a variety of settings, including private practice, schools, Headstart, and outpatient and inpatient mental health settings. She is currently conducting research with sexually abused preschool-age children.

Susan B. Mayman, A.S.W., L.C.S.W., is a licensed certified social worker with a private practice in Bethesda, Maryland. She received her master's degree in social work from Florida State University and has worked in the field of child sexual victimization since 1985. For more than two years, she was a child protection service worker for the Commonwealth of Massachusetts, where she interviewed children to assess and evaluate the possibility of sexual abuse and provide ongoingg services for child sexual abuse victims and their families. For the past two years, she has provided evaluation and treatment for children and adolescents who have been sexually victimized, adults who were sexually abused as children, and their significant others.

Stephen Parker, M.A., L.P., received a master's degree in counseling psychology from the College of St. Thomas and is a licensed psychologist at Northland Therapy Center in St. Paul, Minnesota. He coteaches a course on men in therapy in the graduate Counseling and Psychological Services Program of St. Mary's College of Minnesota in Minneapolis. He also serves as a consultant to the Employee Advisory Resource of Control Data Corporation and to Pride Institute, an inpatient chemical dependence treatment center for lesbians, gay men and bisexuals. He is a member of study groups on men's issues and gay/lesbian issues in the American Orthopsychiatric Association.

Jack Rusinoff, M.A., holds a master's degree in educational psychology (counseling) from the University of Minnesota. His has a Minnesota graduate social worker license and is working toward becoming a licensed psychologist. He provides long-term psychotherapy for male survivors of sexual violence at the Rape and Sexual Assault Center, where he has worked for more than four years. He also rehabilitates men who batter at the Domestic Abuse Program (DAP). He was instrumental in redesigning the DAP men's program and wrote its current *Men's Treatment Handbook*.

Katherine Steele, M.N., R.N., C.S., is a psychotherapist in private practice in Atlanta, specializing in the treatment of sexual abuse, posttraumatic stress disorder, multiple personality disorder (MPD), and other severe dissociative disorders. She also provides training, consultation, and supervision in these areas. She has published a number of articles on dissociation and MPD. She is active in a number of organizations involved in the treatment of abuse victims, including the International Society of the Study of Multiple Personality and Dissociation (ISSMP&D), the American Professional Society on the Abuse of Children, and the Georgia Board for the Survivors Program of the Georgia Council on Child Abuse, Inc.

Robert Timms, Ph.D., is a clinical psychologist in private practice in Atlanta. He is cofounder of the Atlanta Center for Integrative Therapy, a treatment research and training center for adults who were sexually abused in childhood. He is a member of the American Academy of Psychotherapists and the American Group Psychotherapy Association and has led workshops at the national meetings of both organizations. He is the author of several articles on abuse, survivors, and treatment. He and Patrick Connors are working on two books about the treatment of physical and sexual abuse survivors and provide other professionals with training in body work and psychotherapy.

About the Editor

Mic Hunter, M.A., M.S., L.P., L.M.F.T., C.C.D.C.R., N.C.A.D.C., is licensed both as a psychologist and a marriage and family therapist and is certified as a chemical dependence counselor (reciprocal). He is also a national certified alcohol and drug counselor. Currently, he is in private practice in St. Paul, Minnesota. Prior to this, he was employed by several outpatient mental health centers and chemical dependence treatment programs. His formal education includes an undergraduate degree in psychology from Macalester College in St. Paul; a master of arts degree from St. Mary's College in Winona, Minnesota; a master of science in education/psychological services from the University of Wisconsin–Superior; and completion of the University of Minnesota's Alcohol/Drug Counseling Education Program, the Program in Human Sexuality's Chemical Dependency and Family Intimacy Training Program, and the Intensive Post-Graduate Training Program at the Gestalt Institute of the Twin Cities. He started his doctoral studies at the Minnesota School of Professional Psychology in the Fall of 1990. In addition to articles for other helping professionals and the general public, Mr. Hunter is the author of *Abused Boys: The Neglected Victims of Sexual Abuse* and *The Twelve Steps and Shame*. He also is co-author of *The First Step for People in Relationships with Sex Addicts*. His current project is a book on the identification and expression of emotions.